2011
NEW PLAYWRIGHTS
THE BEST PLAYS

2011
NEW PLAYWRIGHTS
THE BEST PLAYS

Edited and with a Foreword
by Lawrence Harbison
Introduction by Adam Bock

NEW PLAYWRIGHTS SERIES

SMITH AND KRAUS PUBLISHERS
177 LYME ROAD, HANOVER, NH 03755
EDITORIAL 603.643.6431 TO ORDER 877.668.8680
www.smithandkraus.com

Published by Smith and Kraus, Inc.
177 Lyme Road, Hanover, NH 03755
www.SmithandKraus.com

First Edition: April 2012
10 9 8 7 6 5 4 3 2 1

Manufactured in the United States of America
Cover design by Emily Kent, emilygkent@gmail.com
Book design by Nathan Spring

ISBN 10-1-57525-779-3 ISBN 13- 978-1-57525-779-2
ISSN 1545-7281

CONTENTS

FOREWORD

The 2010-2011 theatre season was the strongest in recent memory. I was a member of the Nominating Committee of the Drama Desk, and we saw and evaluated over 200 eligible productions from Off Off Broadway to Off Broadway to Broadway. In April alone, we saw 30 new shows! There were the Broadway debuts of two playwrights whose work has appeared in my New Playwrights books previously, Rajiv Joseph's *Bengal Tiger at the Baghdad Zoo* and Stephen Adly Guirgis' *The Motherf**cker with the Hat,* and, amazingly, both managed successful Broadway runs, as did Jez Butterworth's epic comic drama *Jerusalem,* which featured a titanic performance by one of the world's greatest actors, Mark Rylance. Eric Simonson's *Lombardi,* featuring a terrific performance by Dan Lauria in the title role, managed a successful Broadway run, as did Emma Rice's enchanting stage adaptation of Noël Coward's *Brief Encounter,* which lit up Broadway's Studio 54.

Off Broadway, there were successful productions of plays by veteran playwrights such as Charles Busch *(The Divine Sister),* Sarah Ruhl *(Orlando),* Lisa Kron *(In the Wake),* Richard Nelson *(That Hopey Changey Thing),* Neil LaBute *(The Break of Noon),* Adam Rapp *(Ghosts in the Cottonwoods and The Hallway Trilogy),* Adam Bock *(A Small Fire),* Jon Robin Baitz *(Other Desert Cities,* which moved to Broadway in the fall of 2011), Rajiv Joseph *(Gruesome Playground Injuries)* and A.R. Gurney, *(Black Tie)* who was honored by the Drama Desk with a special Lifetime Achievement Award; and, there were exciting productions of plays by less well-known playwrights, some of whom are included in this book.

Even the Humana Festival, for several years in decline due to Actors Theatre of Louisville's regrettable recent predilection for experiment over substance, stepped it up several notches in 2011, with a lineup of terrific new plays by Molly Smith Metzler, Adam Rapp, A. Rey Pamatmat, Peter Sinn Nachtrieb and Jordan Harrison.

Now, to the plays in this book.

Bachelorette, by Leslye Headland, had an extended run Off Broadway, produced by Second Stage as part of their Uptown series at the McGinn/Cazale

Theatre. The fur flies fast and furiously as a group of women at a bachelorette party in the suite of a swank hotel confront the truth about their lives and the lies they have told themselves.

I have included several ten-minute plays by Bekah Brunstetter in my annual anthologies of these short plays. I was chatting up a cute bartender at a restaurant in the Village, who told me that her roommate (maybe it was her roommate's friend) wrote 10-minute plays. She passed on my e-mail address to the playwright, and that's how I came across Bekah Brunstetter. *Be a Good Little Widow* knocked me out when I saw it at Ars Nova, one of the better Off Off Broadway companies in New York. When we think of a "widow," we think of an old lady whose husband has passed away. The central character of Brunstetter's play, however, is a 20-something woman, only recently married, whose husband is killed in a plane crash. She and her husband's mother, a more traditional widow, try to cope with this tragedy. Brunstetter's writing is fresh, funny, poignant and intensely theatrical.

Samuel D. Hunter's *A Bright New Boise* also was produced Off Off Broadway, by another fine company called Partial Comfort Productions. It was nominated by our committee as Best New Play, and won an Obie Award in the same category. It takes place in the employee lunch room of a pet products superstore in Boise, Idaho. Its central character is a man who has come from another town in the state to escape the notoriety of a religious cult with which he was involved, but also to find and re-connect with his son, whom he hasn't seen in years, who works at the store. A Bright New Boise is a wonderful example of classic American Realism, a genre out of favor these days but one with which I have more than a partial comfort.

Carly Mensch's *Now Circa Then* also comes from Ars Nova. It's a delightful two-hander about a man and woman who work as historical re-enactors at the Tenement Museum

LaByrinth Theatre Co. had another hit with Melissa Ross' comedy *Thicker Than Water*, which is about three adult siblings with the same father but different mothers who come together because of the terminal illness and later death of their father.

Matthew Lopez' *The Whipping Man*, produced by Manhattan Theatre Club, won the Outer Critics Circle's John Gassner Award, given annually to a new playwright. It's an unusual Civil War drama. A seriously-wounded Confederate soldier makes it back to his family's plantation house, only to find it a burned-out shell, inhabited solely by one of the family's slaves. We learn that his family is Jewish; so, of course are the slaves. When another former slave shows up, the young soldier learns the truth about himself and his family.

David Davalos' witty *Wittenberg*, produced regionally before turning up at the Pearl Theatre Co., is a comedy about a young Danish Prince named Hamlet, at Wittenberg University to study philosophy with an irreverent professor named Faustus, who engages in theological tugs of rope with Martin Luther, often with young Hamlet as the rope.

I have no doubt that each of this year's New Playwrights will soon become Household Names (at least in households which know, and care about, the theatre). I think theirs are wonderful plays. I Hope you agree.

Lawrence Harbison
Brooklyn, New York

INTRODUCTION

Spells and plays work like this: describe a door to a prisoner with enough clarity and the prisoner can walk through it. A cool breeze Will ruffle the sand in a desert. A hard woman can cry. Conjure up new endings for old stories and people long entrapped by their own weary imaginations can be set free.

Create a character we've never seen before on stage, and suddenly we can imagine her. And the space for this new person opens up in our community. Or perhaps the person who has been there all this time can finally be recognized.

I think our world is a story we tell ourselves. Looking with dark eyes, we can only see a dark world. As a playwright I'm supposed to remember that other ways of looking exist. To see new possibilities and to try them out on stage. I love being a playwright. I like the work, I like the challenge and I like playing. It's worthwhile and it's fun. The only thing that's hard out here in playwriting land is that it can seem lonely.

This book introduces us to a group of great new writers who have joined the game, laughing and pushing at each other and at us. Look at the amazing stories they are telling us. Look at the wild and interesting worlds they are reminding us to live in!

Adam Bock

A BRIGHT NEW BOISE

Samuel D. Hunter

For John

PLAYWRIGHT'S BIOGRAPHY

Samuel D. Hunter's recent plays include *A Bright New Boise* (2011 OBIE award for playwriting, 2011 Drama Desk Nomination for Best Play; original production by Partial Comfort Productions in NYC, recent production at Woolly Mammoth Theater Company), *The Whale* (The Denver Center), *A Permanent Image* (commissioned and produced by Boise Contemporary Theater) *Jack's Precious Moment* (Page 73 Productions at 59E59), *Five Genocides* (Clubbed Thumb at the Ohio Theater), *Norway* (Phoenix Theatre of Indianapolis; Boise Contemporary Theater), *I Am Montana* (Arcola Theatre, London; Mortar Theater, Chicago). He has active commissions from MTC/Sloan, Seattle Rep, and South Coast Rep. His plays have been developed at the O'Neill Playwrights Conference, Bay Area Playwrights Festival, PlayPenn, Ojai Playwrights Conference, the Lark Playwrights Workshop, Juilliard, LAByrinth, Rattlestick, Seven Devils Playwrights Conference, 24Seven Lab and elsewhere. Internationally, his work has been translated into Spanish and presented in Mexico City and Monterrey, and he has worked in the West Bank with Ashtar Theatre of Ramallah and Ayyam al-Masrah of Hebron. At Ashtar, he co-wrote The Era of Whales which was performed in Ramallah and Istanbul. Awards: 2011 Sky Cooper Prize, 2008-2009 PONY Fellowship from the Lark, two Lincoln Center Le Compte du Nuoy Awards, others. He is a core member of the Playwrights Center, a member of Partial Comfort Productions and is an alum of Ars Nova's Playgroup. He has taught at Fordham University, Rutgers University, and Marymount Manhattan College. A native of northern Idaho, Sam lives in New York City. He holds degrees in playwriting from NYU, The Iowa Playwrights Workshop and Juilliard.

Originally commissioned and produced by Partial Comfort Productions.

Directed by Davis McCallum

CAST

Leroy	John Patrick Doherty
Alex	Matt Farabee
Will	Andrew Garman
Anna	Sarah Nina Hayon
Pauline	Danielle Slavick

CREW

CHARACTERS

Will . . . . Late thirties, male.
Pauline . . . . Late thirties to early forties, female.
Anna . . . . Late twenties to early thirties, female.
Leroy . . . . Early to mid twenties, male.
Alex . . . . 17, male.

TWO MALE VOICES ON HOBBY LOBBY TV

SETTING

Aside from the scenes in the parking lot, the entire play takes place in a windowless break room of a Hobby Lobby in Boise, Idaho. Stark, florescent lighting, white walls. A few cheap chairs and tables are in the space, along with a telephone on the wall, an ethernet port, lockers, maybe a vending machine or mini-fridge, and a mounted television. Some non-ironic corporate slogans or work schedules adorning the walls wouldn't be out of order.

NOTES

"Hobby Lobby TV" should be a recording two men sitting behind a desk, with a very dull background, either completely unadorned or with a very cheap looking "Hobby Lobby" sign behind them. It should always be at an extremely low, barely perceptible volume (except when indicated), and the dialogue should be as plain, boring, and non-descript as possible. No effort should be made to make it funny, ironic, meaningful, etc. It should only be slow, low-pitched, monotonous chatter about new items, sales and promotions, new store locations, etc.

Dialogue written in italics is emphatic, slow, and deliberate; dialogue in ALL CAPS is impulsive, quick, explosive. Dialogue written in BOTH is a combination of the two.

A "/" indicates an overlap in dialogue. If desired, an intermission can be taken between scenes six and seven.

***"A Bright New Boise" was commissioned and first produced by Partial Comfort Productions at the Wild Project in New York City in September, 2010, directed by Davis McCallum.

AGENT CONTACT:
Derek Zasky
William Morris Endeavor Entertainment
1325 Avenue of the Americas
New York, NY 10019
(212) 903-1396
DZasky@wmeentertainment.com

A BRIGHT NEW BOISE

SCENE ONE

Will stands in a parking lot, at night. Sounds of a freeway can be heard: passing semis, car horns, car stereos, etc, as well as the buzzing glow of neon signs and florescent lights overhead.
He stands with his eyes closed, listening to the noise.

WILL:
Now.

…

…

…

Now.

…

…

…

Now.

…

…

…

Now.

(The noise continues.)

SCENE TWO

(The breakroom. Will sits facing Pauline, whose back is to the television. Pauline wears a bright red vest with a nametag and holds a clipboard.)

(An extreme close-up of ear surgery plays on the television.)

PAULINE: So then the black guy comes up to the Asian lady and the white lady, and he's like, "I don't really understand what all this talk about unions is gonna get us. All they wanna do is take our money and decide who were going to vote for." And then the Asian lady is like, shocked, and she says "they choose who you vote for?" And then the white lady says, "that's not what America is all about." And then there's a graphic, or... Shit, what the hell is...? It's like a pie chart. Yeah, it's like—I don't know, something about unions. Do you know anything about unions?

WILL: They're not good.

PAULINE: Yeah, exactly. That's the gist of the pie chart, anyway, so you get it. Sorry you couldn't just watch it, the damn VCR's broken. Everything here is falling apart, including me. Heh, you know.

WILL: Oh. Yeah, heh.

PAULINE: So anyway, don't try to unionize.

WILL: Oh, no, of course not.

PAULINE: They shut down a Hobby Lobby in Kansas City when they tried to unionize, so don't try to unionize.

WILL: I really won't.

PAULINE: Too bad you couldn't see the video, it's actually—it has a funny segment, like a cartoon?

WILL: Oh, okay.

PAULINE: Yeah, it's actually a pretty great company when it comes down to it. And they know how to run a business, everything is hooked up to the corporate office. We can't even turn the air conditioning on without calling South Carolina. I mean—I know that sounds annoying, but it's actually really great. Really, it's just—a well-oiled machine.

WILL: Yeah, I'm really glad you had an open position—

PAULINE: *(holding Wills resume)*
Says here you worked for Albertson's up in Couer d'Alene?

WILL: Uh—yes.

PAULINE: Uh huh. And how was that?

WILL: Oh, it was—fine, I guess.

PAULINE: I used to be assistant manager at Fred Meyer, you know Fred Meyer?

WILL: Oh yeah, of course.

PAULINE: It's kind of like an Albertsons. *(Quick pause)*

WILL: Y—yes.

PAULINE: continues to look through his resume.

PAULINE: You from Couer d'Alene originally?

WILL: The area, yeah.

PAULINE: Beautiful up there.

WILL: Yes, it really is.

PAULINE: What brings you down to Boise?

WILL: I guess—change in scenery more than anything else.

PAULINE: Yeah? Well, Boise's a good town. You'll like it here, it's grown a lot over the past ten years.

WILL: Yes, it really / seems like—

PAULINE: When I was a kid, it was nothing like this. Where we're sitting right now used to be cow pastures. Nowadays, all the surrounding towns just spill right into one another. Friend of mine lives in Caldwell, tells me sometimes it takes him forty minutes to get to work. We have honest-to-god city traffic, you believe that?

WILL: Yeah, I haven't been here since I was a kid, it's much different—

PAULINE: *(looking at the resume)* Why'd you switch to part time in 2004? *(Pause.)*

WILL: What's that?

PAULINE: At Albertson's. You switched to part time in 2004, how come?

WILL: Oh, I had a—sort of a second job.

PAULINE: What was it?

WILL: Uh—I was, it was sort of like, uh—bookkeeping?

PAULINE: Why isn't it on your resume?

WILL: Well, it wasn't really… It was very specific, it was for a church.

PAULINE: So?

WILL: Oh, you just… I don't know, sometimes people—they make assumptions about who you are based on—

PAULINE: Hell, we're not like that, believe me. The guy who founded the company is all, like, Christian. David Green, that's the guys name. You should read the statement of purpose for the company, it's all like—

WILL: Plus, all my other experience is in retail, I thought that was more important.

PAULINE: Huh. Well, anyway, I can get you started as soon as you like. Tomorrow, even. Pays $7.25 an hour, I'll try to put you on full time in nine months if I can, until then you work thirty-eight hours a week. Holidays are time and a half, Sundays are time and a quarter. Possible seventy cent raise after nine months.

WILL: Perfect.

PAULINE: Alright then. I'll go get your W-2, do you have your social security card and driver's license on you? I can take you out on the floor and we can get going on your training. I'll set up an appointment for the drug test for tomorrow morning. You have any questions?

WILL: Yeah, just—is that always on the TV in here?

PAULINE: turns around, sees the television.

PAULINE: Goddammit. Mother fucker. Goddammit.

PAULINE: gets up and goes to the television, looking at it.

PAULINE: Goddammit. What is that, an ear? That's an ear, isn't it? Goddammit.

PAULINE: picks up the phone and dials a few numbers.

PAULINE: (on the phone) Leroy, go up to the roof and—. Yeah, it's an ear or something. Yeah well fuck you too, Leroy. (hangs up) Sorry about that. Goddammit.

WILL: Why is—?

PAULINE: It's the satellite dish, I don't know. Sometimes it gets all screwy, is it raining outside?

WILL: A little bit, yeah.

PAULINE: Figures. The company has it's own dedicated channel—nothing much, just info on products, new stores, stuff like that. Sometimes the signal gets crossed with these medical whatevers.
(looking at the television) Goddamn, would you look at that? How do you think that feels? Jesus Christ.
(Will cringes. Pauline notices.)

PAULINE: Don't worry, you'll get used to it. You're not gonna vomit, are you? Interviewed a girl last month, she almost threw up. I didn't hire her.

WILL: I'm fine, it's fine.
(Alex enters, iPod buds in his ears. He doesn't look at either Pauline or Will and sits down on one of the chairs, facing away from them.)
(Will stares at Alex.)

PAULINE: (re: Alex)
He's twelve. From some former soviet republic, doesn't speak English so we can work him seventy hours a week.

WILL: What?

PAULINE: I'm shitting you. He's a high school kid. Worked here last summer too.

(to Alex)

Hey. Hey, Alex. SAY HI TO WILL. HE'S NEW.

(no response, nearly screaming)

Alex FUCKING SAY HI TO WILL. MAKE HIM FEEL WELCOME.

(Alex barely looks up, does a half-hearted wave toward Will. Will smiles, waves back.)

PAULINE: Good worker, actually. Real accurate register counts.

(P.A. ANNOUNCEMENT) (Anna)

Mandy, personal call on line two. Mandy, line two.

PAULINE: Fuckin' Mandy.

(re: social security card and driver's license)

Can I grab those to make a copy?

(no response)

Will?

WILL: Uh—yeah, here.

(Will hands her his social security card and driver's license, Pauline exits. Will continues to stare at Alex. After a moment, Alex feels someone looking at him.)

(He looks behind him, seeing Will. Will smiles warmly at him. Alex smiles back, then goes back to his iPod.)

(He still feels Will staring at his back, he looks back at Will again.)

WILL: What're you listening to?

ALEX: *(taking off his headphones)*

What?

WILL: Sorry, I—I'm just wondering, what're you listening to?

ALEX: Villa-Lobos.

(Pause.)

WILL: Is that—pop music?

ALEX: He's a composer who mixed traditional Brazilian music with European classical music.

WILL: Oh. Wow. That's impressive.

ALEX: Yeah, well, I'm glad you're impressed, that means a lot.

(Alex looks away, putting his headphones back in. Will keeps looking at him. Finally, Alex looks at him.)

WILL: *(reaching out a hand)*

I'm Will. I just got hired.

(Alex takes out his ear buds.)

ALEX: Wait, you wanna like, talk?
> *(Pause.)*
> I'm Alex.
> *(Pause.)*

WILL: What other kinds of music do you listen to?

ALEX: Lots. Mostly modern composition.

WILL: What does that mean?

ALEX: Like, composers. Who are modern.
> *(Pause.)*

WILL: Are you a / musician?

ALEX: I'm gonna listen to my music now if that's okay.

ALEX: smiles at him, putting his headphones back in. He turns on his iPod, scrolling through the music.

WILL: Alex?
> *(Alex takes off one earbud, annoyed.)*

ALEX: Yeah?

WILL: I'm your father. When you were born your name was William. You were named after me.
> *(Pauline re-enters.)*

PAULINE: Okay, so here we are. If you can get these done fast, I should be able to train you on one of the registers before we close. Should be quick, if you remember anything from Albertson's, you'll be able to pick it up pretty—
> *(With a burst of static, the television flips back to Hobby Lobby TV.)* *(Alex hurries out of the room.)*

PAULINE: Ah, there we go. These two guys, they never say their names on the air for some reason. Everybody has guesses of what their names are. I think they both sound like they're kinda high, so I call this one Woody and this one Harrelson. Get it?
> *(Pause.)*

WILL: No, sorry, I don't.

SCENE THREE

Later that night, back in the breakroom. The room is dark except for the glow of the television, still tuned to Hobby Lobby TV.

Anna enters, cautiously making her way into the room. She sits at a breakroom table and takes out a book and a plastic bag full of jerky. She opens the book and begins to munch on the jerky.

After a moment, Will enters holding a laptop, turning on the lights. Anna lets out a little scream and drops her book. Will, startled, lets out a little yell as well.

WILL: OH—
ANNA: I'm sorry. I'm sorry.
ANNA: *desperately starts grabbing her things.*
WILL: No, I'm sorry—
ANNA: I'm leaving, I'll leave. I'm sorry, I just—
    (quick pause)
    I know this looks weird, but I was just reading, I wasn't doing anything strange, I just...
    (Pause.)
    Are you—? Wait, who are you?
WILL: I'm new, I just got hired today—
ANNA: *(relief)*
    Oh... My God, I thought you were from corporate. Oh my God.
WILL: Corporate?
ANNA: They send—the company, sometimes they send people from corporate to check out the store at night, after closing. Like, a surprise inspection.
WILL: Oh.
ANNA: They have a video about this, you didn't watch the video?
WILL: The—it was the VCR, it wasn't working.
    (Pause.)
ANNA: Just—don't tell Pauline you saw me here after closing, okay?
WILL: As long as you don't tell her you saw me.
ANNA: Right. Ha, ha.
    (Pause.)
    I'm sorry, so what are you—?
WILL: *(holding up the laptop)*
    I don't have internet where I'm staying right now. I noticed the plug-in thing earlier.

(*Pause.*)

How about you?

ANNA: holds up her book, smiles awkwardly.

WILL: You can't read at home?

ANNA: Not really.

(*Pause.*)

I usually stick around until ten or eleven.

WILL: hooks up his computer to the Ethernet jack, Anna awkwardly goes back to reading.

After a moment, Will goes to the television, about to turn it off.

ANNA: Could you—? Sorry, I sort of like to keep it on.

WILL: Oh—

ANNA: I'd just—rather you didn't turn it off. If that's okay.

(*Pause.*)

You know, I can read in my car, I can—

WILL: No, it's—you were here first. I can come back later, I can—sorry, how did you get back in the building?

ANNA: Oh, I… It's silly. I just hide in the silk flower section right before closing. No one seems to notice when I don't leave with them, I don't know. How did you get back in?

(*Pause.*)

WILL: Fabric section.

(*short pause*) They both start laughing, awkwardly at first.

ANNA: Are you serious?

WILL: Yep.

ANNA: That's—that's just ridiculous, isn't it?

WILL: Yes, I guess it is.

ANNA: Pretty bold move on your first day.

WILL: I used to do it at the Albertson's I worked at all the time.

ANNA: And I thought I was the only wacko who did this.

(*Anna smiles, walking toward Will and extending a hand.*)

ANNA: I'm Anna.

WILL: Will.

ANNA: Well hello, Will!

(*a terrible attempt at a joke*)

"Will" you be sneaking in—.

Neither of them laugh. Anna looks away in shame for a moment, then recovers.

ANNA: If you don't mind, you know—we could both stay, I could read, and you could do your—work or whatever. Do you have a job online? That's so interesting. I'm talking too much, am I talking too much?

WILL: No, it's fine—it's not really a job. I mean, it doesn't pay anything. I have a…

(Pause.)

ANNA: What?

WILL: It's just so stupid, I… It's like—a blog. It's stupid, and I'm a big dork.

ANNA: That's not stupid! What are you talking about? A blog, that's so—hip. What kind of blog is it?

WILL: *(hesitating)*
Um. It's…

ANNA: What am I doing? Shut up, Anna.

WILL: No, it's—it's like a story. Like a long story, like—an online novel.

(Pause.)

ANNA: Holy crap you write books?

WILL: Well—

ANNA: I love books! I read books all the time! You're actually a writer?!

WILL: I don't get paid or anything—

ANNA: So?! Holy crap!

(Pause.)

Sorry, I just—you're a writer, that's so neat.

WILL: Well not lately. It's been kind of rough going.

ANNA: Writer's block?

WILL: Something like that. I keep forcing myself to sit down and write, but—nothing comes.

ANNA: Like a process. Like an artistic process, I get that, yep.

(Pause.)

Well, I bet your book is great. A lot better than what I'm reading right here, I bet that much. What's your book about?

WILL: It's, uh—sort of like—Christian Literature?

ANNA: Oh yeah? That's great! I read that one book, what's it called—"The Purpose Driven Life". Yeah, that was good. Anyway, I'm a Christian, I've always believed in Jesus.

WILL: Yeah?

ANNA: Sure, what else is there to believe in?

Will smiles. (Pause.)

ANNA: Well, I need to let you work. You sure you don't need me to leave? I can leave—

WILL: No, I'd… It's nice to have company, actually.

(Pause.) Anna goes back to reading smiles at him, then laughs a little.

ANNA: I'm sorry. I still just can't believe… Both of us hiding in here—

WILL: It's really pretty funny.

ANNA: It's so cute, I…

> *(Pause.)*
>
> Okay. I read, you write.

WILL: *(smiling)*

> Deal.
>
> *(Anna opens up her book, Will opens his laptop.)*

SCENE FOUR:

Early the next morning, in the parking lot. Will stands facing Alex.

WILL: Hi.

    (Pause.)

    Thanks for meeting me. I think I rushed my introduction just a little bit, I didn't want to—scare you.

    (Pause.)

    Did you tell your parents about me?

ALEX: No.

WILL: Okay.

    (Pause.)

    I can't imagine what you're feeling right now, I can't imagine what you've thought about me all these years—

ALEX: I don't believe you.

    (Silence. Will takes a step toward Alex, who backs away.)

WILL: I can tell you that you were born on May 22nd, that's your birthday, right? You have foster parents, their names are John and Cindy McDonald.

ALEX: Any idiot with access to google could figure out all that.

    (Pause.)

WILL: You have a birthmark on your lower back, on the right side. When you were little you had blonde hair, but I guess it got darker as you grew up.

    (Will pulls out his wallet, taking out a weathered photograph.)

WILL: That's you. At two months. That's me, holding you.

    (Alex looks at the photograph, then hands it back to him.)

ALEX: Whatever, all babies look the same.

    (Pause.)

WILL: Look, Alex, I don't know how to prove this to you—

ALEX: How did you find me?

WILL: I tracked down John and Cindy years ago. They didn't want me to have any contact with you, but every year they send me a letter. About you. Like a—status report, I guess.

ALEX: Do you know John and Cindy?

WILL: No, I mean—not really—

ALEX: Yeah well they're assholes. If you are my father, then fuck you, because you gave me to assholes.

    (Pause.)

When I was little I used to have fantasies about my real dad coming to get me. Like he was a prisoner of war, or an FBI guy or something. He didn't work at the Hobby Lobby, that's for sure. Do you at least drive a cool car or live in a big house?

WILL: It's a '94 Subaru. And right now, it's also my house.

ALEX: I'm gonna kill myself.

WILL: What?

ALEX: Nothing, it's just something I say. So if you're really my father—again, if—what do you want from me? You better not need a kidney or something.

WILL: No, I don't, I... I just want to get to know you.

ALEX: Okay, but why now?

(Pause.)

WILL: Look, Alex, things in my life have sort of been turned upside down, and I've had to reconsider a lot of the decisions I've made, the things I believe in... I just want to make a fresh start.

ALEX: Huh. Well, good for you.

(Pause.)

I have panic attacks. Sometimes more than once a week. Do you know what a panic attack is?

WILL: Yeah—

ALEX: No you don't. You think that you might, but you don't. You probably think that it's just about me being stressed out, you think that I have a panic attack when I get a bad grade on a test or something. I get panic attacks over nothing. Absolutely nothing. I'll be at work, or at home, or at school, and suddenly I'll start shaking and I won't be able to breathe.

(Pause.)

School counselor says that it might be a chemical imbalance. Or, she says, it might have something to do with my past. I think it has something to do with my past, so if you're my father, it's probably your fault.

(Pause.)

WILL: Maybe just lunch / sometime?

ALEX: I want a blood test.

(Pause.)

WILL: Okay. I can—I'm not really sure where to go, but I can find out, I can make some calls—

ALEX: Valley Medical Clinic. It's in Meridian, on 17th Street. I have an appointment for six, you have an appointment for seven. We're going separately, and you're paying for it. It's not cheap.

(Pause.)

WILL: Okay.

ALEX: And you need to know that if it turns out that you're my biological father, that doesn't necessarily mean anything. It doesn't mean I have to talk with you or interact with you in any way.

(Pause.)

WILL: Did you know that your real name is William?

ALEX: My real name isn't William.

WILL: It was the name your mother gave you when you were born.

ALEX: Don't ever call me William. If you call me William, I'm gonna kill myself.

WILL: I won't. I'm sorry.

ALEX: And don't talk about my mom unless I tell you to.

(Pause.)

WILL: I listened to some Villa-Lobos last night. Downloaded some albums.

ALEX: You did?

WILL: Yeah. Backa—?

ALEX: Bachianas Brasileiras.

WILL: Yeah.

ALEX: What did you think?

WILL: It was really pretty.

(Pause.)

ALEX: "Pretty"?

WILL: Yeah, and—

ALEX: (under his breath)
    …i'm gonna kill myself…

WILL: Overwhelming.

(Pause.) (Alex looks at him.)

ALEX: If I ask you to quit and move out of Boise, would you?

(Will doesn't answer, staring down at his shoes.)

ALEX: I gotta clock in.

(Alex exits.)

SCENE FIVE.

> *Later that day. Leroy sits in the breakroom reading a newspaper, wearing a T-shirt that reads simply "FUCK" in large block letters. Hobby Lobby TV plays in the background. After a moment, Will enters with some lunch in a Tupperware container. He notices Leroy's shirt, and nods politely at him.*
>
> *Will goes to the microwave, puts in his lunch, and turns it on.*

LEROY: It's a piece of shit.

WILL: *(turning)*
   What's that?

LEROY: The microwave. It barely works, I'd recommend cranking it up to high and leaving it in there for at least three times longer than normal.

WILL: Oh—okay, thanks.
   (Will turns the microwave up.)

LEROY: How's the first day?

WILL: Second, actually. Well, first full day. It's—fine. Slow.

LEROY: It's always like this. You'd think they were losing money, but the profit margin is pretty amazing.

WILL: What do you mean?

LEROY: Think about it. They're just selling all this raw material; fabric, paint, balsa wood, whatever. It's like the customers are paying money to do the manufacturing process themselves. You know those foam balls, the ones we sell for ninety-nine cents, the one the size of a baseball?

WILL: Yeah.

LEROY: Those things cost less than a penny to make.

WILL: Is that right?

LEROY: That's right.

WILL: Wow. Highway robbery.

LEROY: What?

WILL: Oh, I just—that's a big markup.

LEROY: You think it's dishonest?

WILL: Oh, I—I didn't mean that—

LEROY: You didn't?

WILL: No, I was just... It was just a joke.
   (Pause.)

LEROY: I'm deliberately making you uncomfortable.

(Awkward Pause. Will turns off the microwave and takes out his lunch. He sits at a table across the room from Leroy and begins to eat. Leroy grabs his newspaper and sits down next to Will.)

LEROY: *(extending a hand)*
Leroy.

WILL: Oh, it's—

LEROY: Will. I know.

WILL: How do you know my—?
(Leroy points to his nametag.)

WILL: Oh. Heh.
(pointing to Leroy's shirt)
So do you—? You actually wear that to work?

LEROY: For as long as I can before Pauline sees me.

WILL: You don't get in trouble?

LEROY: I'm the only one in this store who knows anything about art supplies, so I can basically do whatever I want. I'm the only one that can answer actual questions.

WILL: Are you an artist?

LEROY: Getting my masters in Fine Arts at BSU.

WILL: What kind of art to you make?
(Leroy points to his t-shirt.)

WILL: I—don't understand—

LEROY: I also have one that says "cunt", one that says "you will eat your children", and one that has a color photograph of my penis on both sides.

WILL: Oh.

LEROY: I'm forcing people to confront words and images they normally avoid. Especially at a place like this.

WILL: You—you mean the Hobby Lobby?

LEROY: Exactly. It's about the interaction between the word and the kinds of people who shop here, deliberately making them uncomfortable. Soccer moms and grade school kids and little old ladies, they all have to confront the reality of the words before they get their arts and crafts supplies. You want a foam ball? FUCK. You want some acrylic paints? CUNT. You want some pipe cleaners? YOU WILL EAT YOUR CHILDREN. It's the only reason I work here, I could have got some boring job on campus just as easy. But where's the art in that?
(Pause.)

WILL: Well I'm just gonna finish up my—

LEROY: You just move to town?

WILL: Um. Yes, actually.

LEROY: Where from?

WILL: Up north.

LEROY: Where up north?

WILL: Outside of Couer d'Alene.

LEROY: Where outside of Couer d'Alene?

WILL: Um. Small town.

LEROY: Beautiful up there.

WILL: Yes, it is, it's really— Have you spent time up there?

LEROY: Little bit. Family trips, you know. Things like that. Kootenai county, right?

WILL: That's right.

LEROY: Rathdrum—that's around there, isn't it?
    (Pause.)

WILL: Yeah, that's actually—well, I grew up in Rathdrum.

LEROY: Is that right? Pretty small town, right?

WILL: Pretty small.

LEROY: Must be hard to be in Boise after such a nice little quiet town like that, huh?

WILL: Boise's actually / very nice—

LEROY: What was the name of that church up in Rathdrum? The one that was in the papers a few months ago—Life Church, New Order—?

WILL: New Life Fellowship.

LEROY: Right, New Life. I kind of lost track of the story after a while—is your pastor in jail yet, or is he still awaiting trial?
    (Pause.)
    You see this? This is me deliberately making you uncomfortable. This is your "FUCK" t-shirt.
    (Pause.)

WILL: Well, I figured this would happen.

LEROY: I actually think this is kind of cool, it's like I'm talking to a survivor of Jonestown or something.

WILL: Is there a reason that you're doing this?

LEROY: Alex is my little brother. Adopted brother, whatever.
    (Pause.)

WILL: I know how this looks. And you're right to be defensive but—honestly, after what happened, I'm just trying to start again.

LEROY: You still believe in all that?

WILL: I still believe in God.

LEROY: What about the other stuff? All that crazy crap your pastor was preaching about, you still believe in all that?
(Pause.)
WILL: I don't know.
(Pause.)
I'm trying to leave all that behind.
(Pause.)
LEROY: Okay, look. I read through some of the articles last night. From what I can tell, you didn't have anything to do with that kid who died. And I get that you coming down here is just your ham-fisted attempt to put your life on a new track. But you're going about this in the creepiest way possible, confronting him at work like this.
WILL: I didn't know what else to do, I was worried your parents wouldn't allow me to see him—
LEROY: Yeah, well, John and Cindy drink enough nowadays that they probably wouldn't even care that you're here. But believe me, I care.
(Pause.)
Just stay away from him, okay? Don't fuck with him. Don't try to "convert" him or whatever.
WILL: I won't. I don't do that anymore.
(Pauline enters with a clipboard, Will and Leroy stop. She senses the tension in the room.)
PAULINE: What?
LEROY: Nothing.
PAULINE: You making enemies already, Leroy?
LEROY: No—
PAULINE: Well, you better not, because the last thing I want to deal with today is fucking conflict resolution and I—
(noticing Leroy's shirt)
Leroy TAKE THAT FUCKING SHIRT OFF.
LEROY: I didn't bring another one.
PAULINE: I CARE?!
Leroy takes the shirt off, putting his Hobby Lobby vest on over his bare torso.
PAULINE: Get out there, you're ten minutes late.
LEROY: Fuck you.
PAULINE: FUCK YOU.
(Leroy exits.)
PAULINE: Fucking hell I wish I could fire that self-righteous little—
Leroy (O.S.)

FUCK YOU.

PAULINE: (screaming)

FUCK YOU!

(to Will)

You didn't completely fill out your contact sheet.

WILL: What?

PAULINE: Emergency contact.

WILL: Oh. Um.

PAULINE: Anybody. Family, friend, girlfriend, whatever. Doesn't have to be local.

WILL: I don't really—…

PAULINE: No family?

WILL: Not that I can—…

(Pause.)

PAULINE: It's for corporate. Gotta put something. Make up a name, I guess.

WILL: Okay.

(Pauline exits. Will fills out the form.)

SCENE SIX.

The next morning. Alex sits at a breakroom table, reviewing a spool of record tape from a register. Two other spools sit in front of him.

Hobby Lobby TV plays on the television.

Will enters, stopping when he sees Alex. Alex looks at him. Awkward silence.

WILL: What's this?
(No response. Alex continues looking through the receipt tape.)
WILL: Sorry.
P.A. ANNOUNCEMENT (Pauline)
(Mandy to frontlines please. Mandy, frontlines.)
(Will goes to a locker, taking out his vest and putting it on. He is about to exit when:)
ALEX: Error in my register countdown yesterday.
(Will turns around.)
WILL: Oh. How much?
ALEX: A hundred and sixty seven dollars short.
WILL: Ouch.
ALEX: I've never been more than a dollar off.
(Pause.)
PAULINE: wants me to look at the receipt logs for the entire day to see if I can figure out where I made the mistake. I don't even know what I'm looking for.
(Pause.)
WILL: Do you want me to—?
(Pause.)
I've done this a hundred times, when I was working at Albertson's I was off all the time.
(Pause.) (Alex puts one of the receipt spools at the seat across from him. Will moves to the table and sits down. Will opens up the receipt tape and starts to read it at an extremely fast pace.)
ALEX: Are you really reading it?
WILL: I told you, I've done it a hundred times. My countdowns were always terrible. Trick is to look for too many zeros on the cash tenders. You can skip all the credits and debits.
(Silence as they examine the record tape.)

ALEX: They called me this morning.
WILL: The blood test?
> *(Pause.)*
> Do you believe me now?
ALEX: It doesn't change anything.
WILL: Okay.
> *(They continue to look.)*
WILL: Is there anything you'd like to know?
ALEX: Like what?
WILL: About me, about—why you were put up for adoption—
> *(Anna enters holding the book from before. She smiles at Will, Will smiles back. Anna sits down at a table.)*
ALEX: John and Cindy said my real parents were neo-Nazis.
WILL: That's not... Um.
ALEX: Well, that's what they said. They said my parents were a couple of neo-Nazis. Are you a neo-Nazi?
> *(Anna looks up from her book.)*
WILL: No. a—
ALEX: Actually, the story about you has changed a few times. When I was little, they told me that you both died in a car accident. Then later, it was that you were neo-Nazis. Then, they said that you beat me.
WILL: *(reading the receipt tape)*
> Maybe we should talk about this somewhere else.
> *(Alex looks at Anna.)*
ALEX: Hi, Anna.
ANNA: Um.
ALEX: This is my father. His name is—
> *(Alex looks at Will's nametag)*
ALEX: Will. He put me up for adoption when I was a baby, and according to my parents he's a child-beating neo-nazi who's dead.
> *(Anna closes her book and exits quickly.)*
> *(Silence.)*
WILL: Found it.
ALEX: What?
> *(Will shows him the receipt tape.)*
WILL: See? It's a cash tendered. You entered two hundred instead of twenty.
> *(Pause.)*
ALEX: I've never made a mistake like that before.
> *(Alex takes the receipt tape from him, circling the mistake.)*

ALEX: *(not looking at him)*
   Thank you.
   (Pause.) (Alex puts down the receipt tape, staring at his hands.)
ALEX: Okay, I want you to start talking. You'll start talking, you'll tell me
   things about yourself but when you say something I don't want to
   hear or don't care about, I'm going to say stop, and you're going to
   stop, and then say something different.
   *(Alex reaches into his backpack and takes out a large notebook and a pen.
   He opens to a page about a quarter of the way through and starts writing.)*
WILL: What's—?
ALEX: Stop.
   (Pause.) (Alex continues to write.)
WILL: You were born in a hospital in Couer / d'Alene—
ALEX: Stop.
   (Pause.)
WILL: Your mother and I / were—
ALEX: Stop. I said things about you. Go.
   (Pause.)
WILL: I grew up in Rathdrum. My parents were from there, too. It's a
   little town, about six thousand people. There's a little grocery store
   that my grandfather started, and my father ran it after he died, but it
   closed when—
ALEX: Stop. Boring.
WILL: I'm thirty-nine years / old—
ALEX: Stop.
   (Pause.)
WILL: I didn't have anything to do with you being put up for / adoption—
ALEX: Stop.
WILL: Your mother left me after you / were born and she—
ALEX: Stop stop STOP. If you don't stop I'm going to kill myself.
   (Alex's breathing speeds up a bit.) (Long Pause.)
WILL: Okay, I—…. I'm allergic to tuna, but it's not a terrible allergy so I
   eat it sometimes.
   (Alex begins to calm down.)
WILL: I don't own any decent pants and I don't know why. I don't like
   movies.
ALEX: *(still concentrating on his writing)*
   Why?
WILL: Because they're too violent.
ALEX: There's violence in the world.

WILL: But we don't need to take pleasure in it.

ALEX: That's a stupid thing to say.

(*Pauline appears in the doorway.*)

PAULINE: MANDY?! You guys seen Mandy?

ALEX: No.

PAULINE: Fuckin' Mandy.

PAULINE: exits. (*Pause.*)

WILL: There are things I regret.

(*Alex stops, looks up at him momentarily, then continues writing.*)

WILL: More than regret. There are things that tear into me. Things that that make me physically ill.

ALEX: Stop. I don't care how you feel.

(*Pause.*)

Why were you hiding in the fabric section at closing the other day?

(*Pause.*)

WILL: You saw me?

ALEX: Yes.

(*Pause.*)

WILL: I just—needed a quiet place to do some work.

ALEX: What work?

WILL: I'd really rather not—

ALEX: Tell me.

WILL: Alex—

ALEX: Tell me or I'm gonna kill myself.

WILL: Why do you say that? You don't really mean that, do you?

ALEX: STOP.

(*Pause.*)

WILL: It's like—a blog. It's sort of a novel that I'm writing online.

ALEX: People read it?

WILL: Yeah.

ALEX: How many?

WILL: Quite a few. I don't know.

ALEX: What's it about?

(*no response*)

What's it about?

WILL: The Rapture.

(*Alex stops writing, looks at Will.*) (*Pause.*)

WILL: You actually know what that is?

(*Leroy enters. He glares at Will and goes to his locker, taking out his vest.*)

ALEX: GO AWAY LEROY I'M DOING SOMETHING.

(Leroy exits.)

WILL: Do you want to be a composer?

(Alex considers for a second.)

ALEX: Yeah. Kind of.

WILL: What instrument?

ALEX: It's not like that, it's like—performance art.

(Pause.)

You wouldn't understand.

WILL: No, but I'd like to.

P.A. ANNOUNCMENT (Pauline)

Will to register four, please. Will, register four.

WILL: Could you—could I hear some of it sometime? Do you have any
recordings of your music, or—?

ALEX: People don't take me seriously. You wouldn't take me seriously.

WILL: I would. I take you seriously.

(Alex considers for a second, then takes out his iPod and some iPod speakers.)

ALEX: Don't look at me.

WILL: Don't—?

ALEX: When I'm performing. Don't look at me.

WILL: Oh, you're going to—?

ALEX: My music isn't meant to be recorded.

WILL: You want to—here, right now?

ALEX: Yeah. Don't look at me.

WILL: Oh—uh, okay.

*(Will turns away from Alex. Alex searches around on his iPod for a second.
He flips around in his notebook a bit, stopping at a page. He hits play on
his iPod. A simple, electronic riff starts to play.)*

ALEX: I got this from a Casio keyboard made in 1989.

WILL: It's pretty.

ALEX: IT'S NOT SUPPOSED TO BE PRETTY.

WILL: Okay, I'm sorry. Sorry.

*(Alex takes a breath. After a moment, Alex starts to read. It shouldn't be
"singing" per se—but he obviously has very specific ideas on volume, tone,
rhythm, etc that make the reading sound vaguely musical.)*

ALEX: FEED YOUR USELESENESS
FEED YOUR USELESSNESS
CLOWN OF CLOWNS
NATION OF TEARS
I AM HUNGRY
I AM HUNGRY

CLOWN OF CLOWNS
NATION OF TEARS
I AM HUNGRY
I AM HUNGRY
(ants and bedbugs)
(ants and bedbugs)
BLOOD AND GUTS AND FLESH AND TRUTH
BLOOD AND GUTS AND FLESH AND LIES
CLOWN OF CLOWNS
NATION OF TEARS
(ants and bedbugs)
(ants and bedbugs)
(CONTINUED:)
Alex *(cont.)*
I'M EATING TOO FAST
WE'RE EATING TOO FAST
WE'RE CHOKING
CHOKING
CHOKING
CHOKING
SWALLOW IT
CAPITALISM
END

(The song ends abruptly, Alex turns off the music right at the last lyric.)
(Long Pause.) (Alex looks at Will.)
ALEX: You can look at me now.
(Will looks at Alex, not knowing what to say.)
ALEX: It's deliberately ironic, it's a statement about consumerism, and—
(Pause.)
Fuck this, you don't get it. No one gets it.
WILL: No, it was… Thank you. Thank you for doing that for me, that
was—neat, it was—really interesting—
ALEX: Interesting? I'm gonna kill myself.
P.A. ANNOUNCEMENT (Pauline)
Will. Register four. Now.
Alex gets up.
ALEX: I'm going back to the floor now.
WILL: Wait—
(Will blocks him from leaving.)

ALEX: What are you doing? Stop.

WILL: Please, just—I just want to talk to you—

ALEX: Stop.

(Alex's breathing becomes quicker.)

WILL: I just want to get to / know you—

ALEX: STOP. STOP.

WILL: I'm your father! / I just want to—

ALEX: STOP STOP STOP STOP

(Alex becoming more and more agitated, stands up, hyperventilating. He grabs his chest.)

WILL: Okay, I'm sorry—what's the matter? Okay, just—calm down, you're okay—

(Will wraps his arms around Alex. Pauline enters. She sees Alex.)

PAULINE: Fuck me. What did you say to him?

WILL: Nothing! I didn't say anything!

PAULINE: rushes to the phone, paging over the PA.

PAULINE: Leroy, breakroom now.

(Alex gets worse and worse.)

WILL: Alex, just take a breath. Take a breath, / you just need to breathe—

PAULINE: Leroy knows what to do, just get away from him.

WILL: Alex, it's alright. / Just calm down.

PAULINE: Goddammit, Will, I said leave him alone!

(Leroy enters. Will still has Alex in his arms, Alex struggles a bit but Will holds onto him.)

LEROY: GET OFF HIM.

(Will backs off of Alex. Alex slumps down to the floor, Leroy goes to him.)

LEROY: Okay, buddy, you ready? Look right in my eyes.

(Alex looks at him. They stare at one another silently for a very long time— finally, Alex starts to shake a little less. Very slowly, his breathing starts to regulate. Finally, Alex stops shaking and breathes normally, still looking straight at Leroy.)

ALEX: Chagall?

LEROY: Nope. Kandinsky.

ALEX: It never works.

LEROY: One day.

(Pause.) (Leroy helps him up.)

PAULINE: Alex, take the rest of the day off, okay?

LEROY: *(to Alex)*
You okay?

ALEX: Yeah.

LEROY: I'll drive you home—

ALEX: I have my bike. I'm fine.

PAULINE: You sure?

(Alex gathers his things.)

ALEX: Yeah.

(Pause.)

Sorry.

PAULINE: Nothing to be sorry for.

(Alex exits, followed by Leroy.)

PAULINE: Fuck I hate it when he does that thing. He'll be fine. But if it happens again, don't fucking go near him, just get Leroy in here as fast as you can, okay?

WILL: Okay.

PAULINE: *(checking her clipboard)*

Alright. Well, now we're sort of fucked, we only have two on front lines, and we've got that whole back-to-school display to—

(Leroy re-enters, going to Will.)

LEROY: I told you to stay / away from him.

WILL: Leroy, honestly, / I didn't do anything, I didn't—

PAULINE: Leroy—

(Leroy gets in Will's face, shoving him into the lockers.) .

LEROY: WHAT DID YOU SAY TO HIM?

PAULINE: rushes over to them, breaking them up.

PAULINE: OKAY OKAY OKAY ENOUGH.

(Leroy moves away from Will.) (Pause.)

PAULINE: Both of you sit down. Now.

(Will and Leroy sit. Pauline turns off the television and pulls out a conflict resolution form, begins to fill it out.)

PAULINE: Fucking conflict resolution, I don't have time for fucking conflict resolution today.

LEROY: Do we have to do this, Pauline?

PAULINE: Fuck you, Leroy. Last year when that guy, what's his name, lazy eye, CARL—when Carl made Mandy cry and Mandy went to corporate and I had to do a FUCKING WEEKEND WORKSHOP, so yes, we have to do this. Alright. Let's just do this as fast as possible. Each of you, state your case or whatever. Leroy you go first.

LEROY: Sure.

WILL: I didn't do anything—

PAULINE: No interrupting. Leroy, go.

WILL: I really don't feel comfortable with—

PAULINE: FUCK YOU, Will. Leroy, go. And try to phrase everything in terms of how you feel.

LEROY: I feel this is stupid.

PAULINE: I FEEL FUCK YOU Leroy.

LEROY: Pauline, do you know who this guy really is?

(Pause.)

PAULINE: What?

LEROY: He's from that crazy end-times church up outside of Couer d'Alene, in Rathdrum? The one from a few months ago, with the pastor who let that kid die out in the forest?

(Pause.)

PAULINE: *(to Will)*

You're in that church?

WILL: New Life Church doesn't even exist anymore, I was just a member of the congregation—

LEROY: You were like the second in command, you lived at the church--

WILL: No, see, this is something the papers all got wrong. I lived at the church because they paid me to be their bookkeeper and janitor. There were over ninety people in the congregation, I was just one of them.

(Pause.)

Pastor Rick is going to jail, and he has to live with the reality of what he did, and I—… I was questioned for months. I had nothing to do with Daniel Sharp's death.

(Silence. Pauline crumples up the conflict resolution form. She paces a bit.)

PAULINE: Why the fuck am I always the last one to know what's happening in this store?

LEROY: Alex is his son. That he abandoned when Alex was a baby.

(Pauline drops her clipboard, exasperated. Silence. After a few moments, Pauline collects herself.)

PAULINE: Leroy, clock out and go home.

LEROY: Me?

PAULINE: Leroy.

(Leroy angrily grabs his bag out of a locker and leaves the room. Pauline stares at Will.)

WILL: I didn't mean to cause trouble.

PAULINE: Be quiet.

(Pause.)

You know I can fire you.

WILL: I'm a good employee. I don't have a criminal record. You can't fire

me because of a church I used to go to.
(Pause.)

PAULINE: I'm gonna say this once, and I hope you understand me.
(Pause.)

I took over this store four years ago.
(CONTINUED)

PAULINE: (cont.)

The first day I was here, four out of six cashiers called in sick, there were rats in the stock room, and a good quarter of all items on the floor were mis-stocked or mis-labeled.

The manager before me, this little pip-squeak from Nampa, he saw there was mold problem in the air ducts so his solution was to puncture an air freshener and toss it inside. It was chaos, you understand? Corporate told me I was taking over as a temporary measure, to oversee the branch for six months before, they said, they would most likely close it completely. And what did I do? I cleaned it up. I stayed here during nights by myself restocking and organizing, cleaning the air ducts, firing and hiring and basically reshaping this entire store from the ground up. I took out ads in the paper announcing new management and grand-reopening sales. Six months later, our profits were up sixty-two percent, and they've been climbing ever since. I, Will, I brought order to chaos.

WILL: That's really—impressive.

PAULINE: Goddam right it's impressive. Damn near miraculous. And it happened because of me. Because I changed everything about this store, I changed the way this store feels, the way it thinks, the fucking ecosystem in this store. And I Will not have you or anyone else disrupting the ecosystem I have painstakingly crafted.
(Pause.)

Listen, personally, I don't give a shit what you believe. But as far as the good people of Boise are concerned, you are a state-wide embarrassment. And if people were to find out that one of our cashiers is from this wacky little cult up north, they may think about buying their silk flowers somewhere else.
(Pause.)

When you're in this store, just—stay away from Alex, understand? And I don't want anyone else finding out about this church of yours. No customers, no co-workers, no one.
(Pause.)

You're on register four.
(Will gets up and starts to exit.)

PAULINE: So you still believe in God?
  (*Pause.*) (*Will turns back to Pauline.*)
WILL: Yes.
PAULINE: After all that?
WILL: Yes.
PAULINE: Why?
  (*Pause.*)
WILL: You'll see.
  (*Will exits.*)

SCENE SEVEN.

Night. Will, in the parking lot, as in scene one. Once again, the sounds of the freeway can be heard as well as the buzzing glow of neon signs and florescent lights overhead.

He stands with his eyes closed, listening to the noise.

WILL: Now.
    …
    …
    …
    Now.
    (silence, then becoming more aggressive)
    Now.
    (long pause, more aggressive)
    NOW.
    (pause, more aggressive still)
    NOW NOW NOW NOW NOW N—
    Will stops himself, opening his eyes. *(Pause.)*
    The noise continues.

SCENE EIGHT.

That night. Will sits in the breakroom, his computer hooked up to the internet jack on the wall. A video of a liposuction plays on the television.

Anna enters, seeing Will. She averts her eyes a bit, but doesn't leave. (Long Pause.)

WILL: I can go.
ANNA: It's fine.
(Short pause, then Anna sits down at a table. She notices the TV.)
ANNA: Oh my God. What is that?
WILL: Oh—I don't know, looks like—I don't even know.
ANNA: That's just disgusting.
WILL: You want me to turn it off?
ANNA: Yes. No. Yes. No, leave it on. Oh my God! Every time I come in here and it's playing these medical things—I just can't stop looking, you know? Oh my God that's disgusting.
(Pause.) (Anna smiles a bit at Will, then opens her book.)
WILL: Where were you hiding tonight?
ANNA: Textiles.
WILL: You were?
ANNA: Yes.
WILL: I was there, too.
ANNA: You were not!
WILL: I was, I was next to the back-to-school display, behind the school desk and the—
ANNA: Shut up.
WILL: What?
ANNA: Shut up!
WILL: I'm—what?
ANNA: I was right next to you!
WILL: You were?
ANNA: I was crouched behind the button kiosk! We were five feet away from each other!
WILL: Oh, wow.
ANNA: That's just creepy! Well that's just creepy. How did we not see each other?
WILL: I'm pretty quiet.
ANNA: So am I. Jesus, it's just so—!

WILL: Please don't—… Sorry.

ANNA: What?

WILL: It's just—I'm sorry, the swearing—it's…

ANNA: Oh. I'm so sorry.

WILL: It's fine—

ANNA: Sorry.

> *(Anna almost goes back to reading, then:)*

ANNA: I just want to say I think it's really great that you're here to re-connect with a son, I think that's a great thing to do. I think that's very mature, and very sweet.

WILL: Thank you.

ANNA: I mean, uprooting yourself and moving here from—where are you from?

> *(Pause.)*

WILL: Up north.

ANNA: Up north, you move here from up north and you want to get to know your son, you want to re-unite? That's just great, it's really sweet.

WILL: Thank you.

> *(Pause.)*

ANNA: I'm sorry for swearing.

WILL: It's completely fine.

ANNA: It's such a bad habit. Working around Pauline , I think that's what does it. I start to sound like her.

WILL: You don't sound like her.

ANNA: I mean, I grew up Lutheran, my mother's very religious. And I go to church sometimes with her, I have respect for… You know, God, and everything. And like I said, I believe in Jesus.

> *(Pause.)*

> Do you go to a church here?

> *(Pause.)*

WILL: I had a church up north, but I haven't really… I haven't found one here yet.

ANNA: Go to the Lutheran church!

WILL: Maybe.

ANNA: I don't mean to be forward, I'm sorry. Am I annoying you? You look like you want to get to work.

WILL: No, it's… I enjoy talking to you.

> *(Anna blushes.)*

ANNA: Oh, shut up, you shut up! You're cute.

WILL: And we both hid in textiles tonight, maybe we're kindred spirits.

ANNA: Oh, shut up!

(Anna hits him with her book, maybe a little too hard.)

ANNA: Oh my God, I'm sorry.

WILL: It's okay.

ANNA: And I just swore!

WILL: Yes, you did.

ANNA: I'm just sort of an idiot.

WILL: No you're not.

ANNA: I really am, believe me. I think Pauline's ready to fire me.

WILL: Why?

ANNA: Oh, I just don't do anything right. I put the wrong barcode on an entire palette of doll heads the other day, do you believe that? I put the arm and leg barcode on every last one of them. PAULINE: says I cost the company over a hundred dollars.

WILL: You just made a mistake.

ANNA: Yeah, well, that's one thing I'm good at. I don't even want to tell you how many places I've been fired from in this city. Barnes and Noble, JC Penney, three McDonald's, two Wendy's, the Super Walmart and the regular Walmart—pretty soon I'm gonna run out. Have to go back to telemarketing, I really hate telemarketing.

WILL: Are you married?

(Pause.)

Sorry, what a dumb thing to just blurt out like that, I just—

ANNA: No, I'm not... I have a boyfriend. Well, sort of, we—you know, we date.

WILL: What does he do?

ANNA: He's a telemarketer.

(Quick pause)

And you're a writer!

WILL: Not—really.

ANNA: Well, you write things and people read them, that makes you a writer, doesn't it? Like I said, it's probably better than this book here. I have to stick with it till it's done, but it's just so awful. It's called "Falling From Grace". You ever read it?

WILL: No.

ANNA: The main character's called "Grace", get it?

WILL: Oh, sure.

ANNA: She lives on this big estate in California, and she has this really rich husband, but all of a sudden he dies in this big car wreck, and turns out that— I'm sorry, what am I doing?

WILL: No, no—keep going.

ANNA: Well, she has to figure out how to live now that she doesn't have this rich husband, and turns out he had all this debt, so she didn't get any money, and then she has to move into this studio apartment and it's hard and blah blah blah. Anyhoo! She's working as a checkout girl, and she falls in love with a customer, and they end up together, and she's happy. And now I'm fifteen pages from the end, so I'm hoping she dies.

(Pause.)

WILL: Wait, I'm sorry, you hope she—?

ANNA: Well c'mon! Why the heck have I read a hundred and eighty pages? To hear about this woman getting married and being happy? This is what I'm reading?! I heard once about that book called Anna—something. Anna Karenia? Is that it? Anyway it's this old Russian novel, someone told me she kills herself at the end and that sounded good but it just looked so long.

(Pause.)

Does anyone die in your book?

WILL: Well, it's—about the end of the world, actually.

ANNA: Oh my gosh, a lot of people die then!

WILL: Yeah, quite a few.

ANNA: That sounds so good!

WILL: Thank you.

ANNA: Read some to me! Is that okay that I said that? I'm sorry.

WILL: Oh, well—it's online, you can just—

ANNA: Oh, we don't have a computer at the house. Well, we do, but my dad is the only one who uses it, he doesn't…

(Pause.)

If you don't wanna read it to me, that's fine. I'm being annoying.

WILL: No, you're not, it's me—I just sort of feel like I've lost faith in what I'm writing.

ANNA: Oh, well, all writers hate their own writing, isn't that a thing?

WILL: Yeah, well. Okay, I can…

(scrolling on the computer screen)

This is funny, I'm a little nervous.

ANNA: You're nervous because of me?

WILL: A little.

ANNA: Oh shut up. That's so cute! I'm sorry, that's just so cute, shut up.

(Pause.)

WILL: Okay.

(reading)

"When Andy woke up that morning to his screeching alarm clock, he knew that something was different. The bedroom in his small apartment was windowless but the darkness he woke up to that morning felt more profound, more deliberate. And as he stumbled his way to the light-switch, his forehead sweating, somehow he knew something greater was happening. The light switch didn't work. He opened his bedroom door and squinted his eyes, expecting to greeted by the same blast of sunshine that hit his face every morning, but felt nothing, and saw nothing."

(stops)

Wow this is just terrible, isn't it? It sounds terrible when I read it out loud.

ANNA: No, it's not at all! Keep going!

WILL: *(reading)*

"His living room was pitch black as well. He fumbled through the darkness, barely able to make out the shape of the front door. 'It must still be night,' he thought to himself. 'Something must be wrong with my clock.' He managed to open the front door, and looking outside he saw—nothing. No sun, no moon, no stars. A blackness had overtaken everything. On a usual morning Andy would open his door to the street and the McDonald's and the Home Depot he lived next to. But today, there was no traffic. There were no billboards and neon signs.

(CONTINUED:)

WILL: *(cont.)*

The whole buzz to the world had been taken away, apart from the faint sound of thousands upon thousands of people wandering the streets of the entire suburb, begging for light, cursing heaven, chewing their tongues, and at that moment Andy lifted his eyes to God and whispered an unconscious prayer of confusion, relief, and optimism."

(Long Pause.)

ANNA: Holy crap. You really wrote that?

WILL: Yeah.

ANNA: That was so good!

WILL: It sounds so terrible to read it out loud—

ANNA: That sounds like a real book! Will, that totally sounds like a real book! That is a real book!

WILL: Thank you.

ANNA: I just... WOW!

(staring at Will)

What are you doing working at a place like this? Why don't you get it published, make some money?

WILL: Oh, it's—sort of complicated—

ANNA: Do you need an agent for that kind of thing? I guess I don't know how all of this works. But you could get an agent, it's so good.

WILL: I never really did this for money, it wasn't about that.

ANNA: Oh, sure. You just love writing, / you're an artist.

WILL: I did it because I thought I was spreading God's word.

(Pause.)

ANNA: Huh?

WILL: Nothing, nevermind.

(Pause.) (Anna tenses up.)

ANNA: So what kind of church did you go to?

(Pause.)

WILL: I'd actually rather not talk about it—

ANNA: Yeah but what kind of church was it?

WILL: It was a non-denominational—

ANNA: No, I mean like Methodist, Lutheran, whatever—

WILL: That's what I'm saying, it was non-denominational. Nevermind, it doesn't—

ANNA: I don't know what that means.

WILL: It means that we weren't part of any huge network or organization, we started just because we wanted to. Because we didn't want a church dedicated to any organization, we just wanted a church dedicated to Christ.

(Pause.)

ANNA: I'm Lutheran.

WILL: Oh.

ANNA: Yeah. I only go sometimes.

(Pause.)

You don't know me.

(Pause.)

WILL: What?

ANNA: I said you don't know me.

WILL: I didn't say that I—

ANNA: You know I've had a lot of co-workers like you, super religious guys who try to get me to go to church with them, these little whattayou-callthem, evangelical churches? I even went a couple times. They'd see me sitting and reading my books or whatever, and they'd think, now there's someone who needs help. But let me tell you, I don't need any help, and these churches? No different from a fucking Hobby Lobby, I'll tell you that much. Everyone wants something. So don't think that you know me.

WILL: I'm really not—I'm sorry. I'm not trying to convert you, believe me.

ANNA: You're not?

WILL: No. Really. I'd rather just—not talk about it.

(Pause.)

ANNA: Well what the hell? I'm not good enough for your church or something?

WILL: No, it's... I'm just gonna take off, I think.

(Will closes his computer, putting it into the case. He stands and is about to exit when:)

ANNA: Sorry. It's not you. I know I can turn on a dime like that, I'm sorry. I live with my dad, and all my brothers, they make fun of me, especially when I read so... Anyway, I'm not good with people.

(Will goes back and sits next to Anna.)

ANNA: Just do me a favor, okay? If you see God coming again, if you see him coming in his cloud or whatever and he's about to kill us unbelievers, you let me know, cause I'll be down on my hands and knees praying for forgiveness then, okay?

(The television goes to static for a split second and then starts playing Hobby Lobby TV. They both look at it.)

WILL: I thought someone had to jiggle the satellite dish.

ANNA: Sometimes it just flips back on. Thing has a mind of its own.

(Pause.)

(I think I'm gonna go. It's nothing you said, just... Do you want to leave together? I'm not saying—Oh, gosh, I didn't mean—)

WILL: No, it's fine, I—think I'll just stick around for a while longer.

ANNA: How much sleep do you get?

WILL: Lately, not much.

(Will goes back to his computer, opening it up. Anna starts to exit.)

ANNA: Maybe one of these nights I could try and read your book. Sometimes I can use the computer after my dad falls asleep.

(They smile at one another. Anna exits. Will looks at his computer for a few moments, then closes it.)

(He turns on the television, Hobby Lobby TV is on. He puts a chair in front of the television and watches it silently.)

SCENE NINE.

Hours later, the middle of the night, in the parking lot. The noise of the interstate is heard. Alex is waiting in the shadows. Will enters.

ALEX: Hi.

WILL: *(startled)*
OH. My— Hi.

ALEX: Hi.

WILL: What are you—?

ALEX: I've been sitting out here for a while. I heard Villa-Lobos, were you playing Villa-Lobos in the breakroom?

WILL: Yeah.

ALEX: You know I don't even really like Villa-Lobos all that much.

WILL: You don't?

ALEX: Not really. I think it's sort of trite.

WILL: Oh. I… I really like it.
(Pause.)
How did you know I was—?

ALEX: Anna told me you've been spending your nights here.
(Pause.)

WILL: I'm sorry if I did something wrong earlier today, I didn't mean for you to get upset—

ALEX: Leroy told me about that church you used to go to. He said you guys called yourselves "evangelical", but he said that's just a code word for a cult.

WILL: It wasn't a cult.

ALEX: So what was it?
(no reply)
My best friend and I used to write music together, all the time. But then he started going to one of those evangelical churches. He said he didn't need music anymore, he said he was happier than music could ever make him. And I'd ask him to tell me about his church, but he said he couldn't talk to me anymore because I was ruining his relationship with God. He doesn't even look at me now. We're in English together, first period, and every fucking morning he looks so happy.
(Pause.)
Tell me what your church was like. Go.

WILL: That church doesn't exist anymore. We don't need to talk about it.

ALEX: Tell me or I'm going home.

(Pause.)

Go.

(Pause.)

WILL: In the beginning, it was—amazing. We were all young and ambitious, we would sit around with one another for hours, studying the Bible and talking about our lives—we started a church from the ground up. We weren't interested in emulating any other church, we wanted to create something that was—brand new. And we did. It was—

ALEX: STOP.

(Pause.)

(If your church was so amazing, why did that kid die?)

WILL: We don't need to talk about / that—

ALEX: Leroy told me the story, but I want to hear it from you.

WILL: Why?

ALEX: Because if you do, I'll tell you some things about me.

(Pause.)

Go.

(Pause.)

WILL: Danny was—… He had just graduated from high school. His parents wanted him to go to school and become a pharmacist, he didn't want to leave the congregation. They basically disowned him. I lived at the church, and since we both worked at the same Albertson's, it just made sense for him to live there too.

ALEX: You lived together?

WILL: Yes. He was looking for spiritual guidance, and in a way, so was I. He didn't want to be a pharmacist, I didn't want to work at Albertson's. We helped one another.

(Pause.)

One night, after work, Danny and I were in the Albertson's parking lot, and he told me that he—was questioning his faith, that he didn't believe in God. I didn't know what to do, I was in over my head. So I went to our pastor, and—I told him what Danny had said to me.

ALEX: You told on him.

(Pause.)

Then what happened?

WILL: You already know the rest of the story—

ALEX: Tell me what happened next. Go.

(Pause.)

WILL: Rick took him into the wilderness. He thought he could help

Danny gain an understanding of his place in God's universe if he—brought him to a point of physical exhaustion. He felt that God was telling him to do it.

(Pause.)

ALEX: Keep going.

WILL: About a week later, Pastor Rick comes back to the church, and he comes to me and says—he says he has Danny in the trunk of his car, and he doesn't know what to do. He says that a day earlier he woke up and Danny was stiff. And blue. And he tried to perform CPR, but it didn't work. And he started to cry, and I called the police.

(Pause.)

Yes, I told on Danny. I told on him and if I would have known that Rick was capable of...I pray for forgiveness every night, every night I—

ALEX: I was molested by my sixth grade teacher.

(Pause.)

Also, I was raped by my fourth grade teacher.

WILL: You were--?

ALEX: And my fifth and third and second grade teachers.

WILL: What are you doing?

ALEX: When I was thirteen I was kidnapped for over a week. I was blindfolded in the trunk of a car, every eight hours they would open it up and feed me and give me water without taking the blindfold off.

WILL: Wait——

ALEX: When I was eight, I was camping with my parents and wandered off, and they found me over a month later, and they still don't know how I survived, and I don't remember any of it.

(CONTINUED:)

ALEX: *(cont.)*

When I was fifteen, I watched my best friend commit suicide with his dad's old army pistol. All my life, my parents have told me that I'm not important because I'm not their real kid.

(Pause.)

WILL: I don't underst—

ALEX: The thing about being raped in the fourth grade I told Pauline when she first hired me. The thing about my friend committing suicide is something I told Anna. The thing about being kidnapped, I told that to my biology teacher. I got an A this semester.

WILL: So none of / that is—

ALEX: The last one about my parents, I told to Leroy. He's confronted my parents about it before, they always deny it. But he believes me.

(Silence.)

WILL: Why did you tell me all that?

ALEX: Because you told me about Daniel Sharp.

(Pause.)

WILL: The story about your friend, the friend who joined a church and stopped talking to you—that one's true?

ALEX: That one's true. I haven't told anyone that. Not even Leroy.

WILL: Was he a good friend?

ALEX: He was my only friend.

(Pause.)

WILL: You don't have any songs you wrote by yourself?

ALEX: I wrote all my songs with him.

WILL: You don't have any songs you wrote by yourself?

ALEX: I don't know. I guess.

(Pause.)

They're dumb.

WILL: I'd really love to hear one. If you—if that's alright.

ALEX: What, right here?

(Alex considers for a minute, then starts flipping through his notebook. He lands on a page, looks at it for a second.)

ALEX: I've—... I've got one, but I've barely even looked at it. No one's heard it.

WILL: That's great.

ALEX: I haven't even set it to music yet.

WILL: That's fine, just—read it to me. You don't need music.

ALEX: It's stupid. It's not like, my real art, it's just something stupid I wrote.

WILL: I don't care. I'd just love to hear you read it.

(Alex hesitates for a second, then reads.)

ALEX: (reading, meek and self-conscious)
"My mind folds into itself
when you pass me
like I'm a dead man pretending to be asleep
like I'm a weed growing into itself
and you pass by me
you're passing by me
just now—
Ah, we once found ourselves
spread out onto the wet grass
in the night."

(long pause)

It's stupid, I don't know why I read this to you. It's not like my other stuff, it's trite and sentimental and stupid and—

WILL: That was overwhelming.

(Will smiles at Alex, near tears.) (Pause.)

ALEX: You still believe in God?

(Pause.) (Will looks away.)

WILL: Yes.

ALEX: A God that let Daniel Sharp die in the forest?

WILL: Yes.

ALEX: Why?

(Pause.)

WILL: Because without God, then all I am is a terrible father who works in a Hobby Lobby and lives in his car. There are—greater things in life. There have to be.

(Pause.) (Alex shuts his notebook, putting it back in his backpack.)

ALEX: Keep going.

SCENE TEN.

The next day. Leroy sits in the breakroom reading a book, wearing a T-shirt that reads "YOU WILL EAT YOUR CHILDREN". Alex enters, not looking at Leroy.

LEROY: Hey.
ALEX: Hi.
  (Alex puts his things in a locker, is about to head out.)
LEROY: Why didn't you want a ride this morning?
ALEX: You didn't get my text?
LEROY: No, I got it. But why didn't you need a ride?
ALEX: Felt like riding my bike. Is that a new shirt?
LEROY: Made it a few weeks ago. You like it? I can make you one.
ALEX: It's sort of overdone. The font is too aggressive.
LEROY: Wow. Okay then.
ALEX: I'm just being honest. You want me to lie? Fine. Leroy, it's amazing, you're fucking Picasso.
  (Alex is about to head out to the floor.)
LEROY: Hold up a sec.
ALEX: I'm gonna be late clocking in.
LEROY: Two minutes.
  (Alex sighs, comes back in.)
LEROY: Mom called me. She said you snuck out last night. I covered, I told her you came over to my apartment.
ALEX: I don't care what your mom thinks.
LEROY: So what'd you do? Get drunk with friends?
ALEX: What friends?
LEROY: Is it a girl?
ALEX: Leroy, cut it out.
LEROY: Were you with this guy? Your dad, whatever? Please tell me you weren't with that guy.
  (no response)
  Jesus, Alex.
ALEX: It's not a big deal. We just talked.
LEROY: About what?
ALEX: I asked him about the church he was in and stuff.
LEROY: What did he say?
ALEX: I don't know. I have to clock in.
LEROY: Seriously, what did he say? Did he tell you about how the earth is

six-thousand years old, or that dinosaurs co-existed with man, or—

ALEX: You know, that kid up in Rathdrum—it wasn't really his fault.

(Pause.)

LEROY: Okay—yeah, I know it wasn't his fault, I didn't…

(Pause.)

Alex—you know this guy is nuts, right?

ALEX: Would you stop it? You have no idea what this is like for me, okay?

LEROY: Oh great, are we doing the poor orphan routine now?

(Pause.)

ALEX: Maybe he has some interesting things to say, did you ever think about that? No, because you're always right, and people who believe different things than you are just stupid, right? Maybe I like hearing about that stuff. Maybe I'm interested, how about that?

(Anna enters. She starts to put her things into a locker.)

ALEX: Hi, Anna.

ANNA: Morning. Watch out for Pauline , she just chewed me out for coming in four minutes late.

LEROY: *(to Alex)*

So what are you saying? You're gonna like—get baptized, or something?

ALEX: I DIDN'T SAY THAT, I JUST SAID—you know, forget it. Anna, I like that shirt.

ANNA: Oh, thanks!

LEROY: No, seriously. You want to be a Christian, is that it?

ALEX: I don't know! Why can't I just talk to him about it?!

LEROY: Because he's a fucking psycho! And he might be dangerous!

ALEX: Anna, do you think Will is dangerous?

ANNA: Dangerous? Why would he be dangerous?

(Will enters.)

LEROY: *(to Will)*

What did you do with him last night?

ALEX: Leroy—

WILL: I—we didn't do anything—

LEROY: I want you to keep away from him, you understand me?

WILL: He came to me, I didn't—

ALEX: Leroy, back off!

LEROY: WHY ARE YOU DEFENDING HIM? AM I THE ONLY SANE PERSON LEFT IN THIS STORE? You know what, fuck this, I'm taking care of all right now.

(Leroy goes to the phone and dials a few numbers, putting himself over the P.A.

LEROY: *(into the PA system)*
  Attention Hobby Lobby employees / and guests.
ALEX: Leroy, stop!
LEROY: *(staring straight at Will)*
  This is just a friendly announcement to let you know that one of our
  new employees, Will Cronin, was directly involved with the scandal
  with the cult up north that killed a kid out in the forest. He's an un-
  apologetic religious fanatic, and he believes that soon—
Pauline enters furiously.
LEROY: —Jesus Will come again and kill everyone who doesn't share his
  fucked up beliefs and—
  *(Pauline heads straight for the phone, hanging it up with her finger. She
  stares at Leroy.)*
LEROY: Fuck this. Alex, come on.
  (Alex doesn't move.)
LEROY: Alex C'MON.
  *(Again, Alex doesn't move. Pauline whips out a keychain, and in one swift
  motion, locks the door.)*
LEROY: Pauline.
  *(Pauline, desperately containing her rage, paces over to the lockers. Leroy
  tries the door, it doesn't open.)*
LEROY: Pauline, unlock the / fucking door—
PAULINE: SHUT UP SHUT UP SHUT UP. No one's leaving. No one's
  quitting, just shut up. I just need to—FUCK. I need to think. I
  just need to think for a minute. Everyone sit down.
  (no one moves)
  EVERYONE SIT DOWN NOW.
  (Everyone sits.)
PAULINE: *(nearly frantic)*
  Is it too much to ask that we have a normal fucking workday around
  here?! Here's a news flash for all of you. What people believe doesn't
  fucking matter. What matters are real things. Real things like money,
  the economy, and a country so beautiful that it can support a chain of
  big box retail stores that makes all it's money off of selling people quilt-
  ing supplies and construction paper. That is what matters.
  (pause, thinking)
  Alright, there's only one way to deal with this. Will, I'm sorry—you can
  finish out the rest of your day, but after that you're gonna have to find
  work somewhere else.
WILL: What exactly am I being / fired for?

PAULINE: Look around! One week ago, this store was doing just fine, and now it's fucking chaos! Alex is my most accurate cashier, Leroy knows more about art supplies than anyone in this entire company. It's either them or you. It's my fault, I should have called your references, that's for damn sure.

(Pause.)

Alright, here's what were gonna do. Anna, go out to the floor. Tell any customer you see that a teenager got on the PA or something.

PAULINE: unlocks the door.

ANNA: Oh—uh, I don't—

PAULINE: Anna GO NOW.

(Anna exits.)

PAULINE: Will, register three.

(Pause.)

Please.

(Pause.) (Will considers, then finally makes his way back to the floor.)

PAULINE: Alright, I need both of you back out on the floor. There's four palettes out there that need to be stocked—

LEROY: We need a minute. Please, just a minute.

(Pauline relents and exits. Leroy nods. Pauline exits. Silence.)

ALEX: You think I'm stupid.

LEROY: No—

ALEX: You think I'm a child.

LEROY: Alex.

(Pause.)

Look, I just—… If you wanna be a—Christian, or whatever—

ALEX: Would you stop? It's not about that, it's…

(Pause.)

Leroy, what the fuck does the rest of my life look like?

LEROY: What? Where is this coming from?

ALEX: Last night he told me that life was meaningless. That the reason that he believed in God was that everything on earth was meaningless.

LEROY: And you believe that?

ALEX: Maybe.

(Pause.)

In less than a year, I'm gonna graduate. What the hell am I gonna do then?

LEROY: You have a plan. You'll go to BSU, if the financial aid doesn't come through—

ALEX: That's your plan, not mine. And even if I do that, go to school and major in music, then what? You think I'm gonna like, be the next fucking big thing?

LEROY: Why not?

ALEX: Okay, so I make a few albums, do some performances, probably wind up teaching or something, and that's like, the best case scenario.

(getting upset)

What's most likely going to happen is that I'm going to be mediocre or fail completely at it, come back to Boise, and end up working at this fucking Hobby Lobby—

LEROY: Okay, calm down.

ALEX: —working at this fucking store, for the rest of my life, and that sounds pretty meaningless to me. And what's the alternative? Believing in what my dad believes in, believing in some magical guy up in the clouds who created us for fun I guess, a guy who is going to come pretty soon to kill us all. And that's just as meaningless. These are my two options in life, and they are fucking meaningless.

LEROY: *(cold)*

OKAY Alex.

(Alex stops. Silence.)

LEROY: Look, just—… Buddy, I wish I could give you some big answer, but the truth is we all just do the best we can.

(Pause.)

ALEX: Think of one.

(Pause.)

LEROY: Right now?

ALEX: Yeah.

LEROY: No, Alex, c'mon.

ALEX: I just feel like it, let's just try. C'mon.

(Pause.)

LEROY: Uh. Okay, I got one.

(Leroy looks into Alex's eyes. Silence. Alex stares into his eyes for a long moment.)

ALEX: Frida Kahlo.

(Pause.)

LEROY: Nope. It's—

ALEX: DON'T TELL ME.

(Pause.)

Pollack.

(Leroy shakes his head.)

ALEX: Rauschenberg.

LEROY: No—

ALEX: Edward Hopper. Georgia O'Keefe.

LEROY: Alex, enough. You're not gonna get it.

> *(Pause.)*
>
> You wanna keep working, or you wanna go home?
>
> Silence.

ALEX: I wanna go home.

LEROY: Okay. Just give me a minute, I'll go talk to PAULINE: and then I'll take you home, alright?

> *(Leroy exits. Alex sits motionless for a second, then looks at Hobby Lobby TV. He sits for a long moment listening to the television, before standing up and turning up the volume. For the first time the voices are discernible. The two men speak very slowly, nearly in a monotone.)*

HOBBY LOBBY TV (MALE 1)

> —and so it's, uh. Yeah, it's I think—what's the retail on this?

HOBBY LOBBY TV (MALE 2)

> It's, uh—

HOBBY LOBBY TV (MALE 1)

> It's really a great / product, you know—

HOBBY LOBBY TV (MALE 2)

> It's ninety-seven.

HOBBY LOBBY TV (MALE 1)

> What's that?

HOBBY LOBBY TV (MALE 2)

> Ninety-seven cents. The unit, it's uh. Ninety-seven

HOBBY LOBBY TV (MALE 1)

> Oh, see and that's—that's down from last year. That same unit, uhhh… That was, I wanna say a dollar ten last year. But we, you know. We talked with our distributor, and he—

> *(Slowly, Alex sits down, keeping his eyes on the television.)*

HOBBY LOBBY TV (MALE 2)

> It's always nice when we can offer these savings.

HOBBY LOBBY TV (MALE 1)

> Yeah, it's. It's good to, you know, point the customers toward savings like these. It's a good thing for our employees to keep in mind. I'll tell you, you know, it's also. It's a good product. It's really—you can really do a lot with something like this. Kids love it, and it's good for kids—they can be so creative with things like this—

HOBBY LOBBY TV (MALE 2)

Durable, too.
HOBBY LOBBY TV (MALE 1)

Oh, yeah. You know, it's popular during back to school, it's. Teachers, you know, art teachers, they pick these up—school districts, they love these, and it's great / when we—

HOBBY LOBBY TV (MALE 2)

This year, for the first time, we've been sending fliers out to individual school districts, and we've been getting a great response. The teachers uh, appreciate it.

Alex continues to watch, becoming more and more upset. His breathing becomes quicker.

HOBBY LOBBY TV (MALE 2)

This is, uh. Store number 1478 in Cedar Rapids, they sent out some fliers to the local school board, and they said they've seen an increase in sales, uh, a four percent increase. For the Fall quarter, four percent. Really good stuff.

HOBBY LOBBY TV (MALE 1)

Well, and you know, when you offer quality products like this, uh. You can—feel proud that we can serve our own community by giving them products like these at such low prices.

HOBBY LOBBY TV (MALE 2)

And that we're helping these kids in their education—art is so important for these kids to learn at an early age, that's really what. It's something this company, it's founded on that.

For a moment, it looks like Alex is having another panic attack—but this changes into a quieter, deeper grief.

HOBBY LOBBY (MALE 1)

And you wanna give kids the best art supplies without going bankrupt.

HOBBY LOBBY TV (MALE 2)

Yeah, exactly. / So this is—

HOBBY LOBBY TV (MALE 1)

This is—yep, this is really just a solid product, great for art classes.
(Pause.)
Another great product here—you see this?

HOBBY TV (MALE 2)

Oh yeah.

HOBBY LOBBY TV (MALE 1)

We had this on the shelves down in store 1089 in Tallahassee—
(Leroy enters.)

HOBBY LOBBY TV (MALE 1)

/ —and it was off the shelves almost immediately, so we started introducing it nation wide starting last year.

LEROY: She says she'll want you to make up the hours this weekend.

Mandy's off.

(Pause.)

You ready?

HOBBY LOBBY TV (MALE 2)

We've been getting, uh. A really—a good response to the item, especially in our southeastern division, midwest division—

(Alex gets up, turning the volume back to its original level. Alex looks at Leroy for a moment, then exits. Leroy follows him.)

SCENE ELEVEN.

Much later that night. Will, looking tired and worn out, stares at the television which plays an extreme close-up of eye surgery.

Anna enters with a book. She sees Will immediately. Will continues to stare at the television. Not knowing exactly what to do, Anna sits down at a table at the other side of the room and starts to read.

WILL: Why are you here so late?

ANNA: Couldn't sleep. I don't live far. Just thought I'd—finish up my book.

WILL: How'd you get in?

ANNA: I stole Pauline's spare key ring this afternoon. Got tired of hiding. I figure if she finds out, who cares, I'll go work somewhere else. This place is kinda boring anyway.
(looking at the TV)
Oh, gosh, that's an eye, isn't it?

WILL: Yeah. I think so.
(Anna moves over to him and sits with him. Will finally looks at Anna.)

ANNA: I read that book of yours. Story, whatever it is.
(Pause.)

WILL: All of it?

ANNA: Not all of it. It's long, I didn't have time to read all of it. I had to sneak into my dad's room to use the computer, he was asleep in front of the TV. I didn't have a lot of time. It's really good.
(CONTINUED:)

ANNA: *(cont.)*
(Pause.)
Listen, I know what getting fired feels like. I know. But there are plenty of other places in town you can get a job. My friend Ally, she just got a job at the Costco in Eagle, I could call her and—

WILL: I don't care about getting fired.
(Pause.)

ANNA: Oh.
(Pause.)
Then what's / the—

WILL: Alex came here last night, to see me. And he asked me about God, and the church, and I thought, this is—so amazing, God is giving me the opportunity to have a relationship with my son through him.

We talked for hours out on the loading dock, and then we watched the sun come up over the highway. He promised me that he would meet me here again tonight. He called me toward the end of my shift, he told me he never wanted to see me again, and he hung up.
(Pause.)
I think I might be a bad person.
(Pause.) (Slowly, Anna goes to Will, wrapping her arms around him in a hug. It's awkward at first, but eventually they settle into it.)

ANNA: You know what part of your book I liked best? I mean, I haven't read the whole thing yet, but you know what part I really liked?
(Pause.)

WILL: What's that?
(Anna breaks the hug, but they remain close.)

ANNA: There was that part with the pilot—what's his name?

WILL: Mark.

ANNA: Yeah! Mark. And Mark was flying over Israel and suddenly he looks out the window and he sees the, uh—the / four—

WILL: Four horsemen of the apocalypse.

ANNA: Yeah, and he knows that the world is gonna end, like, soon. And he thinks back on his life, and he realizes all of the bad things he's done, all of the sex and drugs and lies and whatever, and he all he wishes is that he could have repented everything in time. But it was too late. And then he dies. And no one can help him.
(Pause.)
Anyway, that was my favorite part.
(Pause.)

WILL: Danny and I worked at the same Albertson's, we'd try to get the same shifts so we could drive to work together. Some nights, we would both have closing shifts, be there until after midnight. And we'd hide in the store until everyone had left, and then in the middle of the night we'd would go out into the parking lot, right near I-90 where it's nothing but stores and parking lots and stuff. The last time I saw him we were standing in the parking lot praying for Christ to come again. We prayed for all of it to go away, we prayed for all of it to be swallowed up in divine fire, every disgusting house and parking lot and interstate and car and person on fire turning into ash and reforming as a city of pure light that was brilliant and eternal and unchanging and we prayed dear Jesus now.
…
…

...

Now.

...

...

...

Now.

...

...

...

Now.

...

... .

...

And then nothing happened.

(Long silence.)

ANNA: Would you like to go to church with me on Sunday?

(Pause.) (Will looks at her.)

ANNA: Look, I don't meet a lot of guys, and the ones I do meet are pretty
much terrible. But you come in here at night just like I do, and
you're such a talented writer, and I... And listen, you're not the
only one with a checkered past, okay? When I dropped out of high
school, I—... Anyway, I don't even need to tell you, let's just say
that my father, he has good reason to be the overbearing asshole that
he is. But I just think if you could come to church with me, if we
could go together... The pastor, his name is Edward, but everyone calls him Pastor Eddie, it's really nice. And it's not all about
hell and sin and whatever, it's just a nice community organization.
They're very open-minded, we even have a gay couple that comes to
our church, and no one even thinks twice about it. We have a food
bank, and a youth group, and—...

(Pause.)

Will, you can just believe in something else!

WILL: Believe in what? Believe in the Lutheran Church, some branch
of some branch of some branch of Christianity, some organization
that's going to legislate my belief system instead of looking to God's
word for it? You work at a Hobby Lobby, Anna. Before that you
worked at Walmart, JC Penney, McDonald's, Barnes and Noble, and
now we both work here. Your life is meaningless, my life is meaningless, and the only thing that gives any meaning, that brings any
hope to this life is my unshakeable belief that God Will come again

in glory to replace this disgusting life with something new, and pure, and meaningful—

ANNA: Okay, Will.

WILL: *(rising)*

And you could take the easy route, you could go to a liberal church, and believe in nothing, believe that God is unknowable and we'll never know the meaning of life, you'll go to college and get a degree in English or Philosophy or Art or Economics and you'll spend your life searching in the dark, trying to find meaning in meaninglessness—become one of those people who sit around in their fashionable clothes with their fashionable friends and call us bigots, and fanatics, and hicks, calling us idiots for actually believing in something, for standing for truth—

ANNA: Will, stop!

WILL: *(losing himself)*

AND THESE PEOPLE WILL BURN IN HELL, YOU WILL BURN IN HELL BECAUSE INSTEAD OF SEEKING TRUTH YOU MOCK IT, YOU INSULT IT, YOU SPIT IN THE FACE OF GOD AND HE WILL—

(With a quick burst of static, the television flips back to Hobby Lobby TV. Will stops, looking at television.) (Pause.)

(Anna takes her book and exits.)

(Will watches the television for a moment, then slowly opens his laptop. He sits down, looks at the screen, and for the first time, begins to type.)

SCENE TWELVE.

Later that same night, in the parking lot. Will stands, bathed in florescent light, listening to the interstate. Leroy enters behind him.

LEROY: Hey.
   (Will turns around.)(Pause.)
LEROY: You know, last year I found Alex alone in his room reading a Bible. And I was actually angry. I was surprised, I didn't know I felt that strongly. I mean, I always knew that religion was bullshit, I just didn't…
   (Pause.)
   When he was little, I used to show him art films. Take him to galleries. I gave him the collected Ginsberg on his thirteenth birthday. And then seeing him sitting there reading that thing—it was like someone had invaded my turf.
WILL: You won't believe me when I say this, but I never intended on talking to him about what I believe, or my church, or… I just wanted to be his dad, I just—
LEROY: This afternoon he swallowed an entire bottle of my mom's sleeping pills. He's okay, they pumped his stomach. Doctors said he should be sent to some kind of juvenile mental health facility, something like that. Where he won't be a danger to himself. He won't talk to mom or dad. When I asked him why he did it, he said "hell is all around us".
   (Pause.)
   Get in my truck.
   (Pause.)
WILL: What?
LEROY: You wanna be his dad? Now's your chance. We're going to the hospital, and you're going to talk to him. You're going to tell him that there's no heaven, no hell, no apocalypse. No God.
   (Pause.)
WILL: I'm—I'm sorry—
LEROY: You have a choice right now, do you understand? You can go on believing in this bullshit, or you can give it up right now, and maybe—someday—have a normal relationship with your son.
   (Pause.)
   Well?
   Will, holding back tears, looks away from Leroy. He closes his eyes.

WILL: Now.

LEROY: What are you doing?

(Long silence.)

WILL: Now.

(Will doesn't move. Finally, Leroy exits. Will looks back to the interstate, standing in the light in the same way he did at the beginning of the play. Long pause as he listens. He closes his eyes.)

WILL: Now.

…

…

…

Now.

(The sounds of the interstate start to grow in volume.)

WILL: Now.

(The florescent lights become brighter.)

WILL: Now.

(As the light becomes brighter and brighter, the sounds of the interstate grow in volume and change pitch becoming deeper and more violent.)

WILL: Now.

(The light reaches an uncomfortable level of brightness, and the sound of the interstate becomes increasingly more and more distorted.)

WILL: Now.

(As the light reaches it's brightest point, the sounds of the interstate morph into what sounds like one continuous, monotonous explosion—a low, rumbling, unsettling drone that continues throughout the scene.)

(Alex enters, carrying himself differently than before and speaking in a different manner. Will looks at him.)

ALEX: It never works.

WILL: One day.

(Pause.)

ALEX: I was up early this morning, went for a drive up to those mountains outside of town.

(Pause.)

I felt like I should pray. So I got out of the car, and I knelt down on the ground, and I wanted to pray but I couldn't pray anything.

WILL: We could pray together before work.

ALEX: No, that's not it, I…

(Pause.)

When I wake up in the morning, I feel sick. I just feel sick most mornings. Like I don't want to get out of bed. And then I see you, and you

look so happy. You look perfect.
(Pause.)
WILL: I'm not perfect, Danny.
ALEX: Yes. You are. I think you're...
(Pause.)
I see you, and you're so perfect, and I'm—I'm a bad person.
WILL: No, you're not. You're just letting the world get to you. In God's
eyes, you're—beautiful. You're perfect.
ALEX: Pastor Rick is trying so hard / with me—
WILL: One day none of this Will matter. When all this is swallowed up.
When we become bodies of pure light. Our perfect souls ripped
out of these awful bodies and reborn. Both of us. Can you imagine
what that Will feel like?
(Pause.)
ALEX: Will, I'm not sure I believe in God.
(long silence)
Say something.
(Pause.)
Will. Say something.
(Long Pause.)
ALEX: I'm going to walk home tonight.
(Alex exits.)
*(The lights suddenly return to normal, the drone immediately returns to the
normal sounds of the interstate.)*
(Will stands alone, listening.)

END OF PLAY

BACHELORETTE

Leslye Headland

For my best friend, Melissa

PLAYWRIGHT'S BIOGRAPHY

Leslye Headland is a Los Angeles-based playwright and screenwriter. She is the writer/director of the Seven Deadly Plays series, which was produced by and premiered at the IAMA Theatre Company in Los Angeles. The series includes *Cinephilia* (lust), *Bachelorette* (gluttony), *Assistance* (greed), *Surfer Girl* (sloth), *Reverb* (wrath), and *The Accidental Blonde* (envy). *Bachelorette* also enjoyed a sold-out, extended run at Second Stage Theatre Uptown in July 2010, which the NY Times called "vivid, entertaining and witheringly funny." Other New York credits include *Cinephilia* at Theatre Row and *Assistance,* which premiered Off-Broadway at Playwrights Horizons. Ms. Headland is currently working on her final play for the series (pride), as well as commissions for Second Stage Theatre and South Coast Repertory.

On film, Leslye recently wrapped directing her feature adaptation of her play *Bachelorette* with Gary Sanchez Productions (Adam McKay and Will Ferrell), starring Lizzy Caplan, Isla Fisher, Kirsten Dunst, James Marsden and Adam Scott. The film made its world premiere as a selected feature at the 2012 Sundance Film Festival. She is also writing a remake of *About Last Night* for Screen Gems with Will Gluck (*Easy A, Friends with Benefits*) attached to direct. On television, she wrote for the first and only season of *Terriers,* created by Ted Griffin and produced by Shawn Ryan, on FX. She also wrote a pilot based on Julie Klausner's memoir, *I Don't Care About Your Band,* which is also set up at FX.

She holds a B.F.A. in Drama from New York University's Tisch School of the Arts and studied at Playwrights Horizons Theatre School where she was awarded the Robert Moss Prize.

Produced by Second Stage Theatre, New York, 2010
Carol Rothman, Artistic Director
Director: Trip Cullman

CAST

Tracee . . . . ChimoRegan
Carmen M. Herlihy . . . . Becky
Celia Keenan-Bolger . . . . Katie

Fran Kranz . . . . Joe
Eddie Kaye Thomas. . . . . Jeff
Katherine Waterston . . . . Gena

CREW

Casting . . . . Judy Bowman
Andromache Chalfant . . . . Set Design
Emily Rebholz . . . . Costume Design
Ben Stanton . . . . Lighting Design
Jill BC DuBoff . . . . Sound Design

World premiere production presented by IAMA Theatre, January 2008

"There is nothing like puking with somebody to make you into old friends."
~ Sylvia Plath, The Bell Jar

BACHELORETTE

SCENE ONE

> *Two Girls enter an expensive hotel suite.*
>
> *There is a plush couch, a coffee table, two or three chairs, a desk, a large wall mirror and three doors leading to a bedroom, bathroom and closet. The suite is decorated with many floral arrangements. There are many gifts wrapped in white wrapping paper.*
>
> *The Girls, both a bit drunk, stare in awe for a moment. They do not move. Gena (pronounced "JEH-nuh) is a force to be reckoned with even in her dazed intoxicated state. She is perhaps dressed a little boyishly but she's always the sexiest woman in the room. Her alternatively commanding then compassionate personality recalls a headstrong fifth grader.*
>
> *Katie is a true beauty. Her dress is way too short considering her absurd physicality. Katie is all elbows and knees. She has a child-like unawareness of her sexuality. Her looks and wit have been dulled by years of binge drinking but her naïveté and smile are hard to resist.*
>
> *Having sufficiently taken in their surroundings, they burst into laughter.*

GENA: What—

KATIE: What the fuck!?

GENA: Are you kidding me?

KATIE: You. Are. Kidding! ME.
   (Katie bolts into the room. Immediately jumps on the couch.)

GENA: Don't break anything!

KATIE: Holy crap! *(Gena lights up a cigarette. Leaves the door to the suite ajar.)*

KATIE: Dude! Jump! On! This couch!

GENA: Dude. Chill! *(Katie falls off the couch and stumbles into the bathroom)*
   (offstage). (Gena ignores her and wanders. She looks for something to ash in. She bumps into one of the floral arrangements.)

GENA: *(Gesturing to all the flowers)* Fucking hell… who died? You know?

KATIE: *(Offstage)* Gena. You Will not. BELIEVE what's in the bathroom. Come in here! *(Gena goes into the bedroom, gesturing to the bed as she enters.)*

GENA: *(Offstage)* Her final resting place!

KATIE: *(Offstage)* Come in here!

GENA: *(Offstage)* Why? Are you doing coke?

KATIE: *(Offstage)* What!? What...

(Katie re-enters, holding a bottle of expensive champagne.)

KATIE: Oh my god. Where's the coke? *(Gena re-enters. She is briefly unsure of where the coke might be. Then she remembers and pats her pocket.)*

GENA: I have it.

KATIE: You're like a guardian angel.

GENA: Katie... um --what are you holding?

KATIE: *(A bit mystified)* It's more alcohol.

GENA: THANK GOD!

KATIE: Do you know how to open this kind of--

GENA: Give it here, darling.

KATIE: --kind of device. *(Smiles)* Can you smoke in here?

GENA: Nope.

KATIE: You smoke everywhere. *(Katie exits to the bathroom again)*

KATIE: *(Offstage)* Oh my god! That's what I was going to tell you.

GENA: What! Katie! WHAT?! *(Katie re-enters with another bottle of champagne and an astray for Gena.)*

KATIE: Hey dude. Don't yell at me. I'm not the one getting married, okay?

GENA: My apologies.

KATIE: I was gonna saaaaaaaaaaay that there's like 15 bottles of this shit chilling in the bathtub!

GENA: Fuuuuuck.

KATIE: Oh my god I know. It's like so crazy! This is going to be the BEST night EVER! WOODSTOCK! *(Katie jumps on the couch.)*

KATIE: WOODSTOCK! MILLIONS OF PEOPLE! (Breathes like throngs of people cheering) And Jimi Hendrix is like--

(Katie utilizes her champagne bottle like a guitar. She re-enacts Jimi Hendrix playing the Star-Spangled Banner, vocalizing the riff. Gena lights her lighter and waves it like she's at a concert. Affirming Gena.) Totally!

(Katie continues her re-enactment. Then she suddenly and violently sticks her middle finger up at the imaginary throngs of people)

KATIE: FUCK YOU! FUCK YOU BABYBOOMING PIECES OF SHIT! Jimi Hendrix... If he really meant it... if he REALLY REALLY meant it. He would have killed himself. I don't... mean like snorting some bad shit... Going out by accident, right? I mean like putting the barrel of shotgun in his mouth... looking at a picture of his baby girl... BAM! Pull the trigger.

GENA: Kurt Cobain.

KATIE: Jimi Hendrix wishes he was Kurt Cobain. Quick! Give me… give me the lighter.

GENA: Absolutely not.

KATIE: Dude, I have to light my guitar on fire and like.., the "fuck-you" Will be complete. Wait! If we got some heroin—

GENA: We don't do heroin.

KATIE: We should start. Call what's his—

GENA: *(interrupting)* I can't.

KATIE: Can we do some more coke?

GENA: We're rationing, man. Hard times.

KATIE: I'm depressed. I can't believe Pigface Fat Fatty FAT FUCK— *(Gena checks out the closet.)*

What are you doing? What's in there?

GENA: The dress.

KATIE: *(deflates)* Jesus.

GENA: Yep. It's really happening.

KATIE: What does it look like?

GENA: Expensive. *(Then…)* Beautiful. A beautiful white garbage bag.

KATIE: I hate her.

GENA: You can't hate her.

KATIE: Fat people are so easy to hate though.

GENA: Fat people have enough going on.

KATIE: *(Holding up the bottle)* Can you open this?

GENA: I've already got one. Thank you.

KATIE: Will you open yours then?

GENA: You know where you'll get married? In your parents' backyard in Long Island. Or is it technically your backyard as well since you live with them?

KATIE: Who do you think I'll marry?

GENA: Someone appropriate. *(She pops open her champagne bottle. POP! Lots of foam.)*

KATIE: Yah-ee!! Do mine. Do mine! *(Gena takes Katie's bottle. She exposes the cork.)*

KATIE: I think you'll run off with a Russian novelist. And we'll never hear from you again. We'll be like "What happened to Gena?" And I'll be like *(whispers)* "Russian novelist".

GENA: I don't think Russian novelists exist anymore.

KATIE: Then you'll marry an Arab.

(POP! More bubbles. The girls switch bottles.)

GENA: What should we drink to?

KATIE: Life?

GENA: Sure. *(They both chug.)*
Wow.

KATIE: Fuck.

GENA: Wow. *(They chug again.)*
Can we have one of those moments?

KATIE: Yes… I think we should.

GENA: I just wanna say… that I'm… really…

KATIE: Let's drink more first. *(They chug. Katie gags a little. Gena pats her on the back.)*

GENA: I have…

KATIE: What?

GENA: I've no idea. I haven't been this fucked up since graduation.

KATIE: That was, like, a whole week of vomiting.

GENA: You were vomiting.

KATIE: Yeah but you were like… crying and listening to Mozart.

GENA: *(Sighs)* Yeah.

KATIE: *(Coughs)* Can you believe how much Becky lucked out? She's marrying like the richest guy in the world. And he's good-looking.

GENA: Moderately good-looking.

KATIE: I wish I could kill myself, man.

GENA: Katie, stop it.

KATIE: Gena, seriously. I want to die and I can't bring myself to do it.

GENA: Woman. Chillax.

KATIE: Seriously. Did I ever tell you about the time—

GENA: *(I?nterrupting)* Yes. *(Katie takes a swig of her bottle. Gena follows suit. Katie falls over.)*

KATIE: We were gonna have a moment.

GENA: Oh yeah.

KATIE: Let's have it.

GENA: *(After a moment)* It's gone now.

KATIE: Let's do some coke and it'll come back.

GENA: If you do anymore coke, someone's dick is gonna get sucked.

KATIE: Totally.

GENA: I think I was going to say something about--

KATIE: Becky?

GENA: --getting married

KATIE: To a moderately good looking guy.

GENA: Who would've thought.

KATIE: And rich nonetheless. That word is awesome.

GENA: Nonetheless?

KATIE: Absolutely. I don't think I'm using it right.

GENA: Maybe Cal really loves her. Maybe he looks beyond, you know, "looks" and sees... She scares me Katie. Like I haven't seen her since the thing.

KATIE: What thing?

GENA: Remember...with me...her brother...

KATIE: *(Winces)* Right.

GENA: Then out of the blue last minute she invites you and me to party the night before her wedding and has the decency to refrain from making us bridesmaids. Like that is classy and maybe that's what Cal likes about her.

KATIE: Are you trying to be positive?

GENA: I just think it's weird she invited us tonight. Like, what are we doing?

KATIE: Getting wasted.

GENA: Really though. What are we doing here?

KATIE: Getting wasted. There's free booze. I'm excited.

GENA: I think the whole thing stinks. It's bugging me out. We shouldn't have come.

KATIE: We're bringing the party. She knows that's what we do. Right? I mean, what else would she be doing tonight? Rolling around in that bed wondering when that other shoe's gonna drop. Wondering if tomorrow at the alter Cal is gonna say "I do" and then add "but only if you lose 60 pounds."

GENA: Let's do some coke.

KATIE: Finally. *(Gena finds a clear surface to cut lines. She's a little stoned.)*

KATIE: We gotta do it before anyone else gets here. I don't want to share.
(Regan (pronounced "REEguhn") enters the suite.
Regan is a queen bee if there ever was one. She has a fantastic body and a striking face. She is eerily perfect. If you look closely, it should be clear she was not born this way but has worked diligently to appear flawless. She has a penchant for meanness that no amount of beauty can hide. She rips off her expensive coat and tosses it to the floor. She kicks off her designer heels as if they were flip-flops. She throws her purse on the floor like it smells bad. She collapses in the nearest chair.)

REGAN: Holy hell.

GENA: Where have you been?

REGAN: Are you guys doing some coke?

KATIE: Maybe.

REGAN: Thank god.

GENA: Where have you been?

REGAN: Clam-baking with some guys I met. There's only so much pot a girl can smoke before she gets to that point of not having any clue how she got somewhere. There's only so much Dave Matthews one girl can listen to before she considers throwing herself into oncoming traffic!

KATIE: Where are those guys?

REGAN: Trying to find a parking space.

GENA: Are they coming up?

REGAN: I wasn't sure if Becky would be cool with it. I'm gonna text them.

GENA: Where is Becky? I thought she was supposed to meet us here.

REGAN: Probably eating somewhere. *(Re: champagne)* Where did you get that?

KATIE: There's like bottles and bottles chilling in the BATHTUB.

REGAN: Rich fiancées! If only we each had one of our own. *(Regan exits to the bathroom. Gena does a line of coke and passes a rolled-up bill to Katie who follows suit. They snort lines throughout the following.)*

GENA: Are those guys cute?

REGAN: *(Offstage)* They're repulsive. I was just excited about the pot. I haven't smoked since I was five.

KATIE: You got stoned when you were five?

GENA: Regan? What's the deal? Cuz I was gonna--

REGAN: *(Re-entering with her own bottle)* Do you have a date or something?

GENA: I don't want to dick around.

REGAN: Who's dicking around?

GENA: Why did you tell those guys they could come up here?

KATIE: Why not?

GENA: Because, Katie, this isn't our hotel room. And you don't realize this 'cause you like to check out early but usually Regan's schemes have this fantastic way of unraveling. Becky's supposed to meet us here and I—

REGAN: Don't worry about Becky. I'll take care of her.

GENA: I just wanna see this bitch. Throw some rice at her or whatever and get this shit over with.

KATIE: *(To Regan)* You going to the… the thing tomorrow?

REGAN: What thing?

GENA: The wedding. It's tomorrow, right?

REGAN: Yeah. *(Points to herself)* Maid of honor.

KATIE: How did you manage that?

REGAN: Someone had to fulfill best friend duties after Becky dropped Gena.

KATIE: 'Cause of the thing? With her brother?

REGAN: *(Nods, to Gena)* She read me the email she sent you. Brutally epic.

GENA: Who gets married in a hotel?

KATIE: SO TACKY! Why weren't we invited to the wedding?

REGAN: Consider yourselves lucky. I had to go to the rehearsal dinner. I felt like Truman at Geneva.

KATIE: Is that bad?

GENA: SOMEBODY WENT TO AN IVY LEAGUE COLLEGE!

REGAN: Cal is a piece of work.

GENA: SOMEBODY GOT A SCHOLARSHIP TO PRINCETON!

REGAN: Cal bleaches his teeth. Can you imagine marrying a guy who has whiter teeth and less hair on his body than you?

GENA: Or is like half your body weight?

REGAN: It's one thing to like get engaged after three months of dating. I mean, I get it. But Becky's, like, never had a boyfriend.

KATIE: Never?

REGAN: I mean, she definitely didn't in high school. And I would've picked up on it if she had in college. We were CLOSE. We threw up every meal together. Plus we all heard about it after she met Cal. "I met this guy… At work…"

GENA: I was surprised to hear that he works. I assumed people like that just swam in a pool of money all day.

REGAN: Kind of.

KATIE: What does he do again?

REGAN: Something with hedge funds. Becky was temping.

GENA: Swims in a pool of money all day. Becky was fishing the leaves out.

KATIE: I want a pool of money.

GENA: Don't worry, sweetie. You'll get it.

KATIE: I feel like the world is ending.

REGAN: It's not. It's just the first of us to get married.

GENA: I'm perfectly calm.

REGAN: I mean I was sure I was going to get married before her. But, you know what? We don't always get what we want. You know? I'm gonna break up with Frank.

GENA: Don't.

KATIE: You always SAY that.

REGAN: Why hasn't the idiot proposed to me? It's been three years and I'm like sitting around waiting for him to get through med school so what… so he can dump me when he finds someone who will give him a blow job during football. Fuck that!

GENA: Dude. Just give him the blow job during football.

REGAN: No. I won't do that shit anymore. I know you've got to do it in the beginning. When we first got together, I sucked him off for the entire run time of *True Romance*.

KATIE: You went down on him during *True Romance*?

REGAN: The commentary.

KATIE: That is… gay!

REGAN: Blow jobs before dinner. Blow jobs after dinner. Blow jobs during the news, movies, sporting events. What the fuck? Is the quota ever filled?

GENA: You can't spoil them like that. They're like dogs.

KATIE: Or little children.

GENA: They'll get used to it and they'll expect it all the time.

REGAN: So you don't give head.

GENA: Excuse me! I go to town on those fuckers.

KATIE: Hell yeah!

GENA: You get me a dick and I'm like a fat kid eating cake!

REGAN: But it's a special occasion thing.

KATIE: Everything in moderation.

GENA: Speaking of which… *(Moves the coke away from Katie)* Blow jobs are a delicate thing, my friend. You can't just go all out at the beginning of the relationship or affair or whatever. You gotta savor it which makes them savor it. You gotta make them feel like you're holding something back. You know?

REGAN: *(Pops the cork of her champagne)* No. I don't.

GENA: Look. On a scale of one to ten, one being, like, you blow it kisses and ten being you're choking on vomit and semen. You gotta start out with fours and fives. You're just good enough that they feel like you know what you're doing but you're aloof… right? No enthusiasm. So he'll think "Fine. I'll just fuck her." You start off with a ten and you've got nowhere to go. Why is he gonna spend any time fucking you when he just came all over your face? But if you start small… Then you build it up. Give him a six after a fight. Give an eight when he spends a lot of money on you.

KATIE: Eight is like… in the car. While he's driving.

GENA: On the way to your parents' house for Christmas.

KATIE: Then you can go back to fours and fives when you want him to do something like propose.

GENA: Exactly. He'll sense something's afoot.

KATIE: His dick alarm will go off.

GENA: And his dick alarm will go off. He'll ask "What's wrong baby?" when really he means…

KATIE: "Suck my dick harder."

GENA: This also cuts down on the passive-aggressive routine you've got going on.

REGAN: I'm not passive-aggressive.

KATIE: You are SO passive-aggressive. I know because I'm passive-aggressive and you make me look like the prom queen.

REGAN: You were the prom queen.

KATIE: Oh that's right. I was.

REGAN: But isn't rationing blow job potential passive-aggressive?

GENA: That's where you're wrong. Because this has nothing to do with emotions. This is science.

REGAN: It's Pavlovian.

KATIE: Pav—

GENA: Jesus Christ. *(Pushes coke in front of Katie… to Regan)* You get what I'm saying?

REGAN: Yeah.

GENA: Good. Cuz I feel like my head is going to explode.

KATIE: I want to date someone who has a job.

REGAN: Can you believe I'm not getting married first? I mean I'm the one with the boyfriend. I'm hot! I, like, take care of myself.

GENA: It'll be okay, dude.

REGAN: I like exercise and eat like a normal person. I was totally the one who was going to get married first. Frank and I were gonna get married.

KATIE: Men suck.

GENA: No women suck. Men just taste bad.

REGAN: But, like, Becky!? Why does this get to happen to Becky?

KATIE: Why does what get to happen?

REGAN: Like, marrying a Rockefeller and, like, before me and she's FAT. You know? She's fat!

GENA: She's not that fat.

KATIE: I mean… she's not even like a real size.

GENA: According to who? The Gap?

KATIE: I don't work at the Gap anymore! Fuck off!

REGAN: I mean… she's got a nice face.

KATIE: Don't do that.

REGAN: What?

KATIE: That "I just said something mean so I should say something nice" thing.

REGAN: Yeah. You're right. Fuck her. Becky's gonna be richer than any of us ever will be by three PM tomorrow.

GENA: This is about us. Not Becky.

KATIE: I just hope I'm married by thirty. If I'm not married by thirty, I will kill myself. I know you think I'm kidding but I'm not. I'll fucking put the barrel of a shotgun in my mouth.

GENA: Christ! Everyone needs to calm down.

KATIE: I'm totally calm. I just don't want to be thirty and still working in retail and NOT married. I'll fucking kill myself. I'll be like a bunion on the foot of the human race. I mean, you're complaining about Frank but at least you have those retarded kids to save.

REGAN: They're not retarded. They have cancer.

KATIE: Whatever. You know what I mean. You're interesting. You have a noble, like, crusade at the hospital and… And at least you have a guy. At least you're getting cock. I don't even have prospective cock to passive-aggressively manipulate into marrying me.

GENA: Have you ever thought about getting pregnant?

REGAN: Are you crazy?

GENA: No. But I feel like I should've died ten minutes ago.

REGAN: I can't get fucking pregnant.

KATIE: Gena, that's a terrible thing to say.

GENA: I think we should slow down on the coke.

REGAN: I can't get pregnant. I can't just stop taking my contraception and get knocked up and just ASSUME the fucking bastard will stick around. That's like… like… Russian roulette…

KATIE: Except with human life.

REGAN: Yeah.

KATIE: HUMAN LIFE!

GENA: Is there some form of Russian roulette that DOESN'T involve risking human life?

REGAN: You know what I'm saying.

GENA: I miss Clyde.

REGAN: Gena!

GENA: I know I'll stop talking about it.

REGAN: You have to get over him.

GENA: I can't.

REGAN: It's been two years.

GENA: I can't help it. It's not even him I miss anymore. It's like this feeling he injected me with and I feel it all the time. Like the other day, I just stopped in the middle of Broadway and was looking downtown and the afternoon light was hitting the sides of the buildings in this way that just made my heart break. I almost called him.

REGAN: If you call him, I'll never speak to you again.

GENA: I texted him.

REGAN: Gena!

KATIE: Let's not fight. It's too awful on top of everything else. I don't want to go to work on Monday. I just can't stand going back there after like... being here... and like knowing what I'm missing.

GENA: You knew what you were missing before.

KATIE: *(Nearly crying)* I know. I shouldn't read *US Weekly* anymore. It's too awful. I'm addicted. It's like porn for women. It's not fair. I can't stop. I can't stop. It's the clothes. I love looking at all the clothes.

REGAN: Let's not go into this.

GENA: Nobody wants to go to work on Monday. Even if they work with retarded kids.

REGAN: They have cancer.

KATIE: It's my own fault that I'm in credit card debt.

GENA: It's not your fault. You're a victim of the system. Those magazines and advertisers they target people like you. Young white females with disposable incomes.

KATIE: And like, who said my income is disposable? You know? I need it.

REGAN: This is why Becky and Cal piss me off so much. You know? Why should SHE be the loop hole?

GENA: I don't think she physically IS the loophole.

REGAN: Why does she get to never have to worry about money and do whatever she wants and like... you know...? I hate her. I Hope she dies. Let's set her dress on fire!

KATIE: Like Hendrix!

GENA: Katie's in a mood, Regan. Please don't encourage it.

KATIE: Oh my god. I would love you forever if you did that Regan.

REGAN: I mean, why did she invite us to party in this presidential suite or whatever it is. Like what is this?

KATIE: Give me a lighter, Gena.

GENA: No. Regan, tell her to stop.

REGAN: I agree with her. Burn the bitch's dress.

GENA: No.

KATIE: Then the "fuck-you" Will be complete!

REGAN: Fuck her, Gena. Becks doesn't deserve any of this.

GENA: You'll burn the whole place down. *(Katie dashes into the closet. Gena goes after her.*

Offstage, we hear them struggling to get to the dress first.)
GENA: *(Offstage)* Ow!
KATIE: *(Offstage)* No! My FACE!
GENA: *(Offstage)* No tickling. I'm serious. STOP! *(During this offstage strug-*
gle, Regan picks up her designer bag and pulls out a prescription pill bottle.
She picks out several pills, pops them into her mouth, and washes them down
with champagne. Then she returns the bottle to her purse and throws it on
the floor.)
(Katie re-enters, followed by Gena. She holds Becky's wedding dress. It's a
masterpiece made comical by it's size. Beat)
REGAN: Isn't it ridiculous?
GENA: It's retarded.
KATIE: Two people could fit in this!
REGAN: That dress. Almost broke her. It was altered four times before it
actually fit her.
GENA: Let's put it back.
KATIE: I wanna try it on.
GENA: No!
REGAN: Knock yourself out. *(Katie slips it easily over her head. She swims in it.*
Doubles over with laughter.)
GENA: You look like a *Carrie*-themed parade float.
KATIE: Two people could fit in this.
REGAN: Do you know how much that thing cost?
GENA: A semester of higher education?
REGAN: Practically. $15,000.
KATIE: Ugh! Gena, this thing could pay your rent for a year. And a half!
Like two years. How many months does $800 go into...
GENA: I was told there'd be no math.
KATIE: How can Becky justify spending that on what is basically a tent made
out of the skin of infants?
REGAN: She can afford it. She's paying for rent with her sex hole from this
day forward.
KATIE: Someone get in with me. Let's take a picture, post it on Facebook
and then tag Becky!
GENA: Dude! Take it off.
REGAN: That's a genius idea. I'll get in with you. Gena, take a picture!
GENA: Guys! Stop! *(They struggle. Regan manages to get one foot in. Gena*
pulls her.
Riiiiiiiiiiiiiiiippppppppppp! All three girls freeze.) That... just happened.
Didn't it?

KATIE: Oh my god. *(Katie and Regan try to untangle themselves from the dress. Another…*

Riiiiiiiiiiiiiiiiiiiippppppppp!)

GENA: Making it worse. Making it worse!

REGAN: Stop moving.

KATIE: Fuck. *(Regan trips away from the dress, now a pile on the floor.)*

REGAN: Ok. *(Katie steps gingerly out of the dress. Gena picks it up and surveys the damage.)*

GENA: Tell me this is okay. Tell me she can still wear this.

REGAN: *(Deadpan)* It's okay. She can still wear it.

GENA: Dammit, Regan!

REGAN: Jesus. I don't know. *(She also surveys the damage. It doesn't look good.)*

GENA: What're we gonna do?

KATIE: We should hide it!

GENA: What?

KATIE: Tell her… someone broke in and stole it! *(Katie begins to trash the hotel room.)*

GENA: *(Apoplectic)* Regan!

REGAN: I guess… you just tell her what happened?

GENA: Me? This wasn't my—

(Katie throws a glass vase onto the floor. CRASH!)

GENA: What the fuck—

REGAN: KATIE!

KATIE: We gotta make it look like the place was ransacked.

GENA: Regan. Please. Help me.

REGAN: This is probably a good time to let you know that Becky didn't want you two here tonight.

KATIE: What?

REGAN: Becky asked me not to have you guys over here tonight. I thought "Screw her…" But…

KATIE: Why didn't she want us here?

REGAN: Because stuff like this happens when you two are around.

KATIE: Stuff like what? What happens? What exactly did she say?

REGAN: Becky said that I could use this room tonight 'cause she's staying in Cal's room. But that she really didn't want the whole "entourage" tonight.

KATIE: She said that?

REGAN: If she finds out you guys were here and… that you did this… Well, it's gonna be bad.

KATIE: I didn't do anything.

REGAN: You ripped her dress.

KATIE: But that wasn't my fault.

REGAN: Well…

GENA: What're you saying? That you're gonna blame this on us?

KATIE: We were just playing around. *(To Regan)* You stepped on it.

REGAN: It doesn't really matter. It's ripped now and you can blame me if it makes you feel better but… I'm the only one out of the three of us who's supposed to be here.

GENA: If you think I'm lying under the fucking whatever for you on this one, Regan, you are out of your motherfucking mind.

REGAN: Well, someone needs to fix it and it's not gonna be me.

GENA: Why d'you have to make everyone else miserable just because Frank stopped fucking you when you turned twenty-seven.

REGAN: You're one to talk!

GENA: Go ahead rub fucking Clyde in my face again!

REGAN: Oh come on, Gena. I don't need this shit from you.

GENA: Get off my fucking dick. At least Clyde didn't string me along! At least he had the decency to tell me he didn't love me.

REGAN: Clyde ended with an abortion I had to drive you to. *(Beat.)*

GENA: Why did you just say that?

REGAN: Listen…

GENA: Why did you…

REGAN: It's nothing to be ashamed of, Gena.

GENA: I'm not ashamed.

REGAN: You are. But you shouldn't be. I just don't think its fair for you to pull some sort of "holier than thou" routine with me when you're not being honest.

GENA: But I didn't… I wasn't.

REGAN: You were.

GENA: But that's… It's private.

REGAN: You can't expect me to keep secrets for you when I'm not even sure you're on my side.

GENA: I am.

REGAN: You weren't a second ago.

GENA: I am.

REGAN: Ok, then.

(Beat. No one moves.)

KATIE: You guys had an abortion without me?

REGAN: *(Checks her phone)* Those guys are texting me. They've probably circled the hotel like forty times. Shit. You should… maybe… start working on… *(Gestures to the dress)*

GENA: Oh… yeah. I got this.

REGAN: You sure?

GENA: Yeah. I'll deal with it.

KATIE: Your nose is bleeding. *(Gena touches her nose. Blood drips from her nostrils.)*

GENA: Oh shit… Yeah. That happens. Sometimes.

REGAN: Are you okay?

GENA: Yeah. It doesn't hurt. It's just… You know… Life.

KATIE: What am I supposed to do?

REGAN: Go home. *(Regan gathers her things. As she finds Katie's belongings, she tosses them to Katie.)*

KATIE: I can't go home. The next train isn't until one fifteen. And it stops at, like, every stop. It'll take me three hours!

REGAN: We'll go see those guys. And they can drive you to Penn Station.

KATIE: I can't!

REGAN: Don't be such a baby. We'll smoke another bowl and you'll mellow out. It'll be fine. *(To Gena)* Thanks.

GENA: Easier done than said. *(Katie and Regan exit. Gena takes a moment. She picks up the phone.)*

GENA: Concierge please. *(Waits)* Hi, I need a tailor or something for a rip in a dress. How bad is it? Not that bad. It can be fixed.

BLACKOUT.

SCENE TWO

An hour later.
The hotel room is how we left it. Still a mess. The lights are on.
Noises. We hear the door open.

REGAN: *(Offstage)* No! Leave the door open for the... other people. *(Regan stumbles in. She is much more high than she was before. Spacey. Slower. She kicks off shoes, tosses coat, throws purse. Just as she did before.) Close behind her is Jeff (early 30s), a good-looking guy who actually swaggers. He's practically wearing a suit. But it's not a suit.) Jeff is self-assured with maybe a successful middle management job, probably graduated summa cum laude and definitely has fucked hookers.)*

REGAN: I don't wanna go through that whole ordeal again.

JEFF: You really sweet-talked that guy at the front desk.

REGAN: My idiot friend is the only one with the key. *(shouting)* Gena! *(to Jeff)* I forgot to get it.

JEFF: And the coke.

REGAN: What?

JEFF: She's got the coke too.

REGAN: Did we already talk about this?

JEFF: Yes.

REGAN: Sorry. I'm really fucked up. I never smoke pot. It's so pedestrian.

JEFF: Don't be sorry. *(He touches her seductively. Regan lets him but hardly notices. She gets her cell phone and dials.)*

REGAN: Should've grabbed the coke. I'm about to fall asleep.

JEFF: Whose room is this?

Regan: I gotta order some coffee or something. Before we smoke more. I just- *(Pause, then into her cell)* Gena, where are you? Where's the... um... Becky's thing... I need you... to call me.

JEFF: *(looking out the window)* That's quite a view.

REGAN: What? Oh yeah. See! I told you.

JEFF: Whose room is this?

REGAN: Oh. It's this girl's. A friend. We used to live together in Park Slope. She's getting married here tomorrow. Downstairs. In some "Gold Room" or something.

(During the following, Regan goes to the land line and dials Room Service.)

JEFF: Good for her.

REGAN: You probably don't go in for that sort of thing do you?

JEFF: Do you?

REGAN: Maid of Honor.

JEFF: What do you do as the Maid of Honor?

REGAN: Nothing.

JEFF: So what's the point in having one?

REGAN: What the fuck does the "Best Man" do? *(Into the phone)* Can I get like eight black coffees?

JEFF: I was the Best Man once.

REGAN: *(Into the phone)* As soon as possible. Like immediately.

JEFF: For my friend Albert from Northwestern. We were in this fraternity.

REGAN: *(Into the phone)* Yeah. A pot is fine. Whatever you… usually do.

JEFF: That guy was crazy. Works for Mircosoft now.

REGAN: *(Into the phone)* Yeah. One espresso then. And a pot.

JEFF: Knocked up his girlfriend. So they got married. Now they've got this baby and it's all they talk about. You're. Not. Even. Listening to me.

REGAN: I was. Mircosoft baby. Riveting.

(Joe, late 20's, enters. Slumped over him is a very very very wasted Katie. Joe is a variation of those easy-going stoner types that have become so fashionable to fuck now. Joe is in no way the fashionable version. More like the listens-to-jam-bands-and-John-Zorn version.)

JOE: Thanks for waiting for us.

JEFF: Snooze you lose.

JOE: I had to park and I don't know if you've noticed but I've only got my right arm to work with here.

JEFF: It's not like you're left-handed. Did you bring the weed?

JOE: Yes.

JEFF: You wanna pack a bowl?

JOE: Can you just hang on a second?

JEFF: Why didn't you valet?

JOE: You have to pay for that.

REGAN: Just charge it to the room. I'll be right back *(Regan exits to the bathroom. Joe sits Katie down in a chair. She goes in and out of consciousness. Joe gets his weed and bowl out. He packs it.)*

JOE: Whose room is this?

JEFF: Who cares?

JOE: I'm just making sure we're, like, allowed to be here.

JEFF: You worry all the time. Stop worrying.

JOE: I'm not worrying.

JEFF: This is so typical of you, Joe. Don't you get it? We just hit the proverbial jackpot. We are going to get laid tonight. Probably several times. In a five-star hotel. And you're worried. About what? Getting detention from the hall monitor. That girl in the bathroom was practically going to blow me in the car. Give me 15 minutes. Another bowl. And I'll leave you alone with yours.

JOE: Mine's going to pass out. If she hasn't already.

JEFF: Well, she's hotter than mine so it all evens out.

JOE: I guess so.

JEFF: I know so. *(Regan re-enters with two bottles of champagne.)*

REGAN: Greetings. I bring gifts.

JEFF: *(Taking one)* Thank you.

JOE: *(Declining)* I'm packing a bowl.

REGAN: *(Re: the weed)* The more the merrier. *(When bowl is packed. Joe lights and smokes it. He, Jeff and Regan pass it around during the following dialogue.)*

JEFF: So what do you do?

REGAN: I work at a hospital. It's really boring.

JEFF: Doesn't sound boring.

REGAN: I'm boring when I talk about it.

JEFF: I don't think I would ever use the word "boring" to describe you.

REGAN: Right. Don't do that.

JEFF: I'm not doing anything.

REGAN: You're totally doing it.

JEFF: I'm genuinely interested in what you do for a living. Is that a crime?

REGAN: No.

JEFF: You're really on the offensive.

REGAN: I'm not. I don't mean… mean to be. I'm just stoned.

JEFF: Relax. We're in a beautiful place. Look! *(Indicates the view)* Look at that! Central Park. All those people out there without anywhere to sleep tonight. And we're just floating above them. We're safe. You don't need that armor.

REGAN: Armor?

JEFF: That suit you put on every day. That shield of "fuck off" that protects you.

REGAN: I don't… have… a shield.

JEFF: We all do. Tonight is not yesterday. It's not tomorrow. It's right this second.

REGAN: What were we talking about?

JEFF: Your job.

REGAN: *(Prosaically stoned)* Well… I'm not even a real doctor or anything. I mean, I will be someday. But right now I'm working with these sick kids. These kids who've been diagnosed with cancer and, you know, chemo when you're like twevle sucks. It sucks no matter what but like twevle sucks. twevle sucks in general. Like you don't know... you just don't know. Cuz you're a guy. But like twevle. That's when it happens man... that's when it happens.

JEFF: When what happens?

REGAN: When you start to hate yourself.

JOE: Is your friend going to be okay?

REGAN: Who?

JOE: Um...

REGAN: KATIE! *(Katie lifts her head. Joe offers her the bowl. Katie leans toward it. Joe holds it for her and lights it so she can inhale without using her hands. She coughs.)*

KATIE: *(leaning on Joe)* Thanks. I'm fucked.

JOE: That's okay.

KATIE: I'm tired.

REGAN: You can't sleep.

JOE: Well, I think she's—

REGAN: KATIE! WAKE UP!

KATIE: *(To Regan)* You didn't even say anything about my dress.

REGAN: No sleeping.

JEFF: Wait. I'm really interested in this hating yourself thing.

REGAN: What? Oh...Jeff, you wouldn't understand.

JEFF: Try me.

REGAN: It's a girl thing.

JEFF: Don't be like that.

REGAN: Fine. You start bleeding.

JEFF: Don't cop out.

REGAN: I can't... I can't talk to you about it.

JEFF: Why did you bring it up then?

REGAN: Because I'm wasted.

JEFF: I think you want to talk about it.

REGAN: You don't know what I want.

JEFF: I think you do. I think you want me to tell you not to hate yourself. That you're beautiful and that what you're doing with the kids is awesome. But that's not me. I'm not going to do that. I like to compliment a woman because I feel like it. Not because she needs attention.

REGAN: I don't NEED attention. I have a boyfriend. I get plenty of attention.

JEFF: Then why are you here. Why aren't you with him tonight?

REGAN: It's none of your business.

JEFF: I think you're unhappy and you have no reason to be and that makes you hate yourself.

REGAN: Let me guess. Psych major. Psych major with a lucrative advertising job.

JEFF: That's right. Belittle me. Is that what you do to your boyfriend? Does it work for him?

REGAN: Not really.

JEFF: Maybe you should change your tactics.

REGAN: There is nothing wrong with... with my relationship. And I don't care what you think anyway.

JEFF: Right. That's why you're so calm and unaffected by me. *(Regan glares at him.)*

Oh. You're mad. You're so mad.

REGAN: I am not.

JEFF: You're so mad you can barely restrain yourself.

REGAN: I'm not mad.

JEFF: Fine. I'm glad you're in such a good mood. *(Katie hiccups a little. Joe pushes her hair back.)*

JOE: Are you gonna throw up? You want to go to the bathroom with me? *(Katie spits onto the floor.)*

KATIE: Ugh....

JOE: Let's go to the bathroom. *(Joe briskly helps her to her feet. They exit to the bathroom.)*

JEFF: Your friend is pretty fucked up.

REGAN: She's a light weight.

JEFF: You look beautiful right now.

REGAN: I thought you didn't give compliments.

JEFF: No. said I only give compliments when I genuinely mean them.

REGAN: And I suppose this -- *(Gestures at Jeff's persona)* -- is genuine.

JEFF: Why don't you like me?

REGAN: I do.

JEFF: You have a funny way of showing it.

REGAN: This whole night's been a shitshow. I feel like Truman at Geneva.

JEFF: That doesn't make sense.

REGAN: What?

JEFF: You mean... I think you mean Truman at Potsdam.

REGAN: What?

JEFF: Truman had just inherited the presidency due to the fact that Roosevelt died. He had to jet over to Berlin where he was dealing with Stalin and Churchill. He was completely inexperienced and had very little briefing so I can see how you could make the analogy to your shitshow in that sense. The Geneva conferences are something else all together. One in 1932 and I think Truman was running a hat shop at the time and another in the 50s after he… like wasn't president anymore. So I think you mean Truman at Potsdam. *(Beat.)*

REGAN: Yeah. I mean, I'm wasted so I switched it or… something.

JEFF: But it still doesn't really make sense because Truman had a trump card. He had the atomic bomb. So he was really in control the whole time.

REGAN: Well…

JEFF: What's it like being wrong?

REGAN: It feels great.

JEFF: *(Touching her)* Yeah?

REGAN: Mmmhmm.

JEFF: *(Slips his hand in her dress)* You like that?

REGAN: Yeah…

JEFF: You need someone to tell you.

REGAN: Mmm.

JEFF: *(Groping her)* Yeah?

REGAN: Tell me…

Jeff buries his face in her neck.

REGAN: Tell me what?

JEFF: Just that you're wrong. That you're not as smart as you act. That you're really just a little girl. You just act like a bitch because that idiot lets you.

REGAN: Yes.

(Jeff slips his hand between her legs.)

JEFF: You want someone to put you in your place.

REGAN: Where's that?

JEFF: Where do you want it?

(Joe blusters in from the bathroom. He barely acknowledges Jeff and Regan's position but does acknowledge it. He has some vomit on his shirt.)

JOE: She's asking for her purse. Does anyone… like, know where it is?

(Jeff and Regan look at him coldly.)

JOE: It's probably in the car.

(Joe exits to the bathroom. Jeff attempts to move this into the bedroom.)

JEFF: Let's go lie down.

REGAN: *(Softly)* No. No.

JEFF: Come on. Let's lie down.

REGAN: I don't… I can't… have sex with you.

JEFF: We don't have to have sex.

REGAN: I'll get in trouble.

JEFF: I am not that guy. *(Touches under her skirt, groping softly)* I just want to feel that. Right there. How you tremble like that? I just want to feel that. Can I do that?

REGAN: *(Enjoying it)* Uunnhh…

JEFF: Look at you. That's beautiful. When I do this…

REGAN: Let's go. Come on… let's go.

(They exit to the bedroom. Joe re-enters and goes straight to his weed. Katie re-enters. Her face has been washed and her hair is a little wet. They sit together.)

KATIE: I feel so much better.

JOE: Good.

KATIE: I really feel good now.

JOE: Good.

KATIE: MmmHmm.

JOE: I'm gonna smoke more okay?

KATIE: Ok.

JOE: I just… don't want you to think I'm weird.

KATIE: *(Spacey)* Nooooooo.

JOE: This girl who used to babysit me and my brothers when we were little smoked pot on our patio. And I lost all this respect for her. It looks weird when someone smokes by themselves.

KATIE: I don't think you're weird.

JOE: I'm gonna do it anyway. I don't know why I felt the need to point out how weird it is when I was gonna do it anyway.

KATIE: I'll do it with you.

JOE: You probably should take it easy maybe.

KATIE: Thank you.

JOE: For what?

KATIE: For… helping me.

JOE: *(Taking a hit)* Oh yeah. Sure. You're really cool.

KATIE: You're cooler.

JOE: No. Everyone's been there.

KATIE: Where?

JOE: You know… *(Gestures to the bathroom)* It happens. You party too much…. Then you puke.

KATIE: Party too much. *(She nuzzles his shoulder then leans on it. This makes it hard for Joe to smoke.)*

JOE: Yeah.

KATIE: Do you have a job?

JOE: Yep.

KATIE: Me too.

JOE: Let's not talk about it.

KATIE: I work at a store. Where they sell clothes.

JOE: I hang wallpaper.

KATIE: That's amazing.

JOE: Yeah… (Pause.) Hey. This bowl is done. I have to pack it again.

KATIE: Mmmhmm.

JOE: I need to move my arm.

KATIE: I'm sorry. *(Moves away)* I'm so retarded.

JOE: No. I'm sorry… It's just… I need to move it for a second… then it's all yours. *(He packs the bowl. When he's done, he lights and smokes again.)*

JOE: Is this your hotel room?

KATIE: It's Becky's.

JOE: Is she your friend or something?

KATIE: She's fat.

JOE: Oh.

KATIE: Do I look okay?

JOE: Yes.

KATIE: Even though I just threw up?

JOE: Yes.

KATIE: Do you smoke pot a lot?

JOE: Yes. I do. That girl. I was telling you about. She started smoking me out when I was like…. Smaller than I am now.

KATIE: I bet you were cute.

JOE: Not really.

KATIE: How old?

Joe: She was like sixteen. I guess. *(Pause.)* I'm not saying she like got me addicted or anything. I don't think pot is addictive. I think it's pretty natural. That was when I started and I never stopped. I guess. Just like it too much. *(Katie picks up an open champagne bottle. She chugs it.)*

JOE: You might puke again if you do that.

KATIE: I don't think… that's any of your business.

JOE: Whatever. *(She chugs again.)*

JOE: Why do you drink so much?

KATIE: Why do you smoke even if no one else is?

JOE: Because… I mean, I told you.

KATIE: I like when I can't bring the bottle to my mouth anymore.

JOE: Right.

KATIE: That hasn't happened yet.

JOE: I just don't think you want to puke again.

KATIE: I don't care.

JOE: Okay.

KATIE: I want to get to that point.

JOE: Where you can't lift the bottle to drink more?

KATIE: Yes.

JOE: Does that feel good?

KATIE: It's the best.

JOE: I can respect that.

KATIE: What?

JOE: I can respect wanting that. That feeling.

KATIE: Yeah?

JOE: Sure.

KATIE: I just threw up on you.

JOE: You think that hasn't happened to me?

KATIE: Well...

JOE: One time I passed out on the toilet in my own shit.

KATIE: *(Laughs)* I woke up naked next to a hamburger once.

JOE: *(Laughs)* Awesome.

KATIE: I was like "I just fucked that hamburger."

JOE: I was tripping on shrooms this one time and I was convinced I was Satan. So I lit my friend's couch on fire. *(Katie laughs harder.)*

KATIE: When things get that bad, I feel like Marilyn Monroe.

JOE: I used to be obsessed with her. I read like every book on her ever. And the thing that I always thought was incredible was what... Like people... They think of a white skirt over a subway grate or a pink gown and diamonds. Blond hair. Everything she did to cover up who she really was. They don't think about her vomiting from too many pills or getting wasted and throwing her drink in Peter Lawford's face or something. That's what made her the greatest actor ever. And maybe she had to go that crazy in order to be the perfect woman. You know?

KATIE: I tried to cut my wrists open with a broken bottle. *(Beat.)*

JOE: Tonight?

KATIE: Probably a year ago.

JOE: Of course not tonight.

KATIE: I'm sorry.

JOE: No.

KATIE: I don't know—

JOE: No.

KATIE: —why I said that. I just...

JOE: *(Takes a hit)* I went out drinking one night with my friend, Ethan. We'd been friends since, like, third grade. We got blasted. Stumbled back to my place and passed out in my bed. Lying side by side. He never woke up. He just never woke up. They said it was alcohol poisoning. But it turned out he had hepatitis too. So I don't know. He had started this whole heroin thing. Anyway... Maybe... there's something... he didn't look dead. You know? Even at the funeral, with the entire high school there, he just didn't look dead. It was like at any moment he was going to wake up and tell me I was a pussy for buying into this whole mourning and wearing black thing. I wanted to just get high. I felt like that was what he would've wanted. Not all this eulogizing and sober bullshit. But my parents... it was crappy. I had to pretend to be this person who was really concerned. That's not the right word. But I had to be this, like, adult or something. Why? You know? You can't just magically stop. Ethan fucking never woke up but it doesn't make me magically turn into someone who doesn't smoke or drink or get high or whatever. I resent that shit. Like the so-called "wake up" call. What the fuck? Ethan lucked out. When they put him in the ground, I knew he'd gotten away with it.

KATIE: Got away with what?

JOE: He never... he never had to grow up. I know that's fucked up. But I feel like whatever... it's one of those nights, right?

KATIE: *(Desperately)* Yes!

JOE: I feel like you get it. Look at me. I'm twenty-nine and the only difference between me then and now. The only change in twelve years... is that I'm, like, taller. And it's not because I'm, like, some loser. It's because I saw everyone scurrying off from that grave. Like "Holy Shit! We better all grow up. We better not end up like Ethan fucking Parsons." And why? For what? *(Beat.)* Joe takes a hit. Katie stares at nothing.

KATIE: I can't believe... that I haven't blacked out yet. What time is it?

JOE: *(Checks his phone)* Almost midnight.

KATIE: It's early. I love blacking out. It's like sleeping except... better.

JOE: Are you freaked out by my story?

KATIE: No.

JOE: I just think you're cool and I figured you... would like get it. I guess.

KATIE: I told you I tried to kill myself.

JOE: Lots of people try to kill themselves. Marilyn Monroe pretty much killed herself.

KATIE: Yeah.

JOE: You know who you remind me of?

KATIE: Your sister.

JOE: No. I don't have a sister.

KATIE: The prom queen.

JOE: Well… yeah a little.

KATIE: I was the prom queen. It was great. I was fucking awesome. I got to wear a crown and a dress from Neiman Marcus. And everyone hated me.

JOE: You're not that hateable.

KATIE: Everyone hated me. But you know what? It's better than being ignored which is all anyone does to me now. You know what I hate the most about my job. When I say, "Can I help you?" And people just look at me like I'm a lighting fixture. I mean, even the people who have nothing but disdain for me don't piss me off as much as the people who think I'm part of the scenery. *(Drinks)* Then, of course, they inevitably have to come back to me and ask for some fat size because they're fat.

JOE: Did you used to be fat or something?

KATIE: Excuse me?

JOE: You just keep harping on it.

KATIE: I was never fat!

JOE: I used to be fat.

KATIE: Okay.

JOE: I'm just saying…

KATIE: Well, great! Congratulations!

JOE: Anyway. *(DING DONG! The doorbell of the suite rings.)*
(Joe and Katie freeze. There is a moment without dialogue where Katie crawls underneath some furniture and Joe follows her on all fours.)
(DING DONG! The doorbell rings again.)

KATIE: *(Whispers)* Open the door.

JOE: No way.

KATIE: *(Whispers)* Oh my god. It's Pigface. It's so Pigface. We are so fucked.

JOE: Who?

KATIE: Please open the door.

JOE: I don't know who it is.

KATIE: Neither do I.

JOE: So… Fuck! I left my bowl over there.

DING DONG! *(Another ring.)*

KATIE: *(Screams)* It's the fucking cops! Oh my god!

JOE: Shh! *(Joe wrestles her to the ground and puts his hand over Katie's mouth just as...)*

(Jeff re-enters. He's not naked per se. But, you know, we get it.)

JEFF: *(shouts)* Just a second! *(To himself)* Fucking Christ.

(Jeff opens the door and exits. An offstage altercation. Joe strains to hear. Jeff re-enters with a tray of coffee and sets it down somewhere. He picks up a cup for himself and notices Joe. Katie cannot see Jeff. Jeff stares at them. Then he smiles and gives Joe a "thumbs up". He picks up a cup for Regan and exits.

Joe releases Katie. The entire ordeal has exhausted her. Neither of them move.)

JOE: Sorry I did that to your mouth.

KATIE: I don't care.

JOE: *(Wipes his hand)* You didn't have to keep licking it like that.

KATIE: That's how I would get my brothers to stop smothering me.

JOE: Right. Are you... just gonna be okay down here then?

KATIE: I don't feel like moving. *(He moves to go get the bowl. Katie stops him.)*

KATIE: Where are you going?

JOE: Nowhere.

KATIE: Stay down here.

JOE: But we're on the floor.

KATIE: I think it's romantic.

JOE: To be on the floor.

KATIE: Yeah.

JOE: But it's uncomfortable.

KATIE: No it's not. *(She goes to grab a champagne bottle. Joe stops her.)*

JOE: You're gonna choke if you drink that lying down.

KATIE: I'm fine!

JOE: Let's just go on the couch.

KATIE: Please kiss me.

JOE: But...

KATIE: Please... I really need it.

JOE: Katie.

(She kisses him. He kisses her back. Barely.)

KATIE: Your facial hair is so weird. *(They kiss again. She grinds against his crotch. He tries to get into it but eventually he pulls away.)*

JOE: I really don't think we should do this.

KATIE: Do what?

JOE: Let's just drink some coffee and smoke some weed.

KATIE: Why don't you like me?

JOE: I do like you.

KATIE: Why don't you want to have sex with me?

JOE: I do.

KATIE: Then, let's do it.

JOE: I really don't want to right now, Katie.

KATIE: *(Getting upset)* You think I'm not pretty.

JOE: You're beautiful. You're gorgeous.

KATIE: I'm so gross.

JOE: You're the most beautiful girl I've ever seen.

KATIE: Then PLEASE!

JOE: I want to sleep with you. But you're not okay right now.

KATIE: I'm FINE!

JOE: No you're not.

KATIE: Just kiss me again.

JOE: You taste like vomit. *(Mortified, Katie cries out in a very primal and unfeminine way. It's a howl of embarrassment and defeat. No woman has ever made this sound.)*

KATIE: AAAAAAaaaggghh! *(She turns away from him and is silent. Joe touches her hair.)*

JOE: Katie…

KATIE: *(Flinches away)* You're such a poser.

JOE: I'm what?

KATIE: You're just like the rest of them. You're a phony.

JOE: You have no reason to be mad at me.

KATIE: Oh really?

JOE: I've done nothing but try to help you since I met you an hour ago.

KATIE: Don't you get it, you stupid fucking phony?! THIS is what Marilyn Monroe looks like!! *(They stare at each other for a moment.)*

JOE: Do you want me to go?

KATIE: I stopped caring about you awhile ago.

JOE: I don't get it. What am I supposed to do?

KATIE: Nothing.

JOE: But you just screamed at me—

KATIE: Just make me feel better.

JOE: I don't think I can do that.

KATIE: Please just make this like it was a couple of minutes ago.

JOE: I don't know how.

KATIE: Then get out of here.

JOE: Will that make you feel better?

KATIE: Fine. *(Joe gets his things and exits the suite without lingering. A prisoner being released. He leaves the door ajar.)* Katie cries. *Not like a grown person but like a little girl whose toy is broken. She boxes her own ears. A harsh attempt to snap herself out of feeling.)(To herself, methodically)* Stop it. Stop it. Stop it. You're worthless. You're worthless. You're worthless. Everyone hates you everyone hates you everyone hates you…*(She sees Regan's purse and rummages through it.)*

KATIE: Come on. Come on. *(She finds a pill bottle. A different one than Regan used earlier. A different color.)*

KATIE: Jack. Pot.

(Katie takes a handful of pills. She doesn't empty the bottle. She replaces the bottle in Regan's purse. She swallows the pills and washes them down with champagne. She chokes then chugs again.)

(Suddenly – Joe bursts back into the suite.

He goes straight to Katie and kisses her deep and long. Movie star kisses her. I mean, sweeps her off of her feet.)

JOE: Did that work? *(Katie stares at him.)*

I've always wanted to do something like that. *(Katie sways back and forth for a moment. Then…)*

KATIE: Joe?

JOE: Yeah?

KATIE: It's not working.

BLACKOUT.

SCENE 3

Thirty minutes later.
The suite is empty but as it was. A disaster.
After a moment, Regan emerges from the bedroom. A bed sheet wrapped around her. She goes for the coffee and gulps a mug full. The coffee is ice cold so she instantly opens her mouth and coffee spills all over her chest.

REGAN: Shit. Fuck. *(Her cell phone catches her eye. She looks at it.)*
Douchebag. *(She makes a call.)*
(Into the phone) What?!.... Why the fuck are you calling me a million times?... It was on vibrate.... I'm at Becky's thing. I told you we would be out late... You go out every fucking Saturday with your meathead friends and I go out once... ONCE in the last six months and you give me shit for it... Uh huh... Yeah... Well, I don't care... because you're an idiot...Yeah... I TOLD you we'd be OUT late...
(She sees Joe's bowl. She finds a lighter and takes a hit.)
(Into the phone) You don't care anyway.... Your residency my ass-fuck-face.... No I'm not smoking... I'm NOT SMOKING... I fucking quit three years ago... for you... and you don't trust me... that's what this comes down to... You... you... CAN I SAY SOMETHING?! (Jeff enters from the bedroom. He's practically dressed. He picks up a coffee as well. He spits it back into the cup.)*
(Into the phone) Can I say one thing at this juncture before you start acting like... LISTEN! If you can't trust me, than I don't know what the fucking point of me EVER leaving the house... I'll just bake a casserole and then lie around with my legs open until you feel like... YOU ARE SUCH A BABY!... That's stupid... Well, I think you're stupid... I'll be home when I feel like coming home... FINE! MAYBE I WILL!
(She hangs up and tosses the cell phone away.)
JEFF: Trouble in paradise?
REGAN: That was just... you know...
JEFF: Him?
REGAN: Yeah.
JEFF: Yep.
REGAN: I'm... uh... look. This is weird.
JEFF: Don't make it weird.
REGAN: Excuse me?
JEFF: It's never weird unless you make it weird.
REGAN: Unless I...?

JEFF: Yes.

(Regan works up the courage to say something.)

REGAN: You really shouldn't have…

JEFF: *(Reminiscing their tryst)* I had to.

REGAN: You should've asked me first.

JEFF: Aw… And take all the fun out of it?

REGAN: You're an asshole.

JEFF: Don't tell me that was the first time you ever had a guy…*(Regan is silent.)*

JEFF: That's what I figured.

REGAN: You don't know anything about me.

JEFF: You say that like it's a bad thing.

REGAN: Whatever.

JEFF: Don't tell me you feel guilty?

REGAN: I don't!

JEFF: Good girl.

REGAN: I'm… just tired. It's late. He just chewed me out.

JEFF: I'll make you a deal. I won't tell him if you won't.

Regan: *(Pause.)* Why is it so quiet? *(Then…)* Katie?! *(Regan goes into the bathroom.)*

REGAN: *(Offstage)* Oh for fuck's Sake.

JEFF: What now?

REGAN: *(Offstage)* Katie passed out. And you're stupid friend just left her here.

JEFF: Joe's a good guy. I'm sure he's around… somewhere. She okay?

REGAN: *(Offstage)* I knew she'd fall asleep. I TOLD her NOT to! *(Regan re-enters and gets her cell phone. She dials. During the following, dialogue, her phone call keeps going to voicemail so she ends it and re-dials several times.)*

REGAN: You guys should probably go now.

JEFF: Wow.

REGAN: Wow what?

JEFF: Quite the emancipated woman over here. Use me for sex and then kick me to the curb?

REGAN: Shut up.

JEFF: I feel like I just scored myself a guest spot on *Sex and the City.*

REGAN: All you do is fucking talk.

JEFF: This is the episode where Carrie cheats on her boyfriend only to complain a season later about how men are the ones afraid of commitment.

REGAN: What is wrong with you?

JEFF: You don't really expect me to answer that, do you?

(There is a knock at the door. Jeff goes to answer it as Regan finally leaves a voicemail message.)

REGAN: *(Into the phone)* Gena? Where are you? I just walked into the bathroom and Katie. She's— Fucking call me back, okay? Shit got real. *(Joe enters. He holds Katie's purse.)*

JEFF: Nice purse.

JOE: It's Katie's. She asked me to go get it.

JEFF: Ok. Well, we've been asked to clear out.

JOE: What?

REGAN: Yeah, you guys should probably go soon.

JEFF: Charming AND polite.

JOE: I just need to check on Katie.

REGAN: I just did.

JOE: I just need to give her... give her this. *(He exits to the bathroom.)*

REGAN: I cannot believe I got stuck with her tonight.

JEFF: She got pretty fucked up.

REGAN: She's ALWAYS like this. It's so annoying.

JEFF: I'm gonna go put my shoes on.

REGAN: No one's stopping you.

JEFF: Easy there, Miss "Hit the Road." Surely you won't deny me the proper foot ware for a proper exit.

REGAN: Jeff.

JEFF: Yeah?

REGAN: What's my name? *(A silence. He laughs uncomfortably. He doesn't know.)*

REGAN: Just put your shoes on. *(Jeff exits to the bedroom. Joe re-enters. Regan texts on her cell phone.)*

JOE: Um... where's Jeff?

REGAN: In the bedroom. Leaving. Why?

JOE: Oh my god.

REGAN: What?

JOE: Katie. She won't wake up. I can't get her to wake up.

REGAN: She's a drunk.

JOE: No. This is bad. She's like really not moving or something.

REGAN: Or something? She's breathing...

JOE: I think so.

REGAN: She blacked out. I turned her on her side.

JOE: No. Man. This is bad. She's out. I shook her really hard.

REGAN: She's just fucked up.

JOE: I shook her HARD.

REGAN: I heard you the first time.

JOE: I'm really freaked out. We should call someone.

REGAN: Who?

JOE: Like an ambulance.

REGAN: Katie doesn't need an ambulance. We just throw water on her.

JOE: *(Severely)* Dude.

REGAN: *(Just as severely)* What?

JOE: Listen to me. She's not waking up. This is not good.

REGAN: Okay. I have known this girl since high school. She is ALWAYS like
   this. We just throw water on her.
   (Jeff re-enters.)

JEFF: What's happening?

JOE: Katie's not waking up.

JEFF: Did she drink more?

JOE: Not that much more. I was with her the whole time.

JEFF: You weren't here a second ago.

JOE: Well, when I went to the car. I wasn't here when I went to the car.

JEFF: Was she okay before that?

JOE: She was, like, nodding off. I thought she was tired.

JEFF: Then she's probably doing this thing called "sleep".

JOE: No, man…

REGAN: I'm gonna get dressed. You guys figure it out. *(She exits to the bedroom.)*

JEFF: What's her name?

JOE: Katie.

JEFF: No the other one.

JOE: Um… Regan.

JEFF: Fuck!

JOE: Jeff…

JEFF: Right. Let's just see… if we can get her walking. Okay?

JOE: Okay.
   (They exit to the bathroom. After a few moments…
   Becky (late 20s) enters the room. Holding a plate with a large piece of cake.
   She is indeed technically overweight but very pretty. This is due to the fact
   that she is dressed stylishly and expensively. Her jewelry is stunning includ-
   ing a large diamond engagement ring. She carries herself with confidence
   and dignity.)

BECKY: Regan? *(She takes in the suite. She surveys the mess. In a way, it does not surprise her.)*

BECKY: Regan? Are you here?

(Regan re-enters half-dressed.)

REGAN: Yeah. *(sees Becky)* Becks!

BECKY: Oh. Are you fucking some—

REGAN: No! I was just... changing... back into my dress. I spilled some wine on it at dinner and...

BECKY: Right.

REGAN: You look great.

BECKY: Thanks, bitch.

REGAN: What's going on?

BECKY: I was just gonna ask you that...

REGAN: *(Gestures to the room)* Just...

REGAN & BECKY: *(An inside joke)* Heeeeeeeyyyyyyyyyyy!

BECKY: Well, that's what it's here for. The room. You know? Goin' crazy.

REGAN: I didn't really. I just knocked... over... some stuff.

BECKY: *(Suddenly mean)* My stuff. You knocked over. My stuff.

REGAN: *(Recoiling)* I'm sorry.

BECKY: *(Kind again)* It doesn't matter. *(Re: presents)* I was gonna return all that shit anyway.

REGAN: Yeah... Sweetie, what're you doing here?

BECKY: Cal decided he wants to spend tonight in separate rooms. Adorable, right? I can already tell Christmas with him is gonna be hilarious.

REGAN: Yeah.

BECKY: Is it gay that I'm excited for tomorrow?

REGAN: No. It's... I'm really happy for you, Becks.

BECKY: I totally get why people get married. It's like... Remember our first summer in New York. You and I.

REGAN: We were... out of our minds.

BECKY: Totes. Stayed out as late as we wanted because who fucking cared whether we came home. But now... God! It's weird but I'm, like, ready to come home. You know?

REGAN: Yeah... I do. It's just... So you're gonna stay here then?

BECKY: *(Suddenly mean again)* It's my room.

REGAN: *(Instantly apologetic)* Of course, Becks. Whatever you want.

BECKY: *(Kind again)* Let's order room service and some scotch.

REGAN: I'd love to. But first there's something I have to—

BECKY: I don't care that you trashed the room, Regan. I'm just pissed you did it without me. It's my night. You know?

REGAN: Becks...

(BAM! There is a thud in the bathroom offstage.)

REGAN: …I gotta talk to you.

BECKY: What was that?

REGAN: I know you didn't want anyone else here but… um… Katie…

BECKY: Oh my god.

REGAN: I know.

BECKY: Is she here?

REGAN: She was on this side of the park and gave me this whole guilt-trip about not being invited. And you know how she is.

BECKY: Where is she?

(Jeff and Joe enter, carrying Katie between them. Katie is out cold.)

JEFF: Hey.

BECKY: Dear Lord.

REGAN: This is Jeff and Joe. Um… they're friends of Katie's.

BECKY: Yes. Yes they are.

JEFF: Are you the one who's getting married?

BECKY: *(Ruthless)* What?

REGAN: They're gonna get rid of her now.

BECKY: I don't think they should "get rid of her". We can't just prop her up on a train to Greenport. I mean, fuck, can we? Is she okay?

JEFF: *(Relaxed)* Oh yeah I've seen this a thousand times. She just had an awesome night. That's all.

JOE: *(More concerned)* We need to get her walking.

REGAN: I'm really sorry about this, Becks. I know you didn't want this kind of drama tonight.

BECKY: Is any of this coffee hot?

REGAN: It used to be.

BECKY: How long has she been like this?

JOE: Not long but—

BECKY: Maybe we should put her in the shower?

JEFF: It's full of champagne bottles.

BECKY: Of course you ordered champagne!

REGAN: No! They were there when I got here.

BECKY: *(Tickled)* Cal must've done that. He's always doing stuff like that. Things he thinks Super-Cal would do. I fucking love him. Okay. Let's get those out of there and put her—

JEFF: I'm on it. *(Jeff leaves one side of Katie and exits to the bathroom. Joe cannot support her so Becky grabs Katie's other arm to keep her upright.)*
(Katie's head lolls onto Becky's shoulder. Vomit oozes out of Katie's mouth onto Becky's dress.)

BECKY: Ah! Son of a whore!

REGAN: Oh shit. *(Regan grabs a napkin from the coffee tray. She wipes up the vomit.)*

BECKY: Don't worry about it, Regan.

REGAN: Put her on the couch.

JOE: She'll choke if we lie her down.

REGAN: Don't be so dramatic. This isn't 1968.

JOE: What does that mean?

BECKY: He's right. She's barfing. We shouldn't lie her down. Barfing... is good sign though.

JOE: *(To Becky)* You're awesome. I'm freaking out.

BECKY: It's okay. Katie does this a lot. She's breathing and everything. We just need to get her to wake up so she can keep throwing up.

JOE: *(Down for whatever)* Ok.

BECKY: *(A brilliant idea comes to her)* Regan, you should call Gena. She lives in Brooklyn still doesn't she? Bushwick?

REGAN: Yeah... but—

JOE: Who?

BECKY: Gena. She can get Katie up. She's done it practically every weekend since high school.

JOE: Do you really think we should wait for someone to come all the way from Brooklyn?

BECKY: Honestly, Katie's always—

JOE: *(Overlapping)* –always like this. I know. I heard.

BECKY: *(To Regan)* Call Gena. Tell her to call a car. I'll pay for it.

REGAN: I already tried her. She's probably snorting away her unwanted pregnancy.

BECKY: *(Laughs then serious...)* You shouldn't joke about that.

REGAN: *(Smiles)* I know.

BECKY: It's so sad. You're awful.

REGAN: I know.

JOE: *(To Becky)* I think I got her. If you want to...*(Becky releases Katie. Joe can't support her alone but makes a valiant effort.)*

BECKY: *(To Regan)* Where's your phone?

REGAN: Somewhere. In here. *(The girls look for Regan's cell. Becky in earnest. Regan half-heartedly.)*

REGAN: I'm really sorry. I know you didn't want the circus tonight.

BECKY: You can't help it. They follow you around like dogs.

REGAN: Or little children.

BECKY: It's my fault. I should've bit the bullet and invited them.

REGAN: Nooooo!

BECKY: Yeaaaah. Then, at least, they might've behaved themselves.

REGAN: They couldn't even if they tried.

JEFF: *(Re-enters)* The tub is empty. We should take her clothes off.

BECKY: Here it is!

(Becky finds Regan's phone. She dials Gena. Jeff and Joe undress Katie.)

REGAN: Becky, I already left her a message. Honestly, these guys seem… you know… capable. They're her friends. Let them handle it.

(A cell phone rings.

The ringtone comes from outside the suite. Everyone listens for a moment. The ringtone moves closer. Then…

Gena enters. She holds a garbage bag (containing Becky's wedding dress). She also carries plastic bag from a deli filled with two Red Bull energy drinks. There are bits of tissue paper in her nose.

At first, Gena doesn't notice anyone else in the suite. She fumbles with her purse to find her cell phone. When she does and answers, she sees everyone. Gena and Becky share a tense immediate connection.)

GENA: Hi.

BECKY: Hi. Haven't seen you since…

GENA: The thing. *(They end their call simultaneously.)*

BECKY: What're you doing here?

GENA: You called me. *(Re: Katie)* What the fuck is this?

JEFF: Who are you?

GENA: Who the fuck are you?!

BECKY: *(To Regan)* How did she know to come here?

JEFF: Are you the one getting married?

GENA: What the fuck IS this?

REGAN: Give me. The dress. Please. *(Gena gives the garbage bag to Regan. She charges over to Jeff and Joe.)*

BECKY: *(re: garbage bag)* What dress? Who's dress?

REGAN: Mine. Bridesmaid dress. Taken in last minute. *(Becky turns her attention to Gena who, at that moment, smacks Jeff hard in the face. He lets go of Katie.)*

JEFF: Ow!

BECKY: Gena!

JEFF: We were trying to get her walking.

REGAN: You don't need to fucking hit the guy. *(Gena tickles Joe, trying to get him to release Katie. Joe won't let go.)*

GENA: Get off of her!

JOE: I'm trying to help!

GENA: GET OFF OR I SWEAR TO GOD I WILL KILL YOU! I WILL TAKE A BOTTLE TO YOUR FACE MOTHERFUCKER!

JOE: Jesus.

(He reluctantly lets go of Katie. Gena supports her alone.)

GENA: You touch me or her and I will bash your fucking skulls in! *(Gena, with surprising strength, lugs Katie over to the couch. Gena lies Katie down on her back.)*

BECKY: He was keeping her upright.

REGAN: They were gonna put her in the shower!

JOE: Please don't lie her on the couch like that! *(Joe moves to touch Katie.)*

(Gena turns a champagne bottle upside down and wields it like a baseball bat. It was not empty. Champagne pours out all over the floor. Everyone backs off.)

GENA: You think I'm fucking JOKING, asshole!? *(Gestures to Katie)* Why is she naked? Christ! What IS this? National Date Rape Day?!

BECKY: Nobody's raping anybody. We are trying to help.

GENA: *(To Regan)* Did you leave her with these guys?

REGAN: Calm down, Gena.

GENA: You can't leave Katie with guys!

BECKY: *(To Regan)* You invited Gena too!? I should've know you'd—

REGAN: *(To Becky)* No! They guilt-tripped me.

JEFF: *(To Gena)* Joe was taking care of her.

GENA: I'm sure he did just that.

JOE: Fuck! I was just—

GENA: Hey! John Mayer! Great story! Get some water.

JOE: Fine! *(Joe exits to the bathroom. Gena cracks open a Red Bull and chugs it.)*

BECKY: This is a nightmare.

JEFF: *(To Regan)* Don't you work in a hospital? Do something! Blow in her mouth or…

REGAN: I read them books.

GENA: Regan, I know we can't help the fact that Katie's gonna pull a Sylvia Plath on us every fucking time we go out but all I ask is that you don't break cardinal girl rule number one and leave her with some skeeze-bag. Just turn her over on her side and call me.

BECKY: We did! ˙

REGAN: Gena, please wake her up.

JEFF: Joe's not a skeezebag. *(Joe re-enters with a tumbler of water. Gena finishes her Red Bull in record time.)*

JOE: I was taking care of her and talking to her and she was fine and then… she just couldn't keep her eyes open and—

GENA: *(To Katie)* Katie! WE'RE LEAVING NOW!

JEFF: You guys got it from here right? *(Gena throws the empty can at Jeff. Gena props Katie up in a sitting position.)*

JEFF: *(To Joe)* I think they've totally got it from here.

JOE: Just wait a minute, Jeff.

GENA: *(Screaming)* Katie! YOU GOTTA WAKE UP! WE'RE GONNA GO EAT BURGERS AND FRENCH FRIES AND MILKSHAKES!
*(Gena pours the glass of water very slowly onto Katie's chest. She sings to her. She sings Katie's favorite song. Romantic and old school.
[e.g. "Don't Worry Baby" by The Beach Boys]
This does nothing. Katie remains deadly still. This unnerves Gena.)*

JOE: Has this worked with her before?

GENA: *(To Joe)* Yes. It's her favorite song. It always gets her up.

JEFF: She's not getting up.

GENA: I can see that. *(To Joe)* Get some more water.
(Joe exits to bathroom. Without warning, Gena hits Katie hard across the face. Nothing from Katie.)

GENA: You stupid drunk! Wake up! *(To Regan)* This is your fault!

BECKY: Hey! Regan is not her babysitter.

GENA: But I guess I am. That's why everyone's fucking calling me!

BECKY: Well, where were you all night? Trying to score coke?

GENA: No. Actually. I was saving your fucking—

REGAN: *(Ice cold)* She was fixing your wedding dress.
(Becky snatches the garbage bag from Regan. She struggles to open it.)

REGAN: She got coked up and ripped it. I tried to stop her.

BECKY: Why is it in a bodybag? *(Joe comes back in with the water.)*

GENA: I don't have time for this bullshit. *(Gena pours the water on Katie just like before. She sings to her again. This time, everyone sings along. Katie stays motionless. Gena is now scared.)*

REGAN: Ok, we need to think clearly about this. The best thing to do is get her out of here. The hotel. The wedding guests. The police.

GENA: Something's wrong.

REGAN: Obviously. I just think it's best if this doesn't happen… Here.

BECKY: Then where? The lobby? What happens if she never wakes up?

JOE: Gena, we need to get her to the hospital.

GENA: What'd she take? What'd you all do tonight?

REGAN: She did coke with you.

GENA: I know! What else?

BECKY: Oh Jesus! You brought coke here. Of course.

JEFF: We smoked. Some pot.

GENA: And…

JEFF: And… she drank some champagne.

GENA: The doctors could give her something that could kill her--

BECKY: Does this mean we're calling an ambulance?

GENA: --Unless I can tell them exactly what these guys gave her. *(She looks at Jeff.)*

JEFF: *(Offended)* I don't roll like that—

GENA: Regan?

REGAN: What?

JOE: Regan!

REGAN: What?!

JOE: If she took something, tell us so we can get her out of here.

JEFF: Truth be told, they're gonna stick a tube down her throat so it doesn't really matter what went down. It's all coming up.

GENA: This toolbag is amazing.

JEFF: *(To Joe)* Fuck this! We can totally head out, bro. I've seen this a dozen times. It works itself out.

JOE: Really? Cause I've seen it where it doesn't. Can we call 911?

GENA: Yes. Help me put her clothes back on.

JOE: Jeff?

JEFF: Dude… The police?

JOE: Please!

(Jeff dials 911. Gena and Joe dress Katie and collect their things.)

REGAN: Becks, is the dress okay?

BECKY: *(Livid)* I don't even want to look at it. It's been in the hands of a maniac!

REGAN: Gena promised me she would fix it.

GENA: *(To Becky)* Katie's in serious fucking trouble. Okay?! I'm sorry that it's impinging on your "day"" or whatever but—

BECKY: You have done a lot of thoughtless fucked up selfish things to me but ruining my wedding dress? That's low. Even for you, Gena.

JEFF: *(Cupping the receiver of the phone)* What's the address here?

JOE: 700 5th Avenue.

BECKY: If you don't have any respect for yourself then I can't force you to. I stopped trying to help you a long time ago.

REGAN: I'm really sorry, Becks. I shouldn't have let them come.

BECKY: I didn't want them here because they destroy EVERYTHING.

GENA: Which is exactly why Regan invited us.

JEFF: They're gonna be here in fifteen minutes. Let's jet.

JOE: I'm gonna bring her downstairs, first. Jesus, Jeff.

JEFF: That crazy girl's gonna handle it.

JOE: You can't seriously be ditching me now! *(Gena grabs Regan's purse. Regan wrestles with her for it.)*

REGAN: Hey! That's my stuff. *(The purse strap breaks and several prescription pill bottle tumble out and onto the floor. Gena and Regan scramble for them.)*

JEFF: *(Re: bottles)* Whoa!

GENA: Which one, Regan? Which one. *(Holds up bottles)* Which one? Xanax. Codine. Vicodin. Which one, Regan?

BECKY: Jesus, she just fucking killed herself.

JEFF: Man, we can't be here when the cops get here.

JOE: I'm not leaving her.

GENA: Which bottle is not as full as it was when you got here?

JEFF: I can't do it, bro. None of these bitches are worth it.

BECKY: What the fuck, Regan?

JOE: Jeff!

REGAN: *(To Becky)* It's my medicine!

JEFF: If you wanna stay here, then you certainly don't need me. *(Jeff exits. Gena has gotten most of the pill bottles away from Regan. Joe goes to Katie, readies her to leave.)*

REGAN: I have prescriptions. I need them.

BECKY: *(To Gena)* I... had no idea.

GENA: Cancer patients, my ass!

REGAN: Stop it, Gena!

GENA: I'll flush them if you don't fucking tell me.

REGAN: Don't you dare! *(Regan wrestles the pill bottles away from Gena. Regan carefully but frantically inspects each bottle.)*

GENA: Becky, she WANTED this to happen. She told us you wanted us here. Then proceeded to ruin everything.

REGAN: I'm not some sort of sociopath. I didn't plan this disaster.

GENA: Well, it certainly helps your case that the only person who could back me up is crapshoot over here *(Gestures to Katie)* who is going to DIE if you don't tell me what she TOOK!

REGAN: Klonopin.

*(Joe lifts up Katie to bring her downstairs. Suddenly and subtly...
Katie puts her arms around Joe. Then she goes limp again.)*

JOE: Katie?

GENA: Is she awake?

JOE: She just touched me.

GENA: Put her down.

JOE: *(To Gena)* I got it! *(Softly)* Katie?

KATIE: *(Melodically)* Don't worry… Baby… Alright…

JOE: I don't know if you can hear me but… can you… put your arms around me again?

KATIE: Mmmm…*(Katie very slowly puts her arms around his neck. Despite the fact that Katie is practically comatose, this is a very intimate moment for Joe. Everyone is still.)*

JOE: *(to Gena but without taking his gaze off of Katie)* Let's go. *(Gena gathers up the rest of their things)*

GENA: Ladies. I'd love to stay and play "pass the blame" but Zach Braff and I have an ambulance to catch. Call me when you grow a conscience. *(They exit. Regan and Becky stand silent for a moment. Then, Becky moves to the garbage bag and takes out her dress. She looks at it for a long time.)*

REGAN: Becky—

BECKY: Oh my god.

REGAN: … I can explain.

BECKY: *(Might throw up)* Oh my god.

REGAN: Yeah. I—

BECKY: Shut. Up.

REGAN: Um… Okay. I get that this is a really messed up situation but you don't have to freak out on me.

BECKY: How could you let that happen?

REGAN: Why are you telling me to shut up?

BECKY: Are you some sort of junkie or something that you don't even know your shit—

REGAN: NO!

BECKY: Then why would you do this?

REGAN: First of all, I didn't do anything to you. Second of all, you said I could have the room—

BECKY: Because I wanted to be nice.

REGAN: —so it's actually none of your business what I do in it. It was an accident. I fixed it.

BECKY: Gena fixed it.

REGAN: Whatever.

BECKY: This isn't fair.

REGAN: I know.

BECKY: It isn't.

REGAN: You're going to look fine. *(Pause, Then scoffs, almost to herself)* No one's going to be looking at the dress. *(Becky glares at her.)*

REGAN: You know what I mean. They'll be looking at your… face. How happy you are. All that… fucking… shit.

BECKY: What? Are you talking about?

REGAN: I'm tired. Isn't it like one in the morning?

BECKY: I'm getting married tomorrow!

REGAN: So go to bed.

BECKY: Fuck it.

REGAN: What?

BECKY: I thought when you wanted to be my maid of honor—

REGAN: I didn't want to do this.

BECKY: You said that if I asked anyone else you'd cut my tits off.

REGAN: That was obviously a joke.

BECKY: But I wanted you to do this.

REGAN: To plan everything and stand there next to you. In front of everyone like a—

BECKY: I could've asked someone else.

REGAN: Stop it, Becks!

BECKY: I just thought that— I don't know what I was thinking. I didn't know it was this bad. I thought we could still be friends.

REGAN: We are friends.

BECKY: No we're not.

REGAN: Becky, I'm your friend. Okay? I don't understand why you feel like we're not.

BECKY: Gena really looks out for Katie.

REGAN: They pressured me into letting them come here. I shouldn't've—

BECKY: She's gonna spend the whole night in the emergency room with her. And if Katie doesn't wake up. She's willing to be there for that.

REGAN: Katie's gonna be fine. *(Beat.)*

REGAN: Come on, Becks. Let's take a look at this dress. It can't be that bad.

BECKY: DON'T TOUCH IT!

REGAN: Look, Becks. I don't even need this from you. Okay? I don't have to even be there tomorrow. *(Regan storms into the bedroom. Becky picks up Regan's pill bottles.)*

REGAN: *(Offstage)* I really don't appreciate this shit from you. You know I get this kind of manipulative crap from Frank all day. If you're gonna act like this, then I'm leaving. *(Re-enters)* What are you doing?

BECKY: Are you expecting me to stop you from leaving or something?

REGAN: Excuse me?

BECKY: Honestly?

REGAN: Can you just… put those down so we can talk about it?

BECKY: Why?

REGAN: Please just put them down. *(Maliciously, Becky pretends to put down the bottles. Then, at the last moment, doesn't. She shakes her head.)*

REGAN: Do you know what people think when they look at you? Random people. People on the street. They are… what's the right word… what's the exact phrase… "grossed out." That's what they are. They're grossed out. And if you think that marrying Cal Will fix that… it only emphasizes it.

BECKY: I can't control what people think.

REGAN: Oh but you can, Becks. You just don't try hard enough. I've gotten so good at it that even a fat stupid pig thought I wanted to be her maid of honor. *(Becky coolly pours some pills into the palm of her hand.)*

REGAN: Stop.

BECKY: I get it.

REGAN: Give me those.

BECKY: I finally get you. *(Becky casually throws the pills so they scatter all over the room. Regan's hands turn into fists. Becky pours more pills out into her palm.)*

Yep.

(Becky lets the pills slip through her fingers onto the floor. Regan tries not to move. Becky pours out more pills and scatters them. She dumps the remaining bottles onto the floor. Regan shakes with anger. Beat.)

BECKY: You have to pick them up. Don't you?

REGAN: No I don't.

BECKY: Yes you do. Go on. Pick them all up and put them back in their little bottles. Prove my point.

REGAN: Fuck you, cunt.

BECKY: Weren't you just storming out of here a second ago? *(Opens the main door)* Go on. Go on, Regan. Scott-free!

(Regan doesn't move. Becky stomps on a bunch of pills, crushing them.)

REGAN: No! *(Regan rushes to the crushed pills and maniacally tries to pick their remains up. Becky watches this with the look of a woman who learned evil from the best.)*

(Regan tries to pick up rest of the pills. She is desperate and frustrated. She whips herself into a frenzy until she stops and lets out a moaning sob. Then… The two girls sit. Regan, on the floor, dejected. Becky, in a chair, stoic. Then…)

BECKY: You look great.

REGAN: Thank you.

BLACKOUT.

END OF PLAY

BE A GOOD LITTLE WIDOW

Bekah Brunstetter

PLAYWRIGHT'S BIOGRAPHY

Bekah Brunstetter plays include: *Cutie and Bear* (Roundabout Theater, Fall 2012) *A Long and Happy Life* (Upcoming, Naked Angels), *Be a Good Little Widow* (ARS NOVA, Spring 2011) *House of Home* (Williamstown Theater Festival), *Oohrah!* (Off-Broadway at the Atlantic Theater, 2009), and *Miss Lilly Gets Boned* (Finborough Theater 2010, Lark Playwrights Week 2009, Finborough Theater, June 2010). She is a member of The Primary Stages Writer's Group, the Naked Radio writing team, and a Playwright's Realm fellow. She is an alumni of the Women's Project writer's Lab and the Ars Nova Play Group. She is the 2011 Playwright in Residence at the Finborough Theater, London. BA UNC Chapel Hill; MFA in Dramatic Writing from the New School for Drama. www.bekahbrunstetter.com

Be a Good Little Widow was produced by Ars Nova in New York City (Opening Night 2 May 2011) with the following cast:

CAST

Hope	Jill Eikenberry
Craig	Chad Hoeppner
Brad	Jimmy Orsini
Melody	Wrenn Schmidt

CHARACTERS

Melody:	a young wife, 25
Craig:	her slightly older husband, 30
Brad:	Craigs's friend and co-worker; Melody's age
Hope:	mid-50s, Craig's mother, a window since '82

MUSIC

many ages and many kinds

Director: Stephen Brackett

Revisions April 26th 2011
Commissioned by Ars Nova

C/o Derek Zasky, William Morris Endeavor Entertainment

BE A GOOD LITTLE WIDOW

A nice living room. A couch, a coffee table, a TV.
Melody stands in front of the TV, fork in hand, zoning out, watching TV.

CRAIG: *(V.O. of Voicemail)*
Hey Mel. I'm on my way home finally I'll be there in - seven to ten min-
utes - I don't know if you're getting this, you didn't pick up, it's - 7:43 so
I'll be there by 8 the latest. Love you. Oh, it's Craig.
(Craig enters, weary from a flight, in the crisp French blue of corporate
America. He rolls a sad black suitcase.)
CRAIG: Hey!
MELODY: Hey!
(She goes to Craig, kissing him.)
How was your flight?
CRAIG: Long and stupid.
MELODY: Awwwwwwwwww
(Craig's already on his blackberry checking emails, engrossed in it.)
CRAIG: Sorry – there's this – I just have to check this real fast -
MELODY: You hungry?
CRAIG: Big time.
MELODY: I got Thai!
CRAIG: Score.
MELODY: Pad Thai. *(Beat.)* Witthhhhhhhh tofu.
CRAIG: Ew.
MELODY: It's good for you!
CRAIG: Fine. What'd you do today?
MELODY: I did stuff today.
CRAIG: I know –
MELODY: There's nothing to do.
CRAIG: There are things to do in Connecticut.
MELODY: I checked out that yoga place!
CRAIG: Yeah was it good?
MELODY: Bunch of old ladies queefing.
(pointing to it, it's hideous)
And I found this lamp!!!
CRAIG: Where?
MELODY: Thrift store!
CRAIG: Nice!

MELODY: And I unpacked the last box! It was labeled books but it did not contain books!

CRAIG: Yeah what was in it?

MELODY: Ummm cables and extension cords –
Hold on this bitch is about to get punched –
(Eyes on TV. Punch.)
Nice!
I've seen this one like eight times.
Yeah cables and stuff and I didn't know what to do with it so I put it in the hall closet. Which is kind of like unpacking it.

CRAIG: Thanks for doing that.

MELODY: ALSO I organized my sweaters by color which made me really happy. Which is sad.

CRAIG: Do mine next?

MELODY: It'd take me two minutes. Blue; Gray.

CRAIG: Ahhhhhhhh It's good to be home.

MELODY: For a whole week! You spoil me.

CRAIG: Actually um -
They've got me going to Chicago Monday –
I'm sorry they just dropped it on me –

MELODY: You said you were going to start being gone LESS -

CRAIG: It'll be better after this merger I promise.

MELODY: But it's been MORE. You can't just freaking leave / me here

CRAIG: I know, I just – we just have to give it some time!

MELODY: That's what we've been doing!!

CRAIG: Are you pissed?
(Beat.)

MELODY: I know. It's not your fault.
(Beat.)

CRAIG: Hey c'mere!

MELODY: What?
(Craig puts his arms around her. Melody smiles.)

CRAIG: I wanna a kiss.

MELODY: I kissed you!

CRAIG: No I want like a real kiss. Like a welcome home kiss.
(Melody gives him a kiss, a bit longer and deeper.)

MELODY: Like that?

CRAIG: Yeah that's better –

MELODY: Better than what?

CRAIG: Nothing.

MELODY: What?

CRAIG: I like the big soft kisses not the / like

Melody: *(Hurt for some reason)*
Well sometimes I kiss you and your mouth is all small and tight and it's kind of like I'm trying to make out with a butthole.

CRAIG: Big kiss –
(BIG KISS.)
(He then puts his arms around her, starts to slow dance with her. She's uncomfortable, he's loving it.)s

MELODY: Ha what're you doing?

CRAIG: Dancing with my wife in my new house.
(They dance.)
Because I'm actually here for a minute and not in a stinky hotel room or on a plane squished next to some fat mathematician.

MELODY: Was he really that fat?

CRAIG: I don't wanna be a dick or anything but seriously the guy needed two seats.
(He tries to twirl her. It doesn't work.)

MELODY: If we're gonna do this we need music.
She separates from him, mutes the TV, dashes to her ipod, pink and on a dock, and selects some LOUIS ARMSTRONG – *When we are dancing, I get ideas.*

CRAIG: What's this?

MELODY: Louis Armstrong!

CRAIG: Ohhhhh yeah!

MELODY: I downloaded a bunch!
(She returns to him. They dance, a bit better.
But the moment is not nearly as romantic as the music, as it never can be.)

MUSIC
When we are dancing
And you're dangerously near me
I get ideas
I get ideas

MELODY: I'm hungry.

CRAIG: Just another minute.

MUSIC
I want to hold you so much closer

Than I dare to
I want to scold you
Cause I care more
Than I care to
I get ideas, I get ideas
And after we have kissed goodnight oh you still linger
I kinda think you get ideas too

Your eyes are always saying
The things you never say
I only Hope they're saying, that you could love me too
But that's the whole idea, it's true – lovely idea
That I fall in love with you

MELODY: This song makes me feel like I'm in love.

CRAIG: You're not?

MELODY: No I am, just like moreso.

> *(They dance.)*
>
> Music helps you access your emotions. If you're having trouble – accessing an emotion generally, a song will take you there.

CRAIG: You know what?

> I think you'd be an awesome therapist.

MELODY: Stop it –

CRAIG: What?

MELODY: You don't have to like suggest careers for me.

CRAIG: I know! I didn't say anything!

MELODY: I'm going to do something / I just don't know what for yet okay?

CRAIG: I was just saying

MELODY: I'm only three years outta college it's normal for a person to take some / time to

CRAIG: Maybe my Mom could help you get into real estate?

MELODY: Gross, no.

CRAIG: Speaking of, we gotta have her over for dinner soon or she's just gonna show up. With dinner.

MELODY: I just - want the place to be ready.

CRAIG: It looks great!

MELODY: Yeah?

CRAIG: She's gonna love it.

> *(He kisses her. Tries to start something.)*

MELODY: Weird.

CRAIG: What?

MELODY: Don't talk about your mom then try and make out with me.

(Beat.) (They separate.)

MELODY: Should we eat now, or -

CRAIG: Yeah! I gotta drop a load off first. Drop the kids off at the pool.

MELODY: I hate it when you say that.

CRAIG: You love it.

MELODY: Just use the spray.

CRAIG: I will.

(Beat.)

MELODY: Love you!

CRAIG: Love you.

(The music and its romance swell, but there they are, standing apart from each other, looking at each other like strangers.)

(Melody stands in the living room with her Mother in Law, Hope)

(An uncomfortable silence)

HOPE: Is there – I thought there was a fireplace?

MELODY: No –

HOPE: I love my fireplace, It is HEAVEN. My fireplace and a good book and a nice glass of a Bordeaux.

MELODY: Yeah – no fireplace!

Great weather! We've been having.

HOPE: Yes! Except for all of the rain!

MELODY: Right! Yes! It's been raining!

HOPE: Craig loves the rain.

MELODY: Yeah, he does.

(Beat.)

I like it! It like never rains in Colorado.

HOPE: Yes! It was very dry at the wedding. The air was quite dry.

MELODY: I got some rain boots, they're fun.

(Beat.)

HOPE: *(getting an idea)*

You know what?

My friend Naomi from jazzercise! She has a daughter your age. She does – I think she's dentist? Or works for a dentist?

I'm going to give her your phone number.

MELODY: Aw – that's really sweet / but

HOPE: You'll have lunch! You'll make friends!

MELODY: Okay!

(Craig enters with wine)

CRAIG: How was the drive?

HOPE: Terrible traffic on 84. I left a bit late, the League coat drive ran late –

CRAIG: *(to Melody)*

Mom's huge in the Widow's league, super active –

MELODY: I remember!

HOPE: It's just something I do!

CRAIG: She's a total asset, they wouldn't EXIST without her.

HOPE: We received DOUBLE the coat donations this year. DOUBLE.

MELODY: That's great!

CRAIG: You shoulda taken 91, Shave off 20 minutes!

HOPE: But 84 is much more scenic, God that view of the river I could just eat it for LUNCH! Remember when we used to take that drive to your grandmother's?

MELODY: I'm so excited to finally have you over Mom!

(Hope grimaces at the word, as does Melody a little bit.)

CRAIG: It's true, she's been freaking out / getting the place ready for you to see!

MELODY: I haven't been freaking out –

HOPE: Awwww, you don't have to make a fuss over little old me!

MELODY: I just wanted it to look nice for you.

HOPE: Awwww. Isn't that – that's so sweet.

(Beat.) (Melody waits for Hope to compliment her house, but she doesn't.)

MELODY: Your home is so beautiful I just.....you have such beautiful taste!

HOPE: Awww – thank you -

(Beat.) (Hope looks around the room.)

It is such a lovely little house! It's smaller than I remember.

CRAIG: C'mon Mom it's not that small –

HOPE: *(A Hope joke)*

Where will you fit the grandchildren?

MELODY: The hall closet!

(Craig laughs, Hope does not.)

CRAIG: She's kidding

HOPE: Well it's very cozy. Like a little fairy tale.

CRAIG: I think she did a fantastic job.

HOPE: Very eclectic. Like a movie set!

MELODY: What kind of movie?

HOPE: You know one where there's – things. In the house.

Honey is your stomach still bothering you?

CRAIG: No it's better!

MELODY: What's wrong with / your stomach?

HOPE: You've got to keep an eye on him.

MELODY: I – I do –

HOPE: You might have a wheat allergy! So many people these days are allergic to wheat!

CRAIG: I'm fine, it was just a / little

HOPE: Well I'm going to talk to my allergist for you.

MELODY: Should I put some music on?

HOPE: If you'd like! I'm enjoying the quiet.

MELODY: Sometimes I can hear silence.

(Hope nods, trying to agree.)

HOPE: Well I loved the band at your wedding! So romantic, the slow songs –

It was fortunate you found a band, so quickly!

It all happened so quickly!

(Beat.)

Craig called me and said you were engaged and I thought April Fools!!!!

CRAIG: It was April second, Mom –

HOPE: I'd only met you the one time! So. But I was very happy.

Very happy.

So nice to have you back where you belong.

CRAIG: I know, it's great!

HOPE: You know what I was remembering?!

CRAIG: Oh God, what –

HOPE: When we played circus?

CRAIG: Ahh c'mon – that's just mean!

HOPE: He was in the backyard in a tutu – I am in a Circus – I am in a Circus –

MELODY: Ah – haha -

CRAIG: She always remembers this, I don't remember this –

HOPE: I'll never forget it.

MELODY: I used to pretend like I was homeless!

(Hope gives her a look.)

HOPE: So what's for dinner, it smells delicious!

MELODY: I roasted a chicken. There is also a salad.

HOPE: That sounds just gorgeous!! Do you like to cook?

MELODY: Yeah I love it, I kind of just throw stuff together though, I'm not so much into recipes, I usually just –

but I love that cookbook you gave me for Christmas. I love that!

There's a Whole Foods down the – I love Whole Foods.

(Beat.)

MELODY: See can you hear that?

CRAIG: What?

MELODY: Silence!

HOPE: I hear the dishwasher?

MELODY: We don't have a dishwasher.

HOPE: How can you not have a dishwasher?

MELODY: I'm the dishwasher!

I'm just usually broken!

(Beat.) (Hope puts a hand on Craig's knee.)

HOPE: What time's your flight tomorrow?

CRAIG: Ungodly, 6 AM.

HOPE: How do they expect you to function?! That's ridiculous!

CRAIG: I'm a pro!

MELODY: He is a pro he's got like a whole / system

CRAIG: And then the next day Detroit

HOPE: Oh heavens why?

MELODY: That's what I / said

HOPE: Then Chicago then back home to the wife for a whole week!

MELODY: He calls me 'The Wife.'

CRAIG: She likes it.

MELODY: I do!

HOPE: It's a big word to live up to!

MELODY: Yes it is!

HOPE: When you pack him tonight, make sure he has plenty of socks. My boy has sweaty feet!

MELODY: When I p –

HOPE: When you pack him. Tonight.

(Beat.)

May I offer you some brie?

HOPE: No thank you, dear.

MELODY: Okay.

(Beat.)

Why not?

HOPE: Pardon?

CRAIG: Saving room for dinner, huh?

HOPE: Indigestion.

MELODY: You love brie. Craig said it was your favorite.

HOPE: That was very sweet of you! It just looks a little – under-ripe.

CRAIG: *(to Melody)*

The, um. You're supposed to take it outta the fridge, a few hours before.

HOPE: At least three hours before.

MELODY: *(to Craig)*
Why didn't you tell me?

CRAIG: I thought you already did!

MELODY: Well I didn't, I wish you had told me –

HOPE: I'm just going to the little girl's room. Wash my hands.
I'll give you two a moment.

MELODY: We don't need a moment.

HOPE: But I do have to use the restroom.

MELODY: Right down the hall, first door on the left – there's plenty of everything!

HOPE: Thank you.
(Hope goes.)

CRAIG: .....what?

MELODY: Oh my God.

CRAIG: What?

MELODY: These pillows suck - why did I get these pillows - When I PACK you?!

CRAIG: Why are you freaking out??

MELODY: Your Mom hates me!!

CRAIG: She does not / hate

MELODY: Okay well she doesn't like me very much.

CRAIG: Yes she does!!

MELODY: She doesn't.
Which really isn't fair because SOME people think I am awesome.

CRAIG: I think you're awesome.

MELODY: You're required to, by law.

CRAIG: Nope, it's my choice.

MELODY: She'll like me. She just has to get to know me.

CRAIG: Just be yourself.

MELODY: What is that?

CRAIG: ....What?

MELODY: Tell me what to be and I'll be that.
(Hope re-emerges, sniffing the air.)

HOPE: Is something burning?

MELODY: Oh crap -
Excuse me –

MELODY: beelines for the kitchen.
*(Hope joins Craig on the couch. Craig puts his arm around her.
A crash from the kitchen.)*

CRAIG: *(off)*
> You okay baby?

MELODY: *(O.S.)*
> Yeah I'm good! Sorry!
> *(Hope smiles.)*

CRAIG: .....What?

HOPE: She is a baby.

CRAIG: Stop.

HOPE: I ran into Stephanie's mother –

CRAIG: Ahhh –

HOPE: She's still not seeing anyone.
> I don't think she ever got over you.
> *(Beat.)*
> I still think about her sometimes. Stephanie.

CRAIG: Well I don't. So – don't.
> *(Beat.)*

HOPE: Are you happy?

CRAIG: Very much.

HOPE: You sure?
> *(Beat.)*

CRAIG: Yes.

HOPE: Then so am I.
> *(Lights.)*
> *(Hope is gone.)*
> *(In the dark, the sun comes up. Very early in the morning.)*
> *(Craig, in suit, comes in with a suitcase, finishing a cup of coffee.)*
> *(Melody comes in sleepily. He kisses her goodbye.)*
> *(Melody stands alone in the house.)*
> *(Lights shift to day.)*
> *(Still in sleep clothes, She's sitting next to one of the boxes, sifting through it listlessly.)*
> *(She goes to her iPod and selects a song. Dixie Chick's COWBOY TAKE ME AWAY.)*

MUSIC
I wanna touch the earth
I wanna break it in my hands
I wanna grow something wild and unruly
I wanna sleep on the hard ground
In the comfort of your arms

On a pillow of blue bonnets and a blanket made of stars
Oh it sounds good to me Cowboy take me away
Fly this girl as high as you can and to the wild blue
Set me free, Oh I pray
Closer to heaven above and closer to you
Closer to you

(Melody starts to cry, but it is sort of childish and pouty and small.
She gives up, goes to the couch. Sits. Reaches for her phone. Calls.)
MELODY: *(on phone)*
    Hey Dad! What are you doing?
    Oh yeah? What kind? YUM. With pecans? *(She laughs.)* What's Mom doing?
    This morning I invented 'pizza omelet!' Yeah and then it's rolled up like a 'breakfast calzone.'
    (Tears come to her eyes.)
    No, Craig's good, he's fine, I don't know, he's just never here
    But I'm okay.
    No, I'm not crying. I'm fine! I'm fine.
    Go to work.
    Love you. Bye.
    (Melody exits upstairs to her room, we hear VOICEMAILS.)
CRAIG: I love you Melody Oh yes I do
    When I'm not with you
    I'm blue
    Hey. We haven't taken off, we're delayed like two hours now, I just wanna get back to you.
    And I think I left my iPod at home, is it there? Also there's no wireless and I gotta get this proposal in so Brad's gonna come over and grab it off my desktop, okay?
    Love you. Oh, it's Craig.
MELODY: Hey.
    You don't have to say "I love you its Craig" anymore cause I know your voice. Okay? And you don't have to – I mean thank you for doing it but you don't have to update me every second, it's stressing me out, I know when you'll get here okay?
CRAIG: I'm not trying to update you every second I'm sorry I just, I thought you'd want to know. So I was just telling you.
    We're taking off now.
    Bye.

(Lights shift to Melody, watching TV.)
(She is doing yoga on the floor.)
(The TV screen goes out. She futzes with the cable box, turning it on and off.)
(The doorbell rings.)
(Melody lets in Brad, younger and hotter than Craig. Dark, slightly brooding, delicious. Craig's paralegal. He wears workout clothes.
There is subtle tension between them, of the sexy variety. Chemistry, clearly.)

MELODY: Hey Brad.

BRAD: Hey, sorry –

MELODY: Hey! It's okay, come in! How's it going?

BRAD: Good!

   Just got grab this thing off / Craig's

MELODY: Yeah, he told me.

BRAD: We're working on this huge merger and then maybe I'll sleep?

MELODY: Overrated!

BRAD: So where's the –

MELODY: Oh, upstairs. On the left.

   (Brad goes upstairs.)
   (Melody looks in a mirror.)
   (Deliberately fixes herself, for Brad.)
   (Realizes what she's doing. Shakes this off.)
   (Goes back to her mat, stretches. Aware of her shape, her pose.)
   (Brad comes back downstairs. Watches her stretch. He exhales. Clears his throat.)

BRAD: Hey – so – I'm done –

   (Melody gets out of her pose.)

MELODY: Oh, cool!

BRAD: Have you guys tried Bikram?

MELODY: Not yet but I totally want to!

BRAD: There's a great center downtown.

MELODY: Yeah?

BRAD: Yeah and it's so, so intense. The sweat - *mobilizes* you.
   You're slippery like a baby. And you go through the things, and time flies and you come out at the end and it's like you've been fucking or crying for eight years.

MELODY: That sounds amazing!

BRAD: Yeah it totally is.

   (Beat.)

BRAD: I really liked talking to you. At that thing.

MELODY: Yeah me too!

BRAD: God I hate those things.

MELODY: Me too! Well at first I'm like, yay, excuse to wear a dress! But then an hour in my feet hurt and everyone's talking about refinancing their mortgages and I'm just really confused.

CRAIG: bought this house, isn't that crazy?

BRAD: So crazy.

MELODY: *(smiling)*

I got a little drunk at the thing.

BRAD: A little?

MELODY: I got medium a lot drunk.

BRAD: Me too. Um, we were wasted.

MELODY: Yes! Yes we were!

(Beat.)

BRAD: It's the only way to make it through those things without inexplicably bursting into tears or killing yourself.

MELODY: Totally.

I was thinking the other day about that thing you said. About Tibetan Buddhists?

BRAD: Ah! You remember!

MELODY: I remember some parts! Of our conversation!

BRAD: Yeah about how they – um - contemplate their own deaths on a daily basis.

MELODY: Yeah and then this makes them less afraid.

BRAD: Yeah –

MELODY: That's so powerful –

BRAD: I watched a documentary online. I don't personally know any Tibetan Buddhists.

MELODY: That's okay!

BRAD: So you stoked for Craig to come back? Tonight, right?

MELODY: Oh, yeah! Yes.

His flight was super delayed so.

BRAD: He's freaking out, isn't he?

MELODY: How'd you know?

BRAD: Once he was running like ten minutes late for a meeting and he almost had a panic attack.

MELODY: Yeah, he does that!

BRAD: He's a great guy. He's a great guy to work for.

(Beat.)

BRAD: So you having a better time?

MELODY: What?.

BRAD: At the party, you said I hate it here –

MELODY: I did?

BRAD: Yep –

MELODY: Nah, I'm fine.

It's just kind of – it's just hard to be so far from home. And it's – you know it's an okay town / but

BRAD: Whoa, don't talk shit about my hometown!

MELODY: Oh sorry

BRAD: I'm totally kidding I fucking hate it here.

MELODY: I should give it a chance, I haven't given it much of chance.

BRAD: Everyone's pretty lame. I mean like really good people.

But lame.

MELODY: I should make friends.

BRAD: *(fucking with her)*

Yeah you should.

MELODY: *(cute, kidding)*

Will you be my friend?

BRAD: Maybe.

MELODY: We could go rollerskating.

BRAD: We could get drunk and then also go rollerskating.

MELODY: Well wait, what're you doing here if you don't like it?

BRAD: *(Shrugging, slightly embarrassed)*

Yeah - My Dad's a partner at the firm – so -

MELODY: Ah –

BRAD: Yeah so he got me the job, it's just paralegal bullshit, I'm just – just trying to figure out what I really want to do. Then I'm out.

MELODY: You don't belong in an office, you belong on a boat.

BRAD: Like what kind of boat?

MELODY: Like a dingy, sailing around the world.

BRAD: How'd you know?

MELODY: I just do. Also, You're meant to grow a beard.

BRAD: I had the most EPIC beard, in college.

(Beat.)

MELODY: Guess what, I think I have a brain tumor!

BRAD: No shit! Don't die!

Melody: I have this pain thing in my ear. This stabbing pain. I went to braintumor.org.

BRAD: What it'd say?

MELODY: *(kind of joking)* I don't think I have one really. If I did I'd be seizing.

BRAD: *(smiling with her)*
> I'm sure you don't.

MELODY: Craig thinks I'm crazy.

MELODY: Welp. I should probably get 'dinner on.'

BRAD: What're you making?

MELODY: Oh by get dinner on I definitely meant call a foreigner and ask him or her to bring it to me in containers. That I feel really bad about throwing away.

BRAD: Yeah me too. It's like really wasteful.

MELODY: So I stack them in a cabinet and every time I open the cabinet and look at all the containers I kind of want to die.
> I suck at taking care of him.

BRAD: He can take care of himself!

MELODY: That's what I say! But his freakin mom -

BRAD: Ah, I met her – total Mayberry -

MELODY: I know, right?!
> But she hates me. Or I hate her. I don't even know anymore.
> Oh my God why am I telling you this?
> I feel like I haven't talked to anyone in real life in 3 days. Wait, I haven't.

BRAD: You can talk to me.
> *(Beat.)*

MELODY: Ahhhhhhhh I don't know if it's just being HERE or –
> He's got this hoodie. Like his undergrad hoodie. It's got parmesan cheese crusted on the cuffs and it smells like balls and he won't wash it. He makes jokes but they're like: what's a guy gotta do around here to get a blowjob? And he's kidding, but he's not, And I'm like you're a blowjob. Honestly sometimes I'd kind of rather just watch TV.

BRAD: Personally I'd always pick the blowjob.

MELODY: Yeah you would.

BRAD: What?

MELODY: Ha. Um.

BRAD: I'm sure marriage is like – super intense.

MELODY: It is but it's good.
> *(Beat.)*
> It's just different now.
> *(Beat.)* I look at him and it's like: who're you? Who is this person I sleep next to every night? You know what I mean?

BRAD: Totally.

MELODY: Do you have / a

BRAD: No but I totally know what you mean. About intimacy.

MELODY: You wanna get married?
BRAD: *(kidding)*
> You're married to my boss – awkward –
MELODY: No I mean in GENERAL.
BRAD: No, I mean maybe, like in my 30's or 40's? Once I'm ready?
MELODY: Yeah.
BRAD: Emotionally prepared.
> *(Beat.)*
> Not that you're not like ready I didn't / mean
MELODY: No, I know.
BRAD: Well I guess I better head out –
MELODY: Hey you know anything about cable boxes?
BRAD: Maybe?
MELODY: My 'box' is broken. Ha! I'm funny.
BRAD: Yeah you are!
> *(Brad laughs.)*
BRAD: Let's see here –
> *(He puts down his stuff, crouches in front of the TV.)*
BRAD: I think we just gotta re-boot it – this little button – c'mere, see?
MELODY: joins him.
> *(He presses a button. They sit close together, looking at the box.)*
Brad looks at her.
> *(They look at each other. He looks like he wants to kiss her. Melody leans in to receive it, wanting it.)*
> *(Brad pulls away, clears his throat.)*
BRAD: Ahhhh – well –
> *(Brad clears his throat, futzes with cable)*
BRAD: You just gotta reboot the box, if it does that -
> *(TV turns back on.)*
MELODY: Okay..........
> *(They both stand.)*
BRAD: *(with voice)*
> I don't think you'll be having any future interruptions. Ma'am.
MELODY: Thanks – cable man, sir -
> *(Beat.)*
BRAD: I should / probably go
MELODY: You don't have to -
BRAD: Yeah but I probably should.
> *(Brad goes. Melody: sits on the couch. Looks at her phone. She turns back to the TV. Flips channels. Stops. Melody's eyes focus on the TV screen. They*

grow wide. Bigger than wide. She puts a hand to her mouth.)
MELODY: Oh my God – Oh my God Oh my God –
(She reaches for her phone.)
From the TV

NEWS:*(droning)*
At least 50 passengers were killed when a commuter plane originating in Chicago crashed into a home in the suburbs of Albany. The crash occurred just moments after the pilots lost communication with air traffic controllers. The aircraft began a sudden nosedive just after 9:30 pm, then hit a home and burst into flames, according to witnesses.
MELODY: Please pick up Craig please pick up –
(Melody remains, crouched in front of the TV, eyes glued to the flickering footage.)
Night falls.
(The sound of an airplane crashing into a house.)
(Melody stays glued to the TV, sitting in front of it in a crumpled mess on the floor.)
(She can't take her eyes off of it.)
(She sobs, or tries, but it gets stuck in her throat.)
(She scoots closer to the TV, watches, obsessed.)
(The sun comes up.)
(Hope, poised but damaged, comes in through the front door. She spots Melody.)
(Goes to her, pulls her to her feet.)
(Melody is limp. Hope helps her stand.)
(Melody leans on Hope, starts to sob. Hope lets this happen, pats her gingerly.)
(Pulls Melody away from her, pushes hair out of her face.)
(Hope leads Melody offstage.)
(Hope returns and surveys the room. Begins to Clean.)

The living room, later the next day. Hope sits on the couch. She is a bit somber, but poised. She has a neat legal pad with a massive list.

HOPE: I've booked First Presbyterian for Sunday.
Good thing they were free. It's a lovely church, there's a real pipe organ. A place by the altar where folks can donate flowers,. Lilies, azaleas.
The pastor, it was his father that baptized Craig.
(A moment. Hope starts to cry because no one is looking. She stops. She clears her throat. She tries to relate to Melody.)

We would be picking out the casket, his best suit.

With Craig's father he had gotten – he had gotten so THIN I – I had a new one made.

But there's –

there's not as much to do now with no body.

It's – it's unfortunate.

That there won't be a body.

(Melody emerges in an awful black dress. Her eyes are red but her chin is high. She is still stunned.)

MELODY: Is this black black enough?

Is it gray, or is it black?

HOPE: Yes. That's black.

MELODY: I feel like a lesbian.

HOPE: It's not the prom, dear.

MELODY: This is my first funeral.

It's the only funeral I've ever been to.

HOPE: That dress will suffice.

(Back to her list)

We'll have the lunch at my home after the service.

MELODY: Shouldn't we have it here?

HOPE: Dear, really, are you in any shape to host a lunch? Please, let / me

MELODY: Craig loved this house. This is his house.

HOPE: But my house is much more central for the guests.

MELODY: He'd want to do it here.

(Beat.)

HOPE: Fine.

I'll have the cleaners come by Saturday so we should straighten up first.

MELODY: What do we do now?

HOPE: Well we have a service to plan.

Did you speak with your parents?

MELODY: They're trying to get a flight – they got four feet of snow, the airports closed –

HOPE: Hopefully they'll make it by Sunday.

MELODY: Can we wait for them? If they can't –

HOPE: I'm sorry but it can't wait.

(Beat.)

We have to do it Sunday. It's the only day the church is available.

MELODY: I can make a playlist. For the service. I've been making it in my head, the songs he liked –

(She goes to grab it. It's a bright blue to her pink)

HOPE: I've already hired an organist.

MELODY: Maybe we could put out all of the candies and stuff he liked, Little
    Debbie nutty bars! Skittles! And sour patch kids!

HOPE: Craig doesn't eat trash like that.

MELODY: Um, yes he did. Those are his favorites. He hid them in his car.

HOPE: *(flustered)*
    You can't serve CANDY at a funeral. What would people think?

MELODY: They'd be like: yay! Candy!

HOPE: The caterer will handle the food, I've already placed the order.
    (Melody reaches for pen / paper)

MELODY: I'm going to work on my speech.

HOPE: Your what?

MELODY: For the funeral.

HOPE: A eulogy.......
    It's not expected of the Widow.

MELODY: Yeah but – but I want to.

HOPE: I've asked the pastor to say a few words.

MELODY: What're you doing, can I help with what you're doing?

HOPE: I'm making a list of everyone who needs to be notified.
    (Melody peers over her shoulder)

MELODY: I don't know any of these people.

HOPE: Well they knew Craig.

MELODY: I can call people.

HOPE: I have friends through the League who can take care of the calls.

MELODY: No I can do it.
    I can call people in Boulder. His. The people I know.
    (She grabs her phone. Scrolls through. Dials.)

HOPE: Melody –

MELODY: No it's okay I can do this, this is good –

HOPE: You don't need to do this.

MELODY: hang up the phone. Melody.

MELODY: *(on phone)*
    Hey Jimmy?
    What's up it's Melody –
    How's it going?
    I'm okay.
    Ha – cool –
    Listen um -
    Craig is dead.
    (She pauses, regains herself.)

He was on that plane that crashed –
Okay I'll talk to you later bye!!!!
(She hangs up, tosses the phone like it's on fire.)
MELODY: I can't do this –
(She looses it. She shrieks and sobs.)
MELODY: When do I get to see him?
HOPE: Melody.
MELODY: I wanna see him, where is he?
HOPE: He's gone.
MELODY: HOW DO WE KNOW?!
HOPE: It is – it's unfortunate. With no body.
MELODY: I don't even – we don't even get to – we don't even know where he IS.
HOPE: Melody. Listen to me.

There's a way things are meant to happen. In these - times.

First and foremost You have to keep yourself together.
MELODY: How?!
HOPE: I'll take your dress and iron it.

Try and keep it lint free and pressed. Try and keep a lint roller nearby.
MELODY: I don't - have one -
MELODY: An inside piece of packing tape Will do.
MELODY: I don't know how to do this. Oh my God.
HOPE: I want to hug you. Come on now. Let's hug.

(Melody reluctantly goes towards Hope. They embrace. Hope holds her a bit stiffly.)
MELODY: I can't stop – I can't stop wondering like or SEEING like – what was going through his head when he – did it hurt him, did he hurt?!
HOPE: He's in heaven now. Playing cards with his father.

(Melody settles into Hope's embrace.)
MELODY: But I don't know if I even believe in heaven. I haven't decided yet.
HOPE: You haven't decided?

(There is a knock at the door. Hope ignores it.)
HOPE: Mourners. So persistent.

(yelling to door)

WE AREN"T CURRENTLY RECEIVING!

(Melody goes to the door, opens it to find)

(Brad, disheveled and beside himself – but with an air of tragic hero.)

(Melody freezes when she sees him. He looks deliciously sad but she tries to not notice this.)
BRAD: Oh my God, Melody – I just heard – I came right over -

MELODY: Hi -

MELODY: indicates Hope.

BRAD: Oh – hi – sorry -

MELODY: Um, Hope, You remember Brad, he works at Craig's firm.

This is Craig's mother. Hope.

BRAD: Hello. *(Beat.)*

I'm deeply um - sorry for your loss.

HOPE: *(bowing her head gracefully)*

That's very kind of you. And I'm sorry for yours.

BRAD: Thank you. It's not as big as yours.

HOPE: Probably not.

BRAD: But it's pretty big.

(to Melody)

When I saw it on the news I couldn't believe it, I kept thinking or hoping maybe he had missed the plane like maybe he had too much bourbon at the bar or a flat tire or maybe he was taking a shit and they called his name over and over.

Sorry.

MELODY: He would never miss the plane.

HOPE: He was very punctual, that's how I raised him.

BRAD: I know.

MELODY: I know, too.

HOPE: I also know.

(They look at each other.)

BRAD: He was um – I want you to know he was kind of like a big brother to me.

So you're kind of like my Mom.

I know you're not my Mom but.

He was like my brother.

HOPE: Thank you.

Hope nods. Melody is like, what the fuck.

BRAD: I want to help. There's a lot to do, there are things we need to –

HOPE: I've – Melody, we've – got everything under control.

BRAD: What do you need? I Will literally do anything for you right now.

Literally.

HOPE: That's very sweet of you.

BRAD: I'd be honored to - speak a poem at the service.

Psalm 23.

Or John Donne. 'Death be not proud –'

Or Walt Whitman, Song of Myself.

"Failing to fetch me at first keep encouraged - Missing me one place search another - I stop somewhere waiting for you."
(Beat.)
Those are just suggestions.

HOPE: That's very kind of you Bob / but the service has already been planned.

BRAD: Brad - There's all the stuff at - all of his, um – his stuff, at his office, um, like his stapler and his, he has a drawer full of Tylenol and really nice hand lotions and I don't think he'd want me to throw them away and I should probably – Jesus – Jesus Christ –
(He chokes up.)
And there's this really big jar of Swedish fish –

MELODY: *(softly, weirdly)*
Asshole –

BRAD: And his books – and his things –

HOPE: We'll sort it all out after the funeral.

BRAD: Just – if you need anything – you can call me – any time.

Melody: *(quickly)*
I won't.

BRAD: But if you do.

HOPE: Thank you for coming.

MELODY: nods. Brad goes. Hope studies Melody.

HOPE: Well he's nice young man.

MELODY: I really don't know him all that well.
(Beat.)

HOPE: Mourning is a private affair.
(She looks at Melody, her smeared make up.)
Oh my goodness – you're a mess -
(She wets a thumb and roughly rubs mascara off of Melody's face.)
Dear, you are a widow now –

MELODY: I KNOW

HOPE: Oh my – so much eye make up –

MELODY: I'm not your daughter.

HOPE: *(under her breath)*
Thank God.
(Suddenly, Melody spots Craig at the door.)
(He waves to her.)
(She waves back.)
(Hope returns to her list.)
(Craig is gone.)

(Melody, late that night, alone in the house, still wearing the frumpy black dress. Over it, the crusty hoodie.)
(She has a pen and legal pad. Her eyes are shut, tight, she is thinking, so hard.)
(She listens to the remnants of Craig, his last voicemail, over and over. We hear this.)
I love you. Oh, it's CRAIG.
I love you. Oh, it's CRAIG.
I love you. Oh, it's CRAIG.
(She stops herself. Puts on music, Willie Nelson from Craig's blue iPod, Low.)

MUSIC
Can I sleep in your arms tonight, lady
It's so cold, lyin' here all alone
And I have no hold to hold on you
And I'll show you I'll do you no wrong

Don't know why but the one I love left me
Left me lonely and cold and so weak
And I need someone's arms to hold me
Til I'm strong enough to get back on my feet

(Her eyes burst open. She writes.)
MELODY: He was a person – who –
What kind of person was he? What kind of person is anyone? Survived by his wife Melody. 26 years of age. 26 years old. Also survived by his mother, Hope, fifty something. Of Connecticut. His father, Frank, died when he was young. Of cancer?
Craig was a corporate lawyer. He merged and - purchased things.
(Beat.) *(She closes her eyes and listens to the music.)*
He liked….
He liked coconut cake very much? No, Red Velvet better.
Also, he liked Willie Nelson and Seinfield re-runs. He makes the best Fettuccine Alfredo
And when he makes it he – *(she smiles, starts to laugh)* he does this thing he's like – FETTUCINE MONSTERR and I'm like FETTUCINE MONSTERRRRR
(She laughs. She stops.)
He liked Boxer briefs and he folded them.
My underwear is in bunches in a drawer. Next to his folded.

It's so weird. To know someone.

He has no hair on his back or shoulders. His hair recedes on millimeter a year. Sometimes if he can't get it up you have to put your face on his stomach or call him Papi.

He doesn't like Brussels sprouts or pearl onions, he thinks they're like eyes.

He is the nicest man. He is the nicest, nicest man and he has the nicest, nicest hands that anyone would be so lucky to be all wrapped up in.

Had.

Had the nicest hands.

(Beat.)

I knew him but I didn't but I did.

But I loved him.

I think.

We loved each other.

(Beat.)

When he asked me to marry him - I said – I said yes.

She stops. She can barely breathe. She smiles, remembering.

(Craig turns on the light. Melody is there waiting.)

MELODY: Surprisseeeeeeeeeeee

CRAIG: How'd you get in here?!

Melody: I'm sneaky. Told the guy at the front desk that I was your Mrs and that I lost my key card.

CRAIG: Liar.

MELODY: You okay?

CRAIG: Yeah, just - Today was freaking NUTS.

MELODY: How so?

CRAIG: Just a lot.

Going on. Hold on sorry –

MELODY: It's okay, You can do work and ALSO pay attention to me.

CRAIG: Yes. *(Blackberry.)* I. *(Blackberry.)* Can.

(tosses it.)

Fini!!!

MELODY: Oui oui!

CRAIG: I thought you were going out tonight?

MELODY: It felt stupid all the sudden. "Going out."

Also I'm sick of my roommates. I'm sick of roommates.

I like it better here.

CRAIG: It's getting old.

I want like a "home." I wanna put stuff on the walls, I wanna leave my things somewhere.

MELODY: Can I come?

CRAIG: Sure you can.

MELODY: Yay, can I wear an apron? Can it have cats on it?

CRAIG: You bet.

(*She burrows into his hoodie.*)

CRAIG: Ah! I see you found my sweatshirt.

MELODY: It's mine now, I'm cold!

(*Melody yawns, burrowing into Craig.*)

CRAIG: Are you serious?

MELODY: Maybe, about what?

CRAIG: About being sick of roommates –

MELODY: Uh yes. If you're going to fight with somebody about who's taking the trash out you should at least also be having sex with them.

(*Craig laughs. Looks at her with intensity.*)

MELODY: …What?

CRAIG: I uh – I got this job offer, I um – in Connecticut –

MELODY: Well are you gonna take it?

CRAIG: Well you know I've been wanting to get back closer to my Mom eventually / and –

MELODY: (*pouting a bit*)
Yeah –

CRAIG: What if you came with me?

MELODY: To Connecticut?
Like - ?

CRAIG: We could actually live together! Like in a house! Like normal people!

MELODY: Yeah!

(*Craig pulls a ring box out of his pocket.*)

CRAIG: So I was thinking- so – I got you this –

MELODY: I look like shit right now –

CRAIG: Melody, Will you marry me?

(*Melody tears.*)

CRAIG: I had this whole – thing – planned, but you don't need a thing, and now just seemed like the right

MELODY: No, this is perfect!

CRAIG: So – Will you -

MELODY: Yes! Yes!

(*Craig pulls her to her sock-ed feet.
He hugs her. He holds her.*)

CRAIG: Are you freaking out?

MELODY: No! – I mean we haven't even talked / about it. Sorry, it's just kind of, but YAY!

CRAIG: You happy?

MELODY: Yeah!

How long have you had the ring?

CRAIG: It was my grandma's. You like it?

MELODY: It's so pretty!

CRAIG: Really, you like it?

MELODY: I love it.

CRAIG: *(nuzzling her)*

My fiancée –

MELODY: I'm a fiancée!!

(They kiss. Melody pulls away, looks at a frozen Craig.)

MELODY: Can we do it again? Do over – do over –

I didn't show you enough. How excited I was. That wasn't enough.

MELODY: Come on, ask me again.

I'm very excited!

CRAIG: snaps back into pre-proposal position, on one knee.

CRAIG: Melody, Will you / marry me?

MELODY: YES I Will MARRY YOU!

Sorry – that was –

One more time? sorry -

(Lights shift again. Craig gets to one knee.)

CRAIG: Melody:, Will you marry me?

(Melody hesitates)

MELODY: Why did you? Ask me? Was it because of me, or?

(Craig carries on with post-proposal.)

CRAIG: You hungry?

MELODY: It was like: "Hey Mel, what's up. Oh, I was wondering, would you marry me?" "Golly, sure!"

CRAIG: I already ate, you wanna order something?

What do we need, do we need cake? Do fiancées eat cake?

MELODY: "May wedding sound good?"

"Yay, May!"

CRAIG: We need waffles. Chocolate chip waffles.

MELODY: "Then we'll start trying for kids – year after?"

"Naturally!"

"Perfect. Cause After I make partner, I'm gonna need some kids."

CRAIG: I can't wait to tell my Mom.

She's gonna be THRILLED.

(Craig moves towards the stairs.)
MELODY: Where're you going?
CRAIG: Run a bath!
MELODY: You wanna take a bath right now? You're ruining this -
CRAIG: For us.
MELODY: No – not yet –
Stay here with me – let me look at you!
CRAIG: Calm down, I'll just be in the bathroom!
MELODY: No I wanna be where you are!
CRAIG: Then come with me!
MELODY: I CAN'T.
(Craig is gone. Lights shift back to normal.)
MELODY: Craig: -
(The house is quiet.)
(She tries to shake this off. She thinks of something.)
(She grabs her car keys and goes.)
(Sirens, flashing lights, smoke and fire, far away.)
(Lights.)

(The living room, the next night. The house is a Mess.)
(Hope is trying to clean up. You know, for the Cleaners.)
(Melody: sits on the couch, in a daze. She's an even bigger mess.)
HOPE: You do realize I have more important things to do than pick you up
from the police station in the middle of the night?
Why on earth did you go there?! Why!
MELODY: I needed to see.
HOPE: Why would you want to see that???
MELODY: I thought he would be there but he wasn't. There were shoes and
there were bags and there were bones but none of it was HIM.
HOPE: You should take a shower, you stink.
MELODY: The fires were still burning.
HOPE: What did you expect?!
MELODY: The house it crashed into, pictures and books and smoke and
limbs -
HOPE: *(dismissing, covering)*
Well now I've lost my appetite.
MELODY: There were these ropes around the whole thing.
HOPE: Because people are not supposed to BE THERE, Melody. You are not
supposed to SEE THAT.
MELODY: But I went right through the ropes and I said *I need to see my hus-*

band! They said you can't be here I said I'M A WIDOW.

HOPE: You're certainly not acting like one.

MELODY: I could see the tail – and the nose. I went to the tail. It was as big as a boat but it was also it was tiny like the end of a match. See Craig was in the back. I checked his ticket confirmation. Seat 31A. I thought maybe there would be a carry-on or a sweater or anything he ate half of?

MELODY: The trees were moving but there was no wind. And all over the ground, everywhere,
I saw – pieces of people. Guts on the shoes of the workers. I saw an arm – it wasn't Craig's arm

HOPE: You mustn't – we must focus on the tasks at HAND.

MELODY: Each piece of a person has a family - and so then, where are they now?! Where is each person now?! Where did they go?!

HOPE: Help me clean up before the cleaners come.

MELODY: People put into bags like leftovers. Craig pieced back together put into these bags. Pieces of him I never knew or saw. It must have hurt – it must have hurt so much!

HOPE: *(about to loose it)*
Please – stop.

MELODY: We FEEL like we are strong, I FEEL like I'm indestructible, I never thought about this but we are about as strong as grass. We can get RIPPED apart. He was RIPPED apart. Before I could even -

HOPE: Stop it.

MELODY: I smelled skin burning and now it's stuck in my nose. It's stuck in my eyes!!!

HOPE: WE WON'T DISCUSS IT.

MELODY: Don't you miss him?!
(Beat.)

HOPE: I understand what you're going through, I really do but – *(Beat.)* It's important that you just own it. Your grief. Wear it like a brassiere, like something you'd wear every day.

MELODY: I don't wear a bra everyday.

HOPE: MY POINT IS, It's important you don't use it to justify irrational behavior. There are rules.
When I lost my husband they were very useful.
(Melody sobs.)

MELODY: I want my Mom – I want my Mom and my Dad.

HOPE: They're not going to be here forever.

MELODY: Yes – I know I just this I just I've never lost anybody before

HOPE: You have to try and keep it together.

MELODY: I feel like getting drunk.

HOPE: It doesn't help. Trust me, It doesn't drown, it accentuates.

I was looking in your kitchen.

You're going to need some sturdy non-stick pans.

For Bundt cakes, for funerals, after other deaths.

There Will be other funerals. I've gotten you a membership with the Widow's League, it's a valuable resource. It's very – it's very important to have fellowship with other widows.

(Beat.)

MELODY: These 'rules' work for you?

HOPE: YES.

MELODY: How, how do they work?!

HOPE: They provide great comfort.

MELODY: You don't seem very comfortable.

HOPE: I – I am just trying to keep it together.

MELODY: So am I but it's HARD.

HOPE: Oh, it's hard for you? It's hard.

MELODY: you have NO idea what you're talking about. You have NO CONCEPT of the – of what it takes!

MELODY: What WHAT takes?!

HOPE: Honoring your husband after his death.

And before it.

MELODY: I TRIED.

HOPE: You have NO idea.

MELODY: I'm sorry you don't like me / I'm really sorry, but CRAIG married ME, and I married HIM / and

HOPE: I don't not like you! I just doubt your ability to take care of him!

MELODY: No, you're right. I was a shitty wife, I'm a shitty widow.

HOPE: MELODY: –

MELODY: No, your son and my husband is DEAD and you want to pick lint off my dress?! Fuck your rules.

MELODY: You're not even remembering him you're not even THINKING about him.

HOPE: YOU SHUT YOUR FUCKING FACE.

(A tiny glimpse into the depth of her pain.)

(Melody has no idea what to do.)

(Beat.)

I'll be by Sunday morning. We must arrive together in the limo.

There's a song.

It is well.

It is well, it is well, with my soul.

A man wrote it after his wife and four daughters sank on a boat, and died.

His whole family.

Think about that, Melody.

(Hope is gone. Melody goes for vodka.)

(Later that night. The living room.)
(Melody has been drinking vodka. A small, sad party of one.)
(She's wearing her dress as a skirt. Fortunately, she's still wearing a bra.)
(LOUD music shakes the walls, coming from Craig's iPod. She is dancing.)

MUSIC

Bone bone bone bone

Bone bone

Bone bone

Now tell me whatcha gonna do

When there ain't no where to run

When judgment comes for you, when judgment comes for you

When judgment comes for you

And whatcha gonna do

When there ain't no where to hide *(tell me what)*

When judgment comes for you *(Cause it's gonna come for you)*

See you at the crossroads, crossroads, crossroads

So you won't be lonely

See you at the crossroads, crossroads, crossroads

So you won't be lonely

(A Knock on the door.)

MELODY: CRAIG?

(The knocks persist.)

MELODY: Let yourself in, ghost.

(A door shuts.)

(Brad enters, disheveled, with bike helmet.)

Melody: You're not my husband.

BRAD: I know. It's Brad.

MELODY: You shouldn't be here.

BRAD: You called me.

Melody: I did?

BRAD: Yeah.

Melody: What'd I say?

BRAD: "Come over."

MELODY: I'M AWESOME.

BRAD: I rode my bike over. I haven't ridden my bike in forever. I was like: I need to ride my bike right now.

MELODY: I had a bike, I miss my bike. I left it in Colorado.

BRAD: These last few days have felt like years.

I went to take a shit and I was like, why?

I don't know what to do with myself.

MELODY: You're not allowed to be sad cause no one is as sad as me. I'm the widow.

BRAD: You're sad.

Melody: Say I'm sadder than you.

BRAD: You're sadder.

MELODY: Do I look like a widow?

BRAD: Totally -

MELODY: I'm really good at it, I know all the rules.

Like the one about how you probably shouldn't be here right now.

BRAD: I shouldnt've ridden over. I've been drinking. I killed like half a bottle of this really nice chianti I've been saving, I almost hit a pole coming over, I ALMOST DIED, my mind isn't right. I should probably just stay here.

MELODY: You can stay but don't fucking touch me or I'll scream.

BRAD: Okay.

(*Brad comes in, takes off his shoes. Melody gives him a drink. Brad takes a piece of paper out of his pocket, looks at it.*)

MELODY: What's that?

BRAD: I wrote a poem. For Craig, for the service, it's really bad.

MELODY: Can I hear it?

BRAD: It's really bad.

MELODY: I wanna hear it.

BRAD: (*reciting, seriously, vulnerably*)

'A poem for Craig.'

(*Long pause.*)

CRAIG: —

You were my friend

Until the end.

And your end

My friend
Came much too soon.
When I saw the news
I was adding ones and twos
With my calculator.
I was doing a report for you.
Through doing I found meaning.
Meaning being the reality of doing,
And doing things for You,
Was Good.
I didn't always like it but I found
Harmony there,
In the doing.

And I stopped what I was doing
And looked and saw and
I felt you fall and I fell to the ground and
My lunch came up in my throat and
My calculator fell onto the carpet.
Like you fell.

So that's the end.
(Melody is moved, connected to him.)
MELODY: I saw the crash. I went and I saw it.
BRAD: Are you serious? You shouldn't have seen that shit.
MELODY: I did.
BRAD: Why'd you do it?
MELODY: I needed to.
BRAD: *(getting it)*
    Part of your process.....
MELODY: Yeah.
BRAD: What was it like?
MELODY: It was awful.
BRAD: Like what?
MELODY: Like a massacre – and this smell – You ever wonder, what does a
    dead body smell like?
BRAD: Yes –
MELODY: It smells like animals.
BRAD: Like what kind of animal?
MELODY: Like a petting zoo maybe but with fire and blood –

BRAD: Can I tell you something, can I be totally honest?

MELODY: YES

BRAD: I used to like it when he was out of town. Oh God -

MELODY: *(needing to talk)*
Me too, II mean I missed him when he was gone but I used to like the alone time –
I like Poptarts for dinner and a lot of Project Runway.

BRAD: Who's your favorite?

MELODY: Bridget.

BRAD: I like Clive.

MELODY: He's okay.

BRAD: He was so he was so good to me - I mean he worked me hard but it was because he cared but I would like RESENT him sometimes when he just asked me to DO something. And it's my JOB to do things for him, that's my JOB.

Melody: I wanna wake up like it never happened.
I want him to walk in the door.

BRAD: Did you ever wonder– what if there was a way I could go to my own funeral?

MELODY: Yes.

BRAD: Me too.

(Melody changes the song to something hard and DMX.)

MELODY: You wanna dance?

BRAD: What kind?

MELODY: Like a party.

(She turns on music.)
His running mix.
Apparently when he was running he liked to feel like he could kill people.

MUSIC:
This is the fuckin shit I be talking about
You think it's a game
You think it's a fuckin game?

(She starts to dance, letting the music move her. It's sloppy and hot. Brad joins her. They are grief – dancing.)

MUSIC:
Come on

What'cha really want
D-M-X
Come on, Ryde or die
What's my name? DMX and I be the best
You see the rest they lookin like they need a rest
One more time, I'mma spit at you some shit
That's gon get at you be fuckin with your mind, stop talkin shit
Cuz you out there runnin' your mouth
And you really don't know who you fuckin with

(They are grinding and sweating, dancing.
Brad starts to move his hands over her.)
MELODY: This is bad – this is so against the rules -
(Melody grabs hold of Brad, hugs him, hard, needing to be held.)
BRAD: puts his arms around her.
BRAD: It's okay, I got you –
Here I am –
(Brad holds her tighter.)
(Brad kisses Melody. For a moment, she kisses him back desperately.
They go for it, hard, and it's hot.)
BRAD: *(turned on)*
Shit -
MELODY: stops, pulls herself away. Tries to get her bearings.
MELODY: Craig –
BRAD: What?
You okay Mel?
MELODY: Don't call me that.
BRAD: Sorry –
(Melody brings her hands to her lips. To her gut. She sits on the couch.)
MELODY: Sorry, I'm sorry.
I think maybe you should go.
BRAD: Okay, are you sure?
(Melody nods.)
BRAD: I don't know if you should be alone right now.
MELODY: No, I want to be.
BRAD: Maybe we could be alone but like also together.
MELODY: We shouldn't be doing ANYTHING right now Brad, we are fuck-
ing crazy right now -
BRAD: I love you, I think –
(Craig laughs.)

MELODY: What?!

MELODY: We can't do this.

We're grown ass adults I think. No, I know.

BRAD: I'm not immature. I am very mature.

(He heads for the door and is gone.)

(Beat.)

(Craig enters.)

MELODY: You came home!!!

CRAIG: I did!

MELODY: He made it!! He finally made it!

CRAIG: Gahhhh that took forever.

(Melody takes his suitcase, kisses him.)

CRAIG: Did you get my / message

MELODY: I was a bitch on the phone, I'm so sorry

CRAIG: I too was a bitch

MELODY: Seriously, I'm sorry

CRAIG: Me too.

MELODY: I love it when you tell me you love me.

I don't care how many times you tell me.

(She kisses him.)

MELODY: How was the flight?

CRAIG: You know, the plane was on the ground, then it finally took off, then it was in the air, then on the ground again, it was pretty standard.

(Melody laughs.)

Melody: Uch, I don't know how you do it so much, I hate flying.

CRAIG: White wine, Sinatra, and Tylenol PM.

MELODY: Oh, you're drunk?

CRAIG: Sobered up. Ate some nuts.

MELODY: Hahahaha –

(They both laugh.)

MELODY: Guess what I had lunch with your Mom!

CRAIG: Aww!

MELODY: Yeah we're going to take a gardening class together. I think we're best friends.

CRAIG: That's great!

MELODY: Yeah and also, I made chili and also, I missed you.

CRAIG: Mmmm feels good to be home.

(Craig grabs her.)

MELODY: I missed you.

CRAIG: Me too.

(She kisses him.)

MELODY: You must be starved.

    (Craig sits on the couch, removes his shoes. He looks around the room like he doesn't belong. He turns on the TV. He watches the news.)

CRAIG: Oh shit, a plane crashed!

    (Melody, now wearing an apron, sauced spoon in hand, pokes her head in.)

MELODY: What?

CRAIG: A plane crashed –

MELODY: *(Her eyes focus on the TV. They watch together for a minute.)*

    You want a salad too?

CRAIG: That'd be great.

    (at news)

    It's all over everywhere. It crashed. That's terrifying, wow.

    (She sits with him. They watch the carnage. Craig is engrossed.)

    At least I wasn't on it right?

MELODY: Yes. You were.

    What am I doing….What am I doing…..

    (Craig goes.)

    (Melody alone in the house. The room seems to brighten. She sees the mess she's made. She straightens up the house. Pulls herself together.)

    The living room. The morning of the funeral.

    The doorbell rings.

    Doorbell rings again. Cautiously, self consciously, Brad lets himself in.

    He stands uncomfortably in the living room with an elaborate bouquet of begonias.

    Melody enters.

    She is a radiant, well-dressed widow in a black dress pressed with grief. She has pulled herself together. Almost too together. Stiff.

BRAD: Good morning.

MELODY: What're you doing here?

BRAD: I'm sorry – the door was open –

MELODY: This is my house. You can't just let yourself into my house.

    I'm about to bury my husband.

    I have a party to prepare for. A lunch.

BRAD: I just wanted to give you these flowers before the – I mean I'll be at church but these are just for you.

    (He holds them out to her. She takes them, frowns at them.)

    They're begonias. They're symbolic of balance and psychism.

MELODY: They don't go with the rest of the flowers.
BRAD: They're for you.
 (Melody gives flowers back)
MELODY: They don't match. Thank you, but they don't match.
BRAD: You're missing the point.
 I wanted to um – apologize.
MELODY: Nothing happened.
BRAD: Why're you being like this?
MELODY: *(proudly)*
 I'll see you at the service.
BRAD: I just wanted to say, I like – feel for you.
MELODY: Brad –
BRAD: I don't know if it's 'for' you it might also be something selfish, which
 is my least favorite thing, selfishness, even though everything I do
 turns out to be selfish and I really hate that.
MELODY: I can't handle this right now.
BRAD: Just – are you okay?
MELODY: Yeah.
BRAD: You promise?
 (Beat.)
MELODY: Yeah.
BRAD: I'll see you at the church.
 You don't have to like talk to me or anything but I'll be there.
 (Hope enters, bedraggled and numb. She heads straight for the couch.)
MELODY: Thanks.
BRAD: Good morning, again
 (Brad goes.)
 (Melody looks at Hope. Something's terribly wrong.)
MELODY: Good / morning –
HOPE: No it's not.
MELODY: He just – he just came by to bring flowers.
 (Hope doesn't respond.)
MELODY: I'm so sorry about yesterday, I -
HOPE: Forgotten.
MELODY: No. It's not. I was completely inappropriate.
 Do you like my dress? I got a new one. I wanted something a little
 longer / so I
HOPE: Melody –
MELODY: It's from Talbotts.
HOPE: Melody, you can stop.

HOPE: Let's just get through today. Then you can live your life, and I can live what's left of mine.

MELODY: I don't want that.

I finished my eulogy.

I loved Craig. I loved him very very much.

(Hope looks like she could sleep for a hundred years. Or die.)

HOPE: You have him still.

MELODY: What?

HOPE: You have him.

MELODY: So do you.

HOPE: No I don't.

I tried to – last night I –

I couldn't get it out my head.

The fire – and and the limbs -

MELODY: I'm so sorry I shouldn't / have

HOPE: So I -

I said Hello Craig but -

And he was in my dream and – and I didn't even know what to say to him! I couldn't say a word! When I opened my mouth, there was sand!

I have nothing.

MELODY: That's not true.

HOPE: No grandchildren.

MELODY: That's not – *(she stops, because it's true.)*

(Hope starts to break down.)

HOPE: I lost my husband and that was terrible but that was fine. Well it wasn't fine but I did it, I got through it for Craig, because he needed me and I couldn't be a wreck, he needed someone to get him out of bed in the morning, and I needed HIM to get me out of bed in the morning, and I don't even remember what Frank smelled like anymore but this is FINE, because I have Craig, and now he's GONE.

There's no word for a woman who looses their husband AND their son.

I forgot how to brush my teeth.

This morning I forgot how to brush my teeth.

So I didn't.

MELODY: It's okay to be sad.

(Beat. Hope starts to break down. Melody has no idea what to do. She peeks out the window.)

(Limo honks.)

MELODY: The limo's here –

HOPE: I can't do this – I don't know if I can do this - Look at me – I'm a mess -

MELODY: It's okay.

HOPE: No it's not -

MELODY: It is.

> *(A moment. Hope sits on the couch. She howls with grief, relief.)*
> *(Melody watches.)*
> *(Slowly, moves towards her to comfort her.)*
> *(Lights shift to later.)*
> *(In the dark, music for the organ and a singer)*

MUSIC:
When peace like a river
Attendeth my way
When sorrows like sea billows roll

Whatever my lot
Thou hast taught me say
It is well
It is well
With my soul

It is well, It is well
It is well, It is well
With my soul

> *(Melody, in the living room, alone. Night. Sitting by herself on the couch. Hope enters and approaches Melody, sits next to her. Melody is a bit more together. Hope is a bit more relaxed.)*

HOPE: There are bowls of skittles everywhere.

MELODY: It's what he would've wanted.

> *(Beat.)*

HOPE: *(admitting)*
I love skittles!

MELODY: So did Craig:!!!!

HOPE: I never let myself have them but I love them so much!!

> *(Hope decides, and eats skittles.)*
> *(Hope exhales, takes off her shoes.)*

HOPE: Your parents –

MELODY: Yes, sorry, I know – they're loud -

HOPE: They're lovely.

(*Beat.*) (*Melody smiles.*)

MELODY: Yeah, they're pretty great.

HOPE: I'm glad they made it in time.

MELODY: Me too.

HOPE: They've invited me to visit. They say I didn't spend enough time at the wedding.

MELODY: You didn't.

HOPE: I – I felt left out.

MELODY: Why?

(*Hope shrugs, embarrassed.*)

HOPE: Your mom wants to feed me, she says I'm too thin. And your Dad wants me to meet his chickens?

MELODY: You should go, you should totally go!!

They would really like that.

I would really like that.

(*An uncomfortable Beat.*)

HOPE: Your eulogy. It was – it was beautiful. I'm very impressed with you Melody.

MELODY: Thank you.

(*Hope nods. They sit there together. Hope starts to get up.*)

HOPE: I should / make sure there's ice

MELODY: I already checked, we're good, I promise.

(*Beat.*) (*Hope sits back down. Melody starts to laugh.*)

HOPE: What?

MELODY: The other night – after you left – I stood in the kitchen in Craig's underwear and I ate a whole pie.

HOPE: A WHOLE pie?

MELODY: Seriously I killed it.

(*Beat.*)

Is it going to feel like this forever?

HOPE: Yes. In a way.

MELODY: Forever forever?

HOPE: It – shifts a bit

MELODY: How so?

HOPE: Some days are better than others.

MELODY: What do we do now?

(*Hope holds a hand out to Melody.*)

MELODY: What's this?

HOPE: Come now. Come here. It's important that you know this.

MELODY: What am I 'knowing?'

(Melody won't move, so Hope goes to her and guides her to the center of the floor, positions her for a polite dance.)

HOPE: You see, chances are, at some point in the future, a man is bound to ask you to dance.

It's their duty as men.

I know it sounds silly but –

MELODY: No, I wanna know! Show me.

HOPE: So you bow gracefully –

(Hope does so. Melody then does, too.)

HOPE: And you accept. Take his hand but don't ever hold too tight or squeeze it.

And then you dance.

If you start to think of your husband, and the way he held you, if tears come to your eyes, focus on something about the gentleman that is gross or unattractive and keep your eyes there.

I prefer the chin or neck, or a mole. Dance with him for the duration of the song, then say thank you.

Come on now, try and keep up -

(Hope teaches Melody to dance.)

Then take a moment and remember your husband.

MELODY: Like right there, or go into a bathroom / and

HOPE: Just for a moment, right there. Say hello to his memory.

Don't flog yourself, don't run through all the things you should have said just –

Look at this new person and maybe – tell him how you feel.

Tell him about Craig.

Then you should probably cry on him and see how he takes it.

If he takes it: let him take you to lunch.

(Melody smiles.)

(Hope goes.)

(Lights shift to later.)

(Melody, cleaning up after the party. Music plays softly. She turns it off. Stands there in total silence. Stands there, listening to the silence.)

(Craig appears.)

CRAIG: First we pitched up at 31 degrees.

Then we pitched left at 45 degrees.

Finally we pitched right at 60 degrees, then dropped twelve hundred feet in about five seconds.

I thought of you.

Then I realized I was hungry and the hunger felt really strange and then I realized it was fear. And I wondered how many times in my life have I eaten when really all I needed to do was say a prayer or talk to somebody?

Then I thought. Mother. Also, I should get my laptop out of my carry on and why didn't I take that baseball scholarship and what does God think of me?

Then I thought, Brad. Brad can't finish that research himself. I thought, Brad is going to fuck this up.

We were plummeting.

I didn't dare look out the window and see the inevitable.

Everyone was sobbing and yelling out names. Fred, oh Fred! My baby, my baby! Mommy!

Then I wanted a cigarette. Screw this, I'm smoking.

But I didn't have any. I've never smoked. Fear of death.

Then I thought, what's Melody doing?

Then I thought, what's Melody going to do?

Then: I love her. Then: Oh my God I love her.

(Craig looks at Melody.)

CRAIG: Did you love me?

MELODY: Yes. So much.

CRAIG: You promise?

(Melody nods. Craig smiles, satisfied.)

CRAIG: We loved each other.

MELODY: We really did.

I didn't recognize it.

It would've gotten better, I would've gotten better I just –

CRAIG: I know. Me too.

MELODY: Are you going to go back to sleep?

CRAIG: Yes.

Melody: Are you going to heaven?

CRAIG: nods.

MELODY: Have you seen it?

CRAIG: Yep! But only from far away.

MELODY: What's it like?

CRAIG: There's a house. Like ours.

MELODY: Do you have a bed?

CRAIG: Yes.

MELODY: Is it a twin or a full?

CRAIG: Full.

MELODY: Is there room for me in it?
(Craig doesn't respond.)
Is there?
CRAIG: We'll see.
G'night Mel.
MELODY: G'night –
CRAIG: I love you.
It's Craig.
(Melody smiles, laughs.)
(Craig kisses her forehead. Melody nods. Craig goes.)
MELODY: Sleep tight.
(Slowly, Craig goes. Melody watches in silence.)
(Dark.)

END OF PLAY

NOW CIRCA THEN

Carly Mensch

PLAYWRIGHTS BIOGRAPHY

Carly Mensch's plays include *Oblivion* (Steppenwolf First Look), *Now Circa Then* (Ars Nova, TheatreWorks), *All Hail Hurricane Gordo* (Humana Festival, Cleveland Play House) and *Len, Asleep in Vinyl* (2nd Stage/Uptown Series). Carly has developed work at Playwrights Horizons, Manhattan Theatre Club, The Kennedy Center, Marin Theatre Company, New York Stage & Film, Center Theatre Group and Ars Nova, where she was the 2008 Playwright-in-Residence as well as a founding member of Play Group. She is currently a co-producer on Showtime's "Weeds." Carly is a graduate of Dartmouth College and The Juilliard School's Lila Acheson Wallace Playwrights Program.

Now Circa Then was presented by Ars Nova (Jason Eagan, Artistic Director and Jeremy Blocker, Managing Director) in New York City (Opening Night: 27 September 2010). The production was directed by Jason Eagan.

CAST

Margie	Maureen Sebastian
Gideon	Stephen Plunkett

Set Design	Lauren Helpern
Costume Design	Jenny Mannis
Lighting Design	Traci Klainer
Sound Design	Ryan Rumery

CHARACTERS

Margie: 26 - a shy and slightly awkward girl; more goose than swan. Non-white.*

Gideon: 27 - a hardcore history buff; passionate and youthful, with a hint of arrogance. White.

SETTING

A restored 19th century tenement on New York's Lower East Side, present. The play is divided into three rooms: the parlor (beginnings), the kitchen (middles), and the bedroom (endings). Margie's character is scripted as Filipino-American, based on the actress who originated the role, but she can be of any race or ethnicity, really, so long as she's an unlikely casting choice for a 19th century Jewish immigrant. There are two scenes where her race is explicitly mentioned -- scene 9 and scene 22. Adjust accordingly.

AUTHOR'S NOTES

This play is schizophrenically split between two worlds: the world of Gideon and Margie (naturalistic) and the world of Julian and Josephine (stylized, theatrical). Actors and designers should go to town distinguishing between these two modes. Make rules and break them as the play gets messier and the two worlds collide.

In terms of how to stylize the reenactments, the main question is how much to include the audience. Two possible broad approaches are: 1) treating these scenes like living dioramas (fourth wall; all questions to the audience are rhetorical) or 2) treating them like snippets of an actual live museum tour. In the Ars Nova production, we opted for the second. Finding moments to ad lib and engage the audience (baiting them to respond at times) without ever putting any specific audience member on the spot. If you go the participatory route, you might want to give the audience clues that they're part of the story (turning the house lights on, for example). Also, be prepared for audience members to chime in at weird times. We had one woman shout in response to Margie's question "Does anyone have any questions?" with "YEAH, WHAT'S GOING ON!?" (Good question.)

Either way, be bold. Aim high. Overshoot. Mess up. Try again.

Carly Mensch

NOW CIRCA THEN

1.

PROLOGUE

Pin-spot on two people in nineteenth century costume—Margie and Gideon. They smile at the audience. Gideon is pert and enthusiastic; Margie looks vaguely uncomfortable.

GIDEON: If everyone could scooch a little closer. No strangers here. Only opportunities!
(They smile and wait.)
Hello. Guten Tag. How is everybody doing today? Yeah, okay. My name is Julian Glockner and over here is my wife, Josephine.
MARGIE: Hi. I'm Josephine.
GIDEON: We are so psyched to see you!
Do we have any immigrants with us today? Anyone? Maybe just someone from out of town?
If people respond -- go with it and skip the next line.
No? That's okay, we don't like to single people out.
We're all fellow travelers. Josephine and I happen to be recent travelers ourselves. That's right. We traveled all the way from a little place called "West Prussia" circa 1890, just to be here with you today, here on the Lower East Side of New York.
MARGIE: *(wooden)*
Yes. Between 1815 and 1915, more than thirty million immigrants came to America. They came from places like Germany, Russia, Austria-Hungary, Italy and Romania. Oh. And Poland.
GIDEON: Our journey begins now. In this hallway.
Margie and Gideon motion to the door behind them.
(slow, deliberate)
Behind this door lies the tenement apartment Josephine and I Will share for over thirty years together. Now. Let us turn the doorknob ourselves and enter into the rooms of the past…
(Gideon does some big, sweeping gesture.)
(Margie smiles, sort of.)
(Blackout.)

PART ONE

2.

The Parlor.
A room with a small fireplace, a dress form and a sewing table.
But also: an EXIT sign, light switches and fire sprinklers.
Margie passes Gideon items from a large suitcase.

MARGIE: One pair ladies stockings.

One pair of shoes, leather.

Two candlesticks.

Three pairs of cotton underwear, men's.

GIDEON: I Hope these are mine, eh Josephine?

MARGIE: One jar of pickled herring.

One photograph of our native village of Moloschnya.

(Gideon pulls out his own laminated version of the photograph. He holds it out to the audience.)

GIDEON: *(nostalgic)*

Yes. Moloschnya.

It seems like only yesterday when we met at Jakkob the Elder's to sign our arranged marriage agreement, eh Josephine?

MARGIE: That's right, Julian.

GIDEON: *(re the unpacking)*

Is that it?

(Margie looks inside the suitcase—it's empty.)

MARGIE: Yup.

GIDEON: *(out to the audience)*

What luck! You've caught us at a fortuitous time, travelers! Josephine and I have only just arrived in the New World.

MARGIE: America.

GIDEON: We left behind many friends and family. My mother, Irina, a dancer. My father Rudolph. The cabbage farmer.

MARGIE: We rode here on a very big boat.

GIDEON: In steerage.

MARGIE: When we arrived at New York harbor, a man loaded our mattress onto his wagon. He said he was going to give us a free ride into the city.

GIDEON: Unfortunately. That ride didn't include us.

MARGIE: Then we came here. To the Lower East Side.

GIDEON: To this apartment.

MARGIE: This room is called the "front room."

GIDEON: One day, when Josephine and I have children, they will sleep in this room.

MARGIE: Not that we have any children.

GIDEON: But we will. Some day.

MARGIE: In the future.

GIDEON: Well, near future.

MARGIE: Or distant.

(Pause.)

GIDEON: This might be a good time to mention that Josephine and I are newlyweds!

The boat-ride over was essentially our honeymoon.

(He smiles lovingly at Margie.)

MARGIE: *(forcing a smile back)*

Yup.

I threw up six times.

And then I got lice.

GIDEON: We both got lice.

3.

(Lunch break.)

(Gideon reads a biography of James Madison. Margie eats a Pop Tart.)

(After a while:)

MARGIE: Hi. Excuse me?

(Gideon looks up.)

This is really embarrassing. I keep forgetting your name.

GIDEON: It's Gideon.

MARGIE: Hi Gideon, I'm—

GIDEON: Margie. I know.

MARGIE: Oh.

(Gideon goes back to reading his book.)

MARGIE: So have you done this kind of thing before?

GIDEON: What kind of thing?

MARGIE: With the costume. And the tour groups.

GIDEON: You mean reenactment?

MARGIE: Sure.

GIDEON: Historical interpretation. Living history.

MARGIE: Either one.

GIDEON: Yeah, I've done a lot of reenactment.

MARGIE: You're really good at it.

GIDEON: It's kind of my thing.

MARGIE: So what other places have you done?

GIDEON: Uh, I've done Gettsyburg.

MARGIE: Cool--

GIDEON: I've done Plymouth.

MARGIE: Okay--

GIDEON: I've done Salem. I've done Shaker Village. I've done Daniel Webster. I did a few Renaissance Fairs back in college. I've done two Air & Space museums. I've done five birthplaces, all politicians, all Republican. I've done the Boston Fire of 1872 and I just got back from doing this amazing hundred acre Living History Farm in Urbandale, Iowa.

MARGIE: Wow.

GIDEON: It's an addiction. My brain is like a twenty-four-hour History Channel.

What's past is prologue, right? That's Shakespeare.

MARGIE: Right.

GIDEON: We all think we're like these orphans, but we're not really.

MARGIE: We...?

GIDEON: People our age. Like we're these invincible orphan children, running around big cities without any family or history of our own. But we're not, right? Orphans. We all come from somewhere. That's why I like this museum. Immigrants, man? That's like our prologue.

What about you. What's your story?

MARGIE: Well. I just moved here. To New York. I'm still a little... aggh! Uh. I'm 26.

GIDEON: You a history major?

MARGIE: English.

GIDEON: And do you have a background in creative role play?

MARGIE: No.

GIDEON: Do you have any experience as a tour guide?

MARGIE: Nope.

GIDEON: No tour guide experience.

MARGIE: No.

GIDEON: None.

MARGIE: Nope.

GIDEON: So like... how did you get this job?

MARGIE: That woman. With the lipstick?

GIDEON: *(under his breath)*
 Way to go, Roberta.
MARGIE: Excuse me?
GIDEON: Nothing. She's just totally loosening her standards. Up on the third floor - you know, the 1920's apartment - she hired this Guatemalan guy who can barely even speak English.
MARGIE: Mario?
GIDEON: I think she's on some post-racial... liberal-guilt kick. No offense.
MARGIE: None... taken.
GIDEON: It's like - no one cares about authenticity anymore. I mean - you seem like a perfectly nice person and whatever, but Josephine - she was a 19th century Jewish immigrant. She was...
MARGIE: White?
 (Beat.)
GIDEON: We're a history museum. That's our whole raison-d' etre: Making history come to life.
 (A short silence.)
MARGIE: I don't know. I think history is sort of bullshit.
GIDEON: Excuse me?
MARGIE: Like--slavery? People need to get over it already. It's not like I'm personally responsible for what a bunch of racist white guys did a hundred years ago. People should just move on already. Stop worshiping boring old facts.
GIDEON: Okay - I um. Sorry.
 I don't understand. Why would you take a job at a museum if you don't believe in history?
MARGIE: I told you. I just moved here. I needed a job.
GIDEON: You don't think that's... irresponsible?
MARGIE: Are you kidding? I'm eating my lunch out of a vending machine. I still don't have a place to live. So to answer your question. No. I don't think it's irresponsible. In fact - it's probably the most responsible thing I've ever done. Ever.
 (Pause.)
GIDEON: This job. It's like super, super important to me.
MARGIE: I see that.
GIDEON: The last Josephine. She only lasted about a month. Just, FYI.

4.

(Later.)
(Gideon sits at a foot-treadle sewing machine.)

(Margie enters carrying heavy buckets of water. She is now extremely pregnant. She takes a seat next to Gideon.)

GIDEON: Josephine—

MARGIE: Yes, Julian.

GIDEON: Do you know the price of potatoes this month?

MARGIE: …No.

GIDEON: Just take a guess.

MARGIE: Uh. A dollar?

(Pause.)

GIDEON: *(out to the audience)*

Anyone else? Any guesses? Sack of potatoes. 1890.

(Field some guesses.)

GIDEON: Ten cents.

MARGIE: Is that a lot?

GIDEON: Are you kidding? It's insanity! Prices go up and wages go down. Don't worry though—I'm a very resourceful man.

MARGIE: Oh, well that's good.

GIDEON: It's time to be frugal, Josephine. No more of those frilly dresses you like to buy from the pages of Sears & Roebuck. We need to start watching our spending. Especially now with the baby on the way. Everything costs money, in these post-industrial times. Any idea how much I spent on this sewing machine over here?

MARGIE: Uh… hold on.

(Margie picks up a laminated sheet of paper from the table. She quickly skims the document.)

MARGIE: *(reading)*

Twenty-six dollars?

GIDEON: Yup. And that's only cause I got it second hand from a Lithuanian street peddler.

MARGIE: *(still reading)*

"This model is significantly smaller than Singer's original version. The aforementioned price includes a built-in table. For further reading, please see Singer and the Sewing Machine: A Capitalist Romance."

(looking up)

Oh.

GIDEON: The point is, Josephine. It's about seizing opportunities. It's about seeing your dreams ahead of you and catching them with your own custom-made…dream-catching net.

(Margie lets out a laugh.)

(forging ahead)

In our native village, I was a lowly shoe cobbler. Here in America—I am an entrepreneur. A man of boundless potential. A man of...
(Margie sneezes loudly.)
(Gideon looks at her, horrified.)

5.

(After work.)
(Gideon sits at the sewing machine, mending a pair of pants. Coincidentally, he's not wearing any himself.)
(Margie enters carrying a large three-ring binder.)

MARGIE: Don't say anything. I know I fucked up.

GIDEON: Didn't say anything.

MARGIE: I've read this stupid manual like five hundred times. You're not wearing any pants.

GIDEON: Got caught on a nail.

MARGIE: I'll just go somewhere else.

GIDEON: Hey. It's your living room too, right?
(Margie takes a seat, reluctantly.)

MARGIE: I didn't know you could sew. In real life.

GIDEON: Eagle scouts.
I'm also just a really resourceful person. In general.
(Margie opens up the binder.)
(Gideon sews.)
(Every once in a while he looks over at her, reading. After a while:)

GIDEON: Can I give you some advice?

MARGIE: Let me guess: Don't suck.

GIDEON: What you're looking for - it's not in the manual.

MARGIE: What are you talking about?

GIDEON: You can read that thing cover to cover. Memorize every single footnote. Still not gonna help.

MARGIE: Thanks. That's very constructive.

GIDEON: Just saying.

MARGIE: So. What would help?

GIDEON: You really want to know?

MARGIE: Yes.

GIDEON: Stand up.

MARGIE: What?

GIDEON: Stand up.
(She does.)
So. Have you ever done any kind of acting before?

MARGIE: Acting? No.

GIDEON: This museum—we get a lot of former actors. It's like where theater people come to die.

MARGIE: I'm not an actor.

GIDEON: That's okay, that's fine.

MARGIE: Sorry- I thought the point is to be educational.

GIDEON: Yeah... Not really. I mean, people can just pick up a textbook if all they want to do is obtain information, right? There's a certain artistry I like to think. Have you ever seen *Apocalypse Now* with Marlon Brando?

MARGIE: Sure.

GIDEON: You know that scene with all the severed heads?

MARGIE: I think so.

GIDEON: I love that scene! Brando wasn't in that one, but you should really watch him. Very instinctual--

MARGIE: I don't understand—what is it you want me to do?

GIDEON: It's not about doing anything. It's about how you hold yourself.

MARGIE: And how do I hold myself?

GIDEON: Just kind of, regular. Like yourself.

MARGIE: So?

GIDEON: So. Josephine should hold herself like Josephine. Not like Margie.

MARGIE: I hate improv if that's what this is going to be. I am a plum tree. I am a tea pot.

GIDEON: It's not improv.
Okay. I'm going to go exit the room and then come back. Just watch.
(Gideon exits the room and comes back.)
Notice anything?

MARGIE: Not really.

GIDEON: Good.
Now I'm going to do it again.
(Gideon exits the room once more. This time, when he re-enters, he walks with heightened energy and pep. The energized body. Yup. That's right. We all know this.)
See the difference?

MARGIE: You're more taut, I guess.

GIDEON: Right. The first time I entered as myself. The second time as Julian Glockner—dressmaker, husband, persona. It's like the difference between resting on your heals and leaning forward on your toes.

MARGIE: It matters how I'm leaning?

GIDEON: Yes! When you don't really inhabit your part. When you're not really giving me anything, then I can't do my job. It's like a push-pull.

Your turn now.

MARGIE: You want me to exit the room and come back?

GIDEON: Yeah.

(Margie walks listlessly out of the room.)

(She re-enters approximately the same.)

GIDEON: Okay... So maybe focus on how you're standing.

(Margie tries to stand up really tall.)

Great. That's.... better.

Now, relax your shoulders a bit.

(She does.)

Your neck too.

(She does.)

Yeah, that makes a huge difference.

MARGIE: Really?

GIDEON: Uh huh.

MARGIE: I just feel more self-conscious now.

GIDEON: That'll go away.

Now maybe try layering something in. Like—is she tired? From a long, hard day of work?

(Margie hunches her shoulders.)

GIDEON: And maybe her hands are clenched, from all that sewing.

(Margie clenches her fists.)

GIDEON: And maybe she has a sense of striving. Like, a woman who is just trying to get by. Survive.

(Margie tries to think of something to do, She drops the pose altogether.)

GIDEON: What? What happened?

MARGIE: I feel like an idiot.

GIDEON: We're all idiots.

MARGIE: It's a comfort thing. I need to get more comfortable with the material.

GIDEON: Forget about the lines.

MARGIE: Besides. I don't even know who this woman is!

GIDEON: She's... Josephine Glockner.

MARGIE: Yeah, but who is she?

GIDEON: She's a nineteenth century immigrant.

MARGIE: *(starting to freak out)*

But why did she move here? What is she trying to prove?

GIDEON: I don't think she was trying to prove anything…
MARGIE: It's not like this city has magical transformative powers. It's not like you move here and poof, you're suddenly a whole different person.
GIDEON: Sure…
MARGIE: Besides—Julian isn't perfect either.
GIDEON: I never said he was.
MARGIE: Personally, I find him a little over the top sometimes. His whole persona.
GIDEON: Character--
MARGIE: That voice he does.
GIDEON: Hey!
(Margie starts taking off her costume.)
MARGIE: I'm sorry. I can't do this.
GIDEON: Do what?
(Margie heads to the door.)
GIDEON: What are you doing?
MARGIE: Just, tell Roberta I'm sorry.
(Margie rushes out.)
GIDEON: *(calling after her)*
Margie? Hey Margie!

6.

(Margie alone in the parlor.)
MARGIE: Hello, I'm Josephine.
Hi. I'm Josephine.
Guten Tag, my name is Josephine.
Hi. I'm Josephine.
Hello I'm…
I'm…
What's my name? Oh my god how can I forget the name part?
Josephine! My name is Josephine. Duh.
My name is Josephine. Hello. Please to meet you. Josephine. My name is Josephine.
I am a strong, self-actualized independent woman.
I am also a poor, marginalized Eastern European immigrant.
I am…
Dammit.

7

(Next day.)
(Gideon is about to start. Margie rushes in and joins him, out of breath.
They share a quick look before launching into the reenactment.)

GIDEON: This is a little segment we like to call: Who Knew?
 Who knew, Josephine, that in 1890, many people didn't use tooth-
 brushes?
MARGIE: Who knew?
GIDEN: Good thing those women at the Settlement House came up with a
 song to help us remember to use them. Remember?
GIDEON: *(singing)*
 "Here we are coming to clean our teeth, clean our teeth, clean our teeth,
 Here we are coming to clean our teeth; and we do it night and morn-
 ing."
 How about another round.
 (Margie joins in, reluctantly.)
Gideon/ MARGIE: "Here we are coming to clean our teeth, clean our teeth,
 clean our teeth, Here we are coming to clean our teeth; and we do it
 night and morning."
 (Pause.)
MARGIE: Who knew, Julian. That Immigrants were often called by their
 derogatory name; "Greenhorns."
GIDEON: Who knew?
MARGIE: Greenhorn referring, obviously, to being green. Clueless. Easily
 taken advantage of.
GIDEON: Who knew!
MARGIE: Who knew.

8

(After work.)
(Gideon sweeps the floor.)
(Margie paces the room on a cell phone.)
MARGIE: *(into the phone; deeply annoyed at whoever she's talking to)*
 I don't care. Why?... Because it's stupid... It is. It's a baby, not a Nobel
 Peace Prize...
 Fine. I'll send her an email. I will. I will. Tell Dad I say hi. Okay.
 Bye. Bye.
 (Margie hangs up.)
MARGIE: Am I supposed to be doing anything right now?

GIDEON: You're supposed to be cleaning up.

MARGIE: Oh. Duh.

(Margie retrieves a bucket and some gloves.)

(She picks up a candlestick and polishes it very gently.)

GIDEON: I thought you were quitting.

MARGIE: I changed my mind.

GIDEON: That was a pretty strong reaction, yesterday.

MARGIE: Yeah. I do that sometimes. Freak out.

GIDEON: Do you suffer from panic attacks?

MARGIE: No. I'm fine.

I guess. Sometimes I get overwhelmed.

GIDEON: That...

MARGIE: That, I don't know. That I'm living this tiny insignificant life? That I'm never going to achieve my full potential as a human being on this earth?

(Pause.)

GIDEON: Oh.

MARGIE: Back in Michigan. I was working for my Uncle and dating this guy and living in my parents basement and I was like: Really Margie? Is this really who you want to be?

(Margie catches Gideon staring at her.)

MARGIE: What?

GIDEON: You look like someone. Remind me of them.

MARGIE: Who?

GIDEON: My mom.

MARGIE: Okay...

(Margie picks up an old clock.)

GIDEON: DON'T TOUCH THAT!

(She puts the clock down.)

That clock. It's from 1802. It was made by this really, really famous colonial clockmaker. It's super delicate.

(Margie slowly puts down the clock.)

MARGIE: Sorry.

GIDEON: It's okay. You didn't know.

(Margie picks up a ceramic tureen with extra caution.)

MARGIE: You're really intense about history.

GIDEON: It's... important to me.

MARGIE: I see that.

GIDEON: Modern times are boring. Besides, the way I see it, our generation is doomed.

MARGIE: Why?

GIDEON: Because we're all culturally bankrupt?

We have no tangible things to pass down to our children. No artifacts. No family heirlooms.

All we have is fleeting virtual moments.

MARGIE: Isn't that what people said with the telegraph? That we'd all turn into robots.

GIDEON: No. This is different. This is epically tragic.

Think about it: We keep all of our memories out in Data Storage Centers in the Midwest. In these massive cement buildings where Microsoft and Google and Facebook back up our identities. These are the temples we're constructing. Data Centers.

It's so sad.

That's why I don't have a cell phone.

MARGIE: How do you stay in touch with people?

GIDEON: I check email on my Dad's computer about once a month. That's enough, trust me.

MARGIE: So your Dad lives in New York?

GIDEON: Yeah. I'm sort of staying with him for a bit. Plus - Upper West - way nicer than whatever I could afford in Brooklyn.

(Margie's cell phone rings again. She picks it up and turns away)

(from Gideon. After a beat:)

MARGIE: NOOOOOOOOOOOOOOO!!!

(She hangs up the phone.)

(Gideon stares at her for a moment.)

MARGIE: What?

GIDEON: Nothing.

9.

(Two weeks later.)

(Margie brushes her teeth, a sleeping bag on the floor beside her. After a bit, Gideon enters.)

(He watches her for a moment in horrified silence.)

GIDEON: Hi.

MARGIE: *(turning around)*

Hi! Gideon. You're... early.

GIDEON: Did you... sleep here last night?

MARGIE: No.

GIDEON: I can see your sleeping bag.

(Beat.)

MARGIE: Here's my reasoning. I don't have enough money for both food and shelter. And since food is more critical to survival than shelter, it makes more sense to spend my money on that. Also, there's no commute. It's 100% efficient. Think of Lighthouse keepers. They sleep in the same place they work, and they're some of the most dedicated and passionate members of the workforce.

GIDEON: In France.

MARGIE: And... Maine.

GIDEON: How long has this been going on?

MARGIE: A few days. A week. Two weeks. Two weeks. I swear, that's it.

GIDEON: I'm going to be fired. Shit. We're both going to be fired.

MARGIE: It's not that bad! And not the bed. I didn't touch the bed.

GIDEON: I have to report this, right?

MARGIE: What? No you don't.

GIDEON: I have a reputation to uphold. I can't be... complicit... I can't--

MARGIE: Gideon.

GIDEON: You realize this violates like every rule of the museum.

MARGIE: No.

GIDEON: Uh, yeah. Pretty much.

MARGIE: Look at you—you break rules all the time!

GIDEON: Name one rule I've broken since you've been here.

(She thinks about it.)

MARGIE: Socks!

GIDEON: What?

MARGIE: Sometimes when I look down I notice you not wearing any socks.

GIDEON: Yeah, they make my ankles sweat.

MARGIE: In the Educator Manual, under the Health Code & Hygiene section, it says all Interpreters are required to wear both socks and underwear beneath their costumes at all times.

GIDEON: No one's going to care whether or not I wear socks, trust me. And I can just put talcum powder in my shoes. Problem solved.

MARGIE: Also—you go completely off-script!

GIDEON: It's a tour. It's supposed to be improvised.

MARGIE: But half the things you say aren't even in the outline.

GIDEON: That's because I have a very specific style of enactment that I have been developing for over five years now. And yeah, maybe it's a little more lax than, whatever, a Ken Burns PBS special, but that's why it's such an effective and ultimately engaging method.

Also, I've been nominated for the Society of Creative Anachronism's Founding Father Award three years in a row now, so I must be up to something.

MARGIE: Then you shouldn't be so nervous about me telling Roberta.

(Pause.)

GIDEON: Wow.

MARGIE: What?

GIDEON: You're a little scary when you're like this.

MARGIE: Like how?

GIDEON: Like, cornered.

MARGIE: *(softening)*

Think about it. It's in the spirit of the museum. Helping people. Providing shelter to newcomers.

GIDEON: I know that. . . I'm not insensitive. You're just putting me in a really uncomfortable position.

MARGIE: I know that.

GIDEON: So. You're homeless?

MARGIE: No!

I've also had a shitty week. I got on the subway going in the wrong direction and I ended up at JFK airport. Which, sucked.

GIDEON: I thought you had a place in Queens?

MARGIE: I did.

GIDEON: What happened?

MARGIE: Nothing.

GIDEON: What?

MARGIE: It just didn't work out, okay?

GIDEON: Did something happen?

MARGIE: No. No.

GIDEON: *(sensing something)*

What?

MARGIE: It's stupid.

Okay—so I don't really know how to say this. But. The landlady. She's this really old senile Polish lady. She used to be a nun but now she just sits in a lawn chair outside our building. Anyhow. I think she thinks I'm Mexican.

GIDEON: What are you talking about?

MARGIE: She brings up Arizona in like every conversation. And Mexican drug cartels. And then this one time - she casually mentioned that her nephew happens to be a Minuteman.

I guess I've been confused with other Asian people. Vietnamese, usually. I'm Filipino. But never Mexican.

GIDEON: Wait. Are you saying you were... what, discriminated against?

This woman kicked you out of your apartment.

MARGIE: No. She just raised the rent. Which, people do all the time in this economy.

GIDEON: How much did she raise it?

MARGIE: Two hundred percent.

GIDEON: That fucking woman.

MARGIE: No—she's really old. I'm probably projecting.

GIDEON: Fucking racist asshole.

You realize you can sue. You can file a formal complaint.

MARGIE: No—I don't even know if that's what happened.

GIDEON: This is New York City. This is supposed the most tolerant, diverse city on the planet.

MARGIE: It is.

GIDEON: My Dad . He can help find you a really good discrimination lawyer.

MARGIE: No. Please. I don't want to make a big deal.

GIDEON: This is exactly why this museum exists. To combat things like this. To educate the unenlightened assholes of the world.

MARGIE: I don't want to be some victim. That is not who I want to be. Please. Just let it go.

(Gideon paces as he thinks about his options.)

GIDEON: Okay. This is what I'm going to do.

I am going to slowly walk away and go hang out in the dressing room. Read a little James Madison, maybe eat a granola bar. And when I return, we'll just pretend that this never happened.

MARGIE: Really?

GIDEON: If Roberta finds out, though. I'm not going to lie.

MARGIE: Understood.

Gideon—you have no idea how much this means.

GIDEON: I'm slowly walking away.

I'm... walking away.

10.

(Enactment.)
(Margie holds up a large textbook.)
(Gideon stands beside her.)

MARGIE: "In 1492, Columbus sailed the ocean blue."

"In 1492, Columbus sailed the ocean blue."

"In 14—"

GIDEON: Josephine--

MARGIE: Yes, Julian?

GIDEON: What exactly are you doing?

MARGIE: I'm learning English!

GIDEON: But why?

MARGIE: Because—we're Americans now.

GIDEON: That's right. Immigrants had to give up many aspects of themselves to become Americans, including their native language.

MARGIE: An important question to ask, however, is Why?

(turning to Gideon; earnest)

Why do we want to be Americans so badly?

Why are we willing to give up so much of ourselves?

GIDEON: *(completely taken off guard)*

Well, Josephine... Uh. It's the land of opportunity!

MARGIE: On paper.

GIDEON: Upward mobility?

MARGIE: For…two percent of the population.

GIDEON: Still - the possibility of it.

MARGIE: I think we left Prussia because we were sick of our old lives. Of
who we had become.

We so badly wanted to reinvent ourselves.

(Margie turns to Gideon, dead serious, fierce.)

Julian. I want you to know - I'm ready to do this.

GIDEON: Okay…

MARGIE: Really be Josephine.

GIDEON: Because you are, her.

MARGIE: Yes! That's what I'm saying. I'm not just some soot-faced pathetic outsider. I'm- a person.

GIDEON: Of course.

MARGIE: Yeah. So. I'm ready. I just wanted to say that.

(realizing she's gotten carried away; out)

Sorry.

(Gideon looks at her. Impressed. Intrigued.)

GIDEON: No.

(Silence.)

Uh. Let's meet over by the fireplace, folks.

11.

(After work.)

(Margie and Gideon change out of their costumes.)

GIDEON: I like what you did back there.

MARGIE: Really? I thought you were going to scream at me.

GIDEON: No. It was raw. Honest.

MARGIE: Did you know she was my age?

GIDEON: Well, people had shorter life spans back then.

MARGIE: She also came from a really small town. Like me.

GIDEON: Sure.

MARGIE: Maybe I'll check out some books. Go the library. Can you--
(She gestures to a hard-to-reach clasp on her costume. He helps her with it.)

GIDEON: Yeah. Hey. What are you up to tomorrow night?

MARGIE: Hanging out at the sketchy youth hostel I'm staying at.

GIDEON: First Friday of every month a bunch of us gather in the museum
after hours.

MARGIE: Oh.

GIDEON: Grab some beers. That sort of thing.

MARGIE: Actually. I would love to meet the other people who work here.
I still don't really know anyone.

GIDEON: I figure. Since you're part of the team now.

MARGIE: Yeah. Okay. What time?

GIDEON: People usually start arriving at around 8 o'clock. Eight thirty.

MARGIE: Cool. I'll be there!
(Gideon has finished changing.)

GIDEON: You coming?

MARGIE: I'm just going to finish up here.

GIDEON: Alright.
(He starts to leave, then stops himself.)
And, really good job today.

MARGIE: Thanks.
(Gideon exits.)
(Margie stands alone for a moment.)
Hello. I'm Josephine.
Nice to meet you. I'm Josephine.
(She relaxes.)
(finally, in her own voice:)
Hi. I'm Josephine.
This works.

12.

(Late night.)
(Margie and Gideon sip fruity wine coolers.)
(The kerosene sconce has been turned on low.)

MARGIE: Do you think anyone else is coming?

GIDEON: I swear this wasn't intentional.

> *(They both sip their drinks.)*

MARGIE: *(re the beverage)*

> What is this?

GIDEON: Tahitian Sunset.

MARGIE: Mmm.

GIDEON: I got it from the Yemenese deli on the corner. Yemen-aye? Ye-meni?

MARGIE: This neighborhood is so weird.

GIDEON: Weird because...

MARGIE: There are like a bajillion different nationalities, and yet we, an immigrant museum, never really talk about any of that.

GIDEON: Sure we do.

MARGIE: How?

GIDEON: It's implied. You know. Julian. And Josephine. Their story.

MARGIE: Okay. But what does that really mean?

GIDEON: You... ask a lot of questions.

MARGIE: Sorry.

GIDEON: No. It's good. I like- questions.

MARGIE: *(laughing)*

> Okay...

GIDEON: Besides – it's important. Knowing where you're from.

MARGIE: Why?

GIDEON: Because. Your heritage—

MARGIE: Is eating corn on the cob and watching Harrison Ford movies?

GIDEON: Really?

MARGIE: Yes.

GIDEON: Oh.

> Well. Fuck heritage then.
>
> *(He holds up his drink.)*
>
> To corn on the cob and Harrison Ford!

MARGIE: Here here!

GIDEON: To... Tahitian Sunset!

MARGIE: Tahitian Sunset!

GIDEON: To... moving to New York! To starting over and... eating pop tarts for lunch.

> *(They clink; drink.)*

GIDEON: You're doing a really good job here, by the way.

MARGIE: Really?

GIDEON: When you first got here I thought you were massively under-
    qualified. But you definitely bring something... unique. So. I
    apologize if I judged you.
MARGIE: It's cool. I judged you too.
GIDEON: You did?
MARGIE: Yeah.
    Are you kidding?
    Yeah.
    (They drink.)
GIDEON: Why did you say you left Michigan?
MARGIE: Because I didn't want to be a pharmacist's assistant my whole life?
    Also. My sister got pregnant.
GIDEON: Congrats.
MARGIE: No. That's what everyone says. Like it's some sort of feat. Per-
    sonally, I find it depressing. She's 28 and now her whole life is over.
    Done. She doesn't even want to go back to work. Just stay home
    and have babies. It's gross.
    (She takes a huge gulp.)
    Ugh! I can't end up like that. Promise me- I will never end up like that.
GIDEON: Okay.
MARGIE: Seriously.
GIDEON: I... promise. You will not stay at home and have babies.
    (Margie downs the rest of her drink. She paces.)
MARGIE: Whatever. Look at me: I work at a museum.
GIDEON: Hey- me too.
MARGIE: I'm a tour guide.
GIDEON: Educator.
MARGIE: *(with anxious energy)*
    I want to... do things. You know?
GIDEON: Sure.
MARGIE: Big, important things.
GIDEON: You should. You should totally do that.
MARGIE: I want to be passionate about something. Give myself com-
    pletely. You know?
    Like - fully commit, with my whole being. Like... like...
    (a realization)
    you.
GIDEON: Me?
MARGIE: Yes. You are so.... How did you become so passionate about
    history?

GIDEON: Uh. My mom, probably. She taught history at Columbia.

MARGIE: See?! Even your family does stuff.

GIDEON: She wrote this controversial book in the 80s that made her super famous. It's on every major grad school reading list. She's dead. Sorry, I don't know if I mentioned that.

MARGIE: Oh. I'm so--

GIDEON: Nah, it's cool. She died a long time ago. When I was in high school.

MARGIE: Must have been hard.

GIDEON: My Dad. He still really hasn't gotten over her. He just sits and watches women's basketball every night.

MARGIE: Do you want to talk about it?

GIDEON: You would have really liked her I think. You actually remind me a little of her.

MARGIE: Yeah, you said that.

GIDEON: That kind of pioneer woman. With messy hair. Strong, but, also really human. Like one of those people you meet and you're like now that's a person. That's somebody whose really lived.
(Suddenly, Margie leans in and kisses him.)
(A long, long silence.)

GIDEON: Wow. So was that like, a pity kiss?

MARGIE: No.

GIDEON: So then—

MARGIE: I don't know. It just came over me.

GIDEON: Okay.
(They sit with this.)
Do you think, it might come over you again? Just, in terms of gauging expectation.

MARGIE: I don't want this to change anything.

GIDEON: Sure, of course. We have to work together.

MARGIE: I'm not looking for a relationship. The last guy I dated - I kind of lost myself in him.

GIDEON: Sure.

MARGIE: And I'm not going to sleep with you.
(They start making out, desperately. Knocking things over.)
(After a while:)
What if? No. Nevermind, it's stupid.

GIDEON: What?

MARGIE: I was just thinking.
Would it be totally weird--

What if we changed into our costumes?

GIDEON: Like. Our work clothes?

MARGIE: Is that an awful idea?

GIDEON: I'm sorry. What?

MARGIE: Just- for fun.

GIDEON: Okay. Yeah.

Wait. Shit. Fuck. I took it home with me. It's at the dry cleaners.

MARGIE: Oh. Nevermind.

GIDEON: Sorry.

(Pause.)

GIDEON: But... you could. f you want. If that's something you're interested in. No pressure though.

MARGIE: Yeah?

GIDEON: Only if that's something you want. I am in no way explicitly requesting this.

MARGIE: Just- something different.

GIDEON: Sure.

MARGIE: I'll be right back.

GIDEON: Alright. I will wait here. Sit.

(Margie exits to the dressing room.)

(Gideon sits nervously and fidgets. He unbuttons his collar. Buttons it back up. Unbuttons it again. Buttons it back up. He takes a huge chug from his cooler. Maybe he contemplates putting on some music.)

(Margie re-enters, wearing her costume.)

MARGIE: I didn't put on the apron.

GIDEON: You look—

MARGIE: Like Josephine?

(She approaches Gideon.)

GIDEON: I'm uh... I'm gonna go turn off the light.

(Gideon turns off the lamp.)

Blackout.

End of Part 1.

PART TWO

13.

Five months later.
The Kitchen. A cramped room with a cast-iron stove, pots and pans.
A small table.
Laundry lines criss-crossing the space
Margie, in a slip and stockings, stands over the stove, stirring a pot.
Gideon, in undershirt and suspenders, sits at the kitchen table reading the newspaper.
A domestic tableau
After a long silence, the two turn to face the audience.

MARGIE:	GIDEON:
Immigrants--	Sweatshops--

MARGIE: Sorry!

GIDEON: No! You first.

MARGIE: No. You go.

GIDEON: Please. I insist.

MARGIE: I was just going to say:

Immigrants spent a lot of time in the kitchen.

GIDEON: Yeah they did!

(They smile out at the audience.)

GIDEON: Hey. Come here.

MARGIE: *(blushing)*

I'm—working.

GIDEON: Come on.

(Margie nods to the audience.)

(re the audience)

Trust me. They've seen married people before

(She takes a seat on his lap.)

GIDEON: Tell them what we did yesterday.

MARGIE: No!

GIDEON: All Sunday. We just stayed in bed.

MARGIE: Not all day.

GIDEON: We were like—breakfast? No thanks. Lunch? Yup, we'll take
    that right here.

MARGIE: We went out for lunch.

GIDEON: We had these amazing—what would you call them?

MARGIE: Pasticotti.

GIDEON: These Italian pastries. With all this cream.

MARGIE: They were very good.

GIDEON: Italian people. What's up with them?

MARGIE: What do you mean?

GIDEON: They're so good at cooking. No wonder they're so fat, right?

MARGIE: *(hitting him)*
    Julian!

GIDEON: I'm kidding. I love Italian people.
    Mobsters?
    I'm kidding!
    (They smile and sigh out to the audience.)
    (Margie stands.)

MARGIE: I should get back.
    (She heads back to the stove.)

GIDEON: I always think kitchens are very warm places. Not just because
    of this authentic coal-burning stove we have here. Something about
    food and family...

MARGIE: But also, routine.

GIDEON: Routine?

MARGIE: All this cooking. And cleaning. It's so easy to forget, outside this
    room, you're still a person. You're still this living, pulsating, breath-
    ing thing.
    (Gideon stares at her admiringly.)

GIDEON: Josephine.

MARGIE: Yes, Julian.

GIDEON: I love you!

MARGIE: I love you too.
    (Margie turns back to the stove.)
    (Gideon continues gazing at her, adoring her, forgetting himself.)
    (He catches himself.)

GIDEON: *(out)*
    I'm sorry. Uh, what were we saying?

14.

(After work. Cleaning up. They're already mid-conversation.)

GIDEON: ... Because history should be immediate. It should feel like get-
    ting slapped in the face.

MARGIE: You don't think we're getting too... personal?

GIDEON: No way.

MARGIE: All that. I love you, I love you.

GIDEON: We love each other, so.

MARGIE: But Julian and Josephine.

GIDEON: They loved each other too.

MARGIE: I just can't imagine them being like that.

GIDEON: Why not? They were human beings...

MARGIE: Sure

GIDEON: You want us to portray them as what, miserable, downtrodden people? Is that it?

MARGIE: No, definitely not.

GIDEON: Poor them. Poor Julian and Josephine.

MARGIE: They're not victims, clearly. Maybe just less... affectionate?

GIDEON: Margie. They had five kids together. I don't think affection was a problem.

MARGIE: But they're middle age now.

GIDEON: So?

MARGIE: So. People grow old. They grow bored with each other.

GIDEON: Are you getting bored with me?

MARGIE: No.

GIDEON: Besides. Boredom's a middle class thing. Julian and Josephine? They fucking, clung to each other. Clasping each other's naked bodies in the cold paucity of their lives. Why do you think immigrants had so many kids?

MARGIE: That is not why...

GIDEON: I know. I'm kidding. Hey. Dinner tonight. Order in?

MARGIE: Let's go out.

GIDEON: Really?

MARGIE: We haven't gone out in months.

GIDEON: We could play a board game.

MARGIE: We always play board games.

GIDEON: How about I cook you something?

MARGIE: You're going to cook.

GIDEON: Yes. I will cook you an elaborate non-spaghetti meal. I'll even break out the placemats.

MARGIE: Fine. But no Prussian music.

GIDEON: No Prussian music. I hate Prussian music.

(Beat.)

Hey – come here.

MARGIE: No. You come here.

(He does. He puts his arms around her waist.)

GIDEON: Look at you. You're all sweaty.

MARGIE: Thanks.

GIDEON: No, I like it. And whatever, I'm sweaty too. It's hot in here.

(She reaches over and picks something off his shoulder.)

MARGIE: You have something --

GIDEON: What?

MARGIE: Oh. It's just dandruff.

GIDEON: Is it bad? To be this comfortable with someone?

MARGIE: No. I don't know.

GIDEON: Were you this comfortable with your last boyfriend?

(Beat.)

MARGIE: Whatever. What about you?

GIDEON: What do you mean?

MARGIE: Other girlfriends.

GIDEON: I haven't had any other girlfriends.

Come on. You knew that.

MARGIE: Yeah. I guess. I just assumed.

GIDEON: I'm not ashamed.

MARGIE: You shouldn't be. I've only really dated two other people. And neither of those were – like, adult.

GIDEON: Think Josephine dated people? Before Julian.

MARGIE: I thought they had an arranged marriage.

GIDEON: Yeah. Probably better that way anyway.

MARGIE: Are you kidding?

GIDEON: Yeah. They didn't have to go through the whole charade of meeting people. Flirting. Putting on fake identities. They could just commit. Start building a future together.

(Beat.)

GIDEON: *(suddenly)*

Oh right! I almost forgot.

MARGIE: What?

GIDEON: I've been carrying this around all day.

(Gideon pulls a crumpled tissue out of his pocket.)

MARGIE: Why…?

GIDEON: It's just something that made me think of you. Here

MARGIE: What is it?

(He hands her the tissue. She unwraps it.)

GIDEON: *(not waiting for her to figure it out)*

It's a brooch.

MARGIE: *(overwhelmed)*

It's...

Did you buy this?

GIDEON: No. It was my mom's.

I think it may have been her mother's or something. It's a family heir-loom. My Dad said I can give it to you.

May I?

(He pins the brooch on her.)

MARGIE: It's like, I've been pinned.

GIDEON: I figured. Since there are no girls in my family.

(She opens her mouth to protest, but then changes her mind.)

MARGIE: I... Thank you. It's beautiful.

15.

(Next day.)

(Margie, now wearing the brooch, irons.)

(Gideon reads the newspaper as before.)

GIDEON: Josephine.

MARGIE: Yes, Julian?

GIDEON: Listen to this Headline:

(reading)

"Man Bludgeoned to Death By Errant Meat Cleaver."

MARGIE: Huh.

GIDEON: "Wife is key suspect."

MARGIE: Wow.

GIDEON: It says here, the motive for murder was "noisy jaw-bone."

"His jaw made this awful clicking sound when he slept. So I killed him."

MARGIE: It's always the little things, isn't it?

GIDEON: What a crazy time we live in, eh Josephine? The nineteenth century.

MARGIE: Pretty crazy.

GIDEON: You would never think of doing that to me, would you?

MARGIE: Kill you? No.

GIDEON: Well that's a relief.

(out)

Right, folks?

(He reads. She irons.)

GIDEON: The American Dream...

MARGIE: Yup.

GIDEON: A good job. A good family.

MARGIE: Well, it's not ideal.

GIDEON: It's pretty close.

MARGIE: Or, you know, a compromise.

GIDEON: God Bless America.

MARGIE: Yes. God Bless America.

> *(A Beat.)*

MARGIE: Ow! DAMNIT—

GIDEON: What? What's going on?

MARGIE: Nothing. I burned myself.

GIDEON: On the stove?

MARGIE: No, on the pantry. Yes the stove.

GIDEON: Do you need ice?

MARGIE: That iron. It's so... fucking heavy.

GIDEON: It's eight pounds. Like most irons of the time...

MARGIE: How are people expected to work in this stupid heat.

GIDEON: I can get you some water.

MARGIE: No, it's fine.

GIDEON: I'll just go down to the pump.

MARGIE: I'm fine! Okay? Just stop.

GIDEON: Okay...

> Are you mad at me?

MARGIE: No. I'm.

> *(recovering, out to the audience)*
> It's my own fault.

16.

> *(The kitchen table.)*
> *(Margie reads New York magazine)*
> *(Gideon eats an apply, loudly.)*
> *(An air of slight boredom.)*
> *(This goes on for an uncomfortably long time.)*

GIDEON: I think I might grow a beard. What do you think?

MARGIE: Go for it.

GIDEON: Something, 1850s.

MARGIE: *(reading)*

> Listen to this: Every Thursday night they have free jazz concerts at the Met. There's champagne and you get to walk around the exhibits. Jerry Seinfeld supposedly goes.

GIDEON: We hate jazz.

MARGIE: So.

GIDEON: I don't understand. Why would you go to something if you don't like the activity?

MARGIE: Because I've never been to the Met.

GIDEON: It's not that exciting.

MARGIE: That's because you grew up here. You take things for granted.

GIDEON: Well, that's what real New Yorkers do. We take things for granted.

MARGIE: Are you saying I'm not a real New Yorker?

GIDEON: You're not.

    (Margie is slightly offended.)

    But that's a good thing, trust me. New Yorkers are assholes.

    (This doesn't help.)

    (Margie goes back to her magazine.)

GIDEON: Hey. I was thinking. We should get our own place.

MARGIE: What?

GIDEON: Instead of you staying over at my Dad's house every night.

MARGIE: Why? Did he say something?

GIDEON: No. I just think we're adults. We shouldn't have to sneak around every night. Maybe some place with a backyard. Grow our own vegetables.

MARGIE: I don't have the money right now.

GIDEON: I can cover the first few months.

MARGIE: I don't want your money.

GIDEON: That's not what I meant.

MARGIE: Gideon- I can't move in with you.

GIDEON: Why not? We already technically live together. We spend like every waking hour together.

MARGIE: I am well aware of that.

GIDEON: Plus. We're already married.

MARGIE: Gideon!

GIDEON: Kidding. Totally kidding.

MARGIE: I don't even know your middle name!

GIDEON: It's Alexander.

MARGIE: See? I didn't know that.

GIDEON: That's good. We still have more to learn about each other.

MARGIE: I can't move in with you.

GIDEON: Why not?

MARGIE: We haven't lived yet. Done anything.

GIDEON: I've done stuff.

MARGIE: Me. I haven't done anything. Accomplished, anything.

GIDEON: So, do it. Accomplish something.

MARGIE: I'm trying.

GIDEON: You should apply for that assistant curator position.

MARGIE: What?

GIDEON: There's a sign in the staff room. I got you an application.

MARGIE: What? I'm not even qualified.

GIDEON: You're super qualified.

MARGIE: I don't even know if this is what I want to do - work in a museum for the rest of my life.

GIDEON: So? It's a good opportunity.

MARGIE: Well, I don't want it.

GIDEON: You don't even want to think about it?

MARGIE: No.

GIDEON: Wow. That's open-minded.

MARGIE: This isn't my dream. Working at museum. This is your, whatever.

GIDEON: Then why are you still working here?

MARGIE: Because. I don't know.

(softening)

I'm sorry – I like working here. I shouldn't have said that. I'm just being crazy.

GIDEON: I might apply. If you don't.

MARGIE: You should.

GIDEON: There's more freedom. Plus you get to decide the exhibits.

MARGIE: Yeah, you should definitely apply.

(Gideon takes a final bite of his apple.)

GIDEON: Hey—how much time do we have?

MARGIE: A few minutes.

GIDEON: I gotta take a shit.

(Gideon tosses her the half-eaten apple and exits.)

(Margie sits, staring at the apple, disgusted.)

17.

(A few days later.)

(Margie sits over a bucket, scrubbing clothes on a washboard. Or with a hand-held wooden agitator, if you can find one.)

(She scrubs. The more she scrubs, the angrier she gets.)

(Gideon enters with a handful of bills and receipts and an account book; he sits down at the table and begins going through them.)

GIDEON: Josephine?

MARGIE: Yes.

GIDEON: Nothing.

   I was just saying hi.

MARGIE: Hi.

   (They work.)

GIDEON: Josephine?

MARGIE: WHAT!?   Why do you always have to say my name. Josephine.
   Josephine. Josephine. I'm right here.

GIDEON: I feel like we don't really talk any more.

MARGIE: We talk all the time. We're talking right now.

GIDEON: Why are you so angry?

MARGIE: I'm not. I'm busy. I'm working.

GIDEON: Is this because of your sister?

MARGIE: What?

GIDEON: Your sister who just gave birth in our hometown of Moloschnya.

MARGIE: What does my sister have to do with any of this?

GIDEON: Maybe you feel bad you weren't there?

MARGIE: I sent her a postcard.

GIDEON: Sometimes. I wonder if you're projecting your hatred of your
   sister onto a hatred of domestic life in general,

MARGIE: I do not hate my sister.

GIDEON: Of course.

MARGIE: *(getting angry)*

   And I don't hate "domestic life in general."

   I just find it pathetic that people succumb to social norms just because,
   whatever, something's been done that way for hundreds of years. That
   like "home" has so much meaning to people and that domestic bliss is
   somehow this inevitable goal. Like it's destiny.

GIDEON: History is destiny.

MARGIE: Oh, please.

GIDEON: What?

MARGIE: You say all these things. These empty things.

GIDEON: No…

MARGIE: Yes.

   I wish you could hear yourself. How ridiculous you sound sometimes.
   How cliché.

   (They work.)

GIDEON: Josephine.

MARGIE: *(tired)*

   Yes, Julian.

GIDEON: I was just wondering.

MARGIE: What?

GIDEON: Last night.

(Beat. Margie sits up a bit.)

GIDEON: Where were you, exactly?

MARGIE: Where was I when?

GIDEON: I woke up in the middle of the night and you weren't there.

MARGIE: I was there.

GIDEON: No you weren't.

MARGIE: Really?

GIDEON: Nope.

MARGIE: Oh. Right. I had to go out for something.

GIDEON: For what?

MARGIE: *(looking out at the audience)*
We shouldn't... you know. Not here.

GIDEON: I think we should. Here.

MARGIE: It's just.
I had some errands to run, that's all.

GIDEON: At eleven o'clock at night?

MARGIE: There was a fabric situation. I forgot to tell you about it. It's a long story.

GIDEON: Give me the short version.

MARGIE: Well, we ran out of fabric for the week. So I went to see Johan, our fabric guy. And he was like, oh, we're also out of fabric. And I was like, really? And he was like, we're getting another shipment in if you can come back later tonight.

GIDEON: Huh.

MARGIE: Yeah. I can't believe I didn't tell you about it.

GIDEON: About the fabric situation.

MARGIE: Right.

(Beat.)

GIDEON: It's just interesting, though, because. I found this ticket stub in your pocket.
(He takes a ticket stub out of his pocket.)
(Margie looks up, caught.)
(Gideon holds up the stub.)
Also—we get our fabric delivered from a supplier. Not Johan. We haven't used him in years. I think he might even be dead.
(He reads the stub.)
"Grizzly Bear Meets Beer Street."

(He looks up to see her reaction; she has none.)
With headliner: "Sargeant Dutchface and the Newsboy Quintet."
(Silence.)
(He shows the ticket stub to the audience.)
GIDEON: What do you think that could be?
(Margie shrugs.)
(Gideon studies the ticket.)
(They stare at each other, face-off style.)

18.

(Meanwhile, back in the real-world:)
GIDEON: Sgt. Dutchface?
(Margie shrugs, defiantly.)
Really, Margie?
Really?
(More silence, more stare downs.)

19.

(Back in reenactment land:)
GIDEON: So you're saying…. Vaudeville!
MARGIE: Uh huh.
GIDEON: As in: Clog dancing. Blackface. Stand-up comedy.
MARGIE: Yes. I go to Vaudeville.
GIDEON: That's the best you could come up with?
MARGIE: I didn't "come up" with anything. It happens to be the dominant
form of populist entertainment in the 19th century.
GIDEON: I know that, Josephine.
MARGIE: It's a vital part of the Lower East Side's history.
(under her breath)
I can't believe you went through my things.
GIDEON: *(whispering back)*
It was on the dresser.
MARGIE: *(whispering)*
It's mine.
GIDEON: *(whispering)*
It's my apartment.
MARGIE: *(whispering)*
It's my life.
(Back to their normal, museum voices.)
GIDEON: So you were saying. Vaudeville.

MARGIE: Yes.

GIDEON: The whole 2nd Avenue circuit!

MARGIE: That's right.

GIDEON: Why didn't you just ask me to come?

MARGIE: Because you hate that kind of thing!

GIDEON: How do you know?

MARGIE: You hate anything that's loud and modern. You would have called it "gaudy" or "grotesque."

GIDEON: Maybe.

MARGIE: And I happen to like going out. I like the people.

GIDEON: Meaning, you prefer the company of strangers to the company of your own husband?

MARGIE: No. I prefer being part of the World instead of retreating from it.

GIDEON: The World being… crazy drunk people.

MARGIE: The World being… millions of strangers , people other than you and me.

That's the point of living in a city. Just FYI.

GIDEON: Yeah, I understand how cities work.

MARGIE: I want to live my life. Get drunk sometimes and stay out late and make bad decisions. Not furrow away in some house with a boyfriend and a vegetable patch.

GIDEON: I don't need to grow vegetables!! That was just an example!!!
(Suddenly, Margie swipes everything off the kitchen table. Plastic food and silverware go flying.)

GIDEON: What are you doing!?

MARGIE: I hate this table! I hate this fruit. And this stupid bowl.…

GIDEON: That's authentic…!

MARGIE: *(holding a doily)*
And this… what is this? I don't even know what this is. It's ugly. I hate it.
(She throws it on the ground.)

MARGIE: *(more frantic now)*
This whole kitchen—I hate it. It's suffocating me. Ugh!
(She grabs the laundry lines and rips them down, creating a tangled mess. She stands -- out of breath, a little wild-eyed)

GIDEON: *(slowly)*
Who… are… you?

MARGIE: I am Josephine fucking Glockner.
(Scary.)

20

(Margie paces the room sipping a Starbucks iced beverage. Something super obnoxious. Think whipped cream. Think Venti.)

MARGIE: *(speaking a hundred miles a minute)*
> … She's stuck. She's trapped in this routine and this life and this marriage. She came here with all these hopes and aspirations. She's disappointed in herself. I get these things. I understand her disappointment.

GIDEON: *(distracted)*
> Uh huh.

MARGIE: She needs to break out. Make changes in her life.

GIDEON: I'm sorry. I can't tell if you're trying to obliterate my soul or if you're just accidentally sipping the most evil beverage on earth.

MARGIE: What?

GIDEON: You know I feel about Starbucks.
> *(Gideon eyes her—Is she doing this on purpose)*

MARGIE: What do you think about my theory on Josephine?

GIDEON: Yeah. Sure. Go with it.

MARGIE: No, really though. I want your opinion.

GIDEON: I think… it sounds like a perfectly competent and viable approach to the character.

MARGIE: Yeah, right? I think so. It was such a release. Playing her this way.

GIDEON: Sure.

MARGIE: This has nothing to do with you, you realize. With Julian. Julian's great.

GIDEON: Oh, well that's good.

MARGIE: I was thinking. For the bath-tub moment. Maybe Josephine contemplates drowning her own infant son. What do you think about that? With her bare hands. Like… grrr.

GIDEON: Can we stop talking about this?

MARGIE: Oh. Sure.

GIDEON: It's kind of all we ever talk about. Here. On break. At the apartment.

MARGIE: You're right. Boundaries.
> *(Pause.)*
> *(Then, unable to help himself:)*

GIDEON: And I really don't think Josephine would do that by the way. Infanticide? She's not fucking, Lady Macbeth. She's a regular, moral person.

MARGIE: You think I'm playing her wrong?

GIDEON: No. I didn't say that.

MARGIE: Be honest.

GIDEON: Honestly. I think she's maybe getting a little self-indulgent. Maybe.

MARGIE: Self-indulgent?

GIDEON: "I hate laundry!" "I feel trapped."
Yeah, a little.

MARGIE: She's angry.

GIDEON: Okay. But why?

MARGIE: Because she's stuck.

GIDEON: So is Julian.

MARGIE: It's different.

GIDEON: Why is it different?

MARGIE: Because.

GIDEON: Because, you, Margie, are terrified of ending up like that?

MARGIE: No!

GIDEON: Because what then? Because you're mad at me? Because you're mad at yourself?

MARGIE: No. This has nothing to do with me.

GIDEON: You're right!
This museum has absolutely nothing to do with you.

MARGIE: What is that supposed to mean?

GIDEON: It means. This museum is not about you or Josephine or whether or not you're playing her like some insane character in a classic melodrama.

MARGIE: So what is it about?

GIDEON: It's about two people. About how they go through life together. About how they figure out how to be decent to each other even as times get rough.
How maybe they lose their way sometimes, but how they help each other make it through and ultimately enrich each other's lives.
And then how ALL of that somehow fits into the larger HISTORY of a place called The Lower East Side CIRCA EIGHTEEN NINETY!!
That's what I think.
(Beat.)
Also. I didn't want to bring this up—but it's weird, when you're having sex with someone, to call them by the name of a character they're playing at a museum.

MARGIE: I do not do that!

GIDEON: Yes. You do it all the time. You did it last night.

MARGIE: No...

GIDEON: Feels great.

MARGIE: You're the one who told me I need to inhabit my part.

GIDEON: Yeah, not completely supplant your own identity.

MARGIE: I'm... figuring a lot of stuff out.

GIDEON: It's not that hard. It's called: Be Yourself. Stop trying on a million different personas.

MARGIE: I'm not--

GIDEON: Yes. You are so insecure--

MARGIE: *(knee-jerk)*

You fart in your sleep!

GIDEON: What?

MARGIE: You do. I never say anything. But you do. And it's gross. It's like a train whistle.

GIDEON: That's real mature.

MARGIE: And you have psoriasis. Your elbows flake off all over the bed, like these little pieces of skin, which is really not very romantic.

GIDEON: I don't understand. If I'm so repulsive, why did you make out with me in the first place?

MARGIE: We were drunk. Whatever. I would have made out with anyone that night. I would have made out with a tree.

GIDEON: You would make out with a tree?

MARGIE: Oh shut up.

GIDEON: So that night-- You were just using me? Was that it?
You were homeless, sleeping on the floor and figured, I bet that kid Gideon will take me in. He looks innocent enough. He seems vulnerable.

MARGIE: No!

GIDEON: What then? Are you saying it was a mistake? These past few months?

MARGIE: No.
I don't know what I'm saying. You're just, springing this on me.

GIDEON: It's called having a conversation, Margie. It's called dialogue.

MARGIE: All I know is I came to this city to be on my own. To be independent for once in my life and become a version of myself I'm actually proud of. But instead I ended up exactly where I was before - in some relationship, spending half my time lying around your apartment like a rag doll and the other half sneaking around, doing all the things I know you secretly disapprove of.

GIDEON: I don't disapprove of you going out at night!

MARGIE: Yes you do—you're very judgmental.

GIDEON: You should just tell me. Gideon—I want to go out.

MARGIE: I tell you all the time! You don't listen. You're stuck in this cocoon of like history and... I hate this, I hate that.

GIDEON: What. So this is my fault?

MARGIE: No. It's no one's fault.

The point is—I got distracted. I got... sidetracked somehow.

GIDEON: Sidetracked from what?

MARGIE: From.... I don't know.

GIDEON: Then how can you be sidetracked from it?

(Margie shrugs, having no answer.)

Alright.

I'm just going to say everything I'm thinking. Lay out all my cards on the table.

Number One. I like you. In fact, I love you. I think I've made that pretty clear. So, whatever I'm about to say should somehow be predicated on that fact.

Number Two. That first night we had together. That was one of the greatest nights of my life. Period.

Number Three. I have psoriasis. You're right. I do. I have this cream I'm supposed to put on it but I never use it. It smells weird and it's cold and I just don't care about those kinds of things and honestly I'm a little surprised that you do but that's besides the point.

Four. Okay, I'm going to stop the list format now.

Bottom line. ~~What the fuck?~~ You used to be this amazing girl and now you're this self-absorbed crazy monster person who drinks Starbucks all the time and talks about killing imaginary children. That first night, you talked all about how you wanted to do something important. I was like: Wow, this girl is going to change the world. This girl is going to do so many noble things.

But you haven't. You've just kind of sat around feeling sorry for yourself ~~and wallowing in the entrapped domestic psyche of "Josephine." Which is weird, since, Josephine lived in a time before feminism and you don't have to be like that.~~ Also - you keep complaining about how you're lost and don't know what to do with your life even though Roberta's given you this like amazing opportunity and you're just wasting it. You're throwing it away.

Okay, I think I'm done.

Oh. Also. I should have gone with you to that thing at the Met. You wanted to go and I shouldn't have been such a jerk about it. I'm sorry.

(A long silence.)

MARGIE: I don't love you.

I used to, I think. But. I don't anymore.

(Silence.)

GIDEON: That's it?

MARGIE: I'm sorry.

GIDEON: Wow.

Okay.

MARGIE: Also. I think you might be in love with your dead mother, which is a little weird.

(Silence.)

GIDEON: Huh.

MARGIE: I'll come get my things later this weekend. I think that would be best.

GIDEON: Yeah.

I'm gonna—

I think gonna go.

MARGIE: Gideon—

GIDEON: No. I think I should…

Yeah.

(Gideon exits; leaving Margie alone onstage. She stands in the mess she's made -- proud, angry, hurt.)

End of Part II.

PART THREE:

21.

The Bedroom.
The most intimate and claustrophobic of the three spaces.
A bed, a dresser, a pair of stockings draped over a chair.
Margie enters to find Gideon sitting on the bed tying his shoes. She freezes
upon seeing him. They share a glance before turning out and launching into
the reenactment.

MARGIE: Hi everyone—
GIDEON: *(cutting her off)*
    Let's start.
    (Uh oh.)
    In 1908, Julian Glockner comes down with Tuberculosis.
MARGIE: What??
GIDEON: Tuberculosis. Consumption. The White Plague.
    For those of you who don't know, Tuberculosis is a disease of the lungs.
    Small tubercles form inside the mucous membranes, causing you to
    slowly drown in a pool of your own blood. Ralph Waldo Emerson once
    described it as: "a mouse gnawing at your chest."
MARGIE: Gideon.
GIDEON: What?
MARGIE: Are you okay?
GIDEON: I'm dying, Josephine.
MARGIE: Not... yet.
GIDEON: It's a long process.
MARGIE: Maybe we should tell them about the bedroom?
GIDEON: *(back to the audience)*
    The funny thing about Tuberculosis is that, historically, it has all this
    social stigma. It was a poor person disease. An immigrant, disease.
    But also, it was a reflection of a person's constitution. Like—delicate
    people. Sensitive people.
MARGIE: This bedroom—
GIDEON: They know what a bedroom is.
MARGIE: Sure... But it's architectural...
GIDEON: *(to the audience)*
    How about it guys? Do you know what a bedroom is? Do you know
    what kind of things go on in here?

MARGIE: This mattress is pretty interesting! Its filled with horsehair.

GIDEON: Let's talk about Death.

MARGIE: Note the authentic hand-made quilt, a gift from Josephine's great Aunt.

GIDEON: Death gives a person perspective. It's like a window into the people around you.

MARGIE: You're not dying.

GIDEON: Yes I am. And you know what? This illness, being confined to this one room—it was like having a new pair of eyes.

MARGIE: But also, it's a space of intimacy.

GIDEON: What?

MARGIE: The bedroom.

GIDEON: Why don't you just stab me?

MARGIE: What?

GIDEON: Intimacy?

MARGIE: Yeah—I just meant. It's the room where people live the most private part of their lives.

GIDEON: I think it's time to take a break.

MARGIE: We're in the middle of—

GIDEON: How about everyone takes a step into the hallway for a few minutes? Check out the rockin' stairwell!

MARGIE: They've already seen the stairwell.

GIDEON: Have they? Right, okay. I think I'm going to step out then. Get some air.

GIDEON: *(on his way out; to Margie)*
      You suck.
      (He storms off.)
      (Margie faces the tour, at a loss of how to handle this.)

MARGIE: *(to the audience)*
      Hi... everyone.
      This is...
      Uh.
      So this is the bedroom.
      This is. . .
      This is the bed.
      This is where they slept.
      In the bed.
      (Pause.)
      Wow. This is surprisingly hard to do alone.
      Does anyone have any questions? That might be... anyone? No. Okay.

(She sits down on the bed)
So, a woman walks into a doctor's office and she says: "Doctor, my arm hurts in two places. What should I do?" And the Doctor replies: "Don't go to those places."
That's an old Vaudeville joke.
Nobody has any questions? Nobody?

22.

(After work.)
MARGIE: Tuberculosis.
GIDEON: It's in the Manual. Look it up.
MARGIE: I know what TB is.
GIDEON: Leading cause of death in the nineteenth century. Plus - the real Julian. He died of TB. That's how he died.
MARGIE: Yeah, but the tour is supposed to end before then.
GIDEON: "Supposed" to. Since when has that mattered?
MARGIE: No one wants to see Julian get sick and die.
GIDEON: Why not?
MARGIE: Because. It's depressing.
GIDEON: Life is depressing.
MARGIE: No it's not. You're just saying that.
GIDEON: It can be.
MARGIE: That's because you, Gideon, are currently depressed.
GIDEON: I am not, depressed. I'm heartbroken. I don't know if you know this, but my heart was broken.

And who does this? Who comes to work the Monday after breaking up with someone?
MARGIE: Okay I admit, I said some really stupid things.
GIDEON: The main thing being: I don't love you?
MARGIE: Yes.
GIDEON: So does that mean, you do love me?
MARGIE: ...No.
GIDEON: You realize that's a pretty damaging statement to say to someone, just FYI.
MARGIE: I do.
GIDEON: And...?
MARGIE: And... I feel really crappy about it. I feel awful.
GIDEON: But?
MARGIE: I don't know what you want me to say. This is hard for me too. I think you're a great guy. You're funny. Passionate. But. Now we're

in this other place and we have to figure out how to work together.
(Beat.)

GIDEON: I'd like the brooch back.

MARGIE: Oh. Okay.

GIDEON: It's a family heirloom, so, I probably shouldn't hand it out to just anyone.
(Margie takes off the brooch and hands it to Gideon.)
Also. I think one of us should consider moving to a different floor.

MARGIE: I don't want to move. I like Josephine.

GIDEON: Well, I like Julian.

MARGIE: So then.

GIDEON: So.
(Stalemate.)
I was here first, you realize.

MARGIE: Yeah, and I have more emotional legitimacy.

GIDEON: Because...

MARGIE: I know what's it like to start over in a new place. Also. I'm... you know, a minority.

GIDEON: Wow. Did you just...?
What happened to "Corn on the cob. Harrison Ford."
(Margie shrugs.)
You don't even consider yourself Filipino.

MARGIE: Yeah, but other people do.

GIDEON: This is such bullshit.

MARGIE: Also. I took your advice and I'm applying for the curatorial position. So. It would look bad to ask for a transfer.

GIDEON: I can't believe this. You're applying?

MARGIE: It's a really good opportunity.

GIDEON: Wow.
Of course. Of course you're applying.
(Beat.)

MARGIE: So I guess I'll see you tomorrow then?

GIDEON: Yup. Can't wait.

MARGIE: Okay.

GIDEON: Yup.

MARGIE: Great.

23.

(Next day.)
(Margie addresses the tour from the bedroom.)

(Gideon, brooding, abstaining, reads the paper alone in the kitchen.)

MARGIE: Last Saturday, there was this awful fire at the Shirtwaist Factory over on Washington Street.

(Gideon coughs loudly from the other room.)

The managers - they locked the doors to the stairwells and many women were trapped inside. Can you believe that? The top three floors--

(Gideon coughs up more phlegm over the next segment.)

(Margie forges on.)

MARGIE: This family who lives in the building. Their daughter, she worked there. How awful, right? There's going to be a demonstration next week. I think I might attend.

WHAT are you doing?

(Gideon stands up and drags himself over.)

GIDEON: I'm sick, so, I need to lie down.

Please, continue.

(He coughs one final time in her ear and lies down in the bed.)

MARGIE: I was telling our guests about the Triangle Shirtwaist incident.

GIDEON: Of 1911.

MARGIE: Yes.

GIDEON: Julian, me. I die in 1910. That's one year before... 19...11.

MARGIE: What?

GIDEON: Sorry. Public records.

Unless you're like... a psychic. Are you.?

MARGIE: No.

GIDEON: Oh.

Night Josephine.

(Gideon goes to sleep, triumphant.)

24.

MARGIE: You embarrassed me out there!

GIDEON: I'm doing exactly what you were doing with Josephine.

MARGIE: You're being shitty.

GIDEON: I'm making it about me.

MARGIE: Lesson learned.

GIDEON: I'm not trying to teach you a lesson. I'm trying to give Julian what he deserves.

MARGIE: By killing him.

GIDEON: By finishing his story. He needs closure, Julian. He's in mourning.

MARGIE: For himself?

GIDEON: Yes. For his brief, truncated life. He was a tragic figure, Julian.

MARGIE: Is this about your mom?

GIDEON: You always bring up my mom!

MARGIE: No I don't.

GIDEON: This is about Julian.

MARGIE: Also - the Triangle Shirtwaist Factory is totally part of this tour.

GIDEON: Not anymore.

MARGIE: You can't just make that decision.

GIDEON: Yes I can.

MARGIE: Roberta, she'll find out.

GIDEON: Roberta hasn't come upstairs once in the year and a half I've worked here.

MARGIE: Last week, you said some things that were painful for me to hear. You said that I needed to stop feeling sorry for myself and suck it up and actually care about something already.

GIDEON: Yeah?

MARGIE: You were right.

And so I am now making a conscious decision to change that. To engage here, to use this opportunity and like, go for it.

But you. Right now you are desecrating the thing that you love.

And - as your friend - I think you should think about that. About if this is how you want to behave. Because if it is. If it is. Then. Maybe this isn't really what you want to be doing with your life.

(Silence.)

(Gideon sits down on the bed, stunned.)

MARGIE: I'm going to get lunch. Want anything?

GIDEON: *(quietly)*

No.

25.

(Margie, alone.)

MARGIE: I'm sure he'll just be another minute.

(She waits.)

He hasn't been feeling well. You know, the TB.

(She waits.)

I've been thinking a lot about this city. About why people move here. Why I moved here.

Why do so many people gravitate to this one place? Is it just money? Jobs? That can't be it, right? There has to be...

Refugees—I guess they come here for asylum. And actors. Lot of ac-

tors…
(She looks over at the door and then at the time.)
This city – it's so big. Where I'm from—there are only like two thousand people. Everybody knows everybody. Here—it's like we're all strangers. We're all pursuing these individual… we're all chasing these…
Which makes it so easy to get lost, you know?
To forgot yourself.
And, to hurt people.
It's so easy to hurt people.
(Beat.)
I'm getting off-track.
  But okay… listen to this. This is going to blow your mind.
(She pulls out a handful of photocopies.)
  I got these from the Public Library. I've been spending a lot of time at the library now that—
  They're from the Department of City Planning. Listen to these numbers.
  Out of the 8.2 million people who live in New York; 37% of them are foreign born. That's almost three million people. Right? Isn't that crazy?
  And do you know what the top groups are? It's like Jamaica, Guyana, the Dominican Republic. Puerto Rico. Ecuador. Trinidad. Columbia. China. India. India's on the rise.
(on a roll now)
  Also. Did you know that Italians are dying off in New York? Yeah, it's true. Italian people are leaving or dying off in huge numbers, especially in Bensonhurst. It's crazy. An entire population is in the middle of being replaced. It's called population churn.
  Are any of you Italian?
  Yeah, people aren't just coming. They're also leaving. Almost as many people come to New York each year leave. So it's like a giant revolving door.
  Yeah.
  It's so exciting, right? I had no idea.
(Looks at the door—Gideon is obviously not coming.)
Looks like Julian will not be joining us this afternoon.
  So. If everyone could just move a little closer. There are no strangers here, right? Only opportunities.

26

(A few days later.)

MARGIE: You're quitting?

GIDEON: Put in my two week notice.

MARGIE: That's not what I meant--

GIDEON: I know.

MARGIE: What happened to applying for the assistant curator position?

GIDEON: I need to get out of this place. Try something different. Maybe Europe.

MARGIE: What are you going to do in Europe?

GIDEON: Climb a mountain. Maybe grow a beard.

Did you know I've never been outside the continental U.S.?

MARGIE: Really?

GIDEON: How messed up is that for a history major? I've been to Pearl Harbor but I've never been to France or Germany.

MARGIE: Is this what you want?

GIDEON: Russia. Never been to Russia.

MARGIE: Gideon?

GIDEON: China.

MARGIE: Gideon – just stop for a second.

GIDEON: I don't know what I want. That's the whole point.

(After a bit:)

GIDEON: I went for this walk. I think I walked the entire length of New York City.

MARGIE: Me too. I mean, I've been spending a lot of time by myself, thinking.

GIDEON: I visited my mother's grave. Like, way out in Staten Island.

When I was there, I saw this guy, this man, and he was facing a tree. And I realized that he was... pissing. Yeah, just peeing on a tree. Nonchalantly. And I screamed at him. I was like Dude, you can't do that! You can't fucking PISS in a GRAVEYARD! IT'S A GRAVE-YARD. THERE ARE PEOPLE BURIED HERE YOU FUCKING ASSHOLE. THIS IS SACRED GROUND.

MARGIE: Did he respond?

GIDEON: No. He just gave me this look. Like he knew some secret that I didn't know.

(Beat.)

MARGIE: I didn't tell anyone you haven't been showing up.

I figure you I owe that much.

GIDEON: That was – very decent of you.

MARGIE: You should, though. Come back.

GIDEON: Nah - it's time for this cowboy to mosey on.

MARGIE: It's a two person job, remember? I can't do it by myself.

GIDEON: Julian's dying. Josephine doesn't need him anymore.

MARGIE: He's part of the history, right?

GIDEON: I don't know if I even believe in that anymore.

MARGIE: In what?

GIDEON: History.

MARGIE: What are you talking about. You love history.

GIDEON: No. Like putting on a costume... ?

I don't even know what that word means. History.

History.

His-tory.

MARGIE: It's just a word.

GIDEON: This morning. I was walking around Seward Park. And I sat
down on this bench across from the statue of who I assume is
Seward. And I was staring at him. At this old, bronze bust of this
dead statesman. And I was like:

Why? Why did we erect a statue for you?

Why statues?

Really, why? Talk to me. Tell me why I am so obsessed with you.

You stupid old statue. Tell me why you're here. Tell me. Tell me.

And then I stood up, and I went up to the statue and I just, kicked it.

MARGIE: You kicked a statue?

GIDEON: Yeah. I kicked it really hard. I think I broke my toe on the base.

(Margie can't help but smile.)

GIDEON: What?

MARGIE: You kicked a statue.

GIDEON: Yeah. He deserved it!

(She laughs.)

GIDEON: It's not funny.

MARGIE: Yes it is.

GIDEON: I was angry.

Okay, maybe it's a little funny.

(He laughs a little too.)

(They laugh together a moment.)

(Then: Gideon switches. He suddenly becomes very serious.)

I've been obsessed with this thing for so long: History. Capital H. But
I have no idea why. I don't even know what it is. I just keep doing it.
Like on autopilot.

MARGIE: You're right. Maybe you should try something else.
GIDEON: Maybe I could be a pencil maker.

> Thoreau. His family made pencils.

> Or a teacher. I could be a good teacher.

MARGIE: Yeah, go for it.
GIDEON: Did you know. Museums - the earliest ones, back in the seven-
    teenth century. They were called "Wonder Cabinets." Cabinets of
    wonder.
MARGIE: And what were they?
GIDEON: Lot of bizarro curiosities. Dead fetuses. Works of art. Inven-
    tions. Maybe that's what I'll do. Open my own Cabinet of Wonder.
    "Gideon's Emporium of Amazingness." Where people can just come
    and wonder about things. No answers. Only questions. And crackers!
    There would definitely be free crackers.
MARGIE: I would totally come to that museum.
GIDEON: Yeah?
MARGIE: Are you kidding? Crackers?

> *(They sit.)*

GIDEON: My mom- She was kind of annoying.
MARGIE: What?
GIDEON: My Dad likes to say she lived with us physically, but her brain
    lived in a different century. She loved her students, but, at home,
    she was like, shut off.
MARGIE: Really? I always thought. They way you talk about her--
GIDEON: No.
GIDEON: Jill.

> That was her name.

27.

(Gideon, still in his street clothes, lies on his death-bed.)
(They are mid-scene.)
GIDEON: I'm dying, Josephine.

> *(Cough. Cough.)*

MARGIE: Can I get you anything?
GIDEON: No. I'm good to just to lie here. Let the TB toxins soak in.
MARGIE: A hot water bottle? Some food?
GIDEON: Just sit with me.

> *(Margie pulls up a chair next to him and sits.)*
> Maybe you can rub my forehead?
> *(Margie begins to very slowly rub his forehead.)*

GIDEON: Josephine?

MARGIE: Yes Julian.

GIDEON: Do you think... if we had met under different circumstances. Things might have turned out differently. . .

MARGIE: Maybe.

GIDEON: Really?

MARGIE: I think we were very young when we met.

GIDEON: I'm scared.

MARGIE: Of what?

GIDEON: Dying.

MARGIE: Everyone's afraid of that.

GIDEON: Are you?

MARGIE: Not really.

GIDEON: What are you scared of?

MARGIE: The opposite. Dying while you're still alive. Maybe that's the same thing though.

GIDEON: I'm scared of that too.

MARGIE: Yeah?

GIDEON: Yeah. Like—Why did I even contemplate buying this cell phone? I hate people with cell phones. I don't want to be like that. Yeah. I think about that stuff all the time.

   (Pause.)

GIDEON: Can I kiss you?

MARGIE: I don't know if that's such a good idea.

GIDEON: Because I'm diseased?

MARGIE: Because...

   (gesturing to the audience)

   You know.

GIDEON: They're seen married people before. Plus, I want to remember what it's like to kiss you. Before I fade into the darkness of the unknown.

MARGIE: Just... one.

GIDEON: Of course.

   (She leans in and kisses him gently.)

   (Beat.)

   (with a huge smile)

   I'm ready to die.

MARGIE: What?

   (He dies instantly.)

MARGIE: Julian?

(No response.)
(He's dead.)
(Margie looks at his body for a moment.)
(Then, slowly, she pulls the blanket over him. She gives him a final kiss on the forehead then stands to address the audience.)
(She takes a moment to find her words.)
(When she does, she speaks with confidence and maturity.)

MARGIE: In the years after Julian's death, I will take over various aspects of the garment shop we set up in our tiny tenement apartment. I will become a very shrewd businesswoman. In fact, I will become one of the first female clothing contractors documented on the Lower East Side. I stopped going to Vaudeville every night. I did all the bookkeeping. I cut back on expenses. And eventually, I was able to support myself and my five children.

I was an incredible woman, I think.

will be, I hope.

(Blackout.)

END OF PLAY

THE WHIPPING MAN

Matthew Lopez

PAST PRODUCTION INFORMATION

Manhattan Theatre Club (Artistic Director, Lynne Meadow; Executive Producer, Barry Grove) Opened February 1st, 2011

Directed by Doug Hughes

Simon.. André Braugher
John .... André Holland
Caleb .... Jay Wilkison

Scenic Design .... John Lee Beatty
Costume Design............................... Catherine Zuber
Lighting Design .... Ben Stanton
Sound Design .... Jill BC DuBoff

Barrington Stage Company (Artistic Director, Julianne Boyd; Producing Director, Richard M. Parison, Jr.) Opened May 29th, 2010

Directed by Christopher Innvar

Simon.. Clarke Peters
John .... Leroy McClain
Caleb .... Nick Westrate

Scenic Design .... Sandra Godmark
Costume Design............................... Kristina Lucka
Lighting Design .... Scott Pinkney
Sound Design .... Brad Berridge

The Whipping Man The Old Globe (Executive Producer, Louis G. Spisto) Opened May 13th, 2010

Directed by Giovanna Sardelli

Simon.. Charlie Robinson
John .... Avery Glymph
Caleb .... Mark J Sullivan
Scenic Design .... Robert Morgan
Costume Design............................... Denitsa Bliznakova
Lighting Design .... Lap Chi Chu

Sound Design .... Jill BC DuBoff

Penumbra Theatre Company (Founder and Artistic Director, Lou Bellamy)
Opened February 19th, 2009

Directed by Lou Bellamy

      Simon... James Craven
      John .... Duane Boutté
      Caleb .... Joseph Papke

      Scenic Design .... Kenneth F. Evans
      Costume Design............................... Kalere A. Payton
      Lighting Design .... Kathy A. Perkins
      Sound Design .... Martin Gwinup

Luna Stage Company (Artistic Director, Jane Mandel)
Opened April 29th, 2006

Directed by Linnet Taylor

      Simon......................... Frankie R. Faison
      John .... Brandon O'Neil Scott
      Caleb .... Douglas Scott Sorenson

      Scenic Design .... Amanda Embry
      Costume Design............... Colleen Kesterson
      Lighting Design .... Jill Nagle
      Sound Design .... Margaret Pine

PLAYWRIGHT BIOGRAPHY

Matthew Lopez's play *The Whipping Man* premiered off-Broadway 2011 at Manhattan Theatre Club in a production directed by Doug Hughes and starring Andre Braugher. For this production, Matthew was awarded the John Gassner Playwriting Award from the Outer Critics Circle. Prior to New York, the play was presented at Luna Stage, Penumbra Theatre Company, Barrington Stage Company and the Old Globe in San Diego, where he is currently Artist-in-Residence. It has become one of the more regularly produced new American plays with productions scheduled at over a dozen theatres across the country this year. His play Somewhere received its world premiere production last autumn at the Old Globe, directed by Giovanna Sardelli. Other plays include Reverberation, Zoey's Perfect Wedding and The Legend of Georgia McBride. His short play The Sentinels was included in Headlong Theatre Company's Decade project, a collection of plays about 9/11, which ran in London in conjunction with the tenth anniversary of the attacks. In addition to his residency at the Globe, he is commissioned by Roundabout Theatre Company, is a New York Theatre Workshop Usual Suspect and is a recent member of the Ars Nova Play Group.

I owe a great debt of gratitude to Linnet Taylor, Lou Bellamy, Giovanna Sardelli and Doug Hughes, the first four directors, each of whose spirit inhabits the play. To all the people who picked it up and carried it when I needed the help: Jane Mandel, Cheryl Katz, Jack DePalma, Lou Spisto, Lynne Meadow and Mandy Greenfield. And finally to Seth Glewen and Brandon Clarke, who carried me when I needed the help.

Matthew Lopez

THE WHIPPING MAN

ACT 1, SCENE 1

Richmond, Virginia. Thursday, April 13, 1865. Around ten o'clock at night.

The lights rise on what was once the front entrance of a grand town home, now in ruins. Craters dot the hardwood floors. The wallpaper is stained with soot and parts of it are burned away. Most of the windows are broken. The railing of the grand staircase leans perilously down to the floor, as if it would collapse with the slightest touch. The steps themselves are broken and jagged. The damage to the house suggests recent destruction rather than years of neglect. This was someone's home not too long ago. But it is now a haunted house.

A violent thunderstorm is raging outside. At the crack of a thunderbolt, the front door swings open. A young man in a tattered Confederate Captain's uniform leans against the doorway. He is bearded, thin and dirty. He hops on one leg toward the center of the room. He then slowly extends his other leg and tries to put weight on it. He lets out a cry of pain and collapses onto the floor in a dead faint.

A few moments pass. Slowly, an older man enters from the kitchen. He is middle-aged, black. He carries a rifle with a lantern dangling from the end. It is too dark to see anything. The older man cautiously approaches.

Lightning and thunder. The room fills with light for a brief moment. Older man sees young man on the floor.

OLDER MAN: Hey you.
  Hey you, there.
  (Older Man approaches the Younger Man, inspecting him from a cautious distance. He then nudges the Younger Man with his foot.)
OLDER MAN: Wake up, soldier. Wake up.
  (Younger Man jerks violently back to life. He turns and sees the figure (but not the face) of Older Man before him.)
OLDER MAN: Easy. Easy.
YOUNGER MAN: Get that rifle out of my face, old man.
OLDER MAN: Seeing as I'm the one holding it, I think I'll make the rules.
YOUNGER MAN: Where am I?

OLDER MAN: That don't matter 'cause you ain't staying.

YOUNGER MAN: Whose home is this?

OLDER MAN: You best be on your way. They ain't nothing left to steal here, if that's what you're thinkin'. If it's dying you're looking to do, you best do that elsewhere. Now get up and--

YOUNGER MAN: Simon? Simon, is that you?

(The Older Man brings his lantern down to the Younger Man's face and takes a good long look at it.)

SIMON: Caleb?

CALEB: *(all tension leaving his body, a wave of relief)*
Yes. Yes. Oh, God. Am I home? Is this, am I, am I home?

SIMON: You are.

CALEB: Oh God, oh God.

(Simon rests his hand on Caleb's head. Caleb flinches at the touch but doesn't fight it.)

SIMON: *Baruch atah adonai elohenu melech haolam mechaye hametim.*

CALEB: Where is everyone? Where's my mother? Where's Sarah?

SIMON: Sarah is with your pa. And my Lizbeth. Your pa took them with him when he left with President Davis. My girls are safe with your pa.

CALEB: And my mother?

SIMON: She went down to Williamsburg to be with your grandma. She's safe, too.

CALEB: When will they be back?

SIMON: No one knows. Just like everyone else from this town. Most folks are gone. They'll be back when it's safe.

CALEB: What about...?

SIMON: Ain't seen him in some time. Probably on a drunk somewhere.

CALEB: Or gone.

SIMON: I'd bet money on a bottle before I'd bet on him leaving.

CALEB: I'm thirsty, Simon. Get me some water.

(Pause.)

CALEB: Simon?

(Another Pause.)

SIMON: Sure. Sure, I'll do that.

(Simon exits to the kitchen. Caleb looks around the room.)

CALEB: What in hell happened here?

(off, to Simon)

What the hell happened here, Simon?

(No answer.)

(He tries to stand. It's not easy for him. He finally gets himself upright on one leg. He cautiously extends the other and tries to put weight on it. He collapses in a heap, crying out in pain.)

(Simon re-enters with a mason jar filled with water, handing it to Caleb.)

SIMON: That you doin' all that yellin'?

CALEB: Yeah.

SIMON: You wounded?

CALEB: It's just a graze. I'll be fine.

SIMON: Can you stand up?

CALEB: Yes, I can stand.

SIMON: Can you walk?

CALEB: Walking's a different matter.

SIMON: When'd this happen?

CALEB: Week? Maybe more? We, ah, we were leaving Petersburg and--

SIMON: Them Federal doctors didn't tend to it?

CALEB: What Federal doctors?

SIMON: When you surrendered.

CALEB: Oh. No, they, ah, they were more concerned with their own, I guess.

SIMON: We'd best take a look at it.

CALEB: It's not that bad.

SIMON: Week-old wounds have a habit of killing people. Might have to take you up to the soldier's hospital.

CALEB: NO!

No, I'm not going there. I'm not going anywhere. I just got here. I'm not leaving.

(Simon begins lighting a few candles and lamps around the room. Not too many. They throw off a weak light.)

CALEB: What happened to this house, Simon?

SIMON: Same thing that happened to all the other houses.

CALEB: What about the furniture?

SIMON: Stolen.

CALEB: By who?

SIMON: People.

Fire happened to this house, too. Upstairs, it...well, I don't go upstairs no more.

CALEB: Why not?

SIMON: Big holes in the roof. Rain's coming in. Artillery shells took out a lot of the roof.

CALEB: The Yanks did that?

SIMON: No, you boys did that. I hear tell that someone told someone else to light all the warehouses on fire so the Yanks couldn't get at any of what was in there. Cotton, tobacco, all up in a blaze. Then, the fire spread to where they stored the munitions and--
(makes an explosion sound)
--right into your mama's sewing room. Whole town looks like this.

CALEB: I saw as I rode up.

SIMON: Hell happened to this town. Looks like hell done happened to you, too.

CALEB: What've you been doing this whole time?

SIMON: Last few months I was living up at Chimborazo with your ma and the women from the temple. Nursing, bandaging, whatever needed doing. Then when the Federals came, your ma left for Williamsburg--

CALEB: And told you to come here and wait for everybody.

SIMON: She asked me.
(Pause.)

SIMON: Best let me take a look.
(Simon pulls out a pocketknife and cuts Caleb's pant leg open at the knee to reveal a rotting bullet wound.)

SIMON: God in heaven. This ain't no graze. This is a bullet hole. You was shot a week ago and you ain't had it cleaned?

CALEB: It was chaos.

SIMON: We need to clean this. Your pa has some whiskey left.

CALEB: Some? He has cases.

SIMON: *Had* cases.
(Simon moves to a section of the torn-up floorboards and begins reaching under.)

CALEB: Where'd all the whiskey go?

SIMON: Same place it always goes when there's trouble.
(He mimes chugging at a bottle. Then he finds a whiskey bottle.)

SIMON: Here she is.
(Simon moves back to Caleb and opens the bottle.)

SIMON: This is gonna hurt, now.

CALEB: I'm sure I've felt worse.
(Simon pours the whiskey on the wound. Caleb lets out a yell, then winces through the pain.)

CALEB: Goddammit, Simon, that hurts!

SIMON: You don't say.
(Caleb grabs the bottle from Simon and takes a healthy swig.)

CALEB: What's there to eat?

SIMON: Not much. Been living off a sack of corn meal and some vegetables from the garden. It's yours if you want it.

CALEB: Where are the chickens?

SIMON: Ain't been no chickens. You gotta understand: things've been bad for a while. People, they...there ain't no food.

CALEB: Market's still open?

SIMON: It's open, so to speak. Those that are left to sell. But what money you gonna buy with? People only taking Federal. Only the rich are eating.

CALEB: Aren't we rich?

SIMON: That's for your father to say. All I know is when he left, he didn't leave nothing behind to live off of. I come home, everyone's gone. The larder's empty. Chickens dead. Carrots, collards and corn meal, that's what we got.

CALEB: I'll eat anything.

SIMON: Well, that being the case, you say you rode here?

CALEB: I had a horse.

SIMON: Had?

CALEB: He's dead. Out front.

SIMON: Just as well. Can't feed a horse, anyway.
Could eat one, though.
That horse have any meat on him?

CALEB: Not much. He spent a week dying.

SIMON: Well, whatever's left, he ain't got no more need for it and God knows we could use a meal.

CALEB: Yes.

SIMON: I've got rags in the kitchen. I need to clean this wound.
(Simon exits to the kitchen.)
(Caleb grabs the bottle and drinks. He then reaches into his coat pocket and pulls out a packet of letters, tied together with string. The sight of them moves him greatly.)
(A figure is seen moving around on the front porch, looking through the windows.)

CALEB: Who's there? Who is that?
(The figure moves away.)

CALEB: Simon! Simon, get in here!
(Simon re-enters.)

SIMON: What? What is it?

CALEB: Something was moving out there, looking in the windows.

(Simon grabs the rifle and moves to the front door. He opens the door and looks about. No one is there. He comes back into the house.)

SIMON: No one there.

CALEB: There was someone looking through the window.

SIMON: Well, if they take a look again, it'll be down the barrel of this gun.

(Simon continues to look out the window for a moment then turns to face Caleb.)

SIMON: You ain't gonna like what I'm about to say.

CALEB: Don't tell me we're out of whiskey, too.

SIMON: Your leg, it...you got the gangrene pretty bad.

CALEB: How bad?

SIMON: Well, it ain't gone above the knee, which is good, but...that leg gonna haveta come off.

(Pause.)

CALEB: No.

SIMON: Caleb.

CALEB: No.

SIMON: I spent three months looking at sick legs--

CALEB: I said no!

SIMON: Caleb.

CALEB: I've been in plenty of hospital tents the last four years. I saw what it was like when they took off those limbs, I--

SIMON: You ever see what it was like when they don't?
We don't cut you leg off at the knee, the gangrene gonna keep crawling right on up, hurting every inch as it goes. It's gonna pass through your privates. They gonna fall off like ripe apples on a tree. There's gonna be a big hole where your Tommy Johnson used to be. It's gonna eat away at your liver, your stomach, your kidneys. Gonna crawl right up to your heart and turn it black. Blacker than my fist. Your blood gonna be so filled with poison, every part of you is gonna hurt. You gonna be in more pain than you ever thought you could stand. You gonna lose your mind with the pain. And then...and only then...will you die. The pain you gonna feel having this leg come off today gonna feel like a tickle compared to the pain you gonna feel when you die of poisoned blood on Sunday. You understand me?

CALEB: If I do this, I'm gonna be better?

SIMON: You gonna have a chance of being better. I wouldn't be saying this if I didn't believe it. Do you trust me?

(Caleb signals his acquiescence by lying back down.)

SIMON: Good. Now, I need to clean this wound and then find some help in the morning to take you up to Chimborazo.

CALEB: No! No hospital. You'll do it here.

SIMON: I can't--

CALEB: If you think this is something I need, then you're gonna do it
yourself.

SIMON: I can't--

CALEB: Yes you can. You've done it before, haven't you?

SIMON: Not by myself. I could kill you.

CALEB: So could they. I'd rather die here than at that hospital.

SIMON: I can't do it.

CALEB: You will. You got tools?

SIMON: Well, I--

CALEB: How much whiskey we have left?

SIMON: Not enough to keep the wound clean and get you as drunk as
you're gonna need to be.

CALEB: How drunk?

SIMON: Dead drunk. Even that ain't gonna be enough.

CALEB: We'll make do with what we've got. Go look for more whiskey.
Find what you can. Check the cellar.

SIMON: Caleb?

CALEB: What?

SIMON: All these things you're telling me to do, by rights now you need to
be asking me to do.

CALEB: Are you asking me to chop off my leg or are you telling me?

SIMON: I'm telling you.

CALEB: Then I'm telling you to go get the fuckin' whiskey. If you're giving
orders, I'm giving orders. That sound fair to you?

SIMON: Fair enough for now.

(Simon exits.)

(The figure appears again at the window.)

CALEB: Who's there? Who is that?

(The figure moves to the door.)

CALEB: Who are you?

(The front door slowly opens. We see the figure standing in the shadows. He
wears a burlap hood over his face with two eye holes cut out, putting him in
likeness of an executioner. He exudes menace.)

MAN: Captain Caleb DeLeon?

CALEB: Who is that?

MAN: Are you Captain Caleb DeLeon?

CALEB: Who are you?

MAN: I am the man asking if you are Captain Caleb DeLeon.

CALEB: What do you want?

MAN: I have a message for you.

CALEB: From who?

> *(No answer.)*

CALEB: What is the message?

> *(A moment, then The Man rips the hood off to reveal the face of John, a young black man close to Caleb's age.)*

JOHN: Nigger John has come home!

> *(John laughs with glee and dances around, delighted with himself. It's is a "boo! I gotchya" moment that John performs with devilish relish. Caleb jumps at this then, knowing he is safe, relaxes.*
>
> > *About John's appearance: he is feral. His clothes are dirty and tattered. His feet are bare. His hair is grown out and a week's worth of beard sits on his face. He also has a cloth bandage wrapped around one hand.)*

CALEB: Godammit John, you scared me half to death.

JOHN: You look at least to be three-quarters there.

This your dead horse here?

CALEB: It is.

JOHN: I don't know which of the two of you looks worse.

> *(John looks behind him as if checking to see that the coast is clear, then he steps inside and closes the door.)*

CALEB: Was that you creepin' around just then?

JOHN: I saw a soldier crawling up to the house and thought he might be up to no good.

CALEB: I thought you were a looter.

JOHN: I was havin' the same thoughts about you.

CALEB: Good to know the house is so well-protected.

JOHN: Not that there's all that much left to protect.

He moves into the room, looking around.

JOHN: Just you and Simon, then?

CALEB: That's right.

JOHN: No one else?

CALEB: You.

> *(John looks Caleb over.)*

JOHN: You wounded?

CALEB: It's just a scratch.

Where've you been? Simon says you've been missing.

JOHN: Oh, I didn't miss a thing.

CALEB: You've been here in Richmond?

JOHN: I have.

CALEB: What's the news? Have you heard anything?

JOHN: I've heard everything. What do you want to know?

JOHN: War's over. You lost. We won.

Whiskey?

CALEB: What?

JOHN: You want some whiskey?

(He reaches into his sack and pulls out a full bottle of whiskey.)

CALEB: Where in hell did you get that?

JOHN: A neighbor.

CALEB: You stole it.

JOHN: I did not steal anything. "Stealing" is when someone has gone to great lengths to protect something. That was not the case with this, although there was a case *of* this. The house was half burned and the doors were wide open. No, this whiskey was liberated and is now being occupied by me.

(He takes a drink then holds it out to Caleb.)

JOHN: Want some?

(Caleb stares at the bottle for a moment then reluctantly gestures for it. John hands it to him and Caleb begins drinking. They pass the bottle.)

JOHN: You were at Petersburg, weren't you?

CALEB: I was.

JOHN: Was it as bad as they say?

CALEB: What'd they say?

JOHN: I wouldn't have wanted to be there.

CALEB: No you wouldn't have.

JOHN: So I guess you surrendered with Lee at Appomattox.

CALEB: I did.

JOHN: That must've stung.

(Silence a moment.)

JOHN: What do I call you now?

CALEB: Call me?

JOHN: "Master" doesn't quite fit anymore.

CALEB: You never called me that.

JOHN: "Sir?" Do I address you as "sir," now?

CALEB: You never called me that, either. I think "Caleb" Will be just fine.

JOHN: Will he?

(Simon enters, carrying a toolbox and a bottle of whiskey.)

SIMON: Well, look who's home.

JOHN: Simon.

(John approaches him. Simon pulls him out of earshot from Caleb, who nurses the whiskey.)

SIMON: John. Where you been, boy?

JOHN: Here, there. Mostly there. This place sure got picked over.

SIMON: You have anything to do with it?

JOHN: I wish I had.

SIMON: I came home thinking you'd be here and you just up and disappeared.

JOHN: Well, now I just up and re-appeared.

SIMON: What'd you do to your hand?

JOHN: It's nothing.

SIMON: Let me take a look at it.

JOHN: I said it's nothing. What's wrong with Caleb?

SIMON: He's got a bullet in his leg.

JOHN: He said it wasn't bad.

SIMON: He ain't a doctor.

JOHN: Neither are you.

SIMON: Closest thing he got to one. His leg's gonna haveta come off.

JOHN: Does he know that?

SIMON: He ain't got no choice. I've been trying to get him to go to the hospital but he won't budge.

JOHN: So...what, then?

SIMON: Well, I told him I'd do it here but it's too much for one man, especially in the dark. I figured if I started laying out all my tools it might scare him into going to the hospital. If that don't work, I just figured to get him drunk. He's half starved as it is. It won't take much for him to pass out. Then we take him to the hospital, whether he wants to go or not.

JOHN: We?

SIMON: I need your help, John.

JOHN: Take him up to Chimborazo?

SIMON: It needs doing.

JOHN: Let me ask you something. How is this our problem anymore?

SIMON: Our problem? That boy is dying. Layin' in his mama's house and dying. That's a problem.

JOHN: So let's leave. Let's get out of here. When they find out, we'll be long gone.

SIMON: And what would happen to Caleb? You see anybody else around here? I need your help, John.

JOHN: Could you do it here? If I helped...could you...could we do it?

SIMON: Could do, but...it ain't an easy thing. He's going to be kicking and screaming. You think you're strong enough to hold him down?

JOHN: Have been since we were kids.

SIMON: It could be done, then.

JOHN: So how do we do this? Just chop it with an axe or something?

SIMON: An axe? You crazy, boy?

JOHN: Well, I don't know! I've never taken off someone's leg before!

SIMON: We use a saw. Saw at his leg right below the knee. Here, see?

(He points to a spot on John's leg. He continues to explain using John's leg as an example.)

SIMON: We gotta cut through the skin, through the muscle, right down to the bone.

JOHN: And then?

SIMON: Then? Clear through the bone. As fast as we can. He's gonna be wiggling and struggling. The more he struggles, the harder it's gonna be for me to cut.

(John grabs the whiskey from Simon and takes a huge gulp.)

SIMON: Through the bone, onto the other side of the leg. The muscle, the skin. Till it comes right off.

JOHN: That's it, then?

SIMON: That's just the beginning. He's got an artery there in his leg. Got to tie that off or else he gonna bleed to death. As it is, he gonna be bleeding all over hisself and us, too.

JOHN: You know how to tie it off?

SIMON: Done it hundreds of times. Then we take the skin from his leg and we cut it, we pull it back. Like pulling the husk off of corn, see? And we cut away at the muscle on the leg 'til the bone's sticking out. We wrap the skin around the bone. We fold them, one over the other and sew it up. That makes the stump, see?

JOHN: He's awake during all this?

SIMON: Without ether? All depends on his strength. Some men pass out at the sight of the saw. Others watch the whole thing.

JOHN: And what about the person holding him down? When does he usually pass out?

SIMON: I need you strong, John.

JOHN: I can do this.

SIMON: It ain't gonna be pretty. We gonna be up all night.

JOHN: So, then...let's get started. You wanna drink first?

SIMON: No.

JOHN: Suit yourself.

(John takes one more swig, then hands the bottle to Simon. Simon goes to Caleb with the bottle, leaving the toolbox behind.)

SIMON: All right, Caleb. We're gonna do things your way. We won't take you to the hospital but we got to do this now. Keep drinking.

CALEB: Goddamnit, Simon, I'm already drunk.

SIMON: Get drunker. Go on. Big ol' gulps.

CALEB: Simon, I--

SIMON: You shoulda had the wound cleaned days ago. You shoulda had that leg off by now.

CALEB: Simon, I changed my mind.

SIMON: You want to go to the hospital?

CALEB: No.

SIMON: Then you ain't got no mind to change. You best start drinking that whiskey. Your bottle is for your belly. My bottle is for your leg. If I finish my bottle before you finish yours, you gonna be in a world a hurt. Drink.

(Caleb hesitates then begins quickly drinking.)

SIMON: John, I need your help over here.
Keep drinking.

CALEB: Simon, I think I'm going to be sick.

SIMON: You gonna be a lot sicker if we don't get this leg off. Drink.

(John hands Simon the chair and Simon sets it on its side. Caleb continues drinking.)

CALEB: Simon--

SIMON: Keep drinking.
I'm gonna grab your leg, now.

(Simon grabs Caleb by his leg and John takes him by the shoulders. They move him over to the chair and rest his leg on it. Simon rips Caleb's pant leg open to above the knee. Caleb's leg is rotting. As this is happening...)

SIMON: Tourniquet.

(John wraps the tourniquet around Caleb's thigh.)

CALEB: Simon, I don't want you to do this.

SIMON: Got no choice, Caleb.

CALEB: I don't want you to.

SIMON: You gonna die if we don't.

CALEB: I'll take my chances.

SIMON: You'll be dead by Sunday.

CALEB: I can't, I can't do this.

SIMON: You ain't gotta do nothing. I'm gonna do all the work.

CALEB: Simon, don't do this.

(Simon takes the bottle and pours the whiskey over the wound. Caleb screams and tries to get away. Simon stops him.)

SIMON: John! You gotta hold him down, now. Hold him down.

(John pins Caleb to the floor.)

CALEB: Let go of me, goddammit!

(Simon repositions Caleb's leg on the chair. Caleb struggles against John.)

CALEB: I said let go!

SIMON: Hold him down, John.

JOHN: He's not going anywhere.

(Caleb continues to struggle but is too drunk and weak to get John off of him.)

(Simon goes to the tool box and pulls out a saw. Caleb sees it and starts to scramble away.)

(Simon brings the knife out.)

CALEB: No, please, Simon. No! Please! Please!

(Simon cuts Caleb's leg with the knife.)

CALEB: SIMON!!! God, please, please, please, please!

(John struggles to keep Caleb pinned. Simon steps on the foot of Caleb's good leg, bearing down with all his weight to keep him from kicking. He then repositions Caleb's bad leg onto the chair. Throughout this:)

CALEB: Simon, no. No, please, Simon. Don't do this.

SIMON: Got no choice, Caleb.

CALEB: Simon, please, please don't do this.

SIMON: It needs doing, Caleb.

CALEB: PLEASEDON'TDOTHISPLEASEDON'TDOTHISPLEASEDO N'TDOTHISPLEASEDON'TDOTHIS...

(Simon breaks off a spindle from the chair and hands it to John.)

SIMON: For his mouth. To bite down on.

(John takes the spindle and tries to put it into Caleb's mouth. Caleb spits it out.)

CALEB: DON'TDOTHISDON'TDOTHISDON'TDOTHIS!
DON'T YOU FUCKING DO THIS!
DON'T YOU FUCKING DO THIS!
DON'TYOUFUCKINGDOTHIS!

(John grabs the spindle again and forcefully puts it into Caleb's mouth, holding it in place.)

(Caleb screams and struggles, his words muffled by the spindle.)

(Simon starts to sing a lullaby to calm Caleb.)

(And then, Simon pulls the saw back, making the first cut into Caleb's leg. The lights immediately fade on them and slowly rise on the rest of the house.

It is our first full look at the ruin. Caleb screams. It is as if his screams were pushing the light upward. His screams echo throughout the empty house as the lights finally fade completely.)

End of Scene 1

SCENE 2

The next morning. Friday, April 14, 1865.
The rain continues.
Caleb is sleeping on a mattress on the floor. His leg is gone and he is covered in quilts and blankets. A few sacks filled with pilfered goods lay around the room. Stacks of books are scattered around, as well.
Simon sits on the floor with a bucket and a scrub brush, cleaning the bloodstains. A cup of what we take to be coffee sits steaming by his side.
John enters from upstairs, carrying a sack. He is dressed in better clothes than in Scene 1. He trudges down and sits on the foot of the stairs, watching Simon scrubbing. After a moment...

JOHN: That coffee?
SIMON: Water. Ain't no coffee.
JOHN: You're just drinking hot water?
SIMON: It warms me.
JOHN: Wouldn't you rather have coffee?
SIMON: I'd rather have flapjacks and some eggs. Some toast, maybe, with some jam. I'd rather have some of Lizbeth's country fried chicken with the thick, white gravy she puts on it. And while we're at it, I'd rather have a soft feather bed to lay down in and have the first decent night's sleep I've had in years. And when I've had all that, then, yes, I wouldn't mind a nice cup of hot coffee.
(He goes back to scrubbing. John rummages through his sack and pulls out a smaller sack of coffee and tosses it over to Simon. Simon opens it and smells deeply.)
SIMON: Where'd you get this?
JOHN: Found it.
SIMON: Stole it.
JOHN: Found it, stole it. What's the difference? Course, if you have an objection, I can always...
(He reaches for the coffee but Simon moves it away from him.)
JOHN: Guess you wouldn't be interested in these, either...
(He pulls a handful of eggs from his coat pocket.)
SIMON: You "found" those, too?
JOHN: These, I "discovered."
SIMON: You best be careful you don't discover yourself staring down the business end of a shotgun.
JOHN: All these houses are deserted.

SIMON: This one ain't.

JOHN: Most of them are. It's like they unlocked the doors of a store and said "welcome."

SIMON: Yeah, but folks will be coming back to these houses eventually. A couple of eggs ain't nobody gonna miss. But them duds you got on...

JOHN: You survive your way, I'll survive mine.

(He reaches into his sack and pulls out a bottle of whiskey.)

SIMON: It ain't barely even noon.

JOHN: I know. I do believe I am behind schedule.

(John looks over at Caleb.)

JOHN: How's Prince Caleb?

SIMON: He's been runnin' a fever this morning. I'm hoping it'll break soon. He lost a lot of blood.

JOHN: I don't want to see anything like that ever again.

SIMON: You'll be a lucky man if you don't. We need to keep an eye on him next few days. You best save some of that whiskey for him once he wakes up.

JOHN: Don't worry about the whiskey. I guarantee we won't run out.

(Pause.)

SIMON: What you got planned for yourself, John?

JOHN: Me? I figure I'll finish this bottle, maybe start a new book. Looking forward to dinner...

SIMON: I mean with your life.

JOHN: Oh.

SIMON: Mr. DeLeon ever talk to you about money?

JOHN: Mr. DeLeon never talked to me about anything.

SIMON: Before the war ended, he told me he was gonna give us money if we was freed.

JOHN: Bullshit.

SIMON: He said.

JOHN: He never told me.

SIMON: He only told me once.

JOHN: Maybe he was drunk.

SIMON: He was sober as a glass of water.

JOHN: How much?

SIMON: Enough.

JOHN: When?

SIMON: When he gets back. Like he done with Bad Eye, remember?

JOHN: No.

SIMON: Bad Eye bought hisself free and Mr. DeLeon bought his train

ticket up North. Gave him some pocket money to get started. Bad
Eye went to New York City with Mr. DeLeon's help.

JOHN: That's what you're here for?

SIMON: That and I'm waiting for my Lizbeth and Sarah to come home.

(John takes a swig.)

JOHN: How do you know he'll keep his word?

SIMON: I don't. If he doesn't, we're no worse off than we are now.

JOHN: Which isn't saying much. That's why you're so keen to help out old
Caleb here?

SIMON: I'm doing it because it's the right thing to do. But if Mr. DeLeon
comes home to find his son dead and we could have helped him...

JOHN: No money.

SIMON: That'd be the least of our troubles.

(Simon stands.)

SIMON: You didn't happen to discover a frying pan, did you?

JOHN: I'll keep an eye out for one.

SIMON: You best be careful.

(Simon starts to exit.)

JOHN: You don't have to worry about me.

*(Simon trudges off to the kitchen. John stands looking at Caleb. He then goes
back upstairs with his loot.)*

End of Scene 2

SCENE 3

Evening. Friday, April 14, 1865.
The rain continues.
Although there are candles and lanterns set around the front parlor, none are lit. Caleb is still asleep.
Elsewhere in the house, the evidence of John's looting is even more apparent. There are some chairs, all mismatched. There are small pieces of furniture; mounds of clothing; the saddle from Caleb's horse; other things that might have been taken from neighboring houses. It is as if John were trying to re-populate the furnishings of this house piece by mismatched piece. The room is still more empty than full. But there is an obvious feeling of addition.
John enters from the front door, wearing his hood again and carrying a burlap sack. His clothes are even nicer than before. He's cleaned himself up. He cautiously looks about, then slips into the house. He makes one more look outside through the window, then removes the hood.
He moves over to where Caleb is sleeping and gets close to Caleb's face, staring at him. After a long moment, Caleb wakes with a violent start and instinctively grabs John by the neck. It is the reaction of a man who still thinks he's at war. John drops the sack. A cacophony of clanging utensils and metal.

CALEB: Who are you?
JOHN: It's me, it's John.
CALEB: John who?
JOHN: Nigger John.
CALEB: Nig--I'm--I'm, where, I'm...
    (He looks around the room and shifts his position, forgetting his leg is gone. Pain shoots up his leg. He screams in agony, grabbing for the leg that isn't there. He looks down at his leg and a wave of realization and memory sweeps over him. He starts to weep and lays back down.)
CALEB: My leg. Oh God, my leg.
    My leg is gone.
JOHN: It is.
CALEB: My leg is gone.
JOHN: Easy, now.
    (He starts to calm down. John carefully moves about the room, lighting the candles and lanterns, keeping a cautious distance from Caleb. It's okay if this takes a little while.)
CALEB: How long was I out?
JOHN: Little more than a day.

CALEB: I was back at the war.

JOHN: When?

CALEB: Just now. I dreamt of Petersburg. I thought I was back. But I'm
not. I'm here. I'm home.
Have they come back?

JOHN: Who?

CALEB: Elizabeth and Sarah? My folks?

JOHN: No. No one's come back yet. Just the three of us still.

CALEB: Has anyone come by?

JOHN: You expecting company?

CALEB: No one's--?

JOHN: No.
*(John sits, takes another drink, then offers it to Caleb. He reaches for it and
a bolt of pain rips through his leg. He falls back and winces/breathes through
it. John watches.)*

JOHN: How'd you get that wound again?

CALEB: Leavin' Petersburg.

JOHN: Funny you didn't get it looked at when you could have.

CALEB: It was chaos.

JOHN: Oh, I've no doubt. But still...

CALEB: What?

JOHN: No, it's just funny, that's all.
(This news causes him to relax a bit. He looks around the room.)

CALEB: What is all this?

JOHN: Things.

CALEB: Whose?

JOHN: Mine, now.

CALEB: What are you going to do with it?

JOHN: Own it.

CALEB: Why?

JOHN: Because I can.
*(John reaches over and hands Caleb the bottle. He drinks. They pass the
bottle back and forth in silence a moment.)*

CALEB: What're you going to do when the folks who used to own it come
looking for it?

JOHN: I'll be long gone by then.

CALEB: Where?

JOHN: I'm glad you asked. You remember Bad Eye?

CALEB: Bad Eye?

JOHN: Bad Eye. He was about ten years older than us. Had that one eye that didn't work so well? Kind of rolled around in the socket like a marble? Used to scare you.

CALEB: He never scared me.

JOHN: So you do remember him, then?

CALEB: We called him "Lawrence."

JOHN: We called him "Bad Eye."

When he left, he told me he was heading up to New York with money in his pockets and a train ticket bought by your father. The day he left, Bad Eye pulls me aside and says to me, "Nigger John..."

CALEB: He never called you that.

JOHN: Oh, he did. Your nickname caught on fast. "Nigger John," he says, "you come up to New York when you get free from here. You come up to New York and I'll set you up with a job and a bed and a way to start your life."

CALEB: That's what you're going to do?

JOHN: That is what I am going to do.

    (Caleb chuckles.)

JOHN: That funny to you?

CALEB: You know how far New York is?

JOHN: I know how far.

CALEB: You're just going to head on up to New York. Out of this town.

JOHN: The hell outta this town.

CALEB: And when you get there, how do you plan on finding him?

JOHN: I'll find him.

CALEB: Just gonna stand on every street corner in New York City, yelling out "Bad Eye, Bad Eye, where are you?"

JOHN: If that's what it takes.

CALEB: "Ten years after you left, here I am."

JOHN: All right.

CALEB: "After four years of war, here I am."

JOHN: Enough.

CALEB: That's about he dumbest thing I ever heard.

JOHN: I SAID ENOUGH!

CALEB: You think my father is going to give you money?

JOHN: He told me he would.

CALEB: When?

JOHN: Several times. Told me, told Simon.

CALEB: He's just gonna give you money?

JOHN: As it says in the Torah: "When you set him free, do not let him go empty-handed."

CALEB: Yeah, well, you better hope he's got some Federal dollars to put in your hand.

JOHN: Oh, I'm not worried about that.

(John moves to the kitchen and yells off...)

JOHN: Hey, Simon...when's dinner gonna be ready?

SIMON: *(OFF)*
You keep askin' like that, the answer gonna be "never."

JOHN: Caleb's awake. If you care to know.

(Simon enters from the kitchen and stops to look at him.)

SIMON: Well...you slept a good long time. How you feel?

CALEB: Like hell.

SIMON: That sounds about on schedule. You gonna be in pain for a while. Gonna try and keep you in as much whiskey as we can find. That'll keep any infection from setting in.

CALEB: How is drinkin' whiskey gonna keep an infection away?

SIMON: Shoot, whiskey'll kill anything. Killed your Uncle Charlie.
You think you can eat? I butchered that horse last night. Meat's tough but there's a lot of it.

JOHN: Horse meat isn't kosher, Simon.

SIMON: Neither is stealin' from your neighbor. You go find me a Rabbi and we'll ask him which is worse. You hungry, ain't you?

JOHN: Yeah.

SIMON: Then it's as kosher as it's gonna get for now.

(Simon heads back to the kitchen, then stops and pulls John aside.)

SIMON: Freddy Cole came around today while you was sleeping off your drunk.

JOHN: Oh yeah? Whatwhatwhat'd he want?

SIMON: He wanted you. Say he been lookin' for you about a week now.

JOHN: Whatwhatwhat did you tell him?

SIMON: Something told me I shouldn't tell him anything. Why do you think I got that feeling?

JOHN: I don't think anyone wants Freddy Cole knowin' where he is.

SIMON: He wasn't lookin' for me, John. You do something make Freddy Cole angry?

JOHN: Doesn't take much.

SIMON: John...

JOHN: You tell Freddy Cole next time he comes round looking for me that you ain't seen me. You tell him I'm long gone and ain't never coming back. You tell him Nigger John says let bygones be bygones and to kiss my emancipated ass!

(He heads up the stairs and off. Simon calls after him.)

SIMON: You done something against Freddy Cole, you got to make it right, boy! You can't run from him forever! You living in this world now, not just servin' in it!

(Simon exits to the kitchen as John re-enters with another sack of looted goods in one hand and a fresh bottle of whiskey in the other.)

CALEB: Freddy Cole is not the kind of man you want looking for you.

JOHN: I ain't scared of Freddy Cole.

CALEB: Then why are you hiding from him?

(Instead of answering, John drinks.)

CALEB: You owe him money? Fuck his woman?

JOHN: He's just a mean ol' cracker who got it out for me, is all. Had one since the day he met me.

CALEB: You're not exactly the ingratiating type.

(Simon re-enters with the cooked horse meat.)

SIMON: Eat it if you're hungry, skip it if you ain't.

(John moves to his sack, pulls out knives and forks and then three dinner plates.)

SIMON: Boy, you stole all that?

JOHN: No one else is going to be eating off it.

SIMON: That's Mrs. Taylor's fine china.

JOHN: That's Mrs. Taylor's *chipped* china. Which was laying on Mrs. Taylor's dirty floor. You want to eat with your hands? Be my guest. I'm using the utensils.

(Simon reluctantly reaches for them. John hands them over. Simon begins serving. As he does...)

JOHN: Never eaten horse before.

SIMON: Ain't nothing to it. Like any other meat. You hungry, right?

JOHN: Yeah.

SIMON: Well, then...

(Simon hands out the food.)

JOHN: *Shabbat Shalom*, Simon.

SIMON: Is it the Sabbath?

JOHN: It is. April 14, to be precise.

SIMON: How do you know that?

(John produces a small datebook from his pocket.)

JOHN: I've been trying to keep track of the days since the town was evacuated. It was hard to do but then I found this datebook.

CALEB: Stole, you mean.

JOHN: Look at Caleb: accusing me of stealing time. Today is Friday, April

14. Took me a while to figure that out but I'm fairly certain it's true.

SIMON: Well, *Shabbat Shalom* to you, then.

JOHN: *Shabbat Shalom.*

(*Simon begins the blessing. John joins in. Caleb does not. Simon notices.*)

SIMON: *Barukh attah Adonai eloheinu melekh ha-olam, shehakol niheyah bidvaro.*

JOHN: Amen.

(*Simon puts a piece of the meat in his mouth. They watch as he chews.*)

JOHN: Well?

SIMON: It's fine.

(*Simon continues chewing. And chewing.*)

JOHN: You've been chewing that piece of meat longer than that horse was alive.

SIMON: It's chewy.

(*Simon continues to chew.*)

SIMON: Very chewy.

(*Simon finally--and with great difficulty--swallows.*)

SIMON: Well?

(*John and Caleb cut into their meat and put a piece to their mouths. They eat in silence for a moment.*)

JOHN: It is chewy.

CALEB: Yes.

(*All three eat in silence, intensely chewing. This lasts a while. Finally...*)

SIMON: John, you say today is April fourteenth?

JOHN: It is.

SIMON: You know that puts us at Passover.

JOHN: Couldn't come at a better time.

CALEB: It comes every year at this time.

JOHN: You know what I'm talking about.

SIMON: I think he's talking about--

CALEB: I know what he means.

SIMON: --the fact that here we are this year, where we are this year, in the middle of all we are this year and Pesach happening at the same time.

JOHN: Why is this year different from all other years?

SIMON: It's a miracle, is what it is.

I noticed, Caleb, that you weren't praying with us when we said the blessing.

CALEB: *(eating)*

So?

SIMON: You forget your Hebrew?

CALEB: No.

SIMON: So, what then?

CALEB: I'm just not big on praying these days, Simon.

SIMON: Since when?

Caleb?

CALEB: Since Petersburg.

SIMON: Why?

CALEB: It's not important.

SIMON: I'd like to know.

CALEB: I said it's not important.

(Silence.)

SIMON: Yes, but still, I'd like to know.

CALEB: It's because I was at Petersburg and He most decidedly was not.

(Caleb goes back to eating. A brief silence, then:)

SIMON: God is not fond of fair-weather friends, Caleb.

CALEB: I don't need a sermon, Simon.

(John snickers.)

JOHN: "Sermon, Simon."

SIMON: No, you don't need a sermon. And you ain't gonna get one. Not from me, at least.

CALEB: Thank you.

(He returns to eating. Another brief silence and then:)

SIMON: But when your mamma finds out you gave up praying...

CALEB: This is starting to sound an awful lot like a sermon to me.

JOHN: It's a "simple Simon sermon!"

SIMON: I just don't understand how can you say you gave up praying just as easy as that, as if that was an easy thing to do.

CALEB: I'm not asking you to understand. I'm asking you to let me eat.

SIMON: But I want to understand, don't you see? You can eat and talk at the same time. God knows you've been doing it all your life.

(Caleb eats and doesn't look up.)

SIMON: We all pray in this house.

JOHN: Yes, we do.

SIMON: And not just on the high holy days, neither, like some families I could mention.

JOHN: The Solomons.

SIMON: Ooh.

JOHN: The Taylors.

SIMON: Yes!

JOHN: The Riveras!

SIMON: To mention just a few.

CALEB: That's enough! From both of you! I don't have to explain anything to either of you. ~~And I don't need a litany of all the under-observant Jews in Richmond.~~ I stopped praying, I stopped believing. It's as simple as that.

SIMON: ~~That is anything but simple. If you ask, He will provide.~~

CALEB: You don't think I asked? I did nothing but ask. For four years, I asked. At Petersburg, I asked. He was silent.

SIMON: ~~War is not proof of God's absence. It's proof of His absence from men's hearts.~~

JOHN: ~~And God didn't start this war, Caleb. You did.~~

CALEB: I did not start this war. I fought to defend my home.

JOHN: ~~From the look of things, I'd say you did a pretty lousy job of it.~~

CALEB: Don't you start with me on why this war was fought, John. You have no idea.

JOHN: ~~I think I may have an inkling.~~

CALEB: Why? Because you've read about it? The northern papers, the abolitionist pamphlets? Oh, yes. You've read all about it, haven't you? But you don't know. You have no idea what this was. I do. I could tell you, if you'd like. I've seen quite a bit these last four years. What have you seen? I was at Sharpsburg, Fredericksburg, Gettysburg. And all the places in between and since. Where were you? I've seen plantations. Have you? I've seen slaves breaking their backs in the fields. When have you ever even broken a sweat? The only cotton you've ever touched is resting comfortably on your back right now. I don't need a lecture from you about what this was. I know better than you do. I know what slavery was. I saw it. I know what war is. I lived it. What did you see? What did you live? I was starving to death at Petersburg and you were safe at home, reading novels. Yes, reading, John. And you have my mother to thank for that, don't forget.

JOHN: I taught myself how to read. Your mama taught me "ABCDEFG" and by the time she got to "H", your father had put a stop to it.

CALEB: Because it was against the law.

JOHN: I wonder if that was the reason. Already before she started to teach me, I was asking questions. Like when was God going to set us free like he did the slaves in Egypt. Or whether Nat Turner was our new Moses. That's when our lessons ended. But I kept reading. I pored over the books of the Torah. And I kept asking questions, if only to myself. You ever read Leviticus?

CALEB: You know I have.

JOHN: Then you'll remember this:

> "Both thy bondman and thy bondmaids, which thou shalt have, shall be of the heathen that are round about you; of them shall ye buy bondmen and bondmaids.
>
> They shall be your possession and ye shall take them for your children to inherit for themselves.
>
> They shall be your bondmen forever.
>
> But over your brethren, the children of Israel:
>
> Ye.
>
> Shall.
>
> Not.
>
> Rule."

You remember reading that?

CALEB: Not enough to memorize it.

JOHN: It certainly got me to thinking. Were we Jews or were we slaves? Were we the children of Israel or we just the heathen that were round about you? Because we couldn't be both, that was clear. And now you say you've given up praying just as easily as that. Because it was yours to discard if you wanted to. It was never ours. It was given to us and it could be taken away with just some careful reading of Leviticus.

SIMON: Is your faith that weak, John? Can't answer one question and it all falls apart?

JOHN: How do you square it, Simon?

SIMON: I can't. I can't square anything I don't understand. It ain't ours to square. That's why we always asking. Like you asked. Both of you asked your questions and sometimes you didn't get answers that you liked. But you kept on asking. That's what a Jew is. We talk with God, we argue with him. Sometimes we even wrestle with him. But we never stop asking, looking, hoping for answers. You don't lose your faith by not getting answers. You lose your faith by not asking questions at all. This is who we are. This is our family.

JOHN: This is not my family!

SIMON: Only family you know.

JOHN: Not by choice.

SIMON: Who chooses their family? Whether you like it or not, we are a family.

JOHN: How?

SIMON: We share a faith. And that faith came to us from Caleb's family.

JOHN: And how did that family treat us, Simon?

SIMON: Better than most.

JOHN: Not good enough.

SIMON: You know all the other slaves from round here. You know we had it a world better than they did. Coming here after your mamma died was the best thing that could have happened to you. You could have been sold to a plantation. You could have been sold to a Christian home. You ever think of that? You think they'da let you be a Jew in a Christian home? You think they'da led you be a Jew in any other Jewish home but this? Boy, you don't know how lucky you are to come from this house. You'da had nothing without it. Instead, you're sitting here quoting scripture. All on account of being brought up in this house.

JOHN: You don't know the first thing about this house.

SIMON: Boy, don't you question me on the history of this house. I could write the history of this house. I could write your history, too.

JOHN: If you could write.

SIMON: Don't need to write to tell your story. You know your story?

JOHN: Better than you.

SIMON: You could put the things you know inside the things you don't and still have room for more. You were born in this house. Did you know that?

JOHN: I wasn't born in this house.

SIMON: You see? Already something he don't know and we just gettin' started. You was born here in this house and then you and your mama was sold to old Mr. Mendez up on the North Side of town. That's how you started out. You was six when your mamma died. I get that right?

(John drinks.)

SIMON: I thought so. And Caleb's mama talked Mr. DeLeon into buying you back to have a mother in my Lizbeth and to be near young folks like Caleb and my Sarah. I remember the day you came here, grabbin' onto a nasty ol' dirty blanket and scared out your mind. But you and Caleb got to be like two peas in a pod. Didn't see one where you'd soon see the other. Always up in Caleb's room, reading your books. Playing out in the yard. Picking on my Sarah like young boys will do. Like two peas in a pod.

JOHN: It wasn't a friendship, Simon. Not when one friend owns the other. Orders him around. Sends him off for whippings.

(The air goes out of the room.)

SIMON: We ain't talking about whippings.

JOHN: Why not? We're talking about everything else. Why, if we were a family, did we get whipped like all the other slaves in town?

CALEB: My father only had his slaves whipped when it was absolutely necessary. He abhors the practice.

JOHN: Didn't stop him from practicing it.

CALEB: Sarah was never whipped. Lizbeth was never whipped. Simon was never whipped. So why were you? If we were so unfair, so malevolent, why were you the only one who was whipped and with so much regularity?

(Pause.)

JOHN: Lizbeth used to say to Sarah and me: "you listen to Mr. DeLeon. You do as you told. Or they gonna send you to the Whipping Man. The Whipping Man gonna take all the skin off your back." He was like the devil, the Whipping Man. Smelled of whiskey, sweat and shit, like he hadn't bathed in years. Probably hadn't. He'd pick up the slaves and put them in chains and take them to his shop. There were blood stains on the walls. And a large collection of bullwhips, too. He used them depending on his mood. First time I was sent there, he used a pearl handled bullwhip.
Didn't he, Caleb?

CALEB: John, you have said enough.

JOHN: Caleb and his father came with me the first time I was sent. Did you know that, Simon?

SIMON: I did.

JOHN: But do you know what happened once we got there?

CALEB: John.

JOHN: Mr. DeLeon felt things were getting too chummy around here between me and Caleb. Between us and the DeLeons. Felt Caleb didn't fully appreciate the true relationship between a master and his slave. So off we all went. To learn.
What happened first, Caleb? You remember?

(No answer from Caleb.)

JOHN: Caleb and his father stood in the corner and watched as the Whipping Man put me on my knees. Didn't you, Caleb? The Whipping Man took off my shirt. He attached my hands to two leather straps. And I was whipped.

(On "whipped," John stomps the floor with his foot then claps his hands together. The sound he makes is a rhythmic "boom-smack.")

(This hurts his injured hand. Perhaps the wound starts to re-open and bleed a bit through the bandage. But the pain is worth it to make this point.)

JOHN: And whipped.

(Boom-smack!)
And whipped.
(Boom-smack!)
And whipped.
(Boom-smack!)
Wasn't I, Caleb?
(Again, no answer.)

JOHN: Then in the middle of the whipping, I heard Caleb's voice. "Stop!" he yelled. "Stop!"

I thought to myself, "Caleb is saving me. Caleb is rescuing me. Caleb cares about me."

And then I heard Caleb say to his father, "I want to do it myself." The Whipping Man handed Caleb the pearl-handled bullwhip. And Caleb whipped me. Didn't you, Caleb? You whipped me.
(Boom-SMACK!)
And whipped me.
(Boom-SMACK!)
And whipped me.
(Boom-SMACK!)
(Boom-SMACK!)
(Boom-SMACK!)
(John walks to Caleb and crouches down in his face. They stare at one another for a moment.)

JOHN: That's when we stopped being as close as you remember, Simon.
(John grabs the bottle and exits to the kitchen.)
(Caleb and Simon sit in silence a moment.)

CALEB: What John said...what I did...

SIMON: You did what you did. We all did what we did.

CALEB: I threw up after. John doesn't know that. And I never went back.

SIMON: John did.

CALEB: My father, he--

SIMON: They ain't no reason to go into it no more.

CALEB: But I want you to know why I did it.

SIMON: You did it because you could. Simple as that.

CALEB: No, it's--

SIMON: Simple as that. John didn't do himself no favors by being, well, by being John. He sassed, he stole, he loafed. Once when you was off at the war, your father found out John was running a whole underground book exchange between all the slaves who could read, what little there were. Your father found John's hiding place in the cellar and you know what he did?

CALEB: Sent him to the Whipping Man?

SIMON: Made him put them in a wheelbarrow and marched him off to the library. Made him give them all away. Only day in that boy's life I ever seen him cry.

CALEB: Why didn't he just take them from him?

SIMON: 'cause he knew John'd just take 'em right back. And the library's the one place he knew a book would be safe from John's hands.

CALEB: John says my father promised you money when he returns. That true?

SIMON: It is.

CALEB: Well, that's good. That's very good.

SIMON: It is good, yes.

CALEB: Think he meant it?

SIMON: One thing I know about your Pa--and I know a bit--he says he's gonna do something, he's gonna do it. Sometimes it works out good for you, sometimes it don't. But he will do it.

CALEB: In that case, how do you plan on spending it?

SIMON: We gonna build a house, Lizbeth and me.

CALEB: A house, really? That's nice.

SIMON: Very nice, yes. Own something. Be something. Nothing too big. Lizbeth and Sarah've been taking care of this big house for so long, I think a small one to come home to every day might be just right. Lizbeth's been saving material for curtains for some time now. God only knows how many windows that woman plans on having. And Sarah, I think she wouldn't mind a small room of her own. A young lady should have her own room.

CALEB: And you?

SIMON: Me? I'd just be happy seeing them happy. Although, I do think I might like to own a chair. If there's any money left over. A nice, comfortable chair.

CALEB: Could I come visit you?

SIMON: We could probably make a space at the table for you. John, too.

CALEB: I don't think John plans to stay around too much longer.

SIMON: Where would John go?

CALEB: Says he's going up to New York.

SIMON: New York? Shoot, that's news to me. I'll believe that when I see it. John talks big, but John acts small.

CALEB: Says he's been planning it ever since my father told him about the money.

SIMON: Your father? He never told John nothing. I told John this morning about the money. Any plans he been making ain't more than a day old.

CALEB: Why would he lie?

SIMON: He is John.

CALEB: So after you've built your house and bought your chair--

SIMON: If there's money left over.

CALEB: If there's money left over. What then?

SIMON: Your father said we could work here, still. For wages. Me, Lizbeth and Sarah.

CALEB: You'd stay here?

SIMON: Ya'll still gonna need a cook, and a maid, and a...well, a Simon. Who else knows this house better than me?

CALEB: No one.

SIMON: You got that right. Shoot, ya'll can't afford to do without us. God knows you can't.

CALEB: It's good that you're staying. It'll be like before.
(Pause.)

SIMON: *(gently, but sternly)*
No. No it will not be like before.
(Pause.)

SIMON: Now, I know we ain't got all that much round here, despite what John's been bringin' in, but I am going to try and have a Seder tomorrow.

CALEB: A Seder?

SIMON: I was thinking God would forgive us if we're a little late this year, seeing as they's special circumstances and all.

CALEB: Simon, I can't. I just...can't anymore.

SIMON: Then don't. I'm not asking your permission. I'm telling you I'm going to have a Seder. I ain't missed a Seder in all my years. I'll be damned if I miss it this year.

CALEB: We'll send John out to steal a Haggadah.

SIMON: Already got me a Haggadah.

CALEB: You do?

SIMON: Gift from your granddaddy, long before you was born. I asked him if Lizbeth and I could have a seder in the kitchen while they were eatin' their meal and the first night of Passover that year, your grandaddy gave me a new Haggadah as a present. Only thing I ever owned in all my life.

CALEB: Can you read it?

SIMON: Not a word. But I have it.

CALEB: But you don't have anything for the ceremony.

SIMON: I've been thinking about that. I think we can make do. Ain't got no parsley but there's some celery growing out back.

CALEB: What about bitter herbs?

SIMON: Collard greens are pretty bitter, if you eat 'em raw.

CALEB: What about the wine?

SIMON: We can just use water. Wish we could make some Charoset. Apples are hard to come by these days. Do have eggs, though. John stole some this morning.

CALEB: Stolen eggs for your Seder. How perfect.

SIMON: None of this is exactly Kosher.

CALEB: And a shank bone.

SIMON: Well, we ain't yet had time to bury yours.

(He gestures to Caleb's leg.)

CALEB: You're joking.

SIMON: *(laughing)*
I'm just looking for ideas.

CALEB: Well, look elsewhere.

SIMON: I got the bones from that old horse. I can use one of those.

CALEB: And the matzah?

SIMON: I already thought of that. You know that hard, cracker stuff the soldiers used to carry with them? Made of flour and water and not much else?

CALEB: Hardtack?

SIMON: That's what it's called! Hardtack, yes!

CALEB: I've been choking down hardtack for four years, you want to serve it at a Seder?

SIMON: It's about as unleavened as you can get.

CALEB: Yeah, but where are we going to find hardtack at...?

(Simon reaches his pocket to remove a handkerchief wrapped around three pieces of hardtack.)

CALEB: Where'd you get that?

SIMON: Hospital. Union fella gave it to me before I left.

CALEB: You could have eaten that.

SIMON: I could have, yes. But then what would we have used for our Seder? No, this hardtack is special. We'll eat it tomorrow.

CALEB: You will.

SIMON: We will.

CALEB: We might.

(A moment, then Simon begins gathering up the dishes and silverware. As he does, John re-enters, drunker than before. He plays out Reveille on a pretend bugle.)

JOHN: On your foot, soldier!

(John laughs and drinks as Simon gathers up the plates and heads for the kitchen.)

JOHN: That's good, there, Simon. Clean all that up.

(Simon stops, looks at John. It is a powerful, withering look. It unnerves John. All the brio disappears for as long as Simon remains on stage. Simon slowly exits to the kitchen.)

JOHN: So we're having a Seder tomorrow?

CALEB: Seems that way.

JOHN: That seems right. That seems right and good that we do. Let's celebrate the freeing of the slaves. Out of Egypt. Out of Richmond. Maybe I'll become a rabbi.

CALEB: That's a sensible idea.

JOHN: You think?

CALEB: You'll have quite a congregation. All the Jewish Negroes in Virginia.

JOHN: I think there'd be enough for a minyan.

I could go to college. Up North. I could go to Harvard.

CALEB: You couldn't get in to Harvard.

JOHN: Then I probably shouldn't go.

Maybe I'll write a book. Like Frederick Douglass.

CALEB: Maybe you will.

JOHN: And maybe I'll even put you in it: Caleb Legree.

CALEB: You're enjoying this, aren't you?

JOHN: What?

CALEB: Settling scores.

JOHN: Is that what I'm doing?

CALEB: I don't know what you're doing. Why are you here?

JOHN: I'm waiting for my money.

CALEB: The money my father said he'd give you?

JOHN: That's right.

CALEB: Simon just told me that my father never said that to you.

JOHN: Did he?

CALEB: You only found out about it this morning when Simon told you.

JOHN: So?

CALEB: So you lied to me.

JOHN: So what if I did? I'm still here waiting for it, aren't I?

CALEB: But why did you come back here in the first place? I know why you're staying. I just don't understand why you came back.

JOHN: I live here.

CALEB: No, you don't. Not anymore. You're free, remember? And what makes you think you're going to see any of that money? Seems like if he meant to tell you, he would've. So why are you here, John? It's not for the money and it certainly isn't to reminisce.

JOHN: Where are all the other Confederate soldiers?

CALEB: I don't know what you're--

JOHN: Why are you here and no one else is? Why are you sneaking home in the middle of the night, riding a dead horse and there are no other Rebs in sight?

CALEB: Why's Freddy Cole lookin' for you? He do that to your hand?

JOHN: No. I cut it.

CALEB: On what?

JOHN: Piece of glass.

CALEB: Breaking into a home?

JOHN: Maybe.

CALEB: Maybe you should have Simon look at it.

JOHN: Maybe you should worry about your own wounds.

CALEB: Maybe the people who you robbed would want to know what you've been up to.

JOHN: If you could find them.

CALEB: They'll be back eventually.

JOHN: Maybe I'll be gone by then.

CALEB: Maybe my father would like to know what you've been up to.

JOHN: Maybe you'd like to know what he's been up to.

CALEB: You know something you're not telling me?

JOHN: Let me see your pardon.

CALEB: My--

JOHN: Your pardon. Officers and soldiers at Appomattox were paroled. If you were there like you said, you'd have a pardon. Piece of paper. Something.

CALEB: I--

JOHN: Where is it?

CALEB: It's hidden.

JOHN: Where?

CALEB: I'm not telling you.

JOHN: Show it to me.

CALEB: No.

JOHN: Why not?

CALEB: Because it's mine.

JOHN: You know what I think?

CALEB: I don't care what you think.

JOHN: I think you weren't anywhere near Appomattox. I think you surrendered long before the rest of your army did. I think you're a deserter.

CALEB: You can think whatever you want.

JOHN: I bet I can prove it, too. It's why you didn't want to go to the hospital, isn't it? You go there, someone's gonna figure out your story. So you have your surgery here. Have Simon care for your wounds, get you food. Oh and, of course, hide you if anyone comes looking for you. That about sum it up?

CALEB: You certainly are the expert on asking Simon to hide you from people who are looking for you. Aren't you, John?

(No answer from John.)

CALEB: And even if what you're saying were true, what difference does it make now? The war is over and--

JOHN: And your side lost and you weren't there when it happened. What about the men you abandoned, the men you were responsible for leading, Captain DeLeon? Deserting the army is one thing, but you deserted your men. They'll hang you from the nearest branch the second they find you.

CALEB: I'm home now. Even if they come here, Simon wouldn't give me up.

JOHN: What if Simon wasn't here?

CALEB: Where would he go?

JOHN: Let's say he goes out looking for Sarah and Lizbeth?

CALEB: Why would he do that? They're with my father.

(John slowly shakes his head "no.")

CALEB: What?

(No answer.)

CALEB: John?

(Still no answer.)

CALEB: Tell me, goddamnit!

JOHN: They're gone.

CALEB: They're with my father.

JOHN: No they are not. They. Are. Gone.

CALEB: Gone where?

JOHN: Sold.

(Dead silence.)

CALEB: You're lying.

JOHN: Your mother was gone. Simon was gone. And he sold them.

CALEB: No. No, that's, that's not possible.

JOHN: Of course it is. He owned them. He could sell them if he wanted to.

CALEB: But he wouldn't have.

JOHN: Why not?

CALEB: Because...

JOHN: Because we're family?

CALEB: No. No, that's not possible. Not Sarah. Not Elizbeth. No.

JOHN: I saw it with my own eyes. Watched them taken away. In chains. Caleb they are gone.

CALEB: Why would he do that?

JOHN: You can't think of a reason? Caleb? Why your father might not want Sarah in the house anymore?

CALEB: Did you tell my father?

JOHN: No.

CALEB: DID YOU TELL MY FATHER???

JOHN: I didn't have to. When was the last time you were home on leave?

CALEB: I don't remember.

JOHN: September. Seven months ago. Things started to become quite... apparent in that time.
    (Pause.)

CALEB: What are you saying?

JOHN: You know what I'm saying.
    (Pause.)

CALEB: Sarah is...?

JOHN: Sarah is.
    (This hits Caleb like a rocket to the chest.)

CALEB: Oh God, Sarah.
    (He buries his face in his hands.)

CALEB: She must have been so scared. This is my fault. This is all my fault. Sarah. My Sarah.

JOHN: Your Sarah?

CALEB: Why did he do it?

JOHN: He is a prominent man. And people do talk.

CALEB: Where are they?

JOHN: Who knows?

CALEB: Who bought them?

JOHN: A trader, headed west away from the Federals.

CALEB: He had to know the war was coming to an end.

JOHN: He didn't sell them for much.

CALEB: You've known all this time and said nothing?

JOHN: What do I owe you?

CALEB: What do you owe Simon? We have to tell him. He has to know.
Simon! Simon, get in here!

JOHN: He'll leave the second you tell him.

CALEB: He has to know.

JOHN: And then you're here, alone and helpless.

CALEB: Well, you--

JOHN: Well I what?

CALEB: You would leave me like this?

JOHN: I would leave you much worse.

CALEB: What are we going to do?

JOHN: We? We are not doing anything. We're not saying anything.

CALEB: But Sarah--

JOHN: If you tell Simon, he will leave. And when Simon leaves, I leave.
That I promise. And then you're on your own. And you will die. Can
you feed yourself? Clean your wound? Hide from anyone who might
be out there lookin' for you? Can you do that?
(Caleb has no answer.)

JOHN: We wait like we have been. We let your father tell Simon when he
gets home. If he gets home.

CALEB: They'll be long gone by then.

JOHN: They're long gone already.
(Simon enters.)

SIMON: Caleb? You wanted something?
(Pause.)

CALEB: Nothing, Simon. I'm sorry.

End of Act 1

ACT 2, SCENE 1

Caleb stands on both feet, facing us.

CALEB: My dearest Sarah:
This is my twenty-fifth letter to you. I fear it will be my last. I do not know what the next few days will bring but the indications are not encouraging. I have only a few minutes and a few pieces of paper to write down all my thoughts.

I am--as I have been for the past two hundred and ten days--sitting in a trench just outside Petersburg, up to my waist in putrid mixture of water, excrement and blood. I am frozen. I am hungry. I am achingly weary.

I woke this morning to a corpse staring at me. He was alive when I fell asleep and today he is blue and lifeless. No one yet has had the strength to remove him. They will do that here: leave a body in place until the rats discover him and only then will they move him to where the other bodies are stacked up. There is no burial in a trench. We are already buried. My men pray daily to God and daily he ignores their prayers.

But oh my Sarah, despite all this, I can still cast my mind back to my last night at home, the last time we were together and the hours we spent, willing the night to fight back the day. How gentle you were with me, despite the roughness the war has caused in me. How effortlessly you smoothed out all my coarseness. How great the calm was that came over me when I was with you. You are home to me. You are warmth.

Were I granted one wish, it would be to grow great wings and to fly far from this place. I would fly over these battlefields, this scarred earth, over armies and governments and wars and cannons until I was back home with you. And books. And fires. And silence.

But daily these thoughts move further and further from me. They recede from my grasp, from my vision, from my mind. These letters are the only things that keep them from disappearing altogether. I want to place them in your hands and watch as you read the words of love I have written only for you. I want your eyes to fall upon them and know their meaning. Know my meaning. Know me. Know me. Know me. I remain now and forever,
Yours.

End of Scene 1

ACT 2, SCENE 2

The next evening. Saturday, April 15, 1865.
The rain continues.
The room is now filled with even more possessions from the neighboring homes: a chandelier, rolls of carpets, paintings and furniture and stacks of silverware. The book collection has grown considerably. There are also more candles about, some in lamps, others bare.
John enters, holding Caleb's packet of letters, reading aloud from the fifteenth.

JOHN: "I long to return home and place them in your hands and teach you how to read the words of love I have written only for you. I want your eyes to fall upon them and know their meaning. Know my meaning. Know me. Know me. Know me."
(The sound of his voice stirs Caleb awake. He catches the end of it, slow at first to register that it's his letter John's reading from.)

JOHN: Pretty flowery stuff, Caleb.

CALEB: Give that to me.

JOHN: Come and take it.

CALEB: You had no right to go through my things.

JOHN: No, I didn't. And yet--
(He holds them up, taunting.)

CALEB: Give them to me, goddamnit. They are not yours.

JOHN: They are not yours, either. They are Sarah's.

CALEB: Those are personal and private.
(John opens another letter.)

JOHN: "My Dearest Sarah, I- -

CALEB: John!
(Caleb starts to get up. Pain zips up his leg. He screams and falls back, fighting the tears that are welling up inside him. These are not tears of pain. Much deeper than that. He fights them off and lays there panting and defeated.)

CALEB: How long are we going to lie to him?

JOHN: That depends on you, I guess.

CALEB: They are out there, John. Sarah and Elizabeth. With my child. He needs to know.

JOHN: Then tell him. And let him go and find them. I'll glad take you to the hospital. Why don't we just grab your pardon and go?
(Silence from Caleb.)

JOHN: Now, if you don't mind, I have a Seder to prepare.

You want a book to read?

CALEB: I want my letters back. Please.

(John looks them over then tosses them to Caleb. Caleb flips through them to make sure they're all there. John continues setting up.)

(There is a noise outside. John and Caleb both freeze. Caleb reaches for something to use as a weapon and tosses it to John, who slowly approaches the door, wielding it. A tense moment. Who is it? The door opens. It is Simon.)

(John instantly relaxes. He and Simon just stare at each other a moment.)

JOHN: Evenin'.

(Simon stands there, motionless.)

JOHN: I set up for the Seder, like you asked.

SIMON: I see that, thank you.

JOHN: It's almost dark. We should probably start soon.

SIMON: Yes.

JOHN: Well, you just gonna stand there or are you gonna come in?

(Pause.)

SIMON: The President's dead.

JOHN: What?

CALEB: Which?

SIMON: President Lincoln. He's dead.

JOHN: How?

SIMON: Shot. Last night. At a theatre. He's gone.

(Silence.)

SIMON: I wouldn't have believed it if I hadn't heard it with my own ears. Right there in the middle of the market, fella rides up and just says it. Announces it like he's callin' a dance. Folks started cheering and whooping. Dancin'. Town started going crazy. Crazier than it's been last few weeks, even. All them folks was so happy. The white folks, anyway. It's crazy out there now. The Federals are all over the place now. More comin' in all the time. They think he come to Richmond, the one who did it. They're blockin' the roads, all the ins and outs. No one's going nowhere 'til they find him.

And Father Abraham is gone.

I met him just the other day, when he came into Richmond.

JOHN: You met Abraham Lincoln?

SIMON: He was a sight to see. Just as tall as they said. Taller. He wore a hat that stretched up to the sky. Made him all that much taller. But when he walked, his shoulders was rounded and he slouched a bit, like he was scared of being up so high. It didn't matter, though. That man had height to spare. He looked to be two hundred years old. His eyes were sunk down in his face and his wrinkles was deeper than any I've ever seen on a man. Like someone took a knife and carved them in. He had a whole crowd of folks around him. Colored folks. They followed him and touched him and kissed his hands. No one had to tell me who he was. Even if I hadn't seen his picture before, I still woulda known. Proudest day of my life. He was coming towards where I was standing. I walked to him. And I stopped right in front of him. And he stopped. And we looked at each other.

JOHN: What'd you do?

SIMON: I bowed.

JOHN: You bowed?

SIMON: Only thing I could think to do.

JOHN: What did he do?

SIMON: He bowed back. Only thing he could think to do, I guess. That was a great man. Father Abraham. Father Abraham, who set us free. There's your Moses, John.

It is only now that we notice that this news has affected Caleb strongly. Indeed, he is silently weeping. One of his sobs becomes audible, getting both Simon and John's attention.

JOHN: What are you blubbering about?

(Caleb cannot answer, he is now sobbing so hard. John just stares. Simon feels compelled to move to him. As soon as he gets close enough, Caleb grabs him and pulls him closer, as if to be saved from drowning.)

CALEB: I'm sorry! I'm sorry, I'm sorry, I'm sorry.

SIMON: Shh...

CALEB: I'm sorry.

SIMON: 'bout what?

CALEB: I'm so, I'm so sorry.

SIMON: It's okay, there. It's okay. Ain't your fault, Caleb. Ain't your fault there's madmen in the world. That ain't your fault.

CALEB: Simon, I'm sorry, I'm sorry.

SIMON: It's okay. It's okay. Calm yourself. Calm yourself. Wash it all away. Like this rain. Wash it all away and start all over.

(Silence a moment as Caleb calms down.)

SIMON: There. That's better. I'm gonna get you some water.

(Simon stands.)

SIMON: John, why don't you finish setting up? Then we'll be ready to start.

JOHN: Okay, Simon.

(Simon exits to the kitchen. John watches him go. Silence a beat.)

JOHN: Careful, Caleb.

CALEB: We have to tell him.

JOHN: Go on and tell him, then. Open his eyes. Then open your own. Did you even hear what he said? The town is crawling with Federal soldiers now, 'cause of Lincoln. You want to be brought to them without a pardon in your hand? Road block in and out of town? Nowhere to go, Caleb. You best make do with what you got here.

CALEB: John, we need to--

(Simon re-enters with a Haggadah and a mason jar of water, which he hands to Caleb.)

JOHN: We need to get started, Simon.

(Simon hands John the Haggadah.)

SIMON: Take this, John. Read along in case I forget. I'm gonna be jumping around a bit. Just make sure I stay on the tracks.

JOHN: You forgot something, Simon.

SIMON: What's that?

(John produces a bottle of wine from his sack.)

SIMON: You discover that, too?

JOHN: Nah, Simon. This I stole.

SIMON: It's already opened.

JOHN: I had to find out if it was any good.

SIMON: Fine, then.

(He gestures for John to place it on the table setting.)

SIMON: Was hoping to find an apple for Kharoset. Something to stand in for mortar. Couldn't find nothing. But I guess this'll do.

(He pulls out a brick from his sack.)

SIMON: We can't eat it but it means the same.

(He sets the brick down on the table setting.)

SIMON: Well, let's start.

Caleb?

CALEB: Yeah?

SIMON: You gonna do this with us?

CALEB: If you'll let me.

SIMON: All are welcome. Good, good.

(Simon moves to the place setting and sits. He takes the wine and pours a small amount into each of the three glasses.)

SIMON: All right, then.

(Simon holds up his glass. Caleb and John follow suit.)

SIMON: "Behold this, the first of our four cups of wine. Let it be a symbol of our joy tonight as we celebrate the festival of Pesach."

(He sets the wine down.)

SIMON: "Praised be you, O Lord our God, King of the Universe, who creates the fruit of the vine. Praised be you, O Lord our God, King of the Universe, who has sanctified us by his commandments."

JOHN: Well done, Simon.

SIMON: Not bad for an old man, huh?

JOHN: Not bad at all.

SIMON: I have no idea what comes next.

JOHN: "As a token of your love..."

SIMON: Yes! "As a token of your love, O Lord our God, you have given us occasions for rejoicing, festivals and holidays for happiness, this Feast of Unleavened Bread, the season of our liberation from bondage in Egypt. Praised be you Lord who sanctifies the people of Israel and the festival seasons. Praised be you, O Lord our God, King of the universe, who has kept us in life, and sustained us, and enabled us to reach this day."

(aside, to John)

If only by the skin of our teeth.

JOHN: Amen.

SIMON: That's right.

(They sit there a moment, waiting for Simon to drink.)

JOHN: You're supposed to drink, Simon.

SIMON: I know.

CALEB: Do you drink?

SIMON: Not a drop in all my life.

(John reaches for it but Simon bats his hand away and takes the glass himself. He looks at it and brings it to his lips. He lets the wine slide down this throat. It tastes like freedom. He closes his eyes. Caleb and John drink their wine.)

SIMON: *(sings)*

WHEN ISRAEL WAS IN EGYPT'S LAND,

LET MY PEOPLE GO!

OPPRESSED SO HARD THEY COULD NOT STAND,

LET MY PEOPLE GO!

GO DOWN, MOSES,

WAY DOWN IN EGYPT'S LAND.

TELL OL' PHARAOH,

LET MY PEOPLE GO!

(Simon then takes the celery off the plate and hands them to John and Ca-

leb, keeping one for himself. They dip them in the salt water.)

SIMON: Praised be you, O Lord our God, King of the Universe who creates the fruit of the Earth.

(They eat the celery.)

SIMON: Caleb, break the hardtack now and read some.

(Caleb picks up the middle piece of hardtack and breaks it in two. John hands him the Haggadah. As Caleb reads, Simon leans back, great satisfaction on his face. He continues to hum the verse of "Go Down, Moses.")

CALEB: "Behold the mazzah, the Bread of Poverty which our ancestors--"

SIMON: Whose ancestors?

CALEB: Our ancestors.

SIMON: Yes, sir.

CALEB: "--our ancestors ate in their affliction, when they were slaves in the land of Egypt. Let- -"

SIMON: "Let all who are hungry come and eat. Let all who are in need come celebrate Pesach. This year we are slaves, next year we may be free." Next year we *will* be free.

(sung)

TELL OLD PHARAOH,

LET MY PEOPLE GO!

(spoken)

Mah nishtanah, ha-laylah ha-zeh, mi-kol ha-leylot.

Phonectic pronunciation: "MAH Neesh-tah-NAH / hah-LIE-lah hah-ZEH / mee-KOL hah-lay-LOAT." Translation: "Why is this night different from all other nights?"

CALEB: You can't ask the questions, Simon, that's my job.

JOHN: I'm the youngest. I should ask.

SIMON: I'll ask. I wanna see if you have any answers for me. A child has questions. A man has answers.

On all other nights we eat either leavened or unleavened bread; why on this night are we eating this hardtack? Caleb?

CALEB: Because our ancestors left Egypt in such a hurry, there was no time for the dough to rise. The first Seder was improvised, like ours.

SIMON: Imagine that.

SIMON: John, on all other nights we eat all kinds of herbs. Why, on this night, do we eat only bitter herbs?

JOHN: To remind us of the bitterness of slavery. As if we needed reminding.

SIMON: Your children will. And their children will. We must not forget. Your children must be taught. Yours too, Caleb.

On all other nights we do not dip any food in any other, even once. Why on this night do we dip twice: the celery in the salt water?

CALEB: To remind us of the tears of slavery.

SIMON: And if we had any Kharoset?

JOHN: To remind us that sweetness can come from bitterness.

SIMON: On all other nights we eat sitting up at the table; why, on this night, do we recline?

JOHN: Because reclining, because rest, is the symbol of the free man.

SIMON: *(sung)*

GO DOWN, MOSES,
WAY DOWN IN EGYPT'S LAND.

(spoken)

Tonight we celebrate the dream and the hope of freedom. The dream and the hope that have filled the hearts of men from the time our Israelite ancestors went forth out of Egypt.

(sung)

TELL OLD PHARAOH,
LET MY PEOPLE GO!

(spoken)

People have suffered and sacrificed to make this dream come true. Father Abraham sacrificed. He sacrificed all he had. Father Abraham. Our American Moses! Lead us from toil and bondage but was not allowed to enter our promised land. Father Abraham. Father Abraham. Father Abraham.

JOHN: That's right.

SIMON: Yes, sir. Father Abraham gave his life to the struggle for freedom and now we must dedicate ours. Though the sacrifice be great and the hardships many, we won't rest until the chains that enslave all men be broken.

CALEB: Broken.

SIMON: *(triumphant singing)*

LET MY PEOPLE GO!

(spoken)

But bein' free means more than just broken chains, you know that, right? It means being free from anything that breaks your spirit or muddies your mind. Because there's more than just one way a man can be a slave. How else?

(Silence from them.)

SIMON: Come on, now.

(Still nothing.)

SIMON: How 'bout all that drinking you been doing, John?

JOHN: What about it?

SIMON: I know that muddies your mind. You a slave to your bottle. How 'bout you, Caleb?

CALEB: I don't know, Simon.

SIMON: Sure you do.

CALEB: I don't think I--

SIMON: How 'bout your leg, there? You're forever branded, just like a slave. You a slave to your old ideas.

(Simon lets this land with Caleb for a moment.)

SIMON: How deeply those enslavements have scarred the world! The wars!

CALEB: Yes.

SIMON: The destruction!

CALEB: Yes.

SIMON: The suffering! The waste!

CALEB: *(more to himself)*
My God, the waste.

SIMON: Pesach calls us to be what?

CALEB: Free.

SIMON: Pesach calls us to freedom. FREEDOM!

CALEB: Freedom.

SIMON: Let freedom ring in this house!

JOHN: Yes, sir.

SIMON: Let freedom ring in this city!

JOHN: Mmmhmm.

SIMON: Let freedom ring in this nation!

JOHN: That's right.

SIMON: Sing it with me.
(sung)
GO DOWN, MOSES!
WAY DOWN IN EGYPT'S LAND.
SIMON & JOHN: (sung)
TELL OL' PHARAOH,
LET MY PEOPLE GO.

SIMON: Okay, good. Let's get back to reading. Caleb, read.
(Caleb hesitates, the takes up the book again.)

CALEB: "Once we were slaves to Pharaoh in Egypt, but the Lord, our God, brought us forth with a strong hand and an outstretched arm. If God had not brought our ancestors out of Egypt, we and our children and our children's children might still be enslaved..."

(He hesitates.)

SIMON: Go on.

JOHN: Caleb.

(Caleb is silent a moment longer.)

CALEB: He sold them.

SIMON: What?

CALEB: He sold them.

SIMON: Sold? Who?

CALEB: Sarah and Elizabeth.

(An eternity.)

SIMON: No.

CALEB: It's true.

SIMON: No.

CALEB: I'm sorry.

SIMON: NO!!!

Why?

WHY!!!

CALEB: She was--

SIMON: WHY?!?

CALEB: She was expecting.

SIMON: Expecting?

CALEB: Yes.

SIMON: Yours?

(Caleb is taken aback by this question.)

CALEB: Yes.

(He gets in Caleb's face.)

SIMON: Where'd they go?

CALEB: I don't know.

SIMON: WHERE'D THEY GO?!?

CALEB: I don't know, I promise you, Simon, I don't.

SIMON: Who bought them?

(Silence.)

SIMON: WHO BOUGHT THEM!!

(Simon grabs Caleb's wound and applies pressure.)

SIMON: You think I'm playin' around?

CALEB: John, tell him!!

SIMON: John?

(He lets go of Caleb and swings violently around, setting his sights on John.)

SIMON: You knew about this?

JOHN: Simon--

SIMON: You knew about this?

(Simon grabs the brick and then John and pins him against the wall, shaking him as he speaks, the brick hovering perilously close to John's skull.)

SIMON: Three days. Three days you knew they was sold and you said NOTHING?

JOHN: Simon, I--

SIMON: You said NOTHING? Three days I coulda been out looking for my family. You said NOTHING.

JOHN: Simon--

SIMON: Where'd they go?

JOHN: I don't know.

SIMON: Who has them?

JOHN: I don't know!

SIMON: Why you keep it from me?

JOHN: Simon, I--

SIMON: WHAT HAPPENED??

JOHN: It was the day Richmond fell. He sold Elizabeth and Sarah -

SIMON: Oh, God!!!

JOHN: --and I tried to stop him. So he sent me to the Whipping Man andandand in the middle of the whipping, thestrapthestrap, the leather strap--

SIMON: (shakes him)
     What about it?

JOHN: It was old, brittle. It just snapped, snapped off. And I grabbed the whip from him, as it was coming to me. Right out of the air, Simon, and I snatched it from him. I don't know why I did it.

SIMON: And?

JOHN: Andandandandandand I whipped him.

SIMON: John...

JOHN: Likelike he whipped me.

SIMON: John...

JOHN: Hehehe was on the ground. Andand I took the handle--the pearl the pearl handle he used on me--and I beat him with it.

SIMON: John...

JOHN: I beat him and beat him and beat him.
     And I I killed him.
     I killed the Whipping Man, Simon.
     I killed him.

SIMON: John, John, John...

JOHN: Freddy walked in, Freddy saw me. I ran. Freddy saw. Freddy saw.

SIMON: You are a dead man, you know that.

JOHN: Simon, I'm scared. Please, Simon...

CALEB: That's why you've done all this. It's because you can't leave, can you?

JOHN: And what have you been doing all this time?

(to Simon)

Caleb, here...the reason he's so afraid to go to the hospital--

SIMON: I don't need no explanations from you. Two lying, deceitful peas in a pod.

JOHN: I was scared, Simon. I had no choice.

SIMON: No. You're free now. For the first time in your life, you do have a choice. You had a choice and you made a choice. When you was beating that man to death, you made a choice. When you hid from Freddy Cole, you made a choice. When you lied to me about my family, you made a choice. I see the choices you made. They tell me all I need to know about the man you are, about the free man you gonna be. You don't get to be free, you work to be free. It's what we been praying for tonight. What you should have learned from all your reading. Were we Jews or were we slaves? I know what you are. You ain't no Jew. You ain't even a man. You just a nigger, John. Nigger, Nigger, Nigger John.

CALEB: Simon, I'm sorry.

SIMON: What good your sorries gonna do me? Your sorries gonna bring back my family?

CALEB: No.

SIMON: Then keep them. I don't need them.

CALEB: I loved her.

SIMON: YOU OWNED HER!

You loved her? How did you love her, Caleb? Like a dog. You love a dog, you feed a dog. But when he acts up, you also--

(boom-SMACK!)

--beat a dog. You might have thought you loved Sarah but you also owned her. And if this hadn't all just happened, you would have owned your baby, too. You would have owned your own child, Caleb.

CALEB: No, that's not how it was.

SIMON: You don't know how it was. You don't know what this was. You don't have any idea. This is what this was.

(Simon takes off his shirt to reveal a horrible patchwork of scars on his back from various whippings through his life.)

SIMON: You see this? From the Whipping Man. Your father sent me. And your grandfather, too. I got your family tree right here on my back. You see? This is your legacy. This is your family's legacy.

CALEB: Simon.

(Simon grabs his hat and coat, a rucksack and his rifle.)

SIMON: I'm leaving. I'm going off to find my family. My wife. My daughter. My grandchild. I lost too much time. God only knows where they might be.

CALEB: It's dark, Simon.

SIMON: Yes, it is. But I will be going.

CALEB: The roadblocks.

SIMON: Let them try and stop me.

(Simon starts to exit. John grabs him by the arm.)

JOHN: Simon, wait.

SIMON: What?

JOHN: Take me with you.

SIMON: Take yourself.

JOHN: I can't.

SIMON: How is that my problem?

JOHN: Freddy's after me.

SIMON: You got to solve this on your own, boy.

JOHN: I can't stay here.

SIMON: Then leave.

JOHN: I can't leave.

SIMON: Then stay.

JOHN: I can't! Simon, please! I don't know where to go. I don't know what to do.

SIMON: You're free now.

JOHN: BUT WHAT AM I SUPPOSED TO DO????

(Simon stops and looks at both of them.)

SIMON: Looks like you two need each other. Both of you need help from each other.

JOHN: I won't help him.

SIMON: Well, that is your choice, ain't it? Help him, don't help him. Stay here, don't stay. Ain't my problem no more. Two peas in a pod.

CALEB: Simon...

(Simon takes his Haggadah.)

SIMON: I wouldn't feel too badly if I were you, Caleb. You ain't the only man in your family to have a baby with a slave. It's time you knew that fact. Things don't change that much from father to son. That much I can see.

Or, I guess, from brother to brother.

That much I can see now, too.

(Simon slowly begins exiting.)

SIMON: When the Lord returns the exiles of Zion, we will have been like dreamers.

JOHN: Simon...

SIMON: Then our mouths will be filled with laughter, and our tongues with joyous song.

JOHN: Simon, please!

SIMON: Then will they say among the nations, "The Lord has done great things for them."

CALEB: Simon...

SIMON: Next year in Freedom!

NEXT YEAR IN JERUSALEM!!!

Simon exits.

John walks to the open door and stands there, watching Simon leave. He charges back into the house and grabs a sack and starts filling it with some of his stolen goods. He heads for the door but stops as he reaches it. He wants to leave but he can't.

John throws the sack to the ground then stalks around the room for a moment, finally grabbing a whiskey bottle and sitting down on the floor to take a drink. After a long moment, he offers the bottle to Caleb. Caleb takes the bottle and drinks, then hands the bottle back to John.

They pass the bottle between themselves.

The rain continues.

The lights slowly fade on them.

END OF PLAY

THINNER THAN WATER

Melissa Ross

PLAYWRIGHTS BIOGRAPHY

Melissa Ross' plays include *Crazy Little Thing, For Dear Life, Thinner Than Water, A Life Extra Ordinary, Do Something Pretty* and *You Are Here.* She has received readings and workshops at 24Seven Lab, Cherry Lane Theater, Dorset Theater Festival, Electric Pear Productions, Labyrinth Theater Company, Manhattan Theater Club, South Coast Repertory, and Rattlestick Playwrights Theater. Melissa is a graduate of Bennington College and the Lila Acheson Wallace American Playwrights Program at The Juilliard School, a two time recipient of the Le Comte Du Nouy Award from Lincoln Center, and a proud member of Labyrinth Theater Company.

ORIGINAL PRODUCTION

Thinner Than Water was originally produced by Labyrinth Theater Company (Stephen Adly Guirgis, Mimi O'Donnell, Yul Vázquez, Artistic Directors: Danny Feldman, Managing Director) in February 2011. It was directed by Mimi O'Donnell; the set design was by Lee Savage; the costume design was by Frederick Tilley III; the lighting design was by Japhy Weideman; the sound design was by Jeremy J. Lee; and the production stage manager was Pamela Salling. The cast was as follows:

Renee	Elizabeth Canavan
Gary	Alfredo Narciso
Cassie	Lisa Joyce
Gwen	Dierdre O'Connell
Henry	Aaron Roman Weiner
Angela	Megan Mostyn-Brown
Mark	David Zayas
Benjy	Stephen Ellis

For Rubin

CHARACTERS
The Family

Renee . . . . Early Forties. Martin's Oldest Daughter
Gary . . . . Mid Thirties. Martin's Only Son
Cassie . . . . Late Twenties. Martin's Youngest Child
Gwen . . . . Early Fifties. Quite possibly Martin's True Love

The Others

Angela . . . . Mid Twenties. A really great mom of a really great kid.
Henry . . . . Mid thirties. Cassie's Boyfriend.
Benjy . . . . Mid Twenties. Gary's Co-Worker
Mark . . . . Mid Forties. Renee's Husband

PLACE
A suburb and an adjacent city.

TIME
The Present

A BRIEF NOTE

A slash in the middle of a line indicates when the next character should begin speaking. The two lines should overlap.

The play should move rather quickly. Beats are quick shifts in thought. And internal punctuation inside of a sentence should serve as a guide for emphasis and intention and not considered true stops.

THINNER THAN WATER

ACT ONE, SCENE ONE

Renee Cassie and Gary in a suburban living room. There is a birthday cake.

RENEE: I can't BELIEVE he called YOU!!!!

CASSIE: You're overreacting!

RENEE: I am not/overreacting!

CASSIE: It's not that big a *deal!* You are *making* it into a / *bigger* deal than you.

RENEE: *I* am not *making* it into anything.

CASSIE: OK.

RENEE: It's *insulting.*

CASSIE: OK.

RENEE: It is *borderline* disrespectful.

CASSIE: OK.

RENEE: Stop it.

CASSIE: Stop *what?*

RENEE: That!

CASSIE: What did I say??? I said OK!! I'm *agreeing*/with you!

RENEE: It's your *tone.*

CASSIE: My tone??? My. Gary? Can you help/me please!

GARY: Not getting involved.

CASSIE: You *suck.*

GARY: Sorry. You're on your own with this one.

RENEE: I'll tell you why. It's because you had the hot mom.

CASSIE: *Excuse* me???

RENEE: Your mom was the hot mom. Gary's mom was the fat mom.

GARY: My mom's not fat!

RENEE: *(Dismissing him.)* Please. And my mom was the pain in the ass. *(Gary laughs.)* What?

GARY: Nothing.

CASSIE: My *mom* -

RENEE: Was hot. And is dead. Dead hot mom trumps fat mom and pain in the ass mom.

CASSIE: Are we really having this conversation?

GARY: Unfortunately yes./Yes we are.

RENEE: I'm just trying to find some *logic* here. Trying to find a little *sense* in the *insanity.*

CASSIE: Are you asking me to *apologize* because my mom's *dead*???

RENEE: Don't be ridiculous. *(Beat.)* Who *actually* called you?

CASSIE: The girlfriend

RENEE: You *talked* to her? She *exists?*

CASSIE: She's not a Yeti.

RENEE: I *know* that. *(Beat.)* What's she like?

CASSIE: I donno. She's fine./She's OK.

RENEE: She must be stupid.

CASSIE: Jesus! I knew you/were gonna.

RENEE: Knew what?

CASSIE: I *knew* you were gonna react/like this.

RENEE: You "knew"???? Gimmie a/fucking break.

CASSIE: GOOD GOD! Could you let me finish a fucking *sentence????* Could you let me *talk* for a minute for a *second* before *interrupting* me!!!

RENEE: Sorry. Go ahead. Talk it out. You have the conch shell.

CASSIE: *(Beat.)* Taking. A break.

RENEE: *(Pause.)* I can understand not calling him.

GARY: Excuse/me?

RENEE: He's over 30 and still lives with his fat mom.

GARY: He is also in the room.

RENEE: Whatever.

GARY: I'm saving!

RENEE: For what? A new bong?

GARY: How'd I get dragged into this????

RENEE: You date *underage* girls!!!

GARY: They are not underage!!!

RENEE: In *Georgia* maybe!!!

GARY: Why is this about me????

RENEE: *I* am the one you call in case of an emergency! I'M THE ONE YOU CALL!

GARY: OBVIOUSLY NOT ALL THE TIME!!!!

RENEE: *(Beat.)* I am a mom. *(Gary walks to the window, opens it and lights a cigarette.)* When you are making an "In Case of Emergency" list. And you are choosing who goes first. Are you smoking?

GARY: Is that a real question?

RENEE: (????)

GARY: I mean. Do you really want me to answer you? Are you *genuinely* confused?

RENEE: Stop being an asshole. And you're choosing between a pothead who lives in a garage, a temp and a MOM. You pick /THE FUCK-ING MOM!

CASSIE: Freelancer!

RENEE: Excuse me?

CASSIE: I'm not a *temp*. I'm a *freelancer*.

RENEE: Do you have *health insurance?*

CASSIE: *No.*

RENEE: Is it a *permanent job?*

CASSIE: It's freelancing. It's. I don't have to defend my career to you!

RENEE: *(A little laugh.)* Career?

CASSIE: They happen to love me at my job.

RENEE: Did I say they didn't?

CASSIE: It was your *"tone"*.

RENEE: *(Beat.)* What does Henry think about this?

CASSIE: This isn't about Henry.

RENEE: Henry has a level head. Henry. I'm sure Henry thinks/this is ridiculous.

CASSIE: I don't want to talk about Henry!

RENEE: OK…

CASSIE: He's not family. He's my boyfriend. He's not. I don't care what Henry/ thinks. OK? OK?

RENEE: Fine. OK. OK! *(Long pause.)* It's my fucking birthday.

CASSIE: I *know*…

RENEE: You call me up. Tell me you and Gary wanna come by. I was so excited that someone remembered. *(Beat.)* I hadda get my own cake.

CASSIE: I know./I'm really sorry.

RENEE: Mark's out of town. The kids're at school. I was gonna be spending my birthday alone/and then you called.

CASSIE: I said I'm sorry Renee. Do you want a kidney?

RENEE: Sure. Why not. *(Beat.)* You couldn't have waited a day? *(Long pause.)* What's wrong with him?

CASSIE: Cancer.

RENEE: What kind?

CASSIE: Lung.

RENEE: Ha! That's *brilliant. (Gary puts the cigarette out and throws it out the window.)* Did you just throw a cigarette butt out on my lawn?

GARY: Yup.

RENEE: That's lovely. Thank you, Gary.

GARY: You're very welcome Renee.

RENEE: *(Beat.)* So not only do I not get the call. But then. I get the honor of picking up the/pieces anyway.

CASSIE: Oh my god! LET IT FUCKING GO!!! *(to Gary)* Can you *please* help me???

GARY: Don't look at me. I live in a garage.

RENEE: Why doesn't the girlfriend take care of him?

CASSIE: She is. She works. She needs help.

RENEE: So why doesn't she get him a nurse

CASSIE: He doesn't want/a nurse.

RENEE: Doesn't want? Well wow. I don't always *want* to stick my finger up my husband's ass. But you know what? I do it anyway.

GARY: Unnecessary/ visual.

CASSIE: He doesn't want a nurse!

RENEE: I DON'T CARE WHAT HE *WANTS!!* YOU TELL HIM HE EITHER GETS A FUCKING NURSE OR HE SITS IN HIS OWN STINKING PISS UNTIL HE *DIES!* *(Long pause.)* He is *not* a good person. You are making him into something tragic. You're making him sad and old and sick and helpless. He's not. He's a shitty human being. And he's drowning. And there's a shark eating his leg. And he picked the weakest link out of the three of us to save him because *that* was his best shot and because if nothing else. The man has good survival skills. *That's* why he called you. Because he knew that if he called me? I'dve hung up on his ass.

CASSIE: Maybe you're right./Maybe he's.

RENEE: No not maybe.

CASSIE: All right. *Fine.* Not maybe. He is a cockroach on a toilet. OK? OK? So. So *be* the better person Renee. *Win* the better person contest. Sit around and watch him smoke himself to death and then send him off to hell with a big fat debt to you. Kill him. With fucking kindness. *(Pause.)* Look. I know you hate him. I get it. And you have good reasons to. But. *(Beat.)* This is something I need to do. And so. If you could/help me.

RENEE: It is always something.

CASSIE: This is the last time. This is the last time I will ask you for *anything.* I promise. I swear. This is it. You can hold me to it. OK? This is the last time.

RENEE: *(Pause.)* What would I have to do?

CASSIE: They need about fifteen hours a week. I figure we can each do five.

GARY: Wait. I've gotta do this too? I can't do this/right now.

RENEE: I need to be home by three when my kids come home from school.

CASSIE: Yeah OK./That's fine.

GARY: Did you hear me??? I can't do this. I've got stuff going on.

RENEE: What kind of stuff.

GARY: *(Beat.)* Personal. Stuff.

RENEE: If we can do it - you can do it.

GARY: This/fucking sucks.

RENEE: *(to Cassie)* You owe me. And if you. You know. Flake out? If you forget. If you lay this/all on me?

CASSIE: I promise I won't.

RENEE: You will not. You will not flake out, Cassie./If you flake out?

CASSIE: I promise. I promise you/I'm not gonna.

RENEE: I have heard this before.

CASSIE: I mean it this time. I swear. I am getting my shit together.

RENEE: Your *shit?* Your *shit* is spread out over the *Interstate.*

CASSIE: I know.

RENEE: You are gonna need a *UHaul* to get your/*shit* together.

CASSIE: I know!

RENEE: So. Good luck with that. *(Pause.)* I am doing this for *you.* Do you understand? I am compromising everything I believe in./For *you.*

CASSIE: I *know. (Beat. And then sincerely.)* I know. *(Beat.)* Thank you Renee.

RENEE: Yeah well. Don't thank me yet. *(Beat.)* Who wants fucking cake.

SCENE TWO

Gary sits at a coffee place. He keeps checking his watch – looking around – fidgeting. Angela enters. She's a little all over the place.

ANGELA: Hi! Hey!/Are you Gary?

GARY: Are you Angela?

ANGELA: Yeah.

GARY: Yeah. Me too. I am. Who you're. *(Beat.)* Hi.

ANGELA: Hey. *(Pause.)* I'm gonna go grab a coffee.

GARY: OK/sure.

ANGELA: You want/something?

GARY: Naw I'm cool.

ANGELA: My treat.

GARY: I'm/fine.

ANGELA: A cookie?

GARY: What kinda cookie?

ANGELA: I donno. Whatever they got. Oatmeal Chocolate Chip Peanut Butter.

GARY: *(Beat.)* Yeah sure. I'll take a cookie. *(Angela takes her wallet out of her bag and then hesitates.)* I can watch your bag.

ANGELA: Oh. *(That's not why she hesitated.)*

GARY: And I won't. Steal anything.

ANGELA: OK. *(Beat.)* I'll. Be right back!

GARY: I'll. Be right here. Watching the bag. Not. Stealing anything.
(She leaves. Gary waits - uncomfortable. He takes a few deep breaths. He fidgets. His cell phone rings. He looks at it, sees who is calling, and decides not to answer it. He fidgets. He takes out a joint, starts to leave and then remembers the bag. He says, "Fuck" under his breath and then sits back down. He decides to smoke under the table. Angela returns.)

ANGELA: Gary?

GARY: *(From under the table.)* Hey! *(He coughs.)*

ANGELA: What are you doing?

GARY: Oh! I uh. *(Beat.)* I wanted to see if I. Fit? Under the table. *(Beat.)* And. I do! *(More coughing. He puts joint out and comes back up.)* Hey.

ANGELA: Hi… *(Beat.)* I thought you'd left my bag alone.

GARY: Oh yeah no. I was. No. I didn't leave it. I promised/I wouldn't.

ANGELA: Were you smoking?

GARY: *No.*

ANGELA: Weed?

GARY: Huh?

ANGELA: Were you smoking *weed*. Under /the *table?*

GARY: No! No!

ANGELA: OK.

GARY: Who'd *do* that? Not me! That's for sure! *(Beat.)* So… *(Beat.)* Whatja get?

ANGELA: A. Frozen Choco-Latte.

GARY: That's funny.

ANGELA: Is it?

GARY: I donno. Maybe? Maybe not. *(Beat.)* Uh. *(Beat.)* You wanna. Sit down?

ANGELA: OK. *(They sit. She hands him a bag.)* They didn't have cookies so I. Got you a brownie.

GARY: OH! *(Not his favorite.)* Thanks…

ANGELA: Sure. *(Beat.)* Soooo. Thanks for meeting up with me, Gary. I've had some bad luck with this and so. I told those guys I need to pre-screen from now on cuz. There's a whole lotta wack-a-doodles out there.

GARY: I'm/sure.

ANGELA: A whole lotta. But you seem nice. *(Beat.)* So far. *(Beat.)* They told me this is your first time doing this.

GARY: Yup.

ANGELA: Why'd you. Why do you, you know. Why do you wanna do this you know? What made you decide to you know.

GARY: Do this?

ANGELA: Yeah uh huh.

GARY: I donno. I wanna. Give back? I guess?

ANGELA: Give what back? Did you steal something?

GARY: No! No! Give *myself* back.

ANGELA: To *who?*

GARY: The. Community?

ANGELA: (???)

GARY: Like volunteering?

ANGELA: Oh. OK. *(Beat.)* Do you have a job?

GARY: Yeah. Yes. I. Work in a store part time.

ANGELA: What kinda store?

GARY: We sell. Graphic novels.

ANGELA: What's that?

GARY: Comic. Books.

ANGELA: Oh. *(Beat.)* How *old* are you?

GARY: Thirty five.

ANGELA: Uh huh. *(She makes a note.)* Thirty. Five.

GARY: I mean. Comic books are. That's kind of a generic term? We sell graphic novels. *And* comic books.

ANGELA: What's the difference?

GARY: What's the difference??? Uh. Well. The difference. The difference is. Kind of a grey area. The difference is. It's like the difference between *movies* and *films*.

ANGELA: OK...

GARY: It's not all Archie and shit. *(His phone begins to ring again.)* I mean some of it is/but not.

ANGELA: Are you gonna answer that?

GARY: Nope.

ANGELA: What if it's important?

GARY: I know who it is. *(He hits the ignore button.)* I hate my cell phone.

ANGELA: Uh huh. *(Beat.)* So. Where were we?

GARY: Comic books.

ANGELA: *Right. (She looks at her notes.)* Do you have any kids?

GARY: Nope.

ANGELA: Married?

GARY: Noooo.

ANGELA: You think you maybe wanna *get* married? Like. Someday?

GARY: I donno./Not sure.

ANGELA: Don't.

GARY: Huh?

ANGELA: Don't get married. It fucking sucks.

GARY: Oh./OK.

ANGELA: I was married. For five years. And it fucking *sucked. (Beat.)* I don't think people are supposed to have to share everything. Like all their shit you know? It's totally suffocating. I was totally suffocated. *(Beat.)* But have a kid. Kids are the best. *My* kid's the best. And I'm not just saying that. Cause he's my kid and all. I'm saying it because people tell me all the time. Teachers. Babysitters. People with their *own* kids still tell me my kid? S'better than their kid.

GARY: Wow.

ANGELA: Yeah he's *awesome.* I *love* him. *(Beat.)* I really thought you'd left my bag.

GARY: I promised you/I wouldn't.

ANGELA: I was about to freak out.

GARY: I'm very glad/you didn't.

ANGELA: I don't often. But when I do? Whoo! Watch OUT! I'm a freakin' freak out *party! (Beat.)* I mean you leave my bag - you could leave my *kid.*

GARY: But I didn't. *(Beat.)* I wouldn't.

ANGELA: Yeah. I don't think you would. I trust you.

GARY: You do?

ANGELA: I feel like I could be a fan.

GARY: Of mine?

ANGELA: Uh huh. I feel like you're honest.

GARY: I am.

ANGELA: That's what I'm feeling. *(Beat.)* I also feel like you're a little fucked up.

GARY: Yeah I'm that too.

ANGELA: But since you're honest? I feel like you own it when you fuck up. It's like. Even though you might be a bit of a nightmare? Your heart's in the right place.

GARY: Usually.

ANGELA: Yeah see? I felt that. *(Beat.)* First guy they sent? Took him out for a day at the zoo. Ice cream. Watch the monkeys throw shit at each other. He had a blast. Came home. Couldn't stop talking about this guy, you know. He's got a convertible. He's gonna teach him how to play golf. He's got a phone that shows movies. And then a week later this asshole decides he's freaked out. It's too big of a commitment. My kid's too *needy.* So he bails. Second guy never shows up. Left him waiting an hour and a half. Staring out the window. Not even a phone call. Third guy gave me the creeps and. *(Beat.)* He's a really good kid.

GARY: Yeah.

ANGELA: And I'm. *(Beat.)* My ex is kind of emotionally retarded. So. I really need a guy who isn't gonna fuck him up more. I need a guy who'se gonna be around if he says he's gonna be around. And I. *(Beat.)* You can't fuck up I guess. Is what I'm saying.

GARY: OK.

ANGELA: And you can't smoke weed in front of my kid.

GARY: I wasn't/smoking.

ANGELA: You can't. Smoke weed. In front of my kid.

GARY: OK.

ANGELA: Or cigarettes.

GARY: OK.

ANGELA: And if you can't commit to this. That's cool. Just tell me right now. He hasn't met you or anything so it's not/a big deal.

GARY: OK.

ANGELA: But if you *do* wanna do this? And for *whatever* reason you break his heart? I swear over my Chocco fuckin Latte that I will kick your ass. Or I will hire someone bigger and meaner than me to come and kick your ass for me. It won't even be an ass anymore. It'll be like. Pulp. On the pavement.

GARY: That sounds like a band.

ANGELA: I'm totally serious.

GARY: *(Beat.)* If I fuck up I will kick my own ass.

ANGELA: OK.

GARY: Or I will hire someone bigger and meaner than both of us to kick it for me. *(Beat.)* I promise I won't fuck up.

ANGELA: Yeah. OK. *(Beat.)* OK. *(Beat.)* Big Brother. Welcome to the family. *(His cell phone begins to ring again.)*

SCENE THREE

An apartment stoop in a city. Cassie is sitting on the steps smoking. It's cold. She's bundled up - a coat over pajamas with a scarf and a hat.

CASSIE: So I thought we said twelve? But maybe we said twelve thirty. Or. I donno. One? Anyway. I'm here. And it's freezing and I'll. *(Beat.)* Maybe you're walking Gidget? Hey if you're getting coffee? Could you get me a hot chocolate? Extra hot. *(Henry enters holding a cup in one hand, a plastic shopping bag in another and a newspaper under his arm.)* No whipped cream. *(He hands her the cup.)* Thanks. *(She hangs up.)*

HENRY: Who was that?

CASSIE: You.

HENRY: Oh yeah? How am I doing?

CASSIE: Don't know. Got your voicemail. *(She lights another cigarette off the one she's smoking.)*

HENRY: Tell me I said hey

CASSIE: Will do

HENRY: *(Beat.)* Thought you quit.

CASSIE: I did. *(Takes a drag.)* I useta smoke two packs a day. Now I only smoke one.

HENRY: Cigarette?

CASSIE: Pack.

HENRY: Huh. Well. Whatever makes you happy.

CASSIE: *(Pause.)* Where's Gidget?

HENRY: Upstairs. She's gonna start whining any second now.

CASSIE: Why?

HENRY: Window's open. She can hear you probably.

CASSIE: *(She looks up.)* Hey Gidg! *(A dog starts barking and whining.)*

HENRY: See. There you go. *(To the window.)* Hey! Shut it! *(The dog stops.)* Good girl. *(Beat.)* She misses you.

CASSIE: *(A little pleased.)* Really?

HENRY: Yeah. And she's pissed at me. She keeps looking at me like "Dude you fucked up in a big way."

CASSIE: *You* didn't fuck up.

HENRY: And she's sleeping on the couch.

CASSIE: Wow she really *is* pissed.

HENRY: I'm telling you. Major Mastiff cold shoulder happenings at my apartment.

CASSIE: *(Beat.)* I miss her too.

HENRY: I'll tell her. *(Beat.)* What's with the pajamas?

CASSIE: I overslept.

HENRY: It's *noon.*

CASSIE: It's *Saturday.* Why are *you* in a *suit?*

HENRY: It's not a suit.

CASSIE: Whatever "business casual".

HENRY: I had a meeting.

CASSIE: On *Saturday???*

HENRY: With my boss. They uh. They wanna put me on "The Partner Track".

CASSIE: Oh my god! That's great!

HENRY: Is it?

CASSIE: It's *fantastic!*

HENRY: Yeah I. Uh. I donno. I may. Hate law. But. *(Beat.)* Anyway. *(Beat.)* You look great.

CASSIE: Really?

HENRY: Yeah. *(Beat.)* Why'dja haveta look so cute. Couldn't you have tried to look busted?

CASSIE: I look totally busted. I haven't showered in a long time.

HENRY: So you stink. You're still cute. Cute and stinky. *(He wipes something out of her eye.)* You've got crap in your eyes. I got it out.

CASSIE: Oh. Thanks.

HENRY: Sure. *(Beat.)* Anyway. So.

CASSIE: Yeah.

HENRY: Huh. *(Pause.)* So uh. Where you living?

CASSIE: Crashing with my brother. Till I find/an apartment.

HENRY: In the garage????

CASSIE: It's OK. /It's nice actually.

HENRY: Does he have *heat???*

CASSIE: Kind of?

HENRY: Do you want to stay here? I could go /to a hotel.

CASSIE: Henry! I'm not gonna kick you out of your apartment!

HENRY: I don't mind. Gidget likes you/better anyway.

CASSIE: No no. My brother's great, actually. It's been. Great. *(Her phone rings. She picks it up looks at it and hits ignore.)* Oh my god go away! *(Beat.)* Renee.

HENRY: She called this morning looking for you.

CASSIE: Sorry.

HENRY: She sounded pissed.

CASSIE: She's always pissed. *(She remembers something.)* Oh no. Oh God fuck. Fuck fuck fuck fuck/ fuck fuck fuck fuck.

HENRY: What?

CASSIE: Shit! I have to start writing stuff down! Fuck. I totally fuck I totally forgot I totally fucking forgot I shit I suck/I totally suck.

HENRY: Why don't you use the schedule in your phone?

CASSIE: Huh?

HENRY: You can program it to /remind you about stuff.

CASSIE: I know! Shit. Fuck.

HENRY: If you'd sit for a minute and figure out how to program it/you wouldn't forget things.

CASSIE: I tried. It's too complicated.

HENRY: Read the manual. *(Beat.)* That was an expensive phone/you know.

CASSIE: I know! I love it. The reception's great.

HENRY: Yeah but. You're not utilizing it to its full capacity. It's not just a phone. I got it so that you'd start to organize yourself a little better. It's got a lot of features. You can make a movie with it. You can download all of your cds onto it. / You can go on the internet.

CASSIE: I like my CDs the way they are in the cases!

HENRY: My grandma likes her 8 tracks too but. Even Tom Jones sounds/ better digital.

CASSIE: OH MY GOD! I don't wanna learn how to program the fucking phone Henry!!!

HENRY: *(Beat.)* Sorry.

CASSIE: It's OK. *(Beat.)* I'll. Tell Renee that I moved out. So she won't call you anymore.

HENRY: Thanks.

CASSIE: Sure. *(Long pause.)* My uh. My dad's sick.

HENRY: Your *dad?*

CASSIE: My whatever. My father. Martin. He's really sick. *(Beat.)* And. I was supposed to do something. And I forgot and. *(Beat.)* I fucked up. I always fuck up. I. *(Beat.)* I need to call Renee and deal/with this.

HENRY: Yeah. Of course. Go. *(Pause.)* I miss you too. *(Beat.)* Me and Gidget. We both miss you. A lot.

CASSIE: That's a shitty thing to say/to me today.

HENRY: That I miss you? How is that a shitty/thing to say?

CASSIE: I'm not moving back. So. It's shitty to try and/say something that will.

HENRY: Woah. Nobody asked you to.

CASSIE: Huh?

HENRY: Nobody asked you to move back.

CASSIE: Oh.

HENRY: Why? *Do* you???

CASSIE: Do I what?

HENRY: Wanna move back.

CASSIE: *(Beat.)* No. I donno. No. I don't think./No

HENRY: Make up your mind.

CASSIE: You make up yours!

HENRY: What is this "I know you are but what am I?" /Are we twelve?

CASSIE: This isn't my fault!

HENRY: Whose fault *is* it???

CASSIE: I/donno.

HENRY: Did I ask you to move out?

CASSIE: No but/you.

HENRY: But I what?

CASSIE: Nothing/I just.

HENRY: We have broken up four times in a year/and a.

CASSIE: Five.

HENRY: What???

CASSIE: Five times. We've broken up five times. Including this.

HENRY: I stand corrected.

CASSIE: Yeah well. Don't worry. This'll be the last time. *(Long pause.)* Can
I have my stuff?

HENRY: Cass.

CASSIE: Can I have. My stuff? *(He hands her the bag.)* Thanks.

HENRY: Sure

CASSIE: *(She takes a key off her key ring and hands it to him.)* Here.

HENRY: Thanks.

CASSIE: Sure. *(She looks inside the bag.)* That was all that was left?

HENRY: Yup.

CASSIE: Everything looks so sad. Poor. Sad. Stuff. *(An awkward pause
while they both stand there not knowing what to do next.)* Good luck
making partner.

HENRY: Thanks.

CASSIE: You'll be great. You'll be really. Great. *(She starts to cry.)* I/gotta
go.

HENRY: Cass.

CASSIE: I gotta go. *(She exits.)*

HENRY: *(He sits on the stoop.)* Fuck! *(The dog begins to whine again.)* Gidg! Shut it! *(The dog stops.)* Good girl.

SCENE FOUR

A hospital waiting room. Gwen and Renee sit far apart. Waiting. A long pause.

GWEN: It sure has been a long time.

RENEE: Yup.

GWEN: Since anybody's come out. Do you think someone will?

RENEE: Don't know. *(Beat.)* Eventually I'm sure.

GWEN: I wish *somebody'd* come out. Sooner rather than later.

RENEE: Uh /huh.

GWEN: So we'd know something. So we wouldn't just be. Left hanging.

RENEE: Maybe there's nothing new to say.

GWEN: Probably not. But still. It'd be nice just to get an update. Even if the update isn't news. Good or bad. Even if it's just to say that there's nothing to say. At least that'd be *something*, you know? It's just so hard. Sitting here. Not knowing anything. *(Beat.)* At least if they had a television I could watch my stories. *(Pause.)* Oh lordy. Was that bad/to say?

RENEE: Huh?

GWEN: What I just said? Was that bad to say that I wanna watch TV?

RENEE: It's fine.

GWEN: I kinda thought after I said it that maybe I shouldn'tve said it. I was worried that you'd think poorly of me and I wanna make a good impression.

RENEE: Don't worry about it. I'm not a. Judgmental person. *(Long pause.)*

GWEN: You're the oldest? Is that right?

RENEE: Excuse me?

GWEN: The oldest? You're/Martin's oldest?

RENEE: Far as I know.

GWEN: I've heard so much about you.

RENEE: I've heard absolutely nothing about you.

GWEN: Oh. *(Beat.)* Well that's OK. Your father's not a big talker. I have to pull things/outta him.

RENEE: Excuse me?

GWEN: Huh?

RENEE: What are you. Sorry. I don't wanna be rude but. What are you talking about?

GWEN: Oh! I was just saying that. It's no wonder you haven't heard that much/about me because.

RENEE: Uh huh.

GWEN: Because your father's /not such a.

RENEE: Martin.

GWEN: *Martin. (Beat.) Martin's* not such a big talker. Not like me!

RENEE: Oh.

GWEN: Not unless you push his buttons and ask a lotta questions . Which
I do. All the time so. I'm not surprised that you don't know anything about me was all. Was all I was. Saying. *(Pause.)* On our first
date we. We went to a museum. Oh goodness what was it called?
It was. That museum with all the boats and. The history about the
boats and. The pictures of the boats and. They had the nicest film
strip about boats and a sea captain from/the 1800's who

RENEE: The *Maritime Museum.*

GWEN: Huh?

RENEE: It's the Maritime Museum. That's what it's called.

GWEN: Oh! Yes! That's it! The Maritime Museum! You're so *smart!* Martin's always saying that you're the smartest out of anybody he knows.

RENEE: Oh yeah?

GWEN: The smartest one! In the whole world! Renee! And he sure seems
right about that! I'll say. Anyway. *(Beat.)* So. We were at the
Maritime Museum. And I kept talking in the middle of the filmstrip.
Actually. I kept talking throughout the entire filmstrip. Top to bottom. Talk talk talk.

RENEE: Really?

GWEN: Uh huh. I kept asking a lot of questions. And he. Well he an-
swered the ones he could answer. And the ones he couldn't answer
he didn't. Answer. But he didn't ask me any questions at all. Not
even one. *(Beat.)* Oh no! I'm wrong! He *did* ask me one question.
He asked me if I ever stopped talking. And I said "Nope I do not."
And he said "What about when you're sleeping?" And I said "Nope.
Not even then. I talk in my sleep!". And he said "Well I snore!"
And I said "Well that's OK by me." And he said "Well - we'll both
need to get some earplugs, won't we!" And we both started laugh-
ing. We hadda nice good laugh outta that one. We sure did. *(Beat.)*
Anyway. *(Long pause.)* So. Where are you from?

RENEE: Here.

GWEN: Oh. That's nice. I'm not from here. I'm from Illinois.

RENEE: Uh huh.

GWEN: Have you ever been to Illinois?

RENEE: Nope.

GWEN: Oh but surely you've been to *Chicago!* That's in Illinois you know.

RENEE: Nope. Never been to Chicago.

GWEN: Oh you should *go!* You really should visit *Chicago!* It's so *lovely* there.

RENEE: Maybe I will.

GWEN: It's a nice visit. It's a nice place to bring your family. There's so much to do! But. Not in the winter. It gets real cold. Too cold for little ones I think. And summer's too hot. But springtime sure is nice. And fall. Although it turns real fast. In the blink of an eye. But that's what you should do. You should take a trip to Chicago in the spring or the fall.

RENEE: Sounds good.

GWEN: They have lots of museums in Chicago. Oooh! Or the Aquarium! You could take the kids to the Aquarium! To see all the fishes and the whales! I love whales. They take care of their babies for a whole year! Did you know that?

RENEE: Uh uh.

GWEN: And female killer whales stay with their mothers their entire lives! Can you imagine that?

RENEE: Good god no.

GWEN: Dolphins can understand *language.* And they'll come right on up to you just like puppydogs. I read about this place in Florida where you can dive right into the water and play with 'em. And they have all kinds of personalities. Some of 'em are *tricksters.* They like to play *tricks.*

RENEE: Wow.

GWEN: Oh jeez. Now I lost my train of thought. What were we talking about?

RENEE: Chicago.

GWEN: Oh that's right! Chicago!

RENEE: Uh huh.

GWEN: You could go to the Art Institute. There are lots of famous paintings there. Or the Children's Museum. That's a whole lotta fun. Have you ever been?

RENEE: I've. Never been. To Chicago.

GWEN: Oh that's right. Well I have friends in Chicago so. If you go you should look them up and maybe they could show/you around.

RENEE: Great. Thanks.

GWEN: *(Beat.)* I don't care what they say. Chicago's just as nice as New York City. Nicer even.

RENEE: Uh huh.

GWEN: In my opinion. Not that anybody asked. *(Beat.)* So. *(Long pause.)* I'm. *(Beat.)* Thank you. For coming. Thank you.

RENEE: Oh sure.

GWEN: When your sister didn't show up/ I was a little lost.

RENEE: *(genuinely)* I'm really sorry about that.

GWEN: I tried to call Gary? He was the next one on my list. And. He didn't answer his phone/either and so.

RENEE: Wait you called *Gary????* I'm *third????*

GWEN: Third?

RENEE: I'm *third???* I'm third on the list??? I'm third after *Gary??*

GWEN: I'm sorry/I don't –

RENEE: Nothing nevermind.

GWEN: *(Beat.)* R comes after G.

RENEE: What?

GWEN: In your father's phone book. R comes after G. And G comes after C. And so. I just copied them down in that order. In the order that I found. The numbers. *(Silence.)* You know he hates hospitals. Doesn't ever wanna go. Wants to sweat it out. Whatever he's got. Doesn't trust doctors.

RENEE: Me neither.

GWEN: But he was so confused this morning when he woke up. Didn't know where he was. Didn't know who *I* was. Not sure he even knew who *he* was. He was so scared. I didn't know what else to do.

RENEE: You did the right thing Gwen.

GWEN: Yeah.

RENEE: Uh huh. *(Beat.)* Maybe I should go check in. Try to find out what's going on.

GWEN: OK.

RENEE: What was the doctor's name again?

GWEN: Oh gosh - I don't remember.

RENEE: *(A little laugh.)* Neither do I.

GWEN: Something with a J?

RENEE: Maybe? I'll figure it out. *(Beat.)* Do you need anything?

GWEN: A sedative maybe?

RENEE: I'm sorry a what?

GWEN: My heart. My heart is beating a mile a minute. It feels like it might pop. Like it might just fly on right through my chest. On wings. It feels like it wants to do that. Like it wants to fly around. Like it wants to fly around your father's. Sorry. *Martin's* room. Find

out what's going on and then report back. It doesn't want to stay
here with me. Can you imagine? A heart on wings.

RENEE: I think that's kind of a common picture. It's a logo. Maybe for a
band? A tattoo sometimes.

GWEN: Oh.

RENEE: Something. I know I've seen it. Before.

GWEN: Well that makes a whole lotta sense. I'll bet whoever invented it
felt just like I do right now. *(Silence.)*

RENEE: I'm gonna walk around the corner. See what I can find out.

GWEN: Oh/sure.

RENEE: Try to call my kids.

GWEN: Uh/huh.

RENEE: I left the oldest in charge so. I wanna make sure nobody's dead.
Or. Nearly. Dead. And I uh. Should try and get /ahold of my
sister.

GWEN: You go ahead.

RENEE: You'll be all right here?/ Till I get back?

GWEN: I am just fine. You go on and do what you need to.

RENEE: OK. *(Beat.)* I'll try to find you some drugs.

GWEN: Huh?

RENEE: A sedative.

GWEN: Oh! Thank you! What a dear you are!

RENEE: Sure.

GWEN: OK! Thank you! Bye now! *(Gwen waves as Renee exits. She gets
a piece of candy out of her purse, unwraps it and puts it in her mouth.
She sits. She begins to cry very very quietly. Renee reenters)*

RENEE: If. *(She notices Gwen crying. Gwen doesn't see her. Renee stands and
watches her.)*

SCENE 5

A Comic Book Store.

BENJY: "Its like." A quest for *identity.* Figuring out who you are from the ground up. And. The heroine. Cassandra? Like the Greek myth you know? She's a *prophet.* So. She can see her *future?* But she also has *amnesia.* So she can't, you know. Remember her *past.* So the quest is. A quest to figure out her *past.* Through her visions of her own *future.* Even her *deaths.*

GARY: That's deep.

BENJY: Yeah. Because depending on what she does in her *present.* Her future? Changes. So. The death scenes change, you know? They *evolve.* Depending on. Lots of different shit. I'm still. Fleshing it all out.

GARY: *(Pause.)* That's my sister's name. Cassandra.

BENJY: Huh?

GARY: My sister? The one who's living with me? My little sister? *Cassie?*

BENJY: I don't know man. You've got a lot of sisters.

GARY: I only have two.

BENJY: Yeah but. I don't have *any.* So. Two's a lot to me.

GARY: You want one of mine?

BENJY: Nah. I'm cool with none.

(Gary's phone begins to ring. He looks at it.)

GARY: Speaking of sisters. *Cassandra. (He hits ignore.)*

BENJY: What about that other chick? The one you were telling me about? The one with the kid?

GARY: Angela? She's not my sister.

BENJY: Are you fucking her?

GARY: No.

BENJY: Do you *wanna* be fucking her?

GARY: Not. Really.

BENJY: I don't get it.

GARY: She's a friend. I'm gonna be a big brother to her kid.

BENJY: Oh. That's cool. *(Beat.)* I don't think I have any friends who are girls. I mean I have friends. Who are girls. But I kinda wanna fuck all of them. They just. Don't wanna fuck me back. Does that count?

GARY: You've said fuck like five hundred times. You need a new word.

BENJY: Sorry. *(Beat.)* Do you ever wanna fuck your sisters?

GARY: God no! Benjy!

BENJY: They do it in Greek myth all the time!

GARY: I don't care! I'm not Zeus!

BENJY: Luke Skywalker? *Totally* wanted to fuck Princess Leia!

GARY: New word Benjy. Remember? New word.

BENJY: Right. Sorry.

GARY: You shouldn't just say all the shit that comes into your head. Sometimes you say weird shit.

BENJY: I know.

GARY: You need to censor.

BENJY: Yeah OK. *(Pause.)* I kinda wanna fuck your sister.

GARY: WHAT DID I JUST SAY???

BENJY: Sorry! Shit! Not just. I mean I wanna hang out with her too! She's. I like her.

GARY: *Cassie?*

BENJY: Yeah.

GARY: *Cassandra???*

BENJY: Shut up.

GARY: I don't think you're her type.

BENJY: I *could* be.

GARY: Nah. She likes. You know. Banker guys.

BENJY: I'm an amazing baker!!!

GARY: *Banker.*

BENJY: Oh.

GARY: Like *money.*

BENJY: Right.

GARY: She'll break your heart. She does that. *(Beat.)* But. You should ask her out. Maybe. Sometime.

BENJY: You think?

GARY: Yeah sure. Why not. *(Beat.)* Your story idea? S'fucking brilliant.

BENJY: Thanks. I just. I gotta flesh it all out.

GARY: You will.

(Cassie enters still in her pajamas.)

CASSIE: Did you just hit the ignore button on your phone???

GARY: Nice outfit.

CASSIE: Don't be an asshole.

GARY: Was I being/an asshole?

CASSIE: You know the person??? Calling??? Can tell the difference between the phone ringing into voicemail and someone hitting the IGNORE BUTTON!

GARY: You're yelling.

CASSIE: We *need*/to go to.

GARY: You *need* to stop *yelling.* I'm at work.

CASSIE: There's nobody here.

GARY: You're disrespecting my coworker.

CASSIE: Sorry. *(to Benjy)* Sorry.

BENJY: No problem.

CASSIE: *(to Gary)* Can you. Go?

GARY: Go where.

CASSIE: Have you gotten *any* of your messages???

GARY: Nope. *(He turns to go.)*

CASSIE: GARY! Don't just walk away like that when I'm/talking to you!

GARY: Hey! Baby Renee! I gotta take a piss! I'll be right back!

> *(Gary exits. Cassie's phone begins to ring. She takes it out and throws it against the wall.)*

CASSIE: OH MY GOD LEAVE ME ALONE! *(She collapses on the floor and puts her head in her hands. Silence.)*

BENJY: You. Want a chair?

CASSIE: No.

BENJY: You just wanna sit on the floor?

CASSIE: Uh huh.

BENJY: OK. *(Pause.)* Bad day?

CASSIE: Yeah uh huh.

BENJY: I hope it gets better. *(No response.)* Can't go anywhere but up, right?

CASSIE: If you say so.

> *(Silence.)*

BENJY: Do you remember me?

CASSIE: *(She doesn't.)* Uh huh.

BENJY: Benjy.

CASSIE: Hi Benjy. Cassie.

BENJY: I remember. *(Pause.)* Cassie. Is that short for. Cassandra?

CASSIE: Uh huh.

BENJY: Do people ever call you that?

CASSIE: Nope.

BENJY: They should. It's a. Really pretty name.

CASSIE: *(She looks up at him for the first time.)* Thanks.

BENJY: Sure.

> *(Gary re-enters.)*

GARY: Why are you sitting on the floor?

CASSIE: It was here.

GARY: OK…

CASSIE: Can you get your mom's car?

GARY: Why?

CASSIE: Because I don't drive and I need/a ride to the.

GARY: I'm at work.

BENJY: I can cover for you if you/need me to.

GARY: I can't just drop everything because you're having some/sort of drama.

CASSIE: It's not *about* me.

GARY: I'm trying really hard to be. *Responsible.* I'm up for a promotion. And so I can't, you know. Like what did you/ fuck up?

CASSIE: It's not me. It's Martin. *(Beat.)* He's at the hospital. Renee is at the hospital. Everybody is apparently at the hospital. Except for us. Which is making Renee very unhappy.

GARY: Oh. *(Beat.)* I guess I should start answering my phone.

CASSIE: You think?

GARY: *(Pause.)* Remember when Renee was nice?

CASSIE: Nope. *(She crosses to get her phone.)*

GARY: There was a time? When Renee was the nicest person I knew.

CASSIE: Yeah well. That's what happens when you're nice. *(Cassie's phone starts to ring again.)* Sooner or later you get really. Fucking. Pissed off. *(She hits the ignore button.)*

SCENE 6

The Hospital. Renee, Cassie and Gary. Gwen is curled up on a few chairs, sleeping. Cassie is still in her pajamas.

CASSIE: I'm /really sorry.

RENEE: Not interested.

CASSIE: If you'd just let /me explain.

RENEE: Don't wanna hear it.

CASSIE: I've got a lot of shit/going on.

RENEE: Uh huh. *(Beat.)* What are you *wearing*?

CASSIE: *Excuse* me?

RENEE: I said. What./Are you wearing?

CASSIE: Should I have gone *home* first? Put on a *party* dress?

RENEE: Don't be ridiculous. *(Beat.)* It's just. The image you present to the world that's all.

CASSIE: Thanks for the tip! *(Beat.)* I was trying to apologize.

RENEE: No you weren't. You were making excuses. And I'm not in the mood. Because *I* have been in a hospital all day. Leaving you messages. The first message being "At the hospital. Here's the address. Come immediately." But maybe that wasn't clear? Because you know most people? Would've gotten their ass here. Most people? Wouldn't have spent hours playing phone tag. Leaving messages like "Oh no! What's going on? Call me back!" They would've just dropped whatever it was they were doing and come. To the hospital. But. Maybe you needed more clarification? So. I'm genuinely sorry for that. I'm sorry Cassie. I'm REALLY TRULY SORRY that I *inconvenienced* you today. That I *disrupted* all of the really important "shit" that *you* have going on in *your* life. Because as you can see. MY LIFE? Is really truly fucking BRILLIANT!!!

CASSIE: *(Pause.)* I'm gonna go to the cafeteria.

RENEE: You do that.

CASSIE: You want/anything?

RENEE: Nope.

CASSIE: *(to Gary)* You?

GARY: I'm good.

CASSIE: OK. I'll be/right back.

RENEE: Have fun. *(Cassie exits.)*

GARY: *(Beat.)* A little harsh maybe? Considering.

RENEE: Considering what?

GARY: Where we are.

RENEE: I don't care.

GARY: OK.

RENEE: I don't.

GARY: *(Beat.)* She broke up with Henry.

RENEE: *(A laugh.)* Again?

GARY: I think this time's for good.

RENEE: Oh well. Good for Henry. He's better off.

GARY: Henry's an asshole.

RENEE: Henry was the best thing that ever happened to her.

GARY: Says you.

RENEE: He was getting her shit together.

GARY: He irons his boxer shorts!

RENEE: So. He's neat.

GARY: Uh huh

RENEE: You could use someone like that.

GARY: For the last time, Renee. I'M NOT GAY!!!

RENEE: Didn't say you were.

GARY: It was implied.

RENEE: Clearly you're a little sensitive about that because. *I* didn't say/a thing.

GARY: Whatever.

RENEE: *(Pause.)* When did she break up with Henry?

GARY: I don't know. Couple weeks ago?

RENEE: When did you find out?

GARY: I donno. She's staying with me/ and so I.

RENEE: In the *garage*? Why didn't she come stay with me???

GARY: OH MY GOD DO YOU REALLY HAVE TO ASK????
    (Silence.)

RENEE: I hate this hospital.

GARY: Yeah me too.

RENEE: This is the hospital where people come to die. *(Pause.)* He was. Disoriented? This morning. So. The girlfriend brought him in and. They rushed him into ICU. And. Nobody talked to us. We just sat here. For hours. Waiting. *(Beat.)* And then Asshole Doctor Number One comes out and tells us he's in a coma and declining. Rapidly. Like he's sorry but. They're out of the special of the day. Like it's gonna rain on the day we'd planned a picnic. Like bad news but not. Life changing bad news. Just. Average everyday run of the mill bad news. And then he said his shift was over. Said Asshole

Doctor Number Two would be taking over. *(Beat.)* Can you imagine? Can you imagine *that* being your *life?* Everyday. Sorry. Your father is declining. Your wife is dying. Your child is dead. Sorry to have to be the one to tell you. Don't shoot the messenger. Don't blame me. Not my fault. Not my problem. Not my family. Here's the information. Be well.

GARY: How long has she been asleep?

RENEE: Couple of hours. She doesn't want to go home. *(Beat.)* They won't let her in to see him. Because she's not family. Can you believe that? Only person in the whole fucking world who actually gives a shit about him. Who's *praying* for him. And she's stuck out here. With me. Of all people. *(Beat.)* It's a crazy fucked up world.

GARY: Yeah.

RENEE: *(Beat.)* I want to go home.

GARY: So go.

RENEE: I can't leave her.

GARY: I'll stay.

RENEE: You don't /have to.

GARY: I'll stay.

RENEE: OK. *(Cassie returns with a box of food. She quietly hands out sandwiches and sits in between them. They all eat.)* Peanut butter and jelly? They had peanut butter and jelly?

CASSIE: Uh huh.

RENEE: I love peanut butter and jelly.

CASSIE: I know.

(They sit side by side and continue to eat in silence.)

SCENE 7

Renee and Mark in the living room. Mark is eating leftover cake. There is a suitcase.

MARK: Happy Birthday.

RENEE: Thanks.

MARK: In case you were wondering? Your kids ate candy for dinner.

RENEE: Oh.

MARK: You know when you're eleven? And your mom leaves you in charge? That's what you do. You eat a ton of candy.

RENEE: I was babysitting at eleven.

MARK: Not criticizing. Just informing.

RENEE: OK.

MARK: *(Beat.)* So. You wanna tell me why our kids were alone watching cable and eating stale Halloween candy when I got home?

RENEE: That sounded critical.

MARK: Just curious.

RENEE: Family emergency.

MARK: That's redundant.

RENEE: Excuse me?

MARK: Your family *is* an emergency.

RENEE: *(Beat.)* How was your trip?

MARK: Aren't you gonna tell me what happened?

RENEE: Didn't sound like you wanted to know.

MARK: Not sure I do.

RENEE: So there you go. Thought I'd change the subject. Talk about something you were interested in.

MARK: My trip was OK. I made the deal of the century.

RENEE: Congratulations.

MARK: Thanks.

RENEE: My father's in the hospital.

MARK: Congratulations.

RENEE: That's not funny.

MARK: Wasn't meant to be.

RENEE: So then it was just mean.

MARK: When I left you hated him.

RENEE: Hate's a strong word.

MARK: Semantics.

RENEE: If you say so. *(Beat.)* He's still family.

MARK: Right. Guess no matter how much it's watered down. Blood stays thick, huh? /And red.

RENEE: I really don't. Can we just drop it?/Can we drop it?

MARK: Sure.

RENEE: Thank you.

MARK: *(Pause.)* They want me to move out to California to head up the merger.

RENEE: In California.

MARK: Yeah.

RENEE: Do you wanna go?

MARK: Not sure yet.

RENEE: Which way are you leaning.

MARK: Towards going. *(Beat.)* It's a great opportunity.

RENEE: When would you go?

MARK: Soon.

RENEE: Do you want us to come with you?

MARK: Do you want to come?

RENEE: Don't do that.

MARK: What?

RENEE: Answer my question with another question.

MARK: *(Beat.)* I would like to go. And I would like for my family to come with me.

RENEE: Is it up for discussion?

MARK: I'm putting it on the table.

RENEE: It's not a great time to move right now.

MARK: Why.

RENEE: I don't want to move the kids in the middle of the school year.

MARK: They're *kids*. They're fine. They'll get to wear flip flops to school. *(Beat.)* This isn't about the kids.

RENEE: Fine. Then for *me*. It's not a good time for *me*.

MARK: Why not?

RENEE: Isn't that enough? Can't I want something just for *me*? My family /needs me right now.

MARK: *I'm* your family!

RENEE: It's not an either or thing Mark!/It's not like that!

MARK: *This* is your family! Me Molly and Ben! *We* are your family!

RENEE: I don't want to be so far away right now. I can't leave Gary and Cassie/alone with this.

MARK: Gary is a grown man!

RENEE: I know/but he's.

MARK: Cassie is an adult. They are both adults. You're not their mother. You're barely even related to either of them!

RENEE: I don't have any other siblings.

MARK: So. Be an only child.

RENEE: *(Beat.)* Cassie has nobody.

MARK: Yeah well if she'd stick with something. With *someone*. For longer than a minute and a half. But why should she when she has you to run in at the last second and deal with all of her shit so she doesn't have to? Huh? While your own fucking kids sit at home breaking their molars on jolly ranchers and watching people shoot holes into other people's heads.

RENEE: Your family's not perfect either.

MARK: This isn't about my family!

RENEE: I'm just saying that. Maybe you should acknowledge. Sorry. Not *criticizing*. Just *informing*. That I'm not the only one who has messed up siblings/ and parents to deal with.

MARK: The *difference*. The *difference* Renee??? Is that my siblings and parents don't invade our life on a daily basis! The *difference*. Is that my family lives hundreds of fucking miles away. And we see them once a year at Christmas where we drink too much and fight and say shitty things to each other. And then we pack up all our *metaphorical* baggage into our *literal* baggage. With our useless presents that will be re-gifted to people we hate. And then we get on a plane and LEAVE. The difference is that my fucking family is self contained. And I can HATE THEM. In small microscopic compartmentalized INTERVALS!!!! *(Pause.)* Trust me. You would hate them a whole lot less if we moved to California. You'd turn into the fucking Waltons. *(Silence.)* Do you remember? Do you remember what we promised each other? When we got married? Before we had kids? When it was just the two of us? Do you remember? We promised that we'd be amazing. *(Beat.)* We are the farthest thing from amazing. *(Beat.)* You know what's really depressing?

RENEE: Huh?

MARK: Someday? Someday our kids're gonna feel that way about *us*. Someday our kids are gonna be yelling with their spouses about us. The thought of that makes me want to kill myself. It's so fucking awful. It makes me want to die. *(Pause.)* I want to go to California.

RENEE: OK.

MARK: You can come with. Or you can stay here. Do what you want. *(Beat.)* I'm gonna go to bed.

RENEE: OK. *(Beat.)* Goodnight.
> *(He takes the suitcase and exits. The phone begins to ring. And ring. And ring. She doesn't go to answer it. She sits and eats the cake)*

End of Act 1

ACT TWO, SCENE ONE

The Hospital. Renee and Gwen are in the same clothes from their previous scene. Gwen is wrapped in a battered looking hospital blanket. She has taken off her shoes and has made herself very much at home. She is surrounded by Kleenex, magazines, and candy wrappers. Renee is filling out paperwork. On her lap is a lumpy manila envelope. The painful silence is punctuated by the occasional sigh from Renee, a sniff from Gwen, the shuffling of papers, and the click of the pen on paper.

GWEN: It's. Cold in here.

RENEE: You want me to see/if they can turn up the heat?

GWEN: I don't want to be a bother. Do you think they would?

RENEE: I can ask.

GWEN: No no don't. I'm fine.

RENEE: OK. Let me know if you change/your mind.

GWEN: Uh huh. *(Long pause.)* Where'd your brother go off to?

RENEE: Don't know.

GWEN: He's a lovely person.

RENEE: He's OK.

GWEN: He's your. Half brother?

RENEE: Different moms.

GWEN: It's nice that you're close.

RENEE: *(A little laugh.)* I guess. *(Beat.)* Our mothers are friends.

GWEN: You don't say.

RENEE: They bonded over their poor choice in men.

GWEN: *(Beat.)* We had such a nice chat. Gary and I. We talked about legalizing marijuana.

RENEE: Oh yeah?

GWEN: For people who are sick. And in pain. It's such a shame. That cigarettes are legal. But marijuana isn't. Cigarettes'll kill you. All marijuana does is make people happy. And hungry. No harm in that. Better to be happy and a little hungry than in pain. *(Pause.)* Could I. Look through the envelope?

RENEE: Sure. *(She hands Gwen the envelope and returns to her paperwork.)*

GWEN: Thank you.

RENEE: Uh huh. *(Gwen empties the contents of the envelope on her lap. A wallet, a pen, a ring, a watch, a cell phone. She puts on the ring. She looks at the watch and laughs.)* Did you say something?

GWEN: Oh no. Just laughing.

RENEE: OK. *(She goes back to the paperwork. Silence.)*

GWEN: Do you wanna know what/I was.

RENEE: Look I haveta fill this stuff out and/I need to concentrate.

GWEN: I'm sorry.

RENEE: It's OK. *(A brief pause and then a little sigh.)* Do I want to know what.

GWEN: Huh?

RENEE: You were asking me. What. Do I want to know/what.

GWEN: Oh! Right. I was wondering if you wanted to know what I was laughing about. When I was laughing just now.

RENEE: Sure.

GWEN: I was laughing because. Your father. He's always fifteen minutes late. All the time. Fifteen minutes to the second. And then I just noticed that his watch is fifteen minutes slow! And so. He's actually. He was actually. Always on time! *(Gary enters.)* Isn't that funny?

GARY: Isn't what funny?

GWEN: Oh nothing.

GARY: Private joke? You *two.*

(The phone lights up and starts vibrating. Everybody stares at it.)

GWEN: Should I.

RENEE: Just leave it. *(It finally stops. A beat.)* Where were you?

GARY: Called my mom. She says hi. She wants to bring you a casserole.

RENEE: I don't need a casserole.

GARY: She needs to feel useful.

RENEE: Your mother is not my problem.

GARY: She wants to do something nice.

RENEE: She can make *you* a casserole.

GWEN: I like casseroles.

RENEE: She can make *Gwen* a casserole.

GARY: Just let her do it.

RENEE: I don't want a casserole. Why is this an issue?

GARY: It's just weird that you're being so./*Weird.* About it.

RENEE: It's not *weird.* I'm not *weird.*

GARY: Yeah OK. *(Beat.)* Renee doesn't like casseroles because she doesn't like it when her food touches. When we were kids? She useta separate/her M&Ms by color.

RENEE: Can we drop this please? *(Beat.)* Did you call Cassie?

GARY: Yup.

RENEE: Is she coming?

GARY: I told her not to.

RENEE: OK.

GARY: Why does she need to be here?

RENEE: Because *I'm* here. Because it was her idea to get involved with this fucking mess in the first place. So *she* should have to sit here if *I* have to sit here because that's *fair*.

GARY: So should I call her?

RENEE: *No.*

GARY: So what do you want me to do?

RENEE: Nothing *(Beat.)* What I *would've* /liked.

GARY: Here we go.

RENEE: Is if you'd taken care of all of this instead of calling me. Not sure why you couldn't've sat here with her – sorry Gwen.

GWEN: It's/OK.

RENEE: And signed forms and decided what went where and who gets his liver and does he want to be cremated or buried and do we want a biopsy. Are you not capable of that?

GARY: It's not about being *capable*. Of course I'm *capable*.

RENEE: Really?

GARY: I happen to be *extremely* capable. I'm up for a promotion at work, actually.

GWEN: Congratulations!

GARY: *Thank* you.

RENEE: At the comic book store? What does that mean? Do you get a new super power?

GARY: Martin named *you* as his person who makes decisions when decisions need to be made and so. They wouldn't tell us he was dead. They told us to call *you*. And so that's what I did. *(Pause.)* Just want to point out that you *really* wanted to be the in case of emergency call. Not being an asshole. Just. *Illuminating* the *irony*.
(Martin's phone lights up and vibrates again.)

GWEN: It's a restricted number.

RENEE: Don't answer it. It's probably a creditor.

GWEN: Maybe I should change the message on the. *(Renee takes the phone and turns it off.)*

RENEE: There you go. Problem solved.
(Renee goes back to the paperwork. Gwen goes back to the things from the envelope. Silence.)

GWEN: Isn't it. Odd.

GARY: What's that?

GWEN: Death.

GARY: Oh. Uh. Yeah? I guess.

GWEN: That death comes with *paperwork*. And an *envelope*. It seems like it should be a bigger deal. Like it should have better office supplies. This could've been for. Interoffice mail. *(She hands the ring to Gary.)* You should have this.

GARY: Oh… That's OK.

GWEN: It's a handsome ring.

GARY: Yeah I don't really wear. Jewelry.

GWEN: Renee, how about you.

RENEE: No thanks. You keep it Gwen.

GWEN: Maybe for your kids?

RENEE: That's OK. They didn't really know him.

GWEN: No but *(Beat.)* That's not their fault, is it?

RENEE: *(Beat.)* Fault?

GARY: Oh/noooo…

GWEN: It's not the children's fault they didn't know their grandfather. /So they shouldn't be.

RENEE: I didn't say it was.

GWEN: I'm not saying it's *anybody's* fault. I'm just. *(Beat.)* I know that he made attempts.

RENEE: Attempts?

GWEN: Called. Sent gifts. I know he wasn't a perfect man. But he did want to get to know his grandchildren. And from what I understand you/were not very.

RENEE: Get to know his *grandchildren*???? Are you *high*??? Why should he be allowed to have that??? For a four dollar toy from the drug store? Is that what my kids are worth? What about when they were *born*? Where was he then with his fucking yo yo and his plastic watergun. Fuck that. Where was he when I got *married*? Or when I graduated from *high school*? Or when I was in the *fucking hospital*??? Fuck that. Fuck him. Look I'm sorry he was sad and sick and without. Medicinal marijuana. That really sucks for him. But there was no way in hell he was gonna get the chance to fuck my kids up like he fucked up me. And break their hearts and disappoint them and make them feel unloved and ugly and unwanted and broken into pieces. Because one day? If I had let him in? He would've fucked up. He would've fucked up huge. And he would've disappointed them. He would've broken a promise. Or disappeared. Or left them wondering what they did wrong. And *my* kids? Aren't worth the risk. So no. He doesn't. Didn't. Get the *privilege* of my children. You clearly aren't a parent or you would get that. *(to Gary)* Can I have a cigarette?

GARY: Do you really think that's appropriate?/ Given the circumstances?

RENEE: Can I please. Have. A cigarette.

GARY: In my jacket pocket.

(Renee takes a cigarette and a lighter and exits as Cassie enters. Renee walks past her without acknowledging her.)

CASSIE: Hey.

GARY: Hey. *(Pause.)* How'd you get here?

CASSIE: Henry.

GARY: He still/ here?

CASSIE: No.

GARY: You guys get/back together?

CASSIE: Really don't wanna chat about it.

GARY: Oh. Kay.

(Silence.)

GWEN: I'm Gwen.

GARY: Fuck sorry. Have you met. This is /my other sister.

CASSIE: Cassie. We talked on the phone.

GWEN: Cassie! Come here! Let me look at you! *(She hugs Cassie and then holds her face in her hands.)* You look just like your picture.

CASSIE: What picture.

(Gwen opens Martin's wallet and shows a picture to Cassie.)

GWEN: See that. Like you took it yesterday.

CASSIE: I was in kindergarten.

GWEN: You look just the same. *(Gary laughs.)*

CASSIE: Shut up. *(She flips through pictures.)* Hey Gary look. Nice "slacks".

GARY: *(He looks over her shoulder at the pictures.)* It was the 80's. Those pants were hot.

CASSIE: Yeah OK. Wow your mom really is fat.

GARY: Hey!

CASSIE: I mean *now*. Compared to *then*.

GARY: *(He looks at the picture.)* Wow. Yeah you're right.

CASSIE: *(She takes out a newspaper clipping.)* Look at Renee. Smiling.

(Renee enters.)

RENEE: Look at Renee smiling at what.

CASSIE: Oh. We were. Just looking at pictures.

RENEE: What pictures.

CASSIE: From Martin's wallet. *(She hands Renee the clipping.)* Remember this? *(to Gwen)* Renee was valedictorian of her high school class. Her picture was in the paper.

RENEE: It was no big deal.

CASSIE: Are you kidding? It was a *huge* deal. She gave a speech. It was beautiful. People cried. They gave her a standing ovation. I was only four but. I remember I wanted to be like you so bad.

RENEE: Why???

CASSIE: I don't know. Just did.

RENEE: Well anytime you wanna switch lives Cass? You just let me know. *(Pause.)* You didn't have to come.

CASSIE: I know.

RENEE: It's not like there's anything left to do.

CASSIE: Should I go?

RENEE: Do what you want.

CASSIE: Wow. I can't win.

RENEE: Oh please don't make this about you.

CASSIE: What am I making about *me*?

RENEE: I said do what you want. You said you can't win. I said don't make it about you. What's not clear.

CASSIE: Why are you mad at me?

RENEE: Who says I'm mad at *you*? Maybe I'm just *mad*.

CASSIE: I *came* here. *For* you. I came because I knew you were here and I wanted to support. *You* and. Jesus. If I hadn't shown up you'd be pissed. I'm here and you're/still pissed.

RENEE: What do you want me to do? *Thank* you??? Jump up and down??? Throw a party? Plan a parade? Don't worry Cass. All the messy work is done. Go get a pedicure and polish your tiara. I took care of it.

CASSIE: Who *asked* you to take care of anything?

RENEE: YOU DID! *YOU* asked me to!!! *YOU* came to my house on my *birthday* and dumped/this on me!!!!

CASSIE: You could've said no!

RENEE: Really??? I could have?

CASSIE: I would've taken care of it/on my own.

RENEE: You fucked up on your first DAY!

CASSIE: I *know*/but.

RENEE: You can't take care of *yourself!* You can't take care of a *houseplant!* Get a *job!* Get an *apartment!* Get a *relationship* that lasts six months straight! Put the airbag on yourself before you try to save the person/ next to you.

GARY: Hey!

RENEE: Because sooner or later? If you're not careful? You're gonna have nothing. And you'll be old and dried up and depressed just like your poor sad little waif of a mother. And then. And *then*. We're all gonna have to drop everything once again and be on FUCKING SUICIDE WATCH SO THAT YOU DON'T END UP KILLING YOURSELF JUST/LIKE HER!!!

GARY: HEY!!!!

RENEE: And YOU??? Don't even get me *started* on you!!! Men your age are parents. And you still LIVE WITH YOUR'S!

GARY: I told you - I'm saving!

RENEE: Well it's been almost fifteen years manbaby! You should be a MIL-LIONAIRE by now!!!

GARY: JESUS FUCKING CHRIST WHY ARE YOU SUCH A BITCH!

RENEE: WHY AM I A BITCH??? YOU WANNA KNOW WHY I'M A BITCH??? I'M A BITCH BECAUSE OF THE TWO OF YOU!

GARY: YOU are a bitch because you wanna be! You're a bitch because we let you! You're a bitch because you hate your miserable fucking life and your bratty fucking kids and your husband that you settled for and the road to nowhere that you're driving on! You're a bitch because you hate yourself! You're a bitch because you need to get laid! You're a bitch because your life's over and you know it! You wanna sit there and judge us? Me and Cass? We may not be perfect. But as lame as we are? At least we're not you! We thank FUCKING GOD we're not you! We pray TO FUCKING GOD every night that we never BECOME YOU! Because you know what? If your life was my life? I'd be pissed off all the time too. I'd be a bitch too. Because your life? SUCKS! (*Silence. Gwen begins to quietly cry.*) Fuck. Gwen. (*Beat.*) Gwen I'm./Fuck. I'm so.

GWEN: Oh it's OK! I'm fine! Don't you worry about me!

GARY: Dammnit./Gwen I'm.

GWEN: (*Keeping up a smile through the tears.*) No I'm fine really! I've never been better. I'm having a splendid day! And a splendid visit with you all. Its been a real pleasure meeting all of you and. We should do this again! Maybe. Maybe Gary? Maybe your mom could bring a casserole next time? What do you think?

GARY: Uh.

GWEN: Whadya think? Sound good?

RENEE: Gwen.

GWEN: But don't let me stop your. Your chat. You all go right on back to what you were doing. You just forget all about me. You all just go right on ahead and do what you need to do. You just keep on being hateful and horrible. You just keep right on just tearing each other to bits. You won't even know I'm here. I'll be. I'll be quiet as a mouse. *(Silence.)*

RENEE: Does he want to be cremated or buried?

GWEN: Buried.

RENEE: OK. *(She finishes her paperwork and hands it to Cassie.)* Here you go. It's all your's. *(Renee puts on her coat and exits. A beat. Gwen takes the cigarettes from Gary's pocket and follows her. A beat. Cassie begins to cry.)*

GARY: You know what?

CASSIE: What

GARY: I think I'm gonna buy a lottery ticket. What do you think? You want in?

CASSIE: Sure. *(Beat.)* I'm so sorry Gary.

GARY: For what?

CASSIE: For being me.

GARY: Yeah. Me too. I'm sorry for being me too.

SCENE TWO

Hospital parking lot. Renee sits alone crying. Gwen enters. She calmly lights a cigarette and hands it to Renee. She lights one for herself. She sits next to her. They smoke silently. They do not look at each other for the entire scene.

RENEE: I thought you wanted cigarettes to be illegal.

GWEN: I do. *(Beat.)* I also think guns should be illegal. Doesn't mean I don't wanna shoot people sometimes.

RENEE: Fair enough. *(Silence. They smoke.)* Hey Gwen?

GWEN: Yeah uh huh.

RENEE: Who would you shoot? If you got a free pass. No repercussions.

GWEN: Anybody at all?

RENEE: Uh huh.

GWEN: Do I only get one?

RENEE: Is there a list?

GWEN: Depends on the day.

RENEE: OK. Today then. Who would you shoot if you got the chance *today?*

GWEN: Today…

RENEE: Uh huh.

GWEN: *(She considers this.)* That doctor.

RENEE: Which one.

GWEN: That one with the name we couldn't remember.

RENEE: Was that Asshole Doctor Number One? Or Asshole Doctor Number Two.

GWEN: The one with the lisp and the shifty eyes.

RENEE: One. That was One.

GWEN: All right then. I would shoot Asshole Doctor Number One.

RENEE: OK. You get One - I'll get Two. We'll take 'em both out, Gwen. You and me.

GWEN: Deal. *(Pause.)* And maybe that nurse?

RENEE: Which one?

GWEN: The one who kept clicking her tongue.

RENEE: The tsk tsker?

GWEN: Yeah her. She was so condescending.

RENEE: She sure was. OK. We can get rid of her too. *(Beat.)* And the cellphone guy!

GWEN: The one breaking up with his girlfriend?

RENEE: Yeah him. *(Beat.)* *And* the girlfriend!

GWEN: *(Pause.)* And the smelly food woman.

RENEE: Oh god yes. Her too. Gone.

GWEN: People shouldn't be allowed to eat tuna in public.

RENEE: I'll smoke to that. *(They smoke. Long pause.)* What about family?

GWEN: What about 'em?

RENEE: Can I shoot my family?

GWEN: Today?

RENEE: Yeah.

GWEN: Today you can shoot anybody you want.

RENEE: OK then. I wanna shoot my family. All of 'em. *(Beat.)* Except my kids. I'll spare my kids.

GWEN: You got it. *(They smoke.)* Doesn't it feel great?

RENEE: Shooting people?

GWEN: Smoking.

RENEE: Ugh. It's disgusting. It's so disgusting. I feel disgusting. *(She takes a drag.)* I only smoke when I already hate myself and wanna die anyway so I figure why the hell not. Like today? Today I wanna shoot everybody in the world and then I wanna shoot myself.

GWEN: You'd regret it tomorrow.

RENEE: Yeah but I'd be dead so. It wouldn't matter. *(Beat.)* You didn't have to come out here.

GWEN: I know. *(Beat.)* You say that a lot. Tell people what they don't have to do.

RENEE: I don't like to be fussed over.

GWEN: I don't believe that. I think you're someone who could use some fussing. *(Beat.)* Maybe you should just try saying thank you. When someone does something nice for you.

RENEE: Maybe. *(Beat.)* Anyway. If I were you Gwen? I wouldn't have followed me. I've been an asshole to you all day long.

GWEN: You were no such thing.

RENEE: Trust me. I was.

GWEN: I was very grateful to have you here.

RENEE: *Why???*

GWEN: You were nice company.

RENEE: How could you say that! I'm *hateful*. A long time ago I useta be nice. But not anymore.

GWEN: *(Beat.)* I used to be a real hideous bitch.

RENEE: *(A little laugh.)* I find that hard to believe.

GWEN: I was! Then I quit drinking and sleeping with married men and smoking two packs a day of Mores and I got a whole lot nicer. Now

I just talk too much. When I smoked and drank and couldn't keep my legs closed? I hardly talked at all.

RENEE: I can't imagine.

GWEN: Oh yes. I was very quiet and mysterious. With my cocktails and my More Cigarettes. But I was also very unhappy. And so. I quit the drinking and the smoking and the screwing around with other people's husbands. And I left Illinois. And I moved here. And when I did? I started talking and talking and talking and I never shut the hell up. Sometimes I hear myself talking and I wish I hadda drink and a cigarette so I'd stop yammering. But Martin? He useta say that that's what he liked about me most. He useta say that I was so friendly that I could talk to anybody. Can you imagine? That's what he liked about me most.

RENEE: It's a nice way to be. *(Pause.)* Hey Gwen?

GWEN: Yeah.

RENEE: What did you like about him the most?

GWEN: Martin?

RENEE: Yeah.

GWEN: You really wanna know?

RENEE: I really do.

GWEN: *(Beat.)* He was funny.

RENEE: *(A small smile.)* Yeah he was.

GWEN: Even when he was pissed as hell.

RENEE: Which was often.

GWEN: But then he was funnier.

RENEE: *(A little laugh.)* Yeah.

GWEN: Useta drive him nuts. He'd be running off about something. And I'd start laughing. And then he'd start laughing too. And he'd curse at me "Damn you Woman! You're putting out my fire!"

RENEE: Sounds like him.

GWEN: Sometimes I liked him best like that. When he was pissed at the world.

RENEE: Huh. *(Pause.)* You OK?

GWEN: *(Beat.)* No.

RENEE: Me neither. I am about as far away from OK as somebody can be. *(Pause.)* I'm sorry, Gwen. I'm sorry for all of us.

GWEN: For what.

RENEE: For the way we were in there. I forget how awful we sound till there's somebody listening.

GWEN: *(Pause.)* Death and family brings out the worst.

RENEE: Yeah.

GWEN: That's why I left mine in Illinois. With my cigarettes. *(Silence.)* I came out here because. You remind me of Martin. *(Beat.)* Can't put my finger on why. But you do. And today? That meant the world. And so. I came out here because you were his daughter. And that matters. At least it matters to me. *(Beat.)* I'm not sure that's something you wanna hear. And I'm sorry to say it if it isn't. But. I mean it as something good. So. I hope you can take it like that. *(Gwen lights a cigarette for Renee, hands it to her, and then lights one for herself. Silence. They smoke.)*

RENEE: Thanks Gwen.

GWEN: Oh. Sure thing hon. Sure thing. *(They sit side by side smoking.)*

SCENE THREE

Henry's stoop. Cassie is pressing the buzzer and waiting. Frustrated – she lights a cigarette. Waits. Presses the buzzer again. Waits. Sits on the stoop and takes out her cell phone. Dials. Waits. Buzzes again. It goes to voicemail.

CASSIE: Hi. Hey. It's me. I've been buzzing you – and. And. Uh. I don't know what I'm saying. I'm downstairs. And. If you get this? I'll be here for a/ little bit longer.
(The intercom is suddenly on. There is loud chaotic barking in the background.)

HENRY: *(Through the intercom.)* Hello? *(To the dog.)* Gidg! *(Through the intercom.)* Hello?

CASSIE: Oh hi! *(To the phone.)* That's /you – so.

HENRY: Cassie?

CASSIE: Uh huh! *(To the phone.)* OK I'm gonna go. Bye.

HENRY: *(He struggles to talk over the barking.)* Bye? / Gidg! Jesus Fucking Christ!

CASSIE: No! Your voicemail! *(To the phone.)* OK. I'm hanging up now.

HENRY: Cass? You still/ there?

CASSIE: Yeah. Hi! Here I am. I'm still here. Can you buzz/me in?

HENRY: GIDG!!! /SHUT IT!!! *(The barking finally stops.)*

CASSIE: Is it a bad time?

HENRY: It's. It's *two*. In the morning.

CASSIE: I know I just. Can I / come up? It's kinda cold.

HENRY: Hold on. I'm coming down.

CASSIE: OK. *(She sits on the stoop. Waits. Finishes the cigarette. Puts it out. Henry opens the door. He's wearing a button down shirt and suit pants. She laughs.)* Where's the tie?

HENRY: *(Looks at what he's wearing.)* Oh. I just grabbed what was there.

CASSIE: I think this is the messiest I've ever seen you.

HENRY: OK…

CASSIE: Why didn't you bring Gidget down?

HENRY: I think she needs to forget you.

CASSIE: Right. Sure yeah.

HENRY: She's this close to forgiving me. *(Beat.)* How're you doing? You OK?

CASSIE: Been better.

HENRY: Yeah.

CASSIE: Been worse. *(Beat.)* Thanks for. Driving me to/the hospital.

HENRY: Oh. Yeah sure. *(Beat.)* Sorry I had to leave I. Had someplace/I had to be.

CASSIE: No no. I didn't. Expect you to stay.

HENRY: Yeah I know but. I would've./If I.

CASSIE: I know.

HENRY: *(Beat.)* How'd you get here?

CASSIE: Gary drove me.

HENRY: Gary has a driver's license?

CASSIE: He's not retarded.

HENRY: I *know* that I just. I always see him on his *bike* /that's all.

CASSIE: He doesn't have a *car* – but he has a *license*. I think. *(Beat.)* *I* don't have a license.

HENRY: I know.

CASSIE: You don't have to be a genius to have a license. Any moron can have a license. I could get one if I want one/I just don't.

HENRY: OK.

CASSIE: It's a lot of responsibility to drive. You know? It's a big/responsibility.

HENRY: Responsibility. I know. I know. *(Beat.)* You get a State ID yet?

CASSIE: Nope.

HENRY: You're still carrying around your passport????

CASSIE: Uh huh.

HENRY: What did I tell you? You can't *do* that.

CASSIE: OK.

HENRY: You need to go to the DMV/and get a Non Driver's ID.

CASSIE: Uh huh.

HENRY: Just do it/already.

CASSIE: Look I promise you that the minute. The *second*. After I bury my father I will race on over to the DMV and I will get a Non Driver's State ID!!! OK???
(Silence.)

HENRY: Why're you here?

CASSIE: Huh?

HENRY: Why. Are you here?

CASSIE: I wanted to see you.

HENRY: Why?

CASSIE: I don't. I'm *sorry*. I don't get what/ you're asking.

HENRY: Why did you want to see me?

CASSIE: Why? I don't know. I. I didn't want to be alone I guess.

HENRY: I thought you were staying at Gary's.

CASSIE: I *am*. I just./I wanted.

HENRY: So you're not alone.

CASSIE: Wow. I'm *sorry*. I wanted to see *you*, OK? Today's been kind of the absolute worst. And I wanted. I needed. To not be broken up today.

HENRY: Cass.

CASSIE: Yeah uh huh.

HENRY: *I* need to be broken up today.

CASSIE: Oh.

HENRY: *I* need to be broken up for good. *(Beat.)* Didn't we just have this conversation?

CASSIE: Yeah.

HENRY: So why are we having it again? Outside. At two in the fucking morning.

CASSIE: I/don't.

HENRY: I wanted to work it out. *You* were the one /who wanted "space".

CASSIE: Yes. I know./I know.

HENRY: So you got what you wanted. You have space. And I have an apartment that feels empty and a dog that whines all the time. Which was not what/ *I* wanted.

CASSIE: I *know*. I just.

HENRY: So what do you want now?

CASSIE: Now?

HENRY: From me. *(Cassie doesn't respond.)* Huh. Well how bout this. When you figure it out you let me know.

CASSIE: Henry.

HENRY: But till then no more. OK? I. I gotta go back upstairs.

CASSIE: Why?

HENRY: Because I'm done with this conversation and. I don't have to tell you why./I just do.

CASSIE: Do you have someone up there????

HENRY: Cass…

CASSIE: *Do* you??? Oh my God! *Do* you????

HENRY: That's not /the point.

CASSIE: I am such an asshole! Oh my God I'm such/an asshole!

HENRY: It's not/what you.

CASSIE: Fuck that. *You're* the asshole!

HENRY: How am I the asshole??

CASSIE: *Because.* You dropped me off at the hospital on the day that my father died. And THEN YOU WENT OUT ON A DATE? Knowing that I'd need a friend. That I'd need/you to be.

HENRY: We are no longer dating! Do you get that??? I am no longer responsible for you!

CASSIE: I *know!*/I *know* that!

HENRY: Do you?

CASSIE: I do! But. You're still the only person I want to see when I'm.

HENRY: When you're what?

CASSIE: I don't know!

HENRY: Wow - I take care of you I'm an asshole. I don't take care of you? I'm still an asshole. Somehow I'm always the bad guy. *(Pause.)* I don't wanna be your friend. I can't be friends with someone I was in love with. Am still in love with. I donno I just. Can't. I'm not that guy. And if that makes me suck. Then I suck. But. I don't want to be your go to guy, Cass. I don't wanna be your safety school. I wanna be the top choice. *(Beat.)* The truth is? Since you've moved out? I have a lot less drama. And I'm kind of liking it. So. Find another chauffeur. And go. I donno. Go get your own damn dog. Fetch your own hot chocolate. Because. I am officially done. *(Pause.)* I would've married you, you know.

CASSIE: Thanks?

HENRY: I'm serious. I would have. *(Beat.)* I useta look at you and see my future.

CASSIE: *(Beat.)* I don't think I want to get married.

HENRY: To me.

CASSIE: To anyone. *(Beat.)* You don't wanna marry me. You really don't. I'm not the kinda girl you marry. I thought maybe I could be. And I tried really hard. But it's just not in me. So. You dodged a big bullet. You dodged a hand grenade. You dodged an atomic bomb. *(Pause.)* You wanna know why I came over? I came over. To see you. Because. I love the way you look at me. Or the way you useta. Look at me. You useta look at me and it was like you could see the potential for good things. And I really wanted to be. A good thing. More than I wanted to be with you. I wanted to be whatever it was you saw when you looked at me. Because all I ever see are the things that make me sick. *(Beat.)* But. I guess you and I are finally on the same page, huh. When you look at me. You just see the same shit I see. You and I are finally looking at. The same exact ugly thing. *(He moves to hug her – but she stops him.)* Don't. Please. Don't.

HENRY: OK. *(Pause.)* I. *(Beat.)* I'm sorry about your dad. *(No response.)*

We should get you in a cab.

CASSIE: I can do it myself.

HENRY: Don't be ridiculous. I'll get you/a cab.

CASSIE: I said I'm good. You should. Get back to your date. *(She lights another cigarette. He goes inside)*

SCENE FOUR

The Coffee Shop. Gary sits. In front of him are two frozen coffee drinks. He waits. His leg bobs up and down. He makes a conscious effort to stop it. He is still. But nervous. His phone rings. He looks at it. He pauses – deciding whether to ignore or pick up. He picks up.

GARY: Not a great time, Cass. *(Angela enters. She stands with her arms crossed.)* Hey Cass? Not a great time. Uh huh. Yeah I gotta. *(He makes a motion to Angela of someone who talks and talks and talks and talks.)* Yeah OK sure. Yeah sure OK. Listen I gotta. I gotta. I gotta go! *(He hangs up and stands up to greet Angela.)* Hi. Hey. *(She doesn't respond.)* Sorry. That was. Family stuff. *(Beat. Still no response from Angela.)* So uh. *(Beat.)* Thanks for meeting me.

ANGELA: Uh huh.

GARY: *(Beat.)* I got you a. *(An attempt to make a private joke.)* Frozen Choco-Latte. *(He laughs. She doesn't.)*

ANGELA: You're lucky you still have an ass.

GARY: Yeah listen./I'm really.

ANGELA: I've got a guy a half a block away waiting for a signal. And if I give him one? He's gonna be here in a heartbeat. And you're gonna haveta get somebody to help you. You're gonna be scraping pieces of your ass offa the sidewalk for like. *A really long time.* You're gonna haveta scrape it all up so you can put your shit back together. So you can have an ass again and not just a pile of. Ass. Pulp.

GARY: Like Humpty Dumpty.

ANGELA: Excuse me?

GARY: Nothing/nevermind.

ANGELA: Not really in a laughy jokey ha ha kinda mood.

GARY: Sorry.

ANGELA: I'm in a watch out get the confetti order the clown and send out the invites cuz. Woo Hoo! Here comes the FREAK OUT party kinda mood.

GARY: I hate clowns.

ANGELA: *What???*

GARY: Nothing.

ANGELA: Did you say you hate *clowns?*

GARY: Just making/conversation.

ANGELA: Cuz I'll tell this guy to kick your ass in a fucking *clown costume.* He'll twist you up like a *balloon animal.* When he's done with you?

You'll. You'll look like a. *(She takes the drink and stands and sips.)* Like a *balloon animal.*

GARY: *(Beat.)* You wanna. You wanna sit maybe?

ANGELA: Nah I'm a little wound up.

GARY: OK.

ANGELA: Not sure how long I'm staying yet.

GARY: OK.

ANGELA: The jury's still. *Deliberating.*

GARY: OK. We can stand. That's cool. *(They stand for a long while. Not saying anything. Sipping in silence.)* So. Uh. *(He reaches down and gets a bag.)* I brought you this.

ANGELA: What is it.

GARY: Comics. Video Games.

ANGELA: Why would I want that???

GARY: It's not for *you.* It's for your son.

ANGELA: I don't want my kid picking up whores and killing people.

GARY: No! I checked. No whores no guns. I promise. It's all pretty much PG rated stuff.

ANGELA: He's eight.

GARY: It's all pretty much. G rated stuff. *(He takes a couple of things out of the bag.)*

ANGELA: Well. Thanks?

GARY: Yeah sure.

ANGELA: You can't buy my kid/you know.

GARY: No! I know. It's just. An apology./That's all.

ANGELA: OK.

GARY: I just wanted. I felt really bad and I./Wanted to apologize.

ANGELA: You should.

GARY: Huh?

ANGELA: You *should* feel bad.

GARY: I do. I really do.

ANGELA: You should hate yourself.

GARY: That's a little./Harsh? Maybe.

ANGELA: You should *hate* yourself.

GARY: OK. I. Hate? Myself?

ANGELA: Good. Maybe now you won't go to *hell.* *(Beat.)* So is that it?

GARY: Is what it?

ANGELA: Is that why you wanted to see me? Cuz if it is. I've got some-place I've gotta be soon. So if we're done. I'll just take my care package/and go.

GARY: Angela look. I'm sorry. I've got a lot going on/right now.

ANGELA: You ripped my baby's heart of his little chest and then you *pulverised* it. He had one hope left. That people weren't assholes. And *you* took that away from him. So. What do you want? Forgiveness? For a bag of comic books and a kid's beat up sad little heart? OK. Fine. You need that to go on with your life? Here you go. Gary? I accept your apology.

GARY: I really/am though.

ANGELA: People like you? You're always apologizing. And maybe you mean it in the moment. But who cares? There's still all this *shit* piled up that you're sorry for in the first place.

GARY: I know.

ANGELA: And it piles up and/it piles up.

GARY: I know.

ANGELA: And pretty soon everybody's buried in shit and *you're* still saying "Sorry! Sorry!" (Beat.) You know what he said when you didn't show up? He said "I knew he wasn't gonna come." And then he went into his room. He didn't cry. He just went into his room. And shut the door. And stayed there for the rest of the day.

GARY: Now I really do hate myself.

ANGELA: Good. You should stay in that.

GARY: I didn't mean to/ disappoint him.

ANGELA: Of course you did. Look. You are a grown ass man. You should know by now who you are and what you do. So. Just stop doing it. *(Beat)* I asked you to be honest with me. I looked you in the eye – and I said "Here's the situation are you *capable?*"

GARY: I /know.

ANGELA: And *you* said yes. You swore up and down that you were. You *promised* me. And even though you're a little rough around the edges I thought "You know what? Who isn't?" And I took a chance on you/anyway and.

GARY: I/know.

ANGELA: Stop saying "I know!" Cuz you clearly *don't* know!

GARY: Sorry.

ANGELA: And stop saying sorry! Sorry's not gonna cut it. You fucked up! In a really big way!

GARY: *I know.* Fuck. Sorry. Fuck. I don't know what to say!

ANGELA: So don't say anything! Just. Shut up!

GARY: I.

ANGELA: Shut it!

GARY: OK!
    (Silence.)
ANGELA: I. Am so fucking. Tired.
GARY: Yeah.
ANGELA: Yeah. *(Pause.)* Good luck to you Gary. I. Really hope you get it
    together someday. /I really do.
GARY: I had a family situation.
ANGELA: *(Beat.)* What kinda family situation.
GARY: My father was in the hospital. And so. I was in and out of the
    hospital all day and. I don't wanna use it as an excuse? So. I wasn't
    gonna say anything. But. I don't want you/to think that.
ANGELA: But you are though.
GARY: Huh?
ANGELA: You *are* using it as an excuse.
GARY: No I'm. Look I'm./Fuck. I'm.
ANGELA: You're what.
GARY: I don't know. I've had a really shitty couple of days.
ANGELA: Yeah. Me too. *(Beat.)* I really hope your dad gets better. I re-
    ally/do but I.
GARY: He's not gonna get better.
ANGELA: OK so. I really hope he doesn't. I donno./Get *worse* then.
GARY: He's not gonna anything cuz. He's kinda dead.
ANGELA: He's what???
GARY: He's dead. Kinda.
ANGELA: What do you mean kinda? There is no kinda? He's either dead
    or/he isn't dead.
GARY: Fine! He's all the way dead. He is really dead. Yesterday morn-
    ing he was still just kinda dead. But now he's really truly officially
    dead. So. There you go. He won't be getting any better. Or worse.
    Anytime soon. Because he's all the way no turning back dead dead.
    (Beat.) It's no big deal. It's just. It is what it is.
ANGELA: *(Beat.)* I'm really/sorry.
GARY: Don't say it. I mean I know that's what you're supposed to say but.
    We weren't pals. We didn't go *fishing* or anything. I have his eyes and
    his shitwater hair and apparently his knack for disappointing people.
    But. Other than that we weren't all that close. So. Don't feel bad for
    me.
ANGELA: OK.
GARY: I'm not grieving or anything. You can still hate my guts if you want
    to.

ANGELA: OK. *(Pause.)* People really fuck their kids up, huh.

GARY: Yeah.

ANGELA: They fuck 'em up huge. *(Beat.)* Not me though. I am a really *awesome* mom.

GARY: I see that.

ANGELA: I am. *(Beat.)* Why didn't you just call me and tell me you weren't gonna show? How hard is that?

GARY: Yeah well I was gonna? And then I didn't. I donno. There was a lot of stuff going on and so. I forgot.

ANGELA: Maybe you should start writing shit down. Stop smoking so much weed.

GARY: I should. Yeah. Probly. Do that.

ANGELA: You think? *(Pause. There's nothing more to say.)* It's too bad things didn't work out, Gary. I'm. I donno I'm. Thanks for the comic books.

GARY: Uh huh. *(Angela turns to go. He almost lets her leave and then decides to stop her. He says "Fuck" under his breath.)* Hey Angela?

ANGELA: Yeah what.

GARY: Listen I know you haveta go somewhere but. Do you have a minute? I promise I won't be long I just. It'll just be a minute. *(She looks at him and waits.)* I. *(Beat.)* I asked you to come here to meet me today. Because I wanted to apologize. Which I did. But I also. I kinda have a favor I need.

ANGELA: From me?

GARY: Yeah.

ANGELA: You wanna ask *me* to do *you* a favor.

GARY: Uh huh. And I didn't want to do it over the phone. I wanted to do it face to face.

ANGELA: I'm probably not your best bet for a favor.

GARY: Yeah/I know.

ANGELA: But go ahead.

GARY: OK. Thanks.

ANGELA: I haven't said yes yet.

GARY: I know just. Thanks for. Letting me ask. *(Beat.)* So I was wondering. If you'd. I was wondering if you'd consider maybe. *(Beat.)* I was wondering if you'd maybe consider giving me. A second chance.

ANGELA: A second chance?

GARY: To prove myself.

ANGELA: To *who*.

GARY: You.

ANGELA: Why would I wanna do that.

GARY: I don't know.

ANGELA: Not a compelling answer.

GARY: Because…

ANGELA: Uh huh.

GARY: Because. I really think I could do it if I had another chance you know. I think I could maybe be good/at this and.

ANGELA: *Could??? Maybe???* What *is* that???

GARY: I think I could maybe. That maybe I could. Sorry. *Can.* Not maybe. That I *can* do it. I just. It was a bad week and I. I donno. If you gave me another chance? If you did. I think I could. I think I *would.* Whichever's better. Could or would. Whatever it is. I'll try to do it. Do that one. The right one. I think I can come through. Second time around? *(Pause.)* Listen. I've got two options right now. I can continue to be the person who fucks shit up. Or I can try and not be. That person. And. I really wanna try and not be. So. *(Beat.)* I know how your kid feels. And it really sucks to feel that way and. I don't wanna be the person who makes people feel like that.

ANGELA: *(Pause.)* My kid's not a roulette wheel. He's not a free trial.

GARY: I know /I just.

ANGELA: He deserves more than a maybe I'll see what I can do. He deserves a hundred percent. Can you give him a hundred percent?

GARY: I can try /the best I can.

ANGELA: Can you give him. A hundred percent?

GARY: I can give. Ninety five.

ANGELA: *(Beat.)* Be good Gary.

GARY: Yeah OK. You too. Thanks for. Coming down.

> *(Angela takes her bag and exits. Gary sits. He drinks. A Pause. Angela re-nters and puts the bag of comic books in front of Gary.)*

ANGELA: Thursday at four o'clock. You're gonna come by my house and bring these to him yourself.

GARY: Uh.

ANGELA: Can you do that?

GARY: I think?/I gotta check.

ANGELA: No I think. Yes or no.

GARY: I gotta /check my schedule.

ANGELA: Yes or no.

GARY: Yes.

ANGELA: Thursday.

GARY: Four o'clock.

ANGELA: You bring these over and you say sorry to him yourself. And if *he* decides to forgive you. Then *he* can. But it's up to him understand?

GARY: Yes.

ANGELA: If he decides to say screw you? He can do that too.

GARY: OK.

ANGELA: And if you fuck up and don't show. It's you and a clown in a dark alley. No third chances. No excuses. You blow this and no more ass for you Humpty Dumpty. OK? OK?

GARY: OK.

ANGELA: OK. OK Good. We're all on the same page then. *(She turns to go.)*

GARY: Hey Angela!

ANGELA: Yeah.

GARY: Thank you. Thank you a lot.

ANGELA: *(Beat.)* Sure. *(She exits.)*

SCENE FIVE

Renee and Mark's living room. The roof is leaking. Badly. There are pots and buckets scattered throughout the room, catching droplets of water in a sort of melodic kerplunking. Mark sits on the couch. It appears that there was a battle between the leak and Mark – and Mark didn't lose – he surrendered. He is drinking a beer. Feet up on the coffee table. Empty beer bottles around him. A little rumpled – but otherwise in good spirits. Renee enters. Soaked through. She had no umbrella. Renee surveys the room – in a bit of shock – taking it all in.

MARK: Welcome home!

RENEE: *(Still taking it all in.)* It's. Raining.

MARK: Uh huh.

RENEE: In. The house.

MARK: Sure is!

RENEE: Why is it raining. In the house.

MARK: I think we may have angered the Gods. *(Beat.)* Beer?

RENEE: No thanks.

MARK: Tequila shot?

RENEE: *(Beat.)* Yeah OK.

MARK: Coming right up! *(He exits to the kitchen.)*

RENEE: Are you drunk?

MARK: *(From off.)* Hammered!

RENEE: You're hammered? Who says *hammered* anymore?

MARK: I do and I am. You are either gonna get lucky or thrown up on.

RENEE: Or both.

MARK: Huh?

RENEE: Nothing.

MARK: Lime and salt?

RENEE: Yes please.

MARK: *(From off.)* I am so hammered – that I am not going to ask you why you never came home last night. *(He returns. She hasn't moved.)* You can do what you want. I can do what I want. This may be the key to a happy and successful marriage. Live separate lives. Sleep in separate beds. And get plastered every night. Just. Like. My parents! *(He hands her a bottle of tequila.)* Here you go. *(He hands her a lime.)* And here you go. *(He licks her hand and shakes salt on it.)* And here you go. *(He raises his beer to her.)* Rock it out babe. *(She licks the salt off her hand, drinks the tequila out of the bottle, and sucks on the lime.)*

RENEE: Listen/I.

MARK: Nope! Don't care. I am on vacation.

RENEE: Vacation.

MARK: In a rain forest. In Hawaii.

RENEE: Mark…

MARK: C'mere. You should join me. *(She does.)*

RENEE: Did you call a roofer?

MARK: I did.

RENEE: And the roofer said…

MARK: We have to wait till it stops raining. And guess what?

RENEE: What.

MARK: It's supposed to rain for the next three days! *(He drinks.)* Starting to get funny – right? On its way to funny.

RENEE: Not yet. *(She takes another drink out of the bottle. He drinks his beer.)* Almost.

MARK: Just sit back and listen.

RENEE: All our stuff's/getting ruined.

MARK: Listen! *(The rain kerplunks.)*

RENEE: *(A little laugh.)* What are we listening to?

MARK: The melodious soprano of. Mother Nature.

   (They drink. They listen. The rain kerplunks again.)

RENEE: Where are the kids?

MARK: Sent them to your mother's.

RENEE: Oh.

MARK: Would you rather them be here?

RENEE: In the *rain forest?*

MARK: Look – if you wanna have a say in where your kids go. You need to be around when the/decision's being made.

RENEE: I know. You're right.

MARK: I'm sorry *what* did you say?

RENEE: You heard me.

MARK: Repeat please.

RENEE: I said. You. Are right.

MARK: Ha! Can we date and stamp this?

RENEE: Sure.

MARK: Create a holiday? A commemorative coin?

RENEE: I'll look into it.

MARK: A Tshirt?

RENEE: Calm down.

MARK: *(Pause.)* You can't do that.

RENEE: Do what.

MARK: Not come home.

RENEE: Oh. *(Beat.)* Yeah I know.

MARK: Not call.

RENEE: I'm sorry.

MARK: I could care less about myself – but it's a shitty thing to do to your kids.

RENEE: I know.

MARK: So. Don't do it again. *(Pause.)* Wherever you were. Whatever you were doing. I'm glad you decided to come back.

RENEE: Me too. *(Beat.)* That's the nicest thing anybody's said to me in weeks. *(Pause.)* Lets go get the kids.

MARK: It's too late.

RENEE: We could just pick them up in our arms and put them in the car? In their pajamas?

MARK: Tomorrow.

RENEE: That seems so far away.

MARK: It's just one night.

RENEE: I miss them.

MARK: We'll go get them first thing.

RENEE: OK.

MARK: Take them for pancakes.

RENEE: OK.

MARK: Go to the aquarium.

RENEE: A perfect day. Can we give them a perfect day?

MARK: Sure.

RENEE: I could use a perfect day.

MARK: Yeah Me too. *(Pause.)* You wanna tell me where you were last night. *(She doesn't answer.)* It's OK if you don't. But if you do? I promise to just listen.

RENEE: *(Pause.)* I was sitting in the car. In the parking lot at the hospital.

MARK: All night?

RENEE: I lost track of time. I started measuring time in cigarettes. I was in the car for three and a half packs. *(Beat.)* Do you know they sell cigarettes at the gift shop in the hospital?

MARK: Really?

RENEE: And booze. And scratch off lottery tickets. So I bought all three. *(Beat.)* I've spent my entire life wondering how I'd react when Martin finally died. I never thought I'd end up stuck in my car

chainsmoking, drinking, and gambling. Like father like daughter.
He woulda been proud. *(Beat.)* Can you believe it's already been
twelve years since Cassie's mom died. In that same hospital.

MARK: I hate that hospital.

RENEE: Yeah me too.

MARK: The doctors there are assholes.

RENEE: *(A little laugh.)* Yeah.

MARK: It's like a job requirement.

(A small shared laugh.)

RENEE: *(Pause.)* She died the same day I found out I was pregnant with
Molly. I hadn't even told you yet. I wanted to tell you in person.
But before I could I got the call to come to the hospital. And you
picked me up. And everything started moving so fast and. I couldn't
tell you like that. So. I put it on hold. And. *(Beat.)* All I could
think was. Fuck them. Fuck them all. The woman had been failing
at suicide for fifteen years. Why'd she have get it right on my fucking
day. And the whole way there I panicked about what to do with
Cassie. I didn't want her. And you dropped me off and you went
to get everybody coffee. And I said to myself "Keep your trap shut
Renee. Don't you dare volunteer. Don't you dare. Even if she ends
up in foster care. Not your problem" And then Gary's mom said
outta nowhere "You'll live with us." And we all looked at her like
she was crazy as she stood up and sat next to Cassie and said "You're
Gary's blood. And so you're my blood too." And she held her in her
arms. And she stroked her pink hair. And Cassie sobbed and sobbed.
And I hated myself for being such a selfish asshole. For not wanting
to share even a second of my happiness. For really not giving a shit
what happened to her. For being *jealous* of a kid with a dead mom.
Because *I* wanted someone to love me like that. Not because they had
to. Because they wanted to. Because they chose to. *(Beat.)* And then
you came back with the coffees. And you handed them out. And you
sat down next to me and picked up my hand and squeezed it. Like we
were sharing a secret. And I thought. "You are my blood. You are my
family. You are my home." And I knew. That for the rest of my life.
As long as you were within reach. I'd be OK. *(Pause.)* How did we
end up. Here.

MARK: I donno.

RENEE: I don't wanna be here anymore.

MARK: Me neither.

RENEE: I wanna run as far away from here as I possibly can.

MARK: Where do you wanna go?

RENEE: *(Beat.)* California. Can we go to California

MARK: Sure. When?

RENEE: Tomorrow.

MARK: OK.

RENEE: In five minutes.

MARK: OK.

RENEE: Right now.

MARK: I'll see what I can do.

RENEE: Thanks.

MARK: You got it. *(Pause.)* Hey.

RENEE: Huh.

MARK: Listen. Just sit here and listen. *(Pause.)* Isn't that just. Isn't that just the most beautiful sound. You've ever heard. *(They sit side by side and listen to the rain.)*

SCENE SIX

Gary and Cassie. He is in a tux. She is in a large and slightly out of control wedding dress. There is a wedding cake.

CASSIE: I think I might puke.

GARY: You're fine.

CASSIE: I think I might puke my guts out.

GARY: Cass.

CASSIE: This dress is cutting off my circulation. I'm gonna pass out. And then I'm gonna puke my guts out. *(Beat.)* What time is it?

GARY: Quarter til.

CASSIE: Everybody's out there, huh.

GARY: Yup.

CASSIE: No turning back now.

GARY: Nope.

CASSIE: Even if I wanted to. Which I don't.

GARY: OK.

CASSIE: OK. *(Pause.)* You got the rings?

GARY: Uh huh.

CASSIE: Lemme see. *(He takes a ring box out of his jacket pocket and shows her.)* There they are.

GARY: Uh huh.

CASSIE: The rings. *(Pause.)* Gary?

GARY: Yeah.

CASSIE: You've gotta get me to the finish line.

GARY: Don't worry.

CASSIE: Straight through. No stopping.

GARY: I told you I would.

CASSIE: Even if I suddenly go crazy and kick you in the balls – you still gotta get me there.

GARY: OK.

CASSIE: Even if I. I donno. Burn you with cigarettes or. Scream profanities. You've gotta make sure I get there.

GARY: I promise I will.

CASSIE: Because I love him. I love him so much it almost hurts.

GARY: I know. *(Beat.)* Don't worry. I'll get you there. No matter what.

CASSIE: Thanks.

GARY: Uh huh. *(Pause.)* You look. Beautiful.

CASSIE: Shut up.

GARY: I mean it. You do. You really do.

CASSIE: I feel a little over the top.

GARY: You're perfect.

CASSIE: I feel like that cake. I match my cake.

GARY: You don't match your cake.

CASSIE: I do. Me and that cake are twins. *(Beat.)* I don't feel like me. I wanted something simple but. Your mom said "You only get to be a princess once." And I got high off the bride fumes.

GARY: I think you made a great choice.

CASSIE: I should've eloped. *(Beat.)* Anyway. *(Beat.)* Thanks for giving me away.

GARY: Sure.

CASSIE: Thanks for being my. Person of Honor

GARY: Uh huh.

CASSIE: Thanks for getting me a little high.

GARY: That's what I'm here for.

CASSIE: You're the best. *(Long pause.)* Hey Gary?

GARY: Yeah.

CASSIE: You wanna hear a secret?

GARY: Sure.

CASSIE: You were my first crush.

GARY: *(A little laugh.)* Really?

CASSIE: Yeah. I was five. And I told Renee I loved you. And she said I couldn't because we'd have kids with three heads. And I cried and cried and cried because I wanted to marry you. So we could live in the same house. Like a real family.

GARY: *(Pause.)* You talk to Renee?

CASSIE: She left me a message.

GARY: What'd she say?

CASSIE: Doesn't matter. She's not here.

GARY: No. *(Pause.)* You think she's ever coming back.

CASSIE: Nope.

GARY: Me neither.

CASSIE: *(Pause.)* It's my *wedding*.

GARY: I know.

CASSIE: It's one day.

GARY: I know.

CASSIE: So. Fuck her. All I got is you.

GARY: She's just working /through her shit.

CASSIE: All I got is you. *(Long pause.)* What time is it?

GARY: Ten of.

CASSIE: You got the rings?

GARY: Uh huh.

CASSIE: Can I see 'em? *(He shows her the rings.)* There they are. The rings. *(Pause.)* I think I'm gonna. I need to take a walk I think. I think I need some air.

GARY: You don't have that much time left you know.

CASSIE: *(Very calmly.)* I'm about to have a panic attack. *(She takes his pack of cigarettes out of his pocket.)*

GARY: OK.

CASSIE: So I think I need some air.

GARY: OK.

CASSIE: OK. *(Beat.)* What time is it?

GARY: Nine of.

CASSIE: You got the rings?

GARY: *(Pats his pocket.)* Right here.

CASSIE: OK. OK. I'll see you in a few. I'm gonna go take a walk.

GARY: Uh huh.

CASSIE: Get some air.

(She exits. She enters again and abruptly and a little awkwardly kisses him on the cheek. They laugh. She exits again. A beat. Gary is alone. He fidgets. He checks for the rings one more time. Opens the box. Satisfied, puts them back in his pocket.)

BENJY: *(from off)* Cass?

GARY: Not here.

BENJY: So can I come in?

GARY: Huh?

BENJY: Bad luck?

GARY: Oh. *(Beat.)* Yeah sure. It's just me.

(Benjy enters.)

BENJY: Hey.

GARY: Hey.

BENJY: Where's my bride?

GARY: Went for a little walk.

BENJY: How's she look?

GARY: She's gonna knock your socks off.

BENJY: Yeah? *(He smiles.)* How's your speech.

GARY: It's OK.

BENJY: Don't fuck it up.

GARY: I won't.

BENJY: You would ruin everything if your speech sucks.

GARY: I know.

BENJY: People remember that shit.

GARY: It'll be great. All the ladies will weep. You'll see. Have a little faith. *(Beat.)* You doing OK?

BENJY: I think so.

GARY: It's the rest of your life!

BENJY: I know. I'm. *(Beat.)* I'm excited!

GARY: Yeah?

BENJY: For the rest of my life! I'm. *(Pause.)* I got the girl!

GARY: You sure did!

BENJY: I'm wearing a fucking tux!

GARY: Yeah you are.

BENJY: I mean. Look at me! I'm like. A spy. I mean. I keep catching myself in the mirror and I'm like. *(He does a sort of Spy-like swagger – and then goes back to himself.)* And then I'm like. *(He pulls a fake gun, shoots a few rounds, and then goes back to himself.)* It's so freaking awesome! *(Beat.)* You got the rings?

GARY: *(He checks one more time.)* Yeah. Right here.

BENJY: Good. *(Beat.)* You're like. You're like wedding party in a box. Give the bride away guy. Best man guy. It's like. It's like we got you on *sale*.

GARY: I feel like I'm not doing a good job.

BENJY: All you gotta do is make sure she makes it down the aisle.

GARY: I think I can do that.

BENJY: And not fuck up the speech.

GARY: Right.

BENJY: That's all you gotta do.

GARY: Yeah. Yeah OK. *(Pause.)* Hey uh Benjy.

BENJY: Yeah.

GARY: Make her happy. OK? Promise me that you'll do whatever you can to just make her really fucking happy.

BENJY: That's the plan.

GARY: Good. Good. *(Long pause.)* I should go be a. Bride giver awayer.

BENJY: OK.

GARY: You've got like two minutes, OK? Not even.

BENJY: Uh huh.

GARY: You know where you're going?

BENJY: I think so.

GARY: So you just do what you gotta do. And then. When you hear the

Earth Wind and Fire – that's your cue to get/in place.

BENJY: Right.

GARY: And then you just get yourself out there. And then. And then we'll get you married. OK?

BENJY: Uh huh.

GARY: Yeah.

BENJY: OK.

GARY: Good. *(Long pause.)* So listen. Uh. Benjy.

BENJY: Yeah?

GARY: Uh. I just wanted. To. Uh. I. *(A deep breath.)* Welcome! Welcome to the family! *(A beat. Benjy impulsively hugs Gary. It is a big huge loving hug without reservation. It is more hug than Gary knows what to do with. He is stiffly uncomfortable with it. But Benjy doesn't let go. He keeps on hugging. A beat. Gary hugs him back tentatively. And then fully. And then as fully as Benjy's hugging him. He hugs him harder than he's ever hugged anybody in his whole life. He doesn't let go. It is a joyous celebratory hug.)*

END OF PLAY

WITTENBERG

A TRAGICAL-COMICAL-HISTORICAL IN TWO ACTS

David Davalos

PLAYWRIGHT'S BIOGRAPHY

David Davalos currently homesteads in the frontier wilds of northern Colorado with his wife and daughter. He is a graduate of the theatre programs of both the University of Texas and Ohio University. Some of his other plays include *Daedalus: A Fantasia of Leonardo da Vinci; The Tragedie of Johnnius Caerson* (a comedy in blank verse chronicling the Late Night TV Wars); and *Darkfall* (a modern sequel to Paradise Lost). For its premiere production at Philadelphia's Arden Theatre, *Wittenberg* received the 2008 Barrymore Award for Outstanding New Play. David was also the recipient of the National Theatre Conference's 2008 Stavis Playwriting Award. The play has gone on to be produced throughout the U.S. from Juneau to Orlando, including an off-Broadway production by the Pearl Theatre. Internationally, *Wittenberg* was produced in London by the Gate Theatre and the German translation has been staged in Berlin and Innsbruck.

Wittenberg was originally produced in 2008 by the Arden Theatre Company (Terrence J. Nolen, Producing Artistic Director; Amy Murphy, Managing Director) in Philadelphia, PA. It was directed by J.R. Sullivan; the set and lighting design were by Michael Philippi; the costume design was by Elizabeth Covey; the sound design was by Jorge Cousineau; the stage manager was Patricia G. Sabato; and the assistant director was Matt Pfeiffer. The cast was as follows:

John Faustus	Scott Greer
Hamlet	Shawn Fagan
Martin Luther	Greg Wood
The Eternal Feminine	Kate Udall

Wittenberg received its New York premiere in 2011 by the Pearl Theatre Company (J.R. Sullivan, Artistic Director; Shira Beckerman, Managing Director). It was directed by J.R. Sullivan. The cast was as follows:

John Faustus	Scott Greer
Hamlet	Sean McNall
Martin Luther	Chris Mixon
The Eternal Feminine	Joey Parsons

Wittenberg is the recipient of the following awards:

Barrymore Award for Outstanding New Play – 2008

Edgerton Foundation New American Plays Award
National Theatre Conference's Stavis Playwriting Award – 2008

Dramatis Personae
John Faustus, M.D., J.D., Ph.D., Th.D., a doctor

Hamlet, Prince of Denmark, a senior, major undecided

Rev.Fr. Martin Luther, D.D., a professor and a confessor

The Eternal Feminine*:
    Gretchen, a working girl
    Helen, a lady of pleasure
    Mary, the Mother of God
    Lady Voltemand, an ambassador

Voices of the Judge and Laertes

*All four women's roles should be played by one actor.

The Time: The last week of October, 1517
The Place: Wittenberg, Germany – the town and its university

Out of love for the truth and the desire to bring it to light, the following propositions will be discussed at *Wittenberg*, under the presidency of the Reverend Father Martin Luther, Monk of the Order of Saint Augustine, Master of Arts and of Sacred Theology, and Lecturer in Ordinary on the same at that place.
– *Disputation of Doctor Martin Luther on the Power and Efficacy of Indulgences (a.k.a. the 95 Theses)*

Then, gentle friends, aid me in this attempt;
And I, that have with subtle syllogisms
Gravell'd the pastors of the German church,
And made the flowering pride of *Wittenberg*
Swarm to my problems as th' infernal spirits
On sweet Musaeus when he came to hell,
Will be as cunning as Agrippa was,
Whose shadows made all Europe honour him.
    – *The Tragical History of Doctor Faustus*

You are the most immediate to our throne;
And with no less nobility of love
Than that which dearest father bears his son,
Do I impart toward you. For your intent
In going back to school in *Wittenberg*,
It is most retrograde to our desire;
And we beseech you, bend you to remain
Here, in the cheer and comfort of our eye,
Our chiefest courtier, cousin, and our son.

— *The Tragedy of Hamlet, Prince of Denmark*

WITTENBERG

ACT ONE

The University of Wittenberg campus quad, specifically the steps in front of the Castle Church's main doors, which are used as a bulletin board. The church bells toll the hour. It is sunrise – stained-glass light. Faustus is nailing up a notice amidst the crowded skein of flyers, bills, et al. He wears a leather pouch stuffed with loose papers slung over his shoulder. Enter Hamlet [dressed in any color but black] carrying a rucksack.

HAMLET: My good Doctor Faustus!

FAUSTUS: His Royal Highness Hamlet Hamletsen!

HAMLET: O, spare me, prithee…

FAUSTUS: My friend, then. Welcome back to Wittenberg! Have you lost weight? New haircut? What is it about you?

HAMLET: A change of mind, methinks.

FAUSTUS: Interesting. I trust you had a productive summer.

HAMLET: 'Twas an exceedingly singular semester abroad indeed.

FAUSTUS: Excellent, most excellent. But, details! We'll have to share some brau soon, yes? And you can illuminate the manuscript of your life for me.

HAMLET: The prospect thereof is a smiling affair.

FAUSTUS: Good, good.
(He produces a flyer from the leather pouch.)
I'll be playing at The Bunghole this week, Wednesday and Friday nights, my usual gig, if you feel like a little light lute. Two-stein minimum, all the tripe you can eat. So: big year. Senior class. Good time to be thinking about declaring a major.

HAMLET: So t'would seem.

FAUSTUS: Decided on your classes yet?

HAMLET: I have decided nothing.

FAUSTUS: I didn't think so. Well, I think you should think seriously about settling on a philosophy degree, and then I think you should think seriously about graduate study with me here afterward.

HAMLET: Seriously?

FAUSTUS: I think so. Plato believed that the world should be run by philosopher-kings, and you're the only student I've had who has a real chance at being both. *(Indicating the notice he has nailed to the door.)*

I'm offering a master's seminar in the philosophy of philosophy this semester. Philosophy as theory which manifests itself in the practice of choice. You are what you choose. Might be worth your time, but it's up to you, which is, of course, the whole point.

HAMLET: No, I would not miss it not for all the gold of newfound 'Merica.

FAUSTUS: O, thank you, but I'd take the gold. Choices!

HAMLET: It likes me well to see thee once again.

FAUSTUS: It likes me likewise. I look forward to our time together.

HAMLET: Ay, truly. Look ye, could I…

FAUSTUS: Yes, what? Could you what?

HAMLET: Nothing, nothing, 'tis a thing of nothing, no more than such like stuff as dreams are made upon. In faith, I am but weary of a-traveling, I will trouble thee no further.

FAUSTUS: No trouble, really.

HAMLET: No, 'tis not the fitting hour for this midnight of my soul. My clock's up-cocked; better rest makes better company.

FAUSTUS: Your brain is sprained and your time is out of joint, I understand. Try leopard's bane.
(He pulls a flyer off the door and jots down a prescription on the back with a pencil.)

HAMLET: I prithee pardon?

FAUSTUS: Leopard's bane. Arnica montana. Stop by the apothecary, give him this, tell him you want leopard's bane prepared for tea.

HAMLET: *(Trying to read the prescription.)* This hand be most inscrutable to me, good doctor sir – thy writing baffles me.

FAUSTUS: Don't worry – the apothecary can read it. Get it, go straight back to your dorm, brew it up, drink it near a bed. When you wake up, you'll be fine.

HAMLET: Leopard's bane.

FAUSTUS: Ask for it by name. The bane for brains of Danes in pain.

HAMLET: Insane.

FAUSTUS: The same.

HAMLET: My thanks.

FAUSTUS: It's what I do. If you need anything else, don't hesitate. I live to serve.

HAMLET: Tut, thou art my master in all things. I take thy hand and take my leave, good sir. Farewell!
(Exit Hamlet.)

FAUSTUS: Exit the Prince, leaving *Faustus* solus. And I'm talking to myself out loud again. Exit

Faustus, mute.

(Exit Faustus, mute. A peal of church bells. The scene is now Luther's theology classroom. Enter Luther, carrying a large, extensively bookmarked Bible. He wears the black habit of an Augustinian monk. He addresses the audience either in his capacity as professor to classroom or as priest to congregation. In either case, he speaks from his pulpit, addressing his listeners from above. A seat in the audience is held for Hamlet, who attends this and the following lecture. [Any latecomers should be seated now.])

LUTHER: Alright, alright, take your seats. Let's go, come on, timeliness is next to cleanliness, and you know what cleanliness is next to. Sit down, sit still – this is Biblical Principles of Theology, and I am your instructor, Professor Doctor Reverend Father Martin *Luther*. You may call me "Professor" or "Doctor" or "Professor Doctor" or "Father" or "Martin", but if you call me "Herr *Luther*", I Will not hesitate to thrash you violently about the neck and face. "Herr *Luther*" is my father.

A reminder that this is Principles of Christian Theology…If you are in league with the Devil, you are in the wrong classroom – and you want instead Doctor Faustus' philosophy seminar: across the quad, down the hall, room 2B, sixth door on the left.

From the breath of life which first animated Adam to the whispered prayer you will find yourself breathing should I call upon you in this room and you are unprepared to respond, theology is simply the study of God's interaction with man. That interaction is documented for us all in the form of God's Holy Word, the only text we require for study. "Take up, and read," as the divine voice told Saint Augustine. Take up, and read.

But we do this only so that we might understand more clearly how the Lord speaks to us, you and me, today. The language of the Lord speaks to our souls, not our minds. In moments of sudden understanding, God speaks to us. In lightning flashes of inspiration, God speaks to us. When you settle on a decision in the absolute certainty that it is the right decision, the best decision, the only decision – that is God whispering the conviction in your ear. *(To Hamlet)* Here, together, through the study of His Holy Word, we will learn how to recognize the voice of God.

So, because the end cometh and we know not when, let's get started. Open your textbooks to chapter one, page one. Let's look at that first verse there: "In the beginning God created the heaven and the earth."

(Lights crossfade to reveal Faustus in his philosophy classroom, addressing

the audience from a lower vantage-point, as though speaking up to students arranged in a series of raked seats. He too reads from a Bible; his first line overlaps Luther's last.)

FAUSTUS: "In the beginning God created the heaven and the earth." So God existed before the beginning. So the truth of the statement "in the beginning" is suspect. So one sentence in, our doubt is aroused. Unless, of course, the statement is not intended to be taken literally, but rather metaphorically. But in that case, the Word of God can be interpreted as poetry and myth. And if we can accept "in the beginning" so easily, why not "the devil" as a name given to man's animal nature, and "hell" as a word describing a state of mind?

Don't get me wrong: I love the Bible. It's a great read. It's got everything: sex, violence, red dragons with seven heads. If you read it closely enough, you can find a justification for anything. That's pretty impressive – one hell of a book. But it's just that, really, only one book, at least in the library of the philosopher. The theologian reads it for the answers; the philosopher for the questions.

I know we have some Jews and Mohammedans auditing the class this semester – shalom, salaam – and I just wanted to make it clear that, despite this being a Catholic university, we are not going to be restricting ourselves to studying the philosophies of the Church. There are, after all, more things in heaven and earth than are dreamt of in its theology. True philosophy is like the insolent child who, regardless of the explanation given by God the Father, will always respond with "why?" "You must not eat from the tree of the knowledge of good and evil, for when you eat of it you will surely die." Why? Isn't "knowledge of good and evil" another way of saying "wisdom"? Is wisdom forbidden? Does that sound right to you? Aristotle, on the other hand, said that "all men possess by nature a craving for knowledge," and Aristotle, of course, wasn't much of a churchgoer.

For those of you pursuing a double major – *(To Hamlet)* and for those of you who remain undecided in your major – keep in mind that a theology degree only serves you when you're talking to God; a philosophy degree is valuable every time you talk to yourself. Of course, in my opinion, what's the difference? But then, that's my philosophy. What's yours? Choose carefully. Read, question, discuss, explore, test, doubt, defy convention. Don't settle for "because I said so," or "because that's the way it's always been." No-one has all the answers. Yet. Above all, think for yourself. Granted, about those things which we cannot think, we must believe. But about those things which we cannot believe, we must think.

(The scene moves to Faustus' study. A desk littered with books, parchments, scrolls and a stack of pamphlets paperweighted with a human skull. A pair of chairs, and/or possibly a chaise lounge. A cabinet from which everything prescribed can be produced. An hourglass, an armillary sphere, and possibly a globe. A hookah. Maybe his four doctoral diplomas, and perhaps a framed Bosch. Faustus examines Luther, initially with his ear against Luther's belly.)

LUTHER: When was your last confession?

FAUSTUS: When was your last check-up?

LUTHER: I worry about your soul.

FAUSTUS: I worry about your bowels.

LUTHER: I've tried and I've tried but nothing is forthcoming.

FAUSTUS: How long?

LUTHER: Six days.

FAUSTUS: O, Martin, come on. God made the universe in six days. I don't think you're really trying.

LUTHER: I'm trying!

FAUSTUS: Are the headaches back?

LUTHER: Yes, of course…my head is throbbing even now.

FAUSTUS: Describe the pain.

LUTHER: The same as always. A metal band clamped around my head. Thorns at my temples. I can hear the movement of my blood. On the nights I sleep, I wake up feeling like someone's hammered a rusty iron spike into the back of my head.

FAUSTUS: How deep does the spike go?

LUTHER: To just behind my eyes.

FAUSTUS: What are you eating?

LUTHER: The usual. Liver. Cabbage. Limburger.

FAUSTUS: The occasional Body-of-Christ.

LUTHER: Yes, if you have to put it that way.

FAUSTUS: It wasn't my idea. What are you drinking?

LUTHER: What is there to drink? Milk, beer, water, beer.

FAUSTUS: And Blood-of-Christ at least twice a week.

LUTHER: Damn it, John –

FAUSTUS: A glass a day is actually good for the heart. So: angsty, much? Any particular sturm blowing? Any source of *drang?*

LUTHER: Well, that damned Tetzel…

FAUSTUS: Tetzel?

LUTHER: John Tetzel, John! Tetzel! Dominican huckster, selling indulgences like lottery tickets. My flock no longer comes to confession!

They have no cause to repent! They believe they've already purchased their salvation from the Church, and have the holy receipt to prove it! They're actually being told they can buy their way out of all their sins committed and those yet to commit! Ridiculous! Tetzel! Shearing the sheep!

FAUSTUS: I take it you have a theological dispute with Tetzel.

LUTHER: I have a theological dispute with the entire idea of it!

FAUSTUS: Martin! Heresy! Good for you!

LUTHER: What? No, no…

FAUSTUS: And what are you doing about it?

LUTHER: What am I doing about it?

FAUSTUS: What are you doing about it?

LUTHER: I'm not doing anything about it!

FAUSTUS: You're not doing anything about it. Well, there's your problem, Martin. There's your blockage. My diagnosis is – you're literally full of shit. It's backed up all the way to your brain in the form of a rusty iron spike.

LUTHER: Useless. You're useless.

FAUSTUS: Seems to be pressing on the free-will portion of your brain, inhibiting it.

LUTHER: You're a quack.

FAUSTUS: But I do have a treatment. Part pharmacological, part occupational.

LUTHER: Just kill me now.

(Faustus prepares Luther's medication of beans.)

FAUSTUS: The pharmacological part is a little something I smuggled out of Mecca over the summer.

LUTHER: O, perfect. Foreign poison.

FAUSTUS: You really need to get out more, you bumpkin.

LUTHER: Wittenberg is world enough for me.

FAUSTUS: "The world is a book, and those who do not travel read only a page."

LUTHER: Yes, yes, don't quote Augustine to an Augustinian.

FAUSTUS: When he's right, he's right. But only when he's right. Behold, magic beans. Grind 'em up, they make a kind of musclebound tea – recommended for headaches, constipation and the general defluxion of humours. It also has the effect of stimulating the attention and increasing mental speed – my colleague Abdullah says it puts the whirl in your dervish and the fizz in your fez. It's called "qahfe," and to the Sultans, it is "the milk of thinkers." Just mix with water and boil.

LUTHER: I'm not drinking any hellfired heathen shitwater.

FAUSTUS: You'll drink what I tell you to drink if you don't want to explode. And you'll drink three cups of it a day: two at Matins, one at Nones. Unclench, Martin, unclench. You're going to like it. It'll keep you awake for all that praying you have to do. Trust me: stick with it for a week, and the problem will be getting you off the stuff.

LUTHER: Does it go with eggs?

FAUSTUS: It goes with everything. Secondly, I want you to make it an exercise to sit down and write a little every day.

LUTHER: What? No...

FAUSTUS: It can be on any topic you like, but at least one page a day.

LUTHER: I don't have time for this...

FAUSTUS: I'm just asking you to cut out fifteen minutes of flesh-mortification and sit down with a quill and parchment. I think you'll find the words will come.

LUTHER: I have nothing to write about...

FAUSTUS: O, no? Shall I give you a topic for the first day? All right, hmm, let's see...the topic is Tetzel.

LUTHER: Tetzel!

FAUSTUS: Tetzel. Write a page about Tetzel.

LUTHER: Tetzel. Profanity acceptable?

FAUSTUS: Use any language you like. It's not for publication.

LUTHER: Tetzel. Anything else?

FAUSTUS: The qahfe and the quill, and that's it. Give the qahfe twenty-four hours, and if it's not producing the desired effects, we'll try it in another orifice.

LUTHER: What?

FAUSTUS: Remember, a page a day is only the minimum. Write as much as you like. There might be more than a page in Tetzel.

LUTHER: Tetzel. I'll see you in confession on Sunday?

FAUSTUS: Well...

LUTHER: I'll see you in confession on Sunday!

FAUSTUS: Ah, that *Luther* charm. Look, Helen's back in town tomorrow. Finally. My appointment book will be full for the next few days.

LUTHER: For the record, I am obligated to object to that...relationship.

FAUSTUS: What does that mean, obligated?

LUTHER: The Church teaches it's a sin. You're sinning. With a sinner. Sinfully. I am forbidden to condone it.

FAUSTUS: You're forbidden?

LUTHER: I am bound by my vows.

FAUSTUS: You're vow-bound?

LUTHER: Stop that! What do you want me to say? I'm trying to be delicate. She's a fallen woman – you should know, because you pushed her. And then you jumped down after her. Into a pool of sin. I have professional reservations.

FAUSTUS: A pool of sin? Come on in, the water's fine. A pool of sin. Well, we're drying off. When next I see her, I'm going to pose the question.

LUTHER: You're going to marry that woman?

FAUSTUS: Joined in the eyes of the Lord.

LUTHER: In a church?

FAUSTUS: Well, that is where they keep the sanctimony.

LUTHER: The sanctity.

FAUSTUS: O, right, sure…Sorry, I still don't know my sanctorum from a hole in the ground.

LUTHER: I can actually feel my patience evaporating.

FAUSTUS: I can actually smell it. Truthfully, I was hoping you would perform the ceremony.

LUTHER: Me? Marry you?

FAUSTUS: O, Martin, I'm flattered, but I'm sure the Church wouldn't approve.

LUTHER: Is this the pretext for another practical joke?

FAUSTUS: I'm hurt. Really. Where is your faith? It's real, it's true…What can I tell you – I'm helpless, it's love.

LUTHER: Hmph. It's a kind of love, perhaps.

FAUSTUS: Every love is a kind of love. "Let the root of love be within, for of this root can nothing spring but what is good."

LUTHER: Yes, and Augustine also said "Love is the beauty of the soul." You see? It always comes back to the soul, you miscreant. And your soul is never beyond redemption, John, no matter how hard you may try. "Sin couches at the door; its urge is toward you, yet you can be its master."

FAUSTUS: Sin's here already? She's early.

LUTHER: Listen, jackass, if you and your…counterpart are serious about this, then take it seriously. I'm serious! Meantime, I'll be praying for you. To Saint Jude, I fear, but praying all the same, damn it. Praying hard.

FAUSTUS: *(As Luther heads out.)* Aren't you even going to congratulate me?

LUTHER: Congratulations. With qualifications.

FAUSTUS: I wouldn't expect it any other way, you sentimental little girl.

LUTHER: Impertinent.

FAUSTUS: Dyspeptic.

LUTHER: Libertine!

FAUSTUS: Tightass!

LUTHER: Dilettante!

FAUSTUS: Drudge!

LUTHER: Save your soul, John!

FAUSTUS: Free your mind, Martin!

> *(Exit Luther, lights down on Faustus. The scene is now Hamlet's dream. He moves warily downstage through an ethereal nightscape. Sound of a beating heart. He reaches the edge of the stage and peers down as if into an abyss. The heart beats louder, faster. A blinding light from above strikes him. He loses his balance and "falls" into the abyss. The heartbeat becomes rapid and deafening. He plummets and finally hits the floor. A sudden sound and light change as Hamlet starts awake, gasping and shaken. Bells toll and daylight warms the stage as he composes himself and makes his way into Faustus' study, waiting for the doctor. He notices the skull on the desk, picks it up and holds it before his face, looking into it. He stands for a moment contemplating it, and then Faustus enters with several pamphlets and printed sheets. Hamlet quickly restores the skull.)*

FAUSTUS: The doctor is in! Thank you for your patience – had to pick these up at the printer's before he closed for the day. Sit down, sit down, make yourself comfortable. I noticed you admiring my skull. Well, not my skull, but my *skull*.

HAMLET: Yes, I mean no liberty to take –

FAUSTUS: No, no, not at all, that's what it's there for.

HAMLET: Wherefore?

FAUSTUS: *Memento mori*, a reminder of our common fate. Professionally speaking, the context of all our philosophical inquiry. What Aristotle called *"on kai me on."*

HAMLET: Being and not-being.

FAUSTUS: Those are the questions, yes. Being and nothingness, the question of existence. *(Indicating the skull.)* Consider this poor bastard. We're told there was a soul in there somewhere. Where did it go? Hell? Heaven? Nowhere? Was it ever really there at all? Him, he's not talking, and all I know for sure is that his head is right here. And that's the start of an answer.

HAMLET: Whose skull is it?

FAUSTUS: It's our skull. No matter whose story, it's the punctuation at the end of the last sentence. Remember that as you write the story of your life.

HAMLET: "And bearing his cross he went forth into a place called the place of the skull, which is called in the Hebrew Golgotha, where they crucified him…"

FAUSTUS: Now, there's a story that ends in an exclamation point! Though, I suppose, for true believers, something more like a semi-colon, endlessly awaiting its second independent statement. So far, silence.

HAMLET: So it seems.

FAUSTUS: Seems? It either is or it isn't. I don't know from "seems." Being. Nothingness. With nothing being in between. *(Beat.)* So what can I do for you?

HAMLET: Father Becker did suggest that I should speak with someone.

FAUSTUS: O? Trouble on the court?

HAMLET: Troubled trouble troubling.

FAUSTUS: And the big tournament against *les français* plays tomorrow.

HAMLET: Hence the urgency.

FAUSTUS: What's wrong?

HAMLET: What's right? My service of late refuses to serve me, and my feet forever find myself at fault. My backhand slaps me i'th'face, my lob's a squab and slobbery. My volleys fire amiss and wound the shooter, and the damn`ed net ensnares me. Today, I rushed it ready to return a fell blow, but lost my footing as I made my swing, and with the racking racquet balled my balls instead, blowing them at the moon, my royal jewels ahoist with mine own petard. 'Twasn't pleasant.

FAUSTUS: Would you like some ice?

HAMLET: It doth subside.

FAUSTUS: Mind if I smoke?

HAMLET: Be thou my guest, as 'twere.

(Faustus smokes from a hookah.)

FAUSTUS: So what's happened to your game, do you suppose?

HAMLET: The motion of bodies through space makes no more sense for me. I can no longer tell if 'tis I who move or if the ball is moving or if it is the court itself that moves. I cannot tell where I stand, or if I stand at all.

FAUSTUS: And what do you think is the source of this problem?

HAMLET: Methinks…methinks mayhap my faith hath been mithlaid.

(Beat.) That is, mislaid.

FAUSTUS: Right. I see…

HAMLET: Of two minds I am of whether I believe in my belief, or only believe that I do, but, either way…

FAUSTUS: To believe or not to believe.

HAMLET: That is the question.

FAUSTUS: Hmm. Well, I thank you for coming to me instead of going to a priest.

HAMLET: I go to thee and to a priest. As I profess, of two minds I am on this.

FAUSTUS: And what did the priest say?

HAMLET: I came here firstly.

FAUSTUS: Good decision. I think I know what the priest will tell you.

HAMLET: So what do ye think?

FAUSTUS: When did you first begin to experience this crisis?

HAMLET: Ay…My dreams…Bad dreams…The first one was the Sabbath day a week ago…I awoke that morn from out a corpse-cold dream, adrench in sweat. Still I see that nightmare even now, as if chisel'd in the table of my memory.

FAUSTUS: Describe it for me, if you would. And spare no detail – the devil's always in the details.

(As Hamlet describes his dream, he relives it in part, and lights and sound help to depict elements of his dream.)

HAMLET: Alone I am upon that skull-white face,
The Moon – The sky a sable canopy
Bestud with diamond fire, the marbled orb
Of Earth a lapis lazuli aloft.
No sound but breathing, and the pounding of
My anxious heart. And as I darkly loom
In moonless lunar gloom entombed, I do
Perceive I stand before the precipice
Of some Tartarean abyss, one foot
Not one foot from the shearing edge. The Sun
Has just begun to break above the gray
Horizon when I now by dawning light
Can see I stand beside a gaping pit,
With corners square, its sides in ratio
Pythagorean perpendicular.
And now the solar lumination casts
Enlightenment upon the surface of
An upright vertick slab obsidian,
A mytholithic finity immense
Of unreflecting black. It darkens me.
(The shadow cast from a huge rectangular monolith falls upon the stage.)
It reacheth up so high it seems to scrape

The vault of distant dark eternity.
Now brighter, brighter now I do discern
The solitary stone stands sentinel
Upon the fathermost – I mean to say,
That is, the *farthermost* edge of the pit,
And as the blinding Sun arrives in full
I stand beneath and understand at last
The monolith doth mark a sepulcher,
A wordless headstone at the gravesite of
Some freshly fallen giant form. And thus
Epiphanized, I sense the Earth above
My head now moving toward the Sun, and feel
The Moon a-spin beneath me, my balance
Unbalanced with footless footing, and pitch
I down toward the pitch, and fall into
That void without, and feel that void within.
Down, down, my heart an anvil hammer'd by
A pounding sledge of fear and trembling:
Pa-PUM, pa-PUM, pa-PUM, pa-PUM, pa-PUM!
(Lights and sound restore to normal.)
And then I wake as one who from the jaws of death is roughly snatched.
And ever since that moment's waking, I have set sail from a sea of tranquility into a sea of crises.

FAUSTUS: Interesting.

HAMLET: What dost thou make of it?

FAUSTUS: What do *you* make of it?

HAMLET: I am afear'd of what lieth in the pit.

FAUSTUS: And what is in the pit?

HAMLET: It hath no name.

FAUSTUS: No face?

HAMLET: I cannot – It hath my face. It hath thy face. *(Indicating the skull.)* It hath his face.

FAUSTUS: What is your relationship to what lies in the pit?

HAMLET: It is – I am its child.

FAUSTUS: Hmm. On the day before this dream, did you do anything out of the ordinary?

HAMLET: In faith, most.

FAUSTUS: O, really? What?

HAMLET: My summer off I spent in Poland studying– but know ye this.

FAUSTUS: I have my spies.

HAMLET: The myst'ries of astronomy have I
    Long long'd to learn; thus travel'd I abroad
    To Polack Frombork-town to study with
    A tutor mathematick'ly advanced,
    One Doctor Nikolai Copernik there –
FAUSTUS: Copernik?
HAMLET: Ay. Dost thou know him?
FAUSTUS: Tall fellow, big hair, horsey face?
HAMLET: 'Tis one way to describe his visage, true.
FAUSTUS: I don't know him, but I heard him speak once in Krakow at a
    symposium on calendar reform. Which is ironic, considering the rest
    of that trip was a vodka-induced lost weekend. But I digress. You
    were studying astronomy…
HAMLET:
    At moonrise, we would scale the parapets
    And have discourse upon the movement of
    Celestial spheres. But when I'd question him
    About the orbit of the Sun around
    The Earth, he'd sigh, and seemed to seek that Sun
    With eyes ablaze with fire of burning love.
    This soulful solarphilia of his
    Confounded me by lengths 'til came it near
    The close of my semester term with him –
    My curiosity o'ermaster'd me
    One night, and forth I blurted out, "Now, tell
    Me, Doctor, sir, I pray – a-prying I
    Mean not to go – but wherefore centereth
    The orbit of thy mind eccentric'ly
    Upon the Sun?" Thence made he me to swear
    An oath upon his astrolabe I would
    Not share the data that he was to share
    With me. Thrice made he swear me thus, and then
    A manuscript he gave to me, and said
    "These theses read, my son, and find my fault,
    If so you can. 'Tis not a challenge, this –
    No, truly, 'tis a very plea. For if
    These my hypotheses herein be sound
    And true – May angels, then, and ministers
    Of grace defend us all." That night I read,
    And sear'd my brains withal. I found no fault.
    At heart, I felt a sickness unto death.

I wept, then with exhausted soul I slept.
The lunic dream which next I dreamt ye know.
And by such like phantasmagoria –
A vengeful Mother Earth disowning me,
Apollo 'pon a wheelless chariot –
By these and other visions hath my sleep
Been sorely vex'd and troubled ever since.

FAUSTUS: Interesting. What was the subject of the manuscript?

HAMLET: 'Tis concerning revolution.

FAUSTUS: Of the oppressed classes?

HAMLET: No, of the heavenly spheres. Revolution of the Earth.

FAUSTUS: O, revolution "revolving", not revolution "revolting".

HAMLET: Ay, though it did to make me pitch the kippers when first its import strook me in the plexus.

FAUSTUS: Revolution of the Earth? Around the Sun?

HAMLET: Verily.

FAUSTUS: Interesting. You know, among the pre-Socratics, the idea that the Earth moved in an orbit around the Sun was put forth by the –

HAMLET: – by the Pythagoreans, yes, I know. Doctor Copernik a-swooned for the Pythagoreans.

FAUSTUS: The Pythagoreans also believed that the Earth itself –

HAMLET: – The Earth itself rotated on its axis, yes, I know. "A complete rotation on its fix`ed poles in a daily motion." Doctor Copernik doth concur in a second opinion.

FAUSTUS: Interesting. The Earth a rotating planet revolving around a central star. Double motion. From standing still to dancing at a gallop!

HAMLET: I can feel it even now.

FAUSTUS: Well, it's revolutionary! Stop the press: "Earth Moves!" But then, of course, two thousand years of institutional knowledge and judgment would have to be wrong.

HAMLET: 'Tis true.

FAUSTUS: The basic assumptions of science, of the nature of physical reality, would have to be turned inside-out.

HAMLET: I fear ye speak the truth.

FAUSTUS: And the Holy Mother Church, the divinely sanctioned repository of all earthly and heavenly wisdom, would prove her testimony fallible and her Scripture unreliable!

HAMLET: A sin it is to even think this, I know.

FAUSTUS: No, no, these are all positive developments. May I read it, do you think?

HAMLET: I thrice swore an oath –

FAUSTUS: Yes, but this is part of your treatment…If the manuscript is at the source of all your troubles, how can I effect a cure without fully understanding it? To do any less than all I can do, after all, would violate my own oath as a doctor. And that is an oath I have made to all mankind, which outweighs the oath you have made to but one solitary man. So. Do you think I might read it?

HAMLET: A Doctor of Law thou art as well, I know.

FAUSTUS: Estates, civil liberties, contracts – unbreakable contracts. My card.

(He produces his business card.)

HAMLET: The manuscript.

(He produces Copernik's six-page manuscript.)

FAUSTUS: Thank you. And you'll be happy to know that our confidentiality is now guaranteed by two oaths, one as your physician and one as your attorney. My recommendation, by the way? Don't mention this to your priest: no priest is ready for this, believe you me. I'll look it over tonight and we'll speak again tomorrow. I can't resolve your spiritual problem overnight, but I can help your physical symptoms. *(He produces a small, full pouch.)* Eat these candies. Moroccan Delights – good mooca from Marrakech. Physically, you are suffering from a form of motion sickness, permeated by a persistent nausea.

HAMLET: Thou hast hit it exactly.

FAUSTUS: One candy every six hours as conditions persist. I think you'll find it will restore your equilibrium. It may also make you hungry. If so, eat.

HAMLET: Wherefore my motion sickness?

FAUSTUS: Wherefore, indeed? If this Polack Copernik is right, then, of course, that changes everything. But, on the other hand, it changes nothing. Everything looks the same and feels the same. The only real effect is the one inside your head. That's what the candies are for. Synchronizing your rotation with that of the Earth's, as it were. My advice: turn in, turn down, turn off.

HAMLET: And tomorrow's tennis tournament?

FAUSTUS: Dose tonight, see how you feel in the morning. If you need it, dose again. I've used those myself. No complaints.

HAMLET: I put my trust in thine Afric sweets. May they ensweeten me.

FAUSTUS: Good, that's the right frame of mind. And now, I wish I could converse further, but I'm getting backed up in my reading. Are you interested in something light from the printer, take your mind off weightier things?

HAMLET: What be this? *Miching Malicho?*

FAUSTUS: Miching Malicho. It means "mischief." Lurid tales of murder and mayhem among the upper classes. That's last week's edition – juicy story of dukicide in Vienna. Enjoy.

HAMLET: "The Murder of Gonzago."

FAUSTUS: Yes – I hear they're making it into a play.

HAMLET: Do tell: I love the theatre. I'll o'erlook these tales tonight with lighter eyes – mayhap I'll stumble 'cross someone I know. Thanks for the sympathetic ear, good sir.

FAUSTUS: Anytime, you know that. And it's my father's, by the way.

HAMLET: Pray what, Doctor – thine ear?

FAUSTUS: The skull. My father's. I've had it since I was a child. He caught plague, killed himself. Never got a decent burial. *(Beat.)* Don't mean to bring the room down – he's smiling now. I'll see you tomorrow.

HAMLET: Good night, then.

FAUSTUS: Sweet dreams.

(Exit Hamlet. The scene moves to "The Bunghole," a popular student tavern. A beat-up wooden bar table with two short stools, or benches. A tall stool to the side where Faustus sits to sing, as he does now – either playing the lute, or accompanied by it.)

FAUSTUS: Department chairs
Autopsy tables
By inches and degrees
I sort the facts and fables

I'm known as The Searcher
I keep asking how and why
Don't know if I'll find what I'm after
But I'm gonna try

I read Bonaventure
I read Saint Beda
I read Thomas Aquinas
But he didn't tell me either

Just call me a Searcher
I want Truth and that's no lie
I can't help the sound of my laughter
Otherwise I'd cry

Don't know if I'll find what I'm after
But damned if I don't try
Thanks, and remember to take care of your wenches.
(He moves to the table, where he is met by the waitress, Gretchen. She is blonde and dirndl'd-up in resemblance to the St. Pauli Girl.)

GRETCHEN: Always so thoughtful, Doctor John. You're a saint.

FAUSTUS: God, I Hope not. Bunghole's booming tonight.

GRETCHEN: You know, another October, another Octoberfest. *(Taking note of his half-empty stein of beer:)* Can I freshen you up?

FAUSTUS: You can certainly try. Another Duvel, if you please.
(Enter Luther with a half-full stein of beer.)

LUTHER: Good evening, Gretchen!

FAUSTUS: Praise God! He is risen!

GRETCHEN: Evening to you, Father. What'd you get from the bar, the usual?

LUTHER: St. Pauli. Keep it flowing.

GRETCHEN: Amen.
(Exit Gretchen.)

LUTHER: Brother John.

FAUSTUS: Father Martin.

LUTHER: Seventy-three books in the Bible, you know how many mention alcohol?

FAUSTUS: How many?

LUTHER: Seventy-two.

FAUSTUS: I'll drink to that.

LUTHER: It's what God would want.
(They toast. Each drains his respective drink.)

FAUSTUS & LUTHER: Ahhh-

LUTHER: -men. Our Lord's first miracle was changing water into wine. If He'd been born a German, He would've changed it into beer.

FAUSTUS: If he'd been born a German, I doubt he would've been a Jew.

LUTHER: Sorry I'm so late, I couldn't tear myself away.

FAUSTUS: O?

LUTHER: I've been up since I last saw you, and I've been on fire!

FAUSTUS: I have a cream for that, if you'd like.

LUTHER: I was up all last night, and I didn't care. I pinned him fast a couple of times, and I gave as good as I got.

FAUSTUS: Interesting. What exactly were you up all night doing?

LUTHER: Wrestling! Grappling! Squeezing the life out of his lying lungs!

FAUSTUS: At least you're getting balanced exercise.

LUTHER: I get exercise.

FAUSTUS: Not balanced exercise – self-flagellation doesn't count, it works the same muscle group over and over again.

(Gretchen returns with a fresh stein for each.)

GRETCHEN: Wet your whistles, boys?

LUTHER: Bless you, angel.

FAUSTUS: A sparkling oasis in the desert, my love. An ever-flowing fountain of delight.

GRETCHEN: O, Doctor John, the things you say…

FAUSTUS: O, Margarita, my pearl of great price, you know if my heart didn't already belong to another, I'd have him marry us here and now.

GRETCHEN: You know it's not your heart I'm interested in.

LUTHER: Easy, child.

GRETCHEN: His mind, Father, his mind. And you get yours out of the gutter.

(Exit Gretchen. As they watch her go:)

LUTHER: Fox.

FAUSTUS: Minx.

LUTHER: That pagan mudjuice you gave me –

FAUSTUS: You like it?

LUTHER: I love it! It's liquid manna! Not half an hour after my first sip, I felt the stirring of the Lord within me.

FAUSTUS: I'm not sure that was the Lord.

LUTHER: I'm absolutely certain of it. I was reading Paul's Letter to the Romans again for Sunday's sermon, and the same verse that always pains me became a thorn in my mind again: "For in the Gospel is the righteousness of God revealed, as it is written: 'The just shall live by faith.'" The righteousness of God – I've always read that and felt fear and anger. A righteous God, judging us all, punishing and casting us down to hell, because of our sins, sins we are damned to commit by Adam's original disobedience! I've always resented a God that would damn us to sin and then damn us for sinning. How could that be the action of a just God? I was reading it over and over, looking for a way out, any way out, and then the Lord began to move within me.

FAUSTUS: The Lord does move in mysterious ways.

LUTHER: I felt something awakening inside me, a quickening, something I couldn't articulate, but the stirrings of what felt like – like a revelation!

FAUSTUS: It's a laxative, Martin.

LUTHER: At last, the moment came upon me. I ran into the privy and sat on the cold stone, but I was hot, I was sweating and my aching mind was aflame, my soul burned! I prayed for the strength to accept God's message, I prayed for wisdom, I prayed for relief! And then as I felt my bowels finally begin to empty, it was as though a bolt of divine lightning exploded in the room, my mind cleared and I felt God's grace fill me up, the cup of my soul overflowing with His sweet mercy and sublime wisdom! I saw it, I saw it writ in letters of fire: the "righteousness" of God doesn't mean God's inexorable justice, the way it has been taught all this time – it means God makes us right with Him, He straightens our crooked lives and justifies us to Him through our faith! As it is written: "The just shall live by faith"! Faith in His holy Word, which He has given to us by His limitless grace! It's not a punishment, it's a gift! It's not about His wrath, it's about His love! I'm telling you, I wept scalding tears of joy, I felt as if I had been born again, as though the gates of Heaven had been opened and I had entered Paradise itself!

FAUSTUS: That's good qahfe.

LUTHER: The just shall live by faith! By faith alone. Faith in the holy Word of God. And then, of course, I know I must be right, because who appears at that blessed holiest moment, condensing from the stink?

FAUSTUS: I'm dying to know.

LUTHER: The old Deceiver himself, the Great Swine, the slandering Ass of Lies, rising up from his shitty pit –

FAUSTUS: The Devil, again?

LUTHER: The same!

FAUSTUS: The Devil appeared to you in your toilet.

LUTHER: He wanted to catch me with my robe up! He wanted to debate, he told me my interpretation went against the church fathers, went against Aristotle! I told him Aristotle never met the Christ, and he could get acquainted with my ass!

FAUSTUS: What's with the anal fixation, anyway?

LUTHER: We argued all night, but he could find no loops or slips in me. I pinned him, I nailed him, dead to rights! My reading of the Word of God was my foundation and my rock.

FAUSTUS: Congratulations on making our toilets safe from the Devil. Did you manage to get any of this down onto paper, as prescribed?

LUTHER: I put down as much as I could until the Serpent's lies enraged me so much I threw my inkwell at him!

FAUSTUS: At the Devil?

LUTHER: Of course at the Devil! Who the hell do you think we're talking about?!

FAUSTUS: We might want to discuss some anger management for you –

LUTHER: I don't need any goddamn anger management! The Lord does not begrudge me a righteous fury in the face of evil!

(Gretchen re-enters with four fresh steins.)

GRETCHEN: Everything all right, doctors?

LUTHER: Fine, fine, damn it, everything's fine!

FAUSTUS: Protect your face, nurse, he's venting spleen! The sedatives, stat! Drink this, quickly!

(Luther takes a big quaff.) You may have just saved his life.

GRETCHEN: Remember that when you tip.

LUTHER: Speaking of salvation, I don't remember hearing you in confession last week, Gretchen.

GRETCHEN: No, Father, but I'm covered for it – Father Tetzel sold me a month of remission.

LUTHER: Tetzel!

GRETCHEN: My indulgence cost me a month of tips, but I have to think it's worth it.

FAUSTUS: Interesting.

GRETCHEN: See? *(She produces a folded indulgence from her cleavage.)* Good for thirty days. "All sins and misdeeds committed therein." Though I'm not sinning, of course, Father.

LUTHER: Lying is a sin!

GRETCHEN: It's covered. *(She recovers the indulgence and tucks it away. Winking and gesturing toward the beer:)* And these are on the house.

LUTHER: Stealing is a sin!

GRETCHEN: It's covered.

(Exit Gretchen. By the end of the scene, all four beers should be consumed and their effects felt.)

LUTHER: Tetzel!

FAUSTUS: Tetzel. But you know, he's only doing what your Papa in Rome is telling him to do.

LUTHER: What?

FAUSTUS: *(Taking a broadsheet from out of a leather pouch.)* Exhibit A, hot off the press – fresh steaming papal bull. I swear: the first Pope cut off a man's ear and denied his Savior three times – and it's been downhill ever since. Read, weep. Leo wants to launch another crusade against the Turks, and he's authorized Tetzel's sale of indulgences to help finance it.

LUTHER: He wouldn't...

FAUSTUS: He would.

LUTHER: He didn't...

FAUSTUS: He did. He has to. Julius leaves him a papal treasury with a four-million-ducat surplus, and Leo spends it dry in four years. When I did that pro bono work with the Lateran Council last year, I sweet-talked my way into one of Leo's banquets. Sixty-five courses, and for dessert, little gold-painted boys jumping out of plum puddings. Now, I'm no expert on gilded-child-filled desserts, but that can't be cheap. And what better way to refill the coffers than to bang the drums of war?

LUTHER: "...and to fund the reconstruction of St. Peter's basilica"?

FAUSTUS: Yes, Gretchen's wages are buying baby Jesus a shinier manger.

LUTHER: He's trafficking in German souls for the sake of Roman contractors?

FAUSTUS: It's a good thing Leo's Pope, otherwise you'd never know he's Christian.

LUTHER: It's outrageous! Haven't we poor sinners enough to suffer without this abuse as well?

FAUSTUS: Indulgences, you mean?

LUTHER: Yes! Treating the salvation of souls like a public bond issue.

FAUSTUS: Indulgences, then. Which is what, exactly – the Church sells slips of paper to poor parishioners, and the slips claim that a certain amount of time they would otherwise spend burning in Purgatory for their sins has now been credited to their account, yes?

LUTHER: Yes, that's the idea.

FAUSTUS: And the greater the payment, the more punishment set aside, yes?

LUTHER: It wasn't my idea.

FAUSTUS: So feelings of remorse, a desire for true penance – the Church doesn't care as long as you've got the gold to pay for it, right?

LUTHER: The Church would prefer your heart were hungry for forgiveness.

FAUSTUS: But if not, cash on the barrelhead will suffice.

LUTHER: What's your point?

FAUSTUS: My point, Martin, and God knows you know the Gospel better than I do, is this: what verse in Romans allows Rome to do this? What does the Bible have to say about getting out of Purgatory?

LUTHER: The Holy Word is silent on the issue.

FAUSTUS: Of getting out of Purgatory?

LUTHER: The Bible doesn't mention Purgatory at all, so it doesn't explain how to get out of it!

FAUSTUS: So where did we get the idea? Is there a Newer Testament I'm not aware of? Or did God just neglect to mention it?

LUTHER: It's – It's not explicit, but the Church interprets several verses as seeming to suggest the possibility of such a place for souls after death…

FAUSTUS: "Seeming to suggest the possibility"? Oh, come on! Objection: Hearsay! Since when has God ever been implicit about anything? He does commandments, not innuendo! How could he neglect to mention a destination in the afterlife where practically every soul seems doomed to end up? Doesn't it seem more likely that it's only one more thing the Church just made up? I mean, for God's sake, Martin, do you believe it?

(Pause.)

LUTHER: When I was there, in that place, in Rome, when I was a younger man – I know I'll regret telling you this – the priests there told me that for a nominal fee, I could scale the steps of the Scala Sancta on my knees, and if I said an Our Father on each step, by the time I reached the top I could save the soul of a loved one suffering in Purgatory. My grandfather had died the week before and I resolved to relieve his suffering, if I could. So I paid, and I kneeled, and pressed my lips to that first step and began, praying and climbing, climbing and praying. Twenty-eight steps, twenty-eight Our Fathers, twenty-eight cold marble kisses. And as I finally lifted my aching knee to that last step, I heard a voice inside my head, a voice as clear as the voice you're hearing now say "But what if it isn't true?" What if it isn't true?

You know, I didn't read the Scriptures until three years after I took my vows. I had to learn the Latin first, the language of the men who crucified our Savior. They had made me a monk, a Brother of Christ, and they didn't care if I had ever read His Gospel for myself. They only cared that I could afford the initiation payment to the Church. They taught me only the lyrics; the music I had to learn for myself.

When I read the New Testament for the first time, I was as far away from Rome as I could possibly be. Twenty-seven books, twenty-seven portraits of the revealed face of the hidden God, twenty-seven tongues of holy fire. My mind felt bathed in the light of the sun. My heart felt as if it would burst with love. And for a brief, sweet blessed moment, the storm in my soul was stilled, and I knew in a way beyond simple knowledge that this, at last, was the Truth. This was the whole Truth. This was nothing but the Truth. So help me God.

Do I believe the Bible? With every fiber of my being. Do I believe the Church? "What if it isn't true?"

FAUSTUS: The just, after all, shall live by faith.

LUTHER: Yes. By faith alone. By Scripture alone.

FAUSTUS: Interesting. So, then, if that's true…who needs indulgences?

LUTHER: That is the issue.

FAUSTUS: No, it's not. The issue is, who needs any of it? Who needs the priests? Who needs the Pope? Who needs the Church?

LUTHER: I don't like what you're intimating.

FAUSTUS: I'm not intimating anything – I'm shouting from the clock tower! Who needs it? Any of it? The just shall live by faith, and the unjust couldn't care less!

LUTHER: I will not be lectured on Scripture by you, Doctor, not now, not ever. The Church is the living body of Christ. The body may be sick from time to time, the body may need treatment, but a moral doctor does not destroy the body when he detects disease!

FAUSTUS: I will not be lectured on medicine by you, Doctor, not now, not ever. Bodies get old and broken, all bodies decay and die, and there is nothing we can do to stop it. We can only slow it down. And sometimes it's a mercy to speed it on its way!

LUTHER: Sounds to me like I want to heal the Church and you want to kill it.

FAUSTUS: Sounds to me like you want to sacrifice the patient to save the cancer!

LUTHER: Pah! Get thee behind me, Satan!

FAUSTUS: Let he who is without sin cast the first stone!

LUTHER: Serpent.

FAUSTUS: Lemming.

LUTHER: Malcontent!

FAUSTUS: Hypocrite!

LUTHER: Extremist!

FAUSTUS: Coward!

LUTHER: Degenerate!

FAUSTUS: Monk!

(Beat.)

LUTHER: I was in such good spirits when I came out here…

FAUSTUS: You're not angry with me, Martin. You're angry with what you know to be true. If I were wrong, you'd condescend to me, but you're angry, so I must be right.

LUTHER: Sometimes I'm angry with you because you're dead wrong!

FAUSTUS: And sometimes – usually – you're just angry! But this isn't one of those times. The logic is inescapable! "The just shall live by faith?" "What if it isn't true?" I'm not making my argument, I'm making yours!

LUTHER: I don't need your help! And your motives aren't pure!

FAUSTUS: I stand for truth. I stand for questioning unquestioned authority. I stand for mankind standing up – to and for everything! Where do you stand?

LUTHER: That's pride, Doctor Faustus, pride! Lucifer's sin! You think you know it all, but the only quantity greater than what you know is what you don't know.

FAUSTUS: I know!

LUTHER: Ach! You always go too far, that's your sin of sins. You always go too far!

FAUSTUS: And you don't go far enough! That's your weakness. Great men always go too far – that's what makes them great! And if they're not crucifying you for your beliefs, then you haven't gone far enough.

LUTHER: Is this about the Church, or are you after bigger game? What exactly are you rebelling against, John?

FAUSTUS: What've you got? What exactly are you submitting to? They've still got you down on your knees, Martin, they've still got you crawling up an endless marble staircase. Stand up! Stand up for yourself! For everyone who's ever asked "What if it isn't true?" Because if it isn't, what are you living for? What Will Leo's crusaders be dying for? What's Gretchen throwing away her last guilder buying indulgences for? You're her shepherd – protect your flocking sheep! And decide who it's more important to protect them from: Tetzel and his Church, or the Devil himself! Because the way you describe it, the Devil sounds like he's less of a threat, loitering around in men's rooms. Indulge me, would you? Name your price. I would sell my soul for one statement from you, one admission that you know your beliefs are different from the Church, and that you know they are truer. That's all I'm asking from you: the truth. One point of debate between you and the Church.

LUTHER: Well, if it's points of debate you want, I could give you around a hundred points of debate. When it comes to indulgences, I have a debate with the Church, I'll admit to that. A friendly collegial debate. That's not heresy, that's dialogue.

FAUSTUS: I'll take it! Call it whatever you like, I'll take it! Around a hundred points of debate, then, an articulation of your conflict with the Church, in detail, yes? There's your page for the day.

LUTHER: Fine. Done. Airtight case.

FAUSTUS: I can't wait.

(Both finish their last beers as church bells toll the hour.)

Already? Trampled by the horses of the night. One last tune, and I must be going.

LUTHER: Early for you.

FAUSTUS: Big day tomorrow. I'm due for a steam and a soak, I want a fresh musk.

LUTHER: Vanity. Pride. Lust.

FAUSTUS: Damn right. Gluttony, if I'm lucky.

LUTHER: Bad enough you corrupted her in the first place, but to persist in defiling her, defiling yourself, God only knows in what kind of depraved and perverted ways…

FAUSTUS: Spoken like a man who needs a nun of his own.

LUTHER: Ex-nun. Fallen nun.

FAUSTUS: There's no accounting for taste.

LUTHER: Sacrilege! O, the sins upon your head…

FAUSTUS: I know – "damned if I do," but I'll be damned if I don't!

LUTHER: Listen, you reprobate, I'm speaking as your pastor, now –

FAUSTUS: O, God…

LUTHER: Damn it, John, I'm speaking as your friend! The reward of sin is death! An everlasting death. Don't be deceived regarding your precious immortal soul, John: I cannot damn you, the Church cannot damn you, even God in all his unimaginable might cannot damn you – only you can damn yourself. You alone. To Hell! Throughout eternity! For your sins! Repent, John. Repent!

FAUSTUS: Sure, sure – later. I'm not done sinning yet and I don't want to go through the whole thing twice. Work, Martin, work, take up and write – and if the Ass of Lies interrupts you, send him my way: I have a few questions for him!

(Gretchen enters with a shot of schnapps. As Luther exits, he admonishes her:)

LUTHER: You! Repent!

FAUSTUS: *(To Luther as he exits:)* You! Relax!

(He knocks back the shot. As he goes to sing, Gretchen cops a feel.)

Hey!

GRETCHEN: *(Waving her indulgence as she exits:)* It's covered.

FAUSTUS: Alright, all you lovesick out there…Heart troubles? Doctor Jack is here with your prescription, to be taken aurally…Good for what ails you…a-fünf-sechs-sieben-acht!

The hot sultry night gave me a sweat
I caught that fever that a man can get
I got this throb in my head
Please confine me to your bed

Doctor, tell me, what can I do
I've gone and caught me the lovebird flu
No dram's gonna ease my jam
She went and gave me the lovebird flu

You've got a habit – you wear it on top
But it's a habit that we're gonna drop

You had me bound, lashed me with your whips
Smile of Judas on your lips
Grab my wrist, nail my wood
I've got it bad, o Lord, so you'll get it good

Doctor, help me, prithee, 'tis true
I've gone and caught me the lovebird flu
No leech gonna heal my breech
I kinda like me this lovebird flu

Good night, Wittenberg!

(Blackout.)

ACT TWO

Lights up on the campus tennis court, on a morning of cloudless sky. Faustus sits up in the bleachers, an air of anticipation about him. He flicks lint off his doublet, checks his breath. Helen, a well-dressed elegant redhead, enters and scans the bleachers. Faustus leaps up and waves, perhaps with a college pennant emblazoned with a "W".

FAUSTUS: Helen!
> *(She smiles, waves, and moves to join him, excusing herself to the other spectators.)*
> Come, Helen, come, give me my soul again.
> Sweet Helen…Make me immortal with a kiss.
> *(They kiss.)*
> O, my divine light. It's autumn at last, and your constellation has re-entered my sky.

HELEN: Mine is a seasonal business, lover. The boys are back in town.

FAUSTUS: My God, look at you. How I've missed you. More and more each time.

HELEN: Darling.

JUDGE: *(from off)*
> Court is in session! Contestants before the judge!

FAUSTUS: I would give you the moon. I'm sure many men tell you they would give you the moon, but I'm the only one who's actually working on it.

HELEN: You're the only one who would really try.
> *(Enter Hamlet onto the court, with a racquet, and dressed in white to play tennis – ideally he should suggest a sixteenth-century Bjorn Borg. He pops a small candy into his mouth, notices Faustus, waves. He is unusually loose. [We see only him and his side of the ensuing tennis game – his opponent LAERTES: and the umpire JUDGE: are both offstage. We hear the ball, but we do not see it.])*

HELEN: Mmm, who's that one?

FAUSTUS: That's my star pupil.

HELEN: What is he, Swedish?

FAUSTUS: Danish.

HELEN: Mmm, I love Danish in the morning.

FAUSTUS: He's not your type.

HELEN: I have many types.

JUDGE: *(from off)*

Call!

HAMLET: Heads.

FAUSTUS: Big surprise.

JUDGE: *(from off)*
> The coin shows heads.

LAERTES: *(from off)*
> Sure, home flip!

HAMLET: I'll take me then the side most easterly.

LAERTES: *(from off)*
> I do not fear the sun, my lord.

HAMLET: Nor do I, sir, if I put him at my back.

HELEN: Mmm, who's the other one, the angry one?

FAUSTUS: Corambisborgensen. Laertes Corambisborgensen. With a temper as puffed up as his name. Funny thing is, he's Danish, too.

HELEN: He looks French.

FAUSTUS: Star athlete of Paris U. I think they issue the greasy hair and the scowl to all the varsity.

LAERTES: *(from off)*
> These racquets have all a length?

HAMLET: Ay, ay. (To Faustus & Helen:) Though 'tis not the length of the racquet, but the bounce in the balls.

HELEN: You've certainly taught him well.

LAERTES: *(from off)*
> Well, then?

HAMLET: Come on, sir!

LAERTES: *(from off)*
> Have at you, my lord!
> *(Laertes serves. They play.)*

HELEN: Beautiful form.

FAUSTUS: Which one?

HELEN: Both.

FAUSTUS: Not at the same time, I Hope.

HAMLET: Long!

LAERTES: *(from off)*
> No!

HAMLET: Judgment!

JUDGE: *(from off)*
> An out! A very palpable out.
> *(Tennis applause.)*

LAERTES: *(from off)*

O, come on! Thou must be jesting me!

JUDGE: *(from off)*
>Love-fifteen.

FAUSTUS: Love, I love you with the love of fifteen.

HELEN: Silly – Love means nothing.

LAERTES: *(from off)*
>Again!

HAMLET: Ay, that's how it's played!

LAERTES: *(from off)*
>For you!
>*(They play.)*

HELEN: Your boy plays well on grass.

FAUSTUS: You have no idea.

LAERTES: *(from off)*
>Out!

HAMLET: Judgment!

JUDGE: *(from off)*
>Line! Inbounds!
>*(Tennis applause.)*

LAERTES: *(from off)*
>Thou canst not be serious! That ball was clearly out!

JUDGE: *(from off)*
>Love-thirty!

LAERTES: *(from off)*
>Knave! Thou art the pits of the world! That ball was in the alley, with
>thy mother!

JUDGE: *(from off)*
>Warning! Unsportsmanlike language!

HAMLET: My racquet shall speak for me, sir!

LAERTES: *(from off)*
>Again!

HAMLET: Thou hast it now!

FAUSTUS: Again and again, thou hast me.

HELEN: And again.

LAERTES: *(from off)*
>*(In French:)* Tenez!
>*(They play, including a sustained rally that ends with Laertes losing the
>point.)*

LAERTES: *(from off)*
>*(In French:)* Foutrez!

(Tennis applause.)
JUDGE: *(from off)*
> Love-forty! Break point! Game point!
LAERTES: *(from off)*
> Damn and damnation! To blackest hell, I say!
HAMLET: Noise, good sir, but yet no racquet!
LAERTES: *(from off)*
> Say ye so, my lord? Come on!
JUDGE: *(from off)*
> Foot fault!
LAERTES: *(from off)*
> 'Swounds! 'Sblood! 'Snails! 'Again!
JUDGE: *(from off)*
> Double fault! Point, game, Wittenberg!
LAERTES: *(from off)*
> 'Sballs! Eat my guts!
> *(A racquet whizzes on from offstage, nearly hitting Hamlet.)*
JUDGE: *(from off)*
> Abuse of the racquet! Second violation! Paris forfeits! Match, Wittenberg!
> *(Applause.)*
LAERTES: *(from off)*
> Marrow-sucking vultures! Trash!
HAMLET: Thou hast clearly lost thy grip, good sir, thou art quite unstrung!
LAERTES: *(from off)*
> Firking woodcocks! I'll be revenged upon thee!
JUDGE: *(from off)*
> Hear ye, hear ye! Court is now in ten-minute recess!
HELEN: *(Tossing a handkerchief down to Hamlet:)* Well played, my lord!
HAMLET: Good lady. Good medicine, good doctor.
FAUSTUS: Good play, good friend.
HAMLET: Thou, good sir, art the man! (As he heads off:) Good day!
FAUSTUS: *(To an exiting Hamlet:)* Good match! *(As he kneels, offering Helen a ring:)* And so are you. For me. Will you make me the happiest man in the world?
HELEN: O, John…
FAUSTUS: Marry me.
HELEN: I've been married – it doesn't agree with me.
FAUSTUS: Bride of Christ doesn't count. It's just a grossly inappropriate metaphor.

HELEN: Believe me, it counts.

FAUSTUS: How exactly did you consummate this marriage?

HELEN: You know I had to wait for you before I ever saw God.

FAUSTUS: I know, I feel the same way. Marry me, let's feel that way forever.

HELEN: O, that's very sweet, but I'm really not in the market for an exclusive relationship right now.

FAUSTUS: You'll never find anyone who could want you more than I.

HELEN: And I'm always yours – for a price.

FAUSTUS: How much for forever?

HELEN: You haven't enough.

FAUSTUS: How much?

HELEN: There isn't enough.

FAUSTUS: Money isn't everything, is it?

HELEN: No, but it buys everything.

FAUSTUS: Everything?

HELEN: You can't own me. My flesh is available for short-term rentals, but my soul is my own.

FAUSTUS: And my soul has become one with yours.

HELEN: O, John...Dear John...You released me from my chains and lit my fire within – my own Prometheus unbound...My first John, my best John, my favorite John...just not my only John. You set me free. I want to remain free.

FAUSTUS: Nothing's free. (He puts away the ring.) Everything has its price.

HELEN: Money makes the sun go 'round.

FAUSTUS: Want to make a bet?

HELEN: I have so loved our time together...

FAUSTUS: (Producing a small purse of coins:) I want you. Now.

HELEN: Now?

FAUSTUS: Now. I want you. I've waited long enough.

HELEN: Now, now...

FAUSTUS: I want you. If I can't have you forever, I'll have you right now. (He places the purse in her hand, kisses her.)

HELEN: Now.

FAUSTUS: Now.

(Lights change as they exit, and we hear an organ playing and perhaps a congregation singing a verse of "Christ Jesus Lay in Death's Strong Bands" [as much as needed for scene change]. The scene now splits between Luther preaching from his pulpit and Faustus and Helen in a dimly-lit encounter in Faustus' bedchamber. Luther's Bible reading, which builds in passion and intensity, inadvertently parallels the shape of the couple's encounter, as he is *likewise ravished by the Holy Spirit.)*

CONGREGATION
So let us keep the festival
  where to the Lord invites us;
Christ is Himself the joy of all,
  the Sun that warms and lights us.
By His grace He doth impart
  eternal sunshine to the heart;
The night of sin is ended! Hallelujah!

LUTHER: Be seated. In today's Scripture, we hear of the passionate love at
    the bless`ed heart of everything our Lord and Master Jesus Christ
    has done for us. Listen, listen now to God's words, from the Song
    of Songs, a rhapsody of our rapture for the Lord God Almighty, and
    His for us.
    (Enter Helen and Faustus.)
    "Let him kiss me with the kisses of his mouth. Come thou south; blow
    upon my garden, that the spices thereof may flow out. I sat down under
    his shadow with great delight, and his fruit was sweet to my taste. His
    left hand is under my head, and his right hand doth embrace me."
FAUSTUS & LUTHER: "O, my love!"
LUTHER: "The joints of thy thighs are the work of a cunning workman.
    My beloved is gone down to feed in the gardens; my beloved, that
    goeth down sweetly. His mouth is most sweet. Honey and milk are
    under thy tongue. Open to me, my love, for my head is filled with
    dew. I rose up to open to my beloved, and my hands dropped with
    sweet-smelling myrrh. My beloved put in his hand by the hole of the
    door, and my bowels were moved for him."
HELEN & LUTHER: "O beloved!"
LUTHER: "I am come into my garden; hearken to thy voice: cause me to
    hear it! Make haste, my beloved!"
HELEN & Faustus & LUTHER: "Come, my beloved!"
LUTHER: "He cometh!
HELEN & FAUSTUS: Ohhhhhhh!
LUTHER: Leaping upon the mountains, skipping upon the hills! The flow-
    ers appear on the earth; the singing of birds is come…
HELEN & FAUSTUS: Ahhhhhhh…
LUTHER: …and the voice of the turtle is heard in our land. Many waters
    cannot quench love, neither can floods drown it: love is strong as

death."

HELEN & FAUSTUS: Mmmm…

LUTHER: This is the word of the Lord. Let us pray.

(Lights down on Luther and up full on Helen and Faustus.)

FAUSTUS: My God…

HELEN: My darling…

FAUSTUS: My love.

HELEN: My great ape…Every time as sweet as the first.

FAUSTUS: And as bittersweet as the last. Stay the night.

HELEN: I can't. This was heavenly, but…it's time for me to leave.

FAUSTUS: What? You just got here!

HELEN: I'm leaving Germany.

FAUSTUS: You're – For how long?

HELEN: Who can say?

FAUSTUS: For where?

HELEN: Everywhere else. You deserved a farewell. I owed you that.

FAUSTUS: Owed me? Why must you always break my heart?

HELEN: I do love you. You know I do.

FAUSTUS: Then what must I do to have you? Tell me, whatever it is, I'll do it.

HELEN: It's beyond your power.

FAUSTUS: It's not beyond yours – you can do whatever you want. Stay with me!

HELEN: You want more than you can have.

FAUSTUS: It's not want – I need you.

HELEN: It's not like you to gush so…

FAUSTUS: No, you don't understand – When I'm with you, everything is different – my mind works faster, my mood is elevated, I tingle. I'm a German, for God's sake, and I tingle! It's not women, it's not love, it's not sex – it's you. I've sampled every mind-altering drug there is from Amsterdam to Zanzibar, but you're the only substance that enlightens me, you're the only craving I can't control. And when I have you with me, that's the only time I sense the presence of the divine. I worship at your temple, you are the center of my universe. I don't believe in anything but I believe in you. I need that taste of God I find only on your lips. It's my only Hope, my only salvation – I'm doomed, lost without it, without you. Don't leave me! I'll give you anything you ask. I'll sell my soul for you.

HELEN: And it's a treasure beyond price. But that's the problem – it doesn't buy me anything. You have a wealth of everything but wealth, and that's the kind of wealth I need.

FAUSTUS: Money, money, it's all just a question of money?

HELEN: It's a question of freedom. That's what this life buys me – a world of choices I can't get anywhere else, a world of peak experience. I've shared the beds of both the Emperor *and* the Pope – and because I can trust you, I can tell you I once shared a bed with the Emperor and the Pope – and once you've lain upon holy sheets, it's hard to go back to sheets with holes. You know? Faculty wife, summer travel on a budget, spring breaks at Baden-Baden? I want more. I choose more. You should understand this – you set me free by teaching me that my choices are mine to make.

FAUSTUS: I set you free so that you could choose me!

HELEN: That's your choice, not mine. If you really loved me, you'd understand that. But you don't really love me, I don't know if you ever have – you only love the idea of me.

FAUSTUS: I will have you, Helen. Believe it. No matter what it takes, I'll find a way.

HELEN: Be content with what you can have, John.

FAUSTUS: I don't want everything. But I want everything I want. And I want you.

HELEN: Don't. I'm the one thing you can't have.

(She leaves behind the purse she was given and exits.)

FAUSTUS: O!

(Exit his Soul, leaving Faustus solus…)

(He despairs. A peal of church bells. Lights down on Faustus and up on Luther's parish office, a much simpler room then Faustus' study: at the very least, it contains a simple chair and writing desk, his large Bible open on a stand and a crucifix hanging prominently on the wall. If there's any art, it's a Dürer woodcut or a Cranach. Luther stands addressing a seated Hamlet, his hand on the Prince's shoulder.)

LUTHER: …So, to put it in a nutshell: in this sea of confusion and doubt we call life, God is the answer. So let His Gospel be your compass, and your faith the wind in your sails.

HAMLET: Thy words are stars to steer my soul by, good Father.

LUTHER: Listen, faith without struggle comes too cheaply. You're not alone. The Christ Himself sweat blood in Gethsemane. I wrestle with my faith every single day, and the struggle strengthens both me and my faith. I submit this thesis, though: our struggle with faith will always end in our surrender – we all believe in something, even if it's nothing. It's only a question of what we choose to surrender to. So choose wisely.

HAMLET: Ay, there's the rub: for choosing comes not easily to me. But here I am to learn, and that I'd learn from thee.

LUTHER: So I can only Hope, my son. Indeed, could I impose upon you for a favor?

HAMLET: Whate'er I can, I shall.

LUTHER: Somewhat rashly, I confess, I have accepted an academic challenge from Doctor *Faustus* to furnish debate points on the issue of indulgences, concerning their power and place in Church teaching. *(He picks a manuscript up from the desk.)* I believe the point-by-point argument I make against them here to be cogent and persuasive, but I am too close to the subject to be an impartial judge. Could I impose upon you to look it over, find any weak points or loopholes before he can? Pray for me, it is the sin of pride, and I am a very sinful man. But I want these ninety-five swings to land ninety-five punches on the good doctor. Would you spar with it?

HAMLET: Good Father sir, 'twould be an honor.

LUTHER: O, thank you, my son. I couldn't ask just anybody. Actually, I don't think I could've asked anybody else. *(Church bells toll.)* O, pray excuse me, but I don't want to be late for my evening Bible study group. It sets a bad example.

HAMLET: I Will read it o'er post-haste immediately, Father.

LUTHER: You are truly a blessing to me, my son. Peace be with you.

(Exit Luther with his Bible. Hamlet follows slowly, reading the manuscript. He pops a candy and reads aloud to himself. The apparition of the Virgin Mary, Our Lady of Wittenberg, is only a voice at first.)

HAMLET: "Our Lord and Master Jesus Christ, in saying 'Repent ye,' intended that the whole life of believers should be repentance."

MARY: Repent ye.

HAMLET: "The true treasure of the Church is the Holy Gospel of the glory and grace of God."

MARY: Glory be to God.

HAMLET: "Christians should be exhorted to strive to follow Christ their Head through pain, death, and Hell, and thus trust to enter Heaven through many tribulations, rather than in the security of peace."

MARY: Peace be with ye. In the name of the Father –

(Blackout.)

– the Son –

(A blinding light from above hits Hamlet, driving him to his knees.)

– and the Holy Spirit –

(Mary, dressed in a blue mantle adorned with gold stars, appears to Hamlet.)

– Amen.

HAMLET: What art thou?

MARY: Mother most pure.

HAMLET: O God!

MARY: Mother most chaste.

HAMLET: Holy Mother!

MARY: Refuge of sinners.

HAMLET: Pray for us!

MARY: Comfort of the afflicted.

HAMLET: Hail, our Queen and Mother blest!
> Be our consolation!
> Holy Mother Church and Son,
> Jesus, our salvation!
> Gracious art thou, full of grace,
> Loving as none other,
> Joy of heaven, joy of earth,
> Mary, God's own Mother!

MARY: Bless`ed be my name. My son, my son, why have ye forsaken me?

HAMLET: I have not forsaken!

MARY: O, but thou hast, thou hast forsaken my Son, my son. But He hath not forsaken thee. He hath died for thee; can ye not live for Him? He is thy Brother in Christ. Be a Brother to Christ, my son. Honor thy Father, as a good son should.

HAMLET: Thus I strive in all ways, Queen Mother!

MARY: Ye strive in the dark night of doubt, my son. Come ye unto the light of the Sun! *(As she fades away [or ascends bodily into Heaven]:)* Repent ye, Hamlet, repent! Remember me!

HAMLET: O all you host of Heaven, no doubt! Remember thee? What else? *(During the following he moves into Faustus' study, speaking to a disheveled and somewhat withdrawn Faustus, who, despite the lateness of the hour, wears what appear to be sunglasses, and drinks red wine throughout the scene.)*
> Sweet Mother of Christ, what more? I had been haunted by these visitations in my dreams, but now my visions come before my eyes awake! No sooner hath my sense of balance been restored to me, but I am struck again! I found my feet upon the earth, but now the ground before me gives way, and I find myself a-teetering –

FAUSTUS: Upon the edge of an abyss.

HAMLET: Yes! Yes!

FAUSTUS: A gaping chasm of despair.

HAMLET: Mine aching soul!

FAUSTUS: It seems to stretch into infinity.

HAMLET: Beyond eternity!

FAUSTUS: But the pit is not bottomless.

HAMLET: No?

FAUSTUS: No. There is a lowermost point, a point of impact.

HAMLET: Yes. Yes!

FAUSTUS: And this point lies deep in the darkness, but not in the unknown. It has a name.

HAMLET: Has it?

FAUSTUS: A name known to you beyond mere knowing.

HAMLET: I know.

FAUSTUS: And what is its name? Tell me, tell me!

HAMLET: 'Tis madness. I stand at the edge of madness.

FAUSTUS: Is that what it is? Do the mad know they're mad?

HAMLET: At the depth of the abyss doth lie a place beyond reason, I feel that in my very bones. And what else doth lie beyond reason but madness?

FAUSTUS: Love lies beyond reason. So does hope. Most of life seems to lie beyond reason. Maybe even the reason why is beyond reason.

HAMLET: I am of a sudden in every way sick...

FAUSTUS: Breathe. We must never despair. Despair is surrender, and we can never surrender.

HAMLET: Can we not? Must the struggle grapple on eternally?

FAUSTUS: Consider the alternative. We all make a basic, binary either/or choice, which informs every other choice we make. When life crushes us, when the future threatens to prove nothing more than a burden followed by oblivion, we respond by making this choice. Do you know what this choice is?

HAMLET: Ay, I remember ye. To believe or not to believe.

FAUSTUS: No, that's not it. To be or not to be.

HAMLET: That is the question?

FAUSTUS: It is the only question, really. Do we go on, or do we give up? And when we choose to *be*, we must really choose to be. It is not enough to simply exist, helpless as a slave to the will of others. We must master ourselves, so that we may master all. That's the other way of dealing with the abyss, you know. If we're prepared to transcend ourselves, to act as something more than merely human, we exert our will to power – and we simply leap over it. Into whatever lies beyond.

HAMLET: A leap beyond?

FAUSTUS: If you have the strength, and the will. But first you must kick off the shackles of convention. You must shuffle off this moral coil. You must overcome yourself. And to do that you must know the truth about yourself. There's something I'd like to – Watching your match this morning, that one rally…The reflexes involved, consciousness as pure instinct and unmediated response…Back! and back! It made me think that – Well, you're good with words, but while language is a tool, it can also be a shield. So I'd like to try to get to the heart of things. I'm going to say a word to you, and I want you to respond with the first word that comes into your head as a result. Just one word. Don't embellish. And the first word, please, your first response. Don't overthink. Yes?

HAMLET: Ay.

FAUSTUS: Good. Ready?

HAMLET: Ay.

FAUSTUS: Very well. Let's begin. Sun.

HAMLET: Father.

FAUSTUS: O, no, I meant "sun in the sky".

HAMLET: Apologies. Moon.

FAUSTUS: No, no, that's not fair, I shouldn't have started with a homophone. My fault. "Foot fault." Let's begin again.

HAMLET: Ay.

FAUSTUS: Father.

HAMLET: King.

FAUSTUS: Mother.

HAMLET: Love.

FAUSTUS: Love.

HAMLET: Death.

FAUSTUS: Flesh.

HAMLET: Death.

FAUSTUS: Sin.

HAMLET: Death.

FAUSTUS: Hope.

HAMLET: Death.

FAUSTUS: Life.

HAMLET: Death.

FAUSTUS: Death.

HAMLET: Sleep.

FAUSTUS: Sleep.

HAMLET: Dream.

FAUSTUS: Dream.

HAMLET: Shadow.

FAUSTUS: Dark.

HAMLET: Tomb.

FAUSTUS: Light.

HAMLET: Fire.

FAUSTUS: Sky.

HAMLET: Cloud.

FAUSTUS: Cloud.

HAMLET: Camel.

FAUSTUS: Camel.

HAMLET: Weasel.

FAUSTUS: Weasel.

HAMLET: Whale.

FAUSTUS: Hawk.

HAMLET: Handsaw.

FAUSTUS: Fool.

HAMLET: Fishmonger.

FAUSTUS: Conscience.

HAMLET: Coward.

FAUSTUS: Frailty.

HAMLET: Woman.

FAUSTUS: Woman.

HAMLET: Queen.

FAUSTUS: Denmark.

HAMLET: Prison.

FAUSTUS: Freedom.

HAMLET: Mind.

FAUSTUS: Mind.

HAMLET: Reason.

FAUSTUS: Reason.

HAMLET: Paradox.

FAUSTUS: Answer.

HAMLET: Mystery.

FAUSTUS: Mystery.

HAMLET: God.

FAUSTUS: Soul.

HAMLET: Damned.

FAUSTUS: Heaven.

HAMLET: Hell.

FAUSTUS: Angel.

HAMLET: Devil.

FAUSTUS: Devil.

HAMLET: Struggle.

FAUSTUS: Peace.

HAMLET: Death.

FAUSTUS: Death.

HAMLET: Silence!

    (Silence.)

FAUSTUS: Good…

HAMLET: Evil!

FAUSTUS: No, no, we're finished – thank you. *(Making some notes:)* Yes. Excellent, fascinating… Words, words, words, right?…Very revealing… Now: I'm noticing a tendency for you to deal with interior chaos by projecting an outward manifestation of order and control, a parental figure – in the case of this vision you describe, a mother. But in the case of your original dream…I'm curious, has your priest weighed in yet with the angelic point of view?

    (Lights reveal Luther addressing Hamlet in the earlier part of their previous conversation – Hamlet is caught between the two doctors, whose advice alternates.)

LUTHER: I've been reflecting on that dream you had –

FAUSTUS: Because I'd like to share my interpretation with you.

LUTHER: As with Jacob and Joseph, I believe God is speaking to you in your dreams.

FAUSTUS: There's a part of the mind that lurks beneath our waking life, an underthought; –

LUTHER: He doesn't always tell us things we want to hear.

FAUSTUS: It sometimes thinks the things we cannot think.

LUTHER: I believe God is speaking to you about the King your father.

FAUSTUS: I think yours is thinking things about God the Father.

LUTHER: God shows you your father's authority ended to ask you what kind of king you will be.

FAUSTUS: Copernik's work put your mind in a cosmic frame when your underthought began considering its theological implications.

LUTHER: The empty wasteland of the Moon shows a world without faith, without meaning.

FAUSTUS: If the Word of God is wrong about the Sun, can it be trusted about anything?

LUTHER: The dead colossus in the pit is the history of all your forefathers as kings.

FAUSTUS: Your crisis of faith took the form of a dead God in a huge grave on a lifeless Moon.

LUTHER: The great empty slab is a yet-unwritten monument to your rule as the next in line.

FAUSTUS: The giant monolith stands as a headstone, but what words could it say of God?

LUTHER: In a way, it is God Himself asking you, "What shall I say of King Hamlet?"

FAUSTUS: In a way, it represents the totality of the unknown, and the unknowable.

LUTHER: "When you join your father in the afterlife, what name will you leave behind?"

FAUSTUS: And now God himself lies lifeless at the foot of the unknown.

LUTHER: The dream asks you directly: when the King is dead, are you ready to be King?

FAUSTUS: The dream challenges you: if God is dead, what rules supreme – you?

LUTHER: You have a duty to be a Christian King, to rule according to Scripture.

FAUSTUS: You have an obligation to think for yourself, beyond such labels as "good" and "evil".

LUTHER: For the world is a battlefield of Good against Evil.

FAUSTUS: After all, there really is no "good" nor "bad", but thinking makes it so.

LUTHER: You must be a faithful servant of the Lord.

FAUSTUS: You must serve nothing but your own judgment.

LUTHER: God has given you a true soul – you have a responsibility to save it.

FAUSTUS: Fate has given you a good mind – you have a responsibility to use it.

LUTHER: You know I feel as though I am more than just your spiritual father –

FAUSTUS: You know I consider you more than just my student –
(Each puts a hand on Hamlet's shoulders.)

LUTHER & FAUSTS: In truth, you're like a son to me.

LUTHER: It's no accident that God has brought us together.

FAUSTUS: Fate has intersected our trajectories.

LUTHER: His Providence is found even in the fall of a sparrow.

FAUSTUS: Destiny is a series of opportunities.

LUTHER: God is everywhere.

FAUSTUS: Everything is a choice.

LUTHER: Be one with God.

FAUSTUS: Be your own god.

LUTHER: For you are nothing without God.

FAUSTUS: For without you, there would be no god at all.

LUTHER & FAUSTS: When the time comes for you to act as King –

FAUSTUS: Act boldly –

LUTHER: Act piously.

FAUSTUS: But don't act rashly.

LUTHER: Let an abiding faith steer you.

FAUSTUS: Let your reason be your guide.

LUTHER: If you need guidance, pray for it – He is listening.

FAUSTUS: The answers are within you – ask yourself.

LUTHER & FAUSTS: So, to put it in a nutshell –

LUTHER: In this sea of confusion and doubt we call life –

FAUSTUS: In this fog of uncertainty and unchallenged assumptions we call reality –

LUTHER: God is the answer.

FAUSTUS: Question everything!

(Lights down on Luther.)

After all, where would we be if your good Doctor Copernik didn't feel the same way?

HAMLET: Standing still at peace in the very center of the universe.

FAUSTUS: Maybe. But in a universe without a fixed central point, every point can be the center. Every man can be the center. Why would you want to be anywhere else?

HAMLET: Perhaps…but Doctor *Luther* would say that man didst usurp the place of God if he placed himself i'the very heart of things.

FAUSTUS: Well, I'd reply that – Wait– You've– Is Doctor *Luther* the priest you've been consulting?

HAMLET: He is.

FAUSTUS: Great Bald Cock of Diogenes! And I suppose he's been advising you to do the exact opposite of everything I've been advising you to do.

HAMLET: Thou couldst say that, ay.

FAUSTUS: Then what are you going to do?

HAMLET: What thou sayst.

FAUSTUS: Good.

HAMLET: Or what he sayst.

FAUSTUS: O.

HAMLET: Or both. Or neither. Or I know not. I pray I'll know when the time to know is upon me.

FAUSTUS: The time to know is always upon us – it's the readiness that's all! Martin. Of course. Who else? *(Beat.)* He should go over the manuscript.

HAMLET: Copernik's?

FAUSTUS: Who else?

HAMLET: But I have sworn an oath –

FAUSTUS: Oaths, oaths, I'm over oaths. *(He produces Copernik's manuscript.)* He deserves to know what we know, don't you think? The truth?

HAMLET: All men, I Hope, deserve such.

FAUSTUS: Good. What other manuscript?

HAMLET: What say thee?

FAUSTUS: I said "the." I made reference to "the" manuscript, and you specified Copernik's. What other manuscript?

HAMLET: I know not what thou meanst.

FAUSTUS: O, come on, it's obvious you're lying. You're a terrible liar. It's a virtue, but it's not very practical.

HAMLET: Doctor *Luther* entrusted unto me the proof perusal of an argument he doth perpend.

FAUSTUS: Arguing what?

HAMLET: Upon the issue of indulgences.

FAUSTUS: Ah! Do you have it on you?

HAMLET: Not at this time.

FAUSTUS: As clear as day, my friend, you're lying.

HAMLET: *(Producing Luther's manuscript:)* Do I not betray his confidence?

FAUSTUS: It's our debate! It's our confidence. I assume he asked you to proof it in preparation for showing it to me, yes?

HAMLET: Ay.

FAUSTUS: Did you read it?

HAMLET: Ay.

FAUSTUS: Did you find fault in it?

HAMLET: O, on the contrary.

FAUSTUS: Then your obligation is discharged, thank you. *(Hamlet surrenders the manuscript.)*
And thank you.

HAMLET: No – thank thee, good doctor, sir, for seeing me at such an untoward time.

FAUSTUS: Not at all. Lately I am possessed of my own demons, and work is the best therapy. Your case is important to me personally, it's why I do what I do. For now, I prescribe rest. *(He produces a small vial of pills.)* Mandragorium, now in easy-to-swallow tablet form. At bedtime, take two of these with water. With red wine, if you've got it. Have you got it?

HAMLET: No.

FAUSTUS: *(Handing a bottle of wine to Hamlet:)* You do now. Good night. Peace be with you.

HAMLET: Ay. And also with thee. *(He heads out, but pauses on the threshold.)* My treatment, sir – What call ye this thy medicine of thought?

FAUSTUS: I call it "mentology": a science of the mind.

HAMLET: Methinks a science of the soul is nearer to the nub of it.

FAUSTUS: Fine. "Psychology." Even better.

(Exit Hamlet. Lights down on Faustusreading and up on Luther preaching.)

LUTHER: When the path seems dark and we fear we may be losing our way, it is vital always to remember that God has a plan. A plan for the world, and a plan for us, and the two are one and the same. He has numbered the stars in heaven and the hairs on your head. *(Touching the top of his head.)* Granted, one is easier than the other.

(He comes down from his pulpit to the audience.)

So take hope. We must never despair – there is a divinity that shapes our ends, rough-hew them how we will. We cannot see the entirety of God's master plan, but we can come to understand our place in it. We have only to open our minds to His Word and our hearts to His love. We have only to listen always to our conscience, and live always by our faith. Let us pray.

(Lights down on Luther and up on Faustusteaching. He is costumed as The Devil.)

FAUSTUS: Boo. Tonight being All Hallows Eve, I know most of you are itching to get out and lift a cup or two – or keg or two – to the memory of dead ancestors. So I'll keep this lecture short, with the reminder that, as you celebrate tonight: if you drink, don't shrive, and if you shrive, don't drink.

As you weigh that choice – I'm sure – consider: what are those voices we hear inside, urging us to make a particular choice? Well, God is one of those voices. His voice says "Thou shalt not." The Devil is one, too.

His voice says *"Do what thou wilt."* But these are not outward influences, an angel on one shoulder and a demon on the other, arguing their points in iambic pentameter – they are the mind talking to itself. Itselves. Whichever voice you choose to listen to at any given moment defines your identity. Opto ergo sum: I choose, therefore I am.

(Bells toll. The scene is now the Church graveyard, under a low, full moon. By lantern light, Faustus digs behind a gravestone bearing the name "George Faustus," excavating a burlap-wrapped bottle of wine. Enter Luther, wearing a black, hooded cloak over a white tunic.)

LUTHER: My God, is nothing sacred, you ghoul?

FAUSTUS: Halloween tradition. Uncle George's secret recipe – one year's fermentation in hallowed ground. *(He uncorks the bottle.)* In vino veritas. Splash of truth?

LUTHER: Not now.

FAUSTUS: O, come on, you prig, get into the spirit of the season. Where's your costume?

LUTHER: I'm wearing it. I'm dressed as a Dominican.

FAUSTUS: Of course – I almost didn't recognize you. *(He drinks copiously from the bottle.)*

LUTHER: Sometimes, because I love you as God commands me to do, because He sees fit to test me – Sometimes I allow myself to forget how dangerous you can be.

FAUSTUS: What?

LUTHER: The Earth moves? The Earth moves around the Sun?

FAUSTUS: O, yes. Interesting idea, isn't it?

LUTHER: The Book of Joshua, chapter ten: "Then Joshua prayed to the Lord, saying in the presence of Israel: Stand still, O Sun, over Gibeon, and Moon, you also, over the valley of Aialon! And the Sun stood still, and the Moon stayed, while the nation took vengeance on its enemies." The Sun stood still! So the Sun moves!

FAUSTUS: That's your evidence?

LUTHER: I don't need evidence, I have the Word of God! "Thou hast fixed the Earth immovable and firm!" That's what the Psalm says!

FAUSTUS: That's not what the math says.

LUTHER: It's heresy!

FAUSTUS: It also happens to be true.

LUTHER: It's irresponsible. And it's grounds for dismissal.

FAUSTUS: Who, me?

LUTHER: Of course! They'd fire you for teaching this blasphemy. And that would be just the beginning.

FAUSTUS: Look, first of all, they can censure me, they can torture me, they can excommunicate me and damn my eternal soul, but they cannot fire me – I have tenure. Secondly, are we here to teach our students that we have reached the end of knowledge, that there's nothing new to learn? Is this your reaction to progress and enlightenment? It's not encouraging.

LUTHER: It contradicts the Word of God!

FAUSTUS: It also happens to be true!

LUTHER: Apostasy! That way lies the road to Hell!

FAUSTUS: Big deal. I've been to Rome in the summer at the height of the tourist season – your idea of Hell holds no fear for me.

LUTHER: Ach! Why must you test me so?!

FAUSTUS: It's my job! Martin, you're a reasonably intelligent man – can't you approach this with an open mind?

LUTHER: "Lead us not unto temptation."

FAUSTUS: The theory's pretty convincing – Look, I'll show you.

LUTHER: "Deliver us from evil."

FAUSTUS: Just hear me out! Do you have it with you?

LUTHER: I burned it.

FAUSTUS: You what?!

LUTHER: Consigned it to the flames.

FAUSTUS: You burned it.

LUTHER: And scattered the ashes.

FAUSTUS: Ah, yes, the religious counter-argument: you burned it! You self-righteous son of a bitch.

LUTHER: I did it for your sake, John, to save you. Your job and your soul. But it wouldn't matter who wrote it.

FAUSTUS: No, of course not. It threatened the dominion of God Almighty! Six sheets of paper.

LUTHER: A profane absurdity.

FAUSTUS: Because you say so.

LUTHER: Because God says so.

FAUSTUS: God provides unforgiving peer review.

LUTHER: God has no peer.

FAUSTUS: There are other copies, you know – that wasn't the only copy.

LUTHER: One man does what he can.

FAUSTUS: Yes, he does. Or he should. Do what he can. Do all he can.

LUTHER: Yes, he should.

FAUSTUS: See, and I rather liked what you wrote. Ninety-five links in a binding chain of reasoning.

LUTHER: You've already read it?

FAUSTUS: Passionately argued, yet always methodical in its approach. Written by a man of conscience and principle. A couple of quibbles with the Latin, but I grade on a curve.

LUTHER: Did he give it or did you take it?

FAUSTUS: Here's my favorite thesis: "Why does not the Pope empty Purgatory for the sake of holy love and of the dire need of the souls that are there – this being the most just of all reasons – if he redeems an infinite number of souls for the sake of that most fatal thing, money, to be spent on building a basilica – this being a very slight reason?" That's an excellent question.

LUTHER: I ask rhetorically.

FAUSTUS: No, you simply ask. And you reason Purgatory out of existence. And you leave the Church with no logical counter-argument. Airtight. Ironclad.

LUTHER: Thank you.

FAUSTUS: You win.

LUTHER: Thank you, that's gratifying, coming from you.

FAUSTUS: And you were debating the Church.

LUTHER: Yes…

FAUSTUS: So the Church loses.

LUTHER: No, that's not the right way to look at it –

FAUSTUS: That's how the Church is going to look at it.

LUTHER: Well, the Church won't read it. That's between me and you.

FAUSTUS: I never assumed that, I took you at your word.

LUTHER: What word?

FAUSTUS: "Out of love for the truth and the desire to bring it to light," those are the first words of the damned thing. Your words, yes?

LUTHER: Yes…

FAUSTUS: Well, the truth must belong to everyone, wouldn't you say? In order to be a universal truth? By definition.

LUTHER: Where are you going with this?

FAUSTUS: You wrote a disputation – that was your word, "let's dispute!" – a disputation to bring to light the truth, a truth which belongs to all.

LUTHER: What did you do with it? Give it back.

FAUSTUS: I don't have it anymore.

LUTHER: Where is it?

FAUSTUS: Which copy?

LUTHER: O, no, no, no,….

FAUSTUS: Because I made some copies at the printer's –

LUTHER: No, no...

FAUSTUS: I posted your original on the door of your office –

LUTHER: God, no...

FAUSTUS: Mailed out some others. Sent copies to the Archbishop, to the Emperor, to the Pope –

LUTHER: No, why, why?!

FAUSTUS: The academic life: publish or perish.

LUTHER: Publish *and* perish! Shit! They'll see it as heresy...

FAUSTUS: I certainly did. Well done! I'd say that would mean big trouble for you in Purgatory, but, then, of course...

LUTHER: But that was – I thought we were – Why in God's name would you do this to me?

FAUSTUS: I didn't do it to you, Martin – I did it for you. And I did it to the Church – a little shock treatment for that sclerotic, ossified cult of yours. It's not just individuals who get sick. Institutions become diseased. Societies, cultures, whole civilizations die from plagues of ignorance. We're doctors. We have the ability, and the responsibility, to treat the illness. What you wrote was a prescription. I filled it.

LUTHER: You are the Devil, aren't you? It all makes perfect sense at last. John Faustus is just your costume the rest of the year. This is who you really are, isn't it?

FAUSTUS: Is it? Am I? Is there a Devil? I'm not so sure. What with all the rotating and revolving and stopping of the Sun and whole regions of the afterlife blinking out of existence, I may have lost my bearings just a little bit!

(He drinks. Enter Hamlet, dressed in the black habit of an Augustinian monk.)

HAMLET: Doctor, Father, I seek and I find. Good friar, my soul is sunned to see thou hast concluded thus to share thy bright and shining words a-wi'th'world. On my way here, I over-read once more thy five-and-ninety theses, there nailed upon the Church's door.

FAUSTUS: O, yes, that's right, I also nailed a copy on the Church's door. Took the liberty of translating that copy into German, so everyone could read it.

LUTHER: God in Heaven! I've got to get to it.

FAUSTUS: Let it stand, Martin! Stand with it!

LUTHER: Damn you, I'm not going to take it down – I need to check your translation! If I'm going to be burned alive, I don't want it to be because of your grammar.

FAUSTUS: Check my translation? That's rich, you hick. I do him a favor, and this is the thanks I get.

LUTHER: A favor?!

FAUSTUS: I'm helping you reform the Church. I'm something of a funda-mentalist, too.

LUTHER: Pah! I want to take the Church back to its roots, and you want to take it back to nothing!

FAUSTUS: And what could be more fundamentalist than that? Look, it's done, Martin: *consummatum est,* already. Clearly it must be the Will of God, right? *(To Hamlet.)*
Or something.

LUTHER: *(To Hamlet.)* My son, I would rather you had not – O, hell, *ego te absolvo,* it's all *mea culpa,* anyway. *(To Faustus.)* As for you – I wash my hands of you. Pray for your soul, Doctor Faustus.

FAUSTUS: Listen to your conscience, Doctor *Luther.*
(Exit Luther. Faustus offers the bottle to Hamlet.)
Swig? An amusing little Trollinger from my uncle's cellar.

HAMLET: No, my brother, thank ye. My wits at last have been restored to me, and I wish to keep them with me awhile longer.

FAUSTUS: Feeling better, good. A good night's sleep? Any interesting dreams?

HAMLET: Nay, thanks be to God, nary a one, for the first night in a fort-night.

FAUSTUS: Good. My explanation of your dream resolved your under-thought's conflicts about it.

HAMLET: But thine explanation drew forth not the true meaning of my dream.

FAUSTUS: No? Don't tell me Martin got it right, please.

HAMLET: Neither wholly true, though half a truth in both. Methinks it was thy wording game that let me finally glimpse the truth out of the corner of my mind's eye.

FAUSTUS: How so?

HAMLET: It did enlighten me this morn – It dawned upon me that, in my dream, the Sun is...the Son. The Son of God. The Light of the world. The Christ.

FAUSTUS: O, Jesus...

HAMLET: All I have learned of late doth show the truth: The Father is in the heavens, and His Son is at the center of all things. Our lives re-volve around the newly-risen Son. And what doth lie in the abyss we stand before is beyond all reason indeed – but 'tis a divine madness: 'tis faith. And we must find the strength to make a leap beyond, 'tis true – but 'tis a leap of faith we make. Into the arms of the Lord.

FAUSTUS: *(Referring to Hamlet's clothing.)* O, God, this get-up, it isn't a costume, is it…

HAMLET: With this kind of leap, one must jump in with both feet. I have decided to give my life to the Holy Mother Church, to live as a Brother to Christ.

FAUSTUS: But you're supposed to be King one day – Are you just throwing that away because I prescribed the right sleeping pills?

HAMLET: The body in the pit I dreamed is what remains of my destiny as King. 'Tis dead to me now. And the eternal stone beside it is the rock of ages, the pillar of my faith, reaching from the grave up to high Heaven. For to be born again one first must die – what else the meaning of the Resurrection?

FAUSTUS: Hamlet, you're sacrificing yourself for a lie! The Church? The Church forever damned my father to Hell for taking his own life. But if the Church is wrong about Purgatory, couldn't it also be wrong about Hell – about our souls, about everything? No, you've got to put your faith in doubt! Believe me! I've searched everywhere for the Truth. I hold four doctorates, for Christ's sake! I thought thinking would lead me to the Truth in the end, but it's only led me to the truth that there *is* no end to the thinking.

HAMLET: Ha! Thou seest?

FAUSTUS: But, for me, no start to the believing. I'm not taking anybody else's word on this, I want to know for myself! If you know, you don't have to believe anymore – you know. And I know that I don't believe. Or at least I believe I don't. You know?

HAMLET: I believe so.

FAUSTUS: So if neither reason nor faith can give us the ultimate Truth, what can? There must be something else, something beyond all this, and I swear to you here and now on my life I will not rest until I find it, whatever it takes! I was so hoping we could seek it out together, as colleagues, as men who are meant to be more than other men… Why, why is it that everyone I choose to live my life for chooses to live their lives without me? If this is the end result of me giving my best to the best who can receive it, then – enough, I'm through with it, the whole thing.

HAMLET: Higher education?

FAUSTUS: Humanity!

HAMLET: O, thy desperate words do touch me deeply, brother, and I can only –

FAUSTUS: Stop calling me that! I'm not your brother. I'm not a part of this dysfunctional family you're so eager to bind yourself to.

HAMLET: Something is rotten in the Papal States, 'tis true. But thou hast read Father Martin's words – I Hope that I may help him heal our ailing family from within.

FAUSTUS: And what of your real family? What's Father Hamlet going to think of this decision, I wonder?

HAMLET: He shall have to see that I must follow the will of a higher Father, one whose Kingdom is not of this world. But it is as it must be – my mind's made up and my soul, at long last, is at peace and settled, and nothing there is that can change that. 'Tis done – clearly 'tis the Will of God, ay?

FAUSTUS: Or something.

(He drinks. Enter Lady Voltemand, ambassador from Denmark, dressed for travel by horse, and bearing a sealed letter.)

LADY VOLTEMAND: Ah! Good my lord! I find thee here at last!

HAMLET: Who's there – How now, my Lady Voltemand?

LADY VOLTEMAND: 'Tis I, my lord.

HAMLET: I bid thee welcome, ma'am. This gentlewoman here doth wait upon My queen and speaks for her in embassy To foreign lands. But say, what brings thee here?

LADY VOLTEMAND: I bear for thee a seal`ed missive from Thy mother-queen at Elsinore, my lord.

HAMLET: What news?

LADY VOLTEMAND: In sooth, I do not know, my lord –
This letter's secret contents did the queen
Entrust to me to show unto thine eyes
And only thine alone, and that post-haste.

HAMLET: O God! From home our court of Elsinore
Comes this most woeful shocking word to me
Of my great father's all untimely-met
Demise! O God! My God! The King is dead!

FAUSTUS: *(Toasting.)* Long live the King. *(He drinks and does not kneel.)*

LADY VOLTEMAND: *(Kneeling.)* King Hamlet 'twas, and now King Hamlet 'tis.

HAMLET: How strange that name becomes me. Prithee, stand.
Save kneeling for the King of Kings, not me.

LADY VOLTEMAND: Condolences upon thy woe, my liege.
But say, how did this sadness come to pass?

HAMLET: While napping in his apple orchard there,
His custom always of the afternoon,

A fatal serpent stung his life away.

FAUSTUS: Interesting. So in your dream – I guess sometimes a dead father is just a dead father.

HAMLET: Was I the killing cause of this? Did I
By dreaming it then will it to be so?

FAUSTUS: No, no, it's just a synchronistic coincidence.

HAMLET: A holy vision of the time to come.

FAUSTUS: An accident.

HAMLET: The divine plan.

FAUSTUS: Whatever. The question is, what are you going to do about it?

HAMLET: I have no choice. I thought God meant me for
The cloth, but now He bids me wear the crown.
I must to Denmark hie me hence forthwith;
The kingdom stands unsure without its king.
Good Lady Voltemand?

LADY VOLTEMAND: I wait thy word.

HAMLET: Pray help me make my preparations here
For to embark for Elsinore tonight.
Go, if ye please, and make ye ready my
Conveyances thereto.

LADY VOLTEMAND: I shall, my lord.
May Denmark's sorrow yield to joy at thee.

HAMLET: My thanks, good Lady Voltemand. Godspeed.
(Exit Lady Voltemand.)
And you, good doctor, sir – despite tonight
I Hope mayhap we part our ways as friends?

FAUSTUS: Mayhap we may, Your Highness…And if I may be so bold, let me offer this last word of advice: with every choice you make, strive always for the Truth – on your own terms, and yours alone. Remember: you write the drama of your life, not some unseen hand. Live your life so that I may never have to read of the tragedy of King Hamlet, yes?

HAMLET: If ye live thine so that the history
Of Doctor *Faustus* is not told by all
To serve them as a cautionary tale.

FAUSTUS: Done. Consider it a deal.
(They seal it with a handshake. Exit Hamlet. A peal of bells. The scene is now later the same night, at The Bunghole, where Faustus is performing.)

FAUSTUS: So, here's one for you…How many Poles does it take to make the world go 'round? Three: the North, the South, and Nikolai Copernik. It's alright: your descendants will appreciate it. Before I close for the night, I have a little announcement to make. This is going to be my last performance for a while. Now, now, your lives will go on. But I'm in dire need of a sabbatical, and I've resolved to finally get some research done that I've been curious about for far too long. Doctor Agrippa will be covering my classes for me, and I'll be going underground for awhile…So for now I want to leave you with a cover of a song my mother used to sing to me. I hope you like it – it goes a little something like this:

When I was just a young schoolboy
I asked my teacher
What will I be
Will I be learn`ed
Will I be wise
Here's what he said to me

Che sera, sera
The things that will be, shall be
Your fate's either bound or free
Che sera, sera
What will be, shall be

Now I have students of my own
They ask me, Doctor
What will I see
Will I find answers
And reasons to be
I tell them truthfully

Che sera, sera
The things that will be, shall be
Our fortune's not ours to see…
(A bell begins tolling midnight. Spotlight on Hamlet, dressed in black from Act V, Scene II of his own tragedy:)
HAMLET: There's a special providence in the fall of a sparrow.
(Spotlight on Luther, confronting the Holy Roman Emperor at the Diet of Worms:)
LUTHER: My conscience is captive to the Word of God.
HAMLET: If it be now, 'tis not to come…
LUTHER: I cannot and will not recant anything…

HAMLET: ...if it be not to come, it will be now...

LUTHER: ...for to go against conscience is neither right nor safe.

HAMLET: ...if it be not now, yet it will come.

LUTHER: Here I stand, I cannot do otherwise, so help me God.

HAMLET: The readiness is all.

LUTHER: Amen.

    (Spotlight on Faustus, which shifts from white to red by the end.)

FAUSTUS: What will be, will be.

    (The song finishes as the last hour tolls. Blackout.)

END OF PLAY

Rights and Permissions

The entire text of each play may be obtained by contacting the rights holder.

MONOLOGUES